云南师范大学
汉藏语研究院文库

跨境语言研究系列丛书

国家社科基金重点项目"东南亚苗语志"（项目编号：16AYY018）阶段性成果

总主编 ◎ 戴庆厦 余金枝

泰国白苗话语法标注文本
ANNOTATED TEXTS OF THAILAND'S WHITE HMONG

余金枝（YuJinZhi）　范秀琳（FanXiuLin）
吴金标（WuJinBiao）　赵　格（ZhaoGe）　◎ 著

中国社会科学出版社

图书在版编目（CIP）数据

泰国白苗话语法标注文本 / 余金枝等著. —北京：中国社会科学出版社，2020.9
（云南师范大学汉藏语研究院文库）
ISBN 978-7-5203-5137-9

Ⅰ.①泰⋯ Ⅱ.①余⋯ Ⅲ.①苗语–语法–泰国 Ⅳ.①H434

中国版本图书馆 CIP 数据核字（2019）第 209012 号

出 版 人	赵剑英
责任编辑	任　明
责任校对	韩天炜
责任印制	郝美娜

出　　版	中国社会科学出版社
社　　址	北京鼓楼西大街甲 158 号
邮　　编	100720
网　　址	http://www.csspw.cn
发 行 部	010-84083685
门 市 部	010-84029450
经　　销	新华书店及其他书店

印刷装订	北京君升印刷有限公司
版　　次	2020 年 9 月第 1 版
印　　次	2020 年 9 月第 1 次印刷

开　　本	787×1092　1/16
印　　张	16.25
插　　页	2
字　　数	355 千字
定　　价	98.00 元

凡购买中国社会科学出版社图书，如有质量问题请与本社营销中心联系调换
电话：010-84083683
版权所有　侵权必究

《云南师范大学汉藏语研究院文库》总序

戴庆厦

建业难，建业苦，建业乐。

为促进我国汉藏语学科的发展，2012 年我们在时任云南师范大学校长杨林教授的积极支持和时任《云南师范大学学报》主编、汉语史专家罗骥教授的倡议和运作下，于 2012 年 4 月 27 日在云南师范大学成立了国内外第一个以汉藏语研究为对象的汉藏语研究院。到现在走过了七个年头。回忆从建院到现在，既有困难缠绕的愁苦，又有取得成绩的欢乐。我们从无到有，从心里没底到如何办成一个有特色的汉藏语研究机构，有了初步的经验。开初，整个研究院只有我（院长）和罗骥（常务副院长）、胡韶星（办公室秘书）三人，后来逐渐调进新人余金枝（副院长）等，目前已有九位专职研究人员，初具规模。

学校给汉藏语研究院的定位是：办成以汉藏语系语言为研究对象的科学研究和高层次人才培养的实体机构。七年来，在学校的支持和老师们的共同努力下，研究院在队伍建设、科学研究、人才培养等方面都取得了显著成绩。研究院已建立起一支结构合理、素质优良、团结实干的科研教学队伍。研究院现有教授 3 人，副教授 3 人。其中，具有博士学位的 7 人，博士后 1 人；博导 2 人，硕导 7 人。

七年来，研究院九名研究人员共获得省级以上的科研项目 20 项。其中省重大招标项目 1 项，国家社科基金重点项目 2 项，国家社科基金一般项目 2 项、青年项目 2 项、西部项目 2 项；部委级项目 3 项；获准建设 1 个省级科研平台。已出版专著 19 部，其中 A 类出版社 14 部；发表论文 83 篇，其中核心期刊 38 篇。研究院已建立起一套高层次人才培养体系。从 2013 年开始招收培养博士研究生，2015 年开始招收培养硕士研究生，2015 年开始招收博士后。已有 3 届博士生毕业；现有在读博士研究生 5 人，在读硕士研究生 28 人；其中外国留学生 5 人。

七年来有一些项目获奖：田阡子的《格西霍尔语动词的时–体范畴》获"李方桂田野调查奖"（2014 年）；余金枝的《湘西矮寨苗语参考语法》（著作），获云南省第 20 届哲学社会科学优秀成果奖三等奖（2016 年）；罗骥的《〈舜典〉三危考》，获云南省第 21 届哲学社会科学成果奖一等奖（2017 年）；和智利的《纳系族群父辈女性亲属称谓的类型及地理分布》，获云南省第 21 届哲学社会科学成果三等奖（2017 年）；彭茹的《汉藏语系语言基数词研究》

（著作），获云南省第 22 届哲学社会科学优秀成果三等奖（2018 年）。陈娥、和智利被评为云南省"万人计划"青年拔尖人才。

这些成绩来之不易。我们的体会主要是：

坚定地树立"实力是硬道理"的理念，团结一致地为提高我国的汉藏语研究的实力而尽力奋斗。研究院始终要求老师们尽力多出有新意的成果。

突出特色。根据国家的总体规划和学科建设的要求，以及研究院的实际情况，安排我们的工作，形成我们的特色。近期，我们把研究院的工作重点放在两个方面：一是云南境内汉藏语系语言研究，特别是研究薄弱或空白的语言；二是研究与云南跨境的语言。

立足本土，眼观四方。我们把焦点聚在云南及我国这块语言学沃土上，努力挖掘本土的"金"资源。但是，我们也重视学习、吸收国内外有关现代语言学、汉藏语言学的研究经验，来丰富、改善我们的视角和方法。

"摸着石头过河"。在学科建设方向、奋斗目标、人才培养、机构设置等方面，我们在继承前人经验的基础上，努力在实践中摸索总结自己的经验。

为了更好地保存、推进我研究院的研究成果，我们决定出版"云南师范大学汉藏语研究院文库"。我希望这一文库能够不断丰富新成果，为我国汉藏语的研究事业贡献力量。

是为序！

2019 年 5 月 26 日
于云南师大新校区青年公寓

内容摘要

本书是国家社科基金重点项目"东南亚苗语志"（16AYY018）的阶段性成果，云南师范大学汉藏语研究院文库"跨境语言研究"的系列成果之一。全书包括 13 篇话语材料，都是基于田野调查所获得的时长共计 104 分钟的视频撰写而成的，属于真实语境的白苗话自然话语材料。其中包括 13 篇话语材料，内容大致分为寓言故事（1—4）、苗族历史文化（5—9）、个人跨国迁徙史（10）、生活经验（11—13）。本书所标注的自然话语材料体现了泰国苗语白苗话真实的语言特征，反映了泰国苗族的历史文化生活。

Texts of Thailand's White Hmong, with grammatical annotation in Chinese and English is one of a series of achievements of the key project of the National Social Science Fund, "Overview of the Hmong language in Southeast Asia" (16AYY018). It is also one of a series of achievements of "Cross-border Language Research" in the Library of the Institute of Sino-Tibetan Studies of Yunnan Normal University. This book consists of 13 discourse materials, which are grammatically annotated texts in Chinese and English, transcribed from audio and video materials with a total length of 104 minutes. The materials represent a sample of natural speech discourse in the White Hmong language. The 13 texts are divided into fables (1–4), Hmong history and culture (5–9), personal history of cross-border migration (10), and life lessons (11–13). The grammatical annotations in Chinese and English reflect the linguistic characteristics of the White Hmong language in Thailand, and the content reflects the culture, history and life experiences of the White Hmong people of Thailand.

前言

本书是国家社科基金重点项目"东南亚苗语志"（16AYY018）的阶段性成果，是云南师范大学汉藏语研究院文库"跨境语言研究"的系列成果之一。全书共包括 13 篇话语材料，是基于时长共计 104 分钟的视频撰写而成的中英文语法标注文本。

话语材料采用国际音标、汉文、英文三行标注。国际音标是根据摄录的音视频转写而成的。中文标注是对国际音标标注的语素的直译，不采用国内有的语法标注所采用的实词用中文标注、功能词用英文的标注方法，使得不懂英文的读者也能够读懂。英文标注采用实词直译、虚词标注其功能。句子翻译和篇章翻译都采用直译法，尽可能体现原文的语义和语法结构。

本书的材料是 2018 年 2 月 4 日课题负责人余金枝教授带着她的硕士龚露、吴志强摄录而来的。发音合作人是泰国清莱府的白苗嘎英才融（苗语音译）。嘎英才融，姓王，在镇政府工作。负责管理村寨。他热爱苗族文化，还参与苗族电影电视的拍摄和表演，懂苗语、泰语和英语三种语言。他性格开朗友善，工作认真，是一个非常好的发音合作人。嘎英才融 1972 年生于老挝，3 岁时由于战乱逃到泰国黎府难民营，7 岁时跑到泰国难府难民营，直到他 20 岁，1992 年才跑到泰国清莱府居住。战争使得嘎英才融的青少年时期一直处于逃难状态，尝尽了颠沛流离、担惊受怕的逃难之苦。嘎英才融见证了 20 世纪七八十年代老挝苗族因战乱而逃离老挝的历史。他的人生经历在泰国北部的泰老边境村寨非常普遍，战争和避难成为他们不可磨灭的人生记忆。

考虑到泰国白苗话语料非常宝贵，将这些语料用中英文进行语法标注具有重要参考价值，我们组成由苗语母语人和英语母语人的团队来进行这项工作。吴金标根据音视频进行国际音标转写和中文翻译。余金枝与吴金标对中文转写的内容进行逐字逐句逐篇审核。中文审核完成后，由吴金标和余金枝配合，交美籍语言学博士范秀琳和云南民族大学英语专业的硕士研究生赵格进行英文翻译。英文翻译完成后，余金枝、范秀琳、吴金标、赵格再一起反复核对中英文翻译。虽然四位作者已经尽了最大努力，但仍难保证没有疏漏和错误。

本书是首部由国内学者编写的境外苗语资料，是国内苗瑶语学者采用记录语言学方法收集境外苗瑶语语料的尝试。该书的亮点是：从方法论上看以真实文本为语料，以服务于苗瑶语深度研究提供材料为理念，为语言类型学研究提供支撑，为读者阅读苗瑶语语料提供了一个高起点的平台。

境外苗族人口约 200 万人，分布在泰国、老挝、越南、缅甸等东南亚国家及欧美各地。本书的出版意味着境内学者开始步入境外苗语口语语料的收集阶段，今后更多的境外苗语话语材料语法标注将不断问世。我们希望，本书的出版能抛砖引玉，带来更多更好的成果问世。

余金枝

2019 年 5 月 30 日

Foreword

Texts of Thailand's White Hmong, with grammatical annotation in Chinese and English is one of a series of achievements of the key project of the National Social Science Fund, "Overview of the Hmong language in Southeast Asia" (16AYY018). It is also one of a series of achievements of "Cross-border Language Research" in the Library of the Institute of Sino-Tibetan Studies of Yunnan Normal University. This book consists of 13 discourse materials, which are grammatically annotated texts in Chinese and English, transcribed from audio and video materials with a total length of 104 minutes.

These discourse materials are annotated with three lines: transcription of International Phonetic Alphabet (IPA), Chinese and English. The IPA transcription was transcribed from the recorded audio and video materials. The Chinese line gives the morpheme-by-morpheme glossing of the Hmong line. We did not adopt the domestic annotation method of annotating content words with Chinese and annotating grammatical morphemes with English; in this way, those readers who do not understand English will still able to use this book. The English line provides the literal translation of notional words and the grammatical category label for the grammatical morphemes. Literal translation is adopted at both the sentence and paragraph levels, to reflect the semantic and syntactic structure of the original texts as much as possible.

The materials in this book were recorded by the project director Professor Yu Jinzhi and her graduate students Gong Lu and Wu Zhiqiang on February 4, 2018. The cooperating speaker is a White Hmong named Garongyingcai (transliteration from Hmong language) in Chiang Rai Province of Thailand. Gayingcairong, surnamed Wang, is now working at the town government and is responsible for the management of the village. He is fond of Hmong culture and actively participates in the filming and performance of Hmong film and television. He also understands Hmong language, Thai language and English. He is outgoing, friendly, hard-working, and is an excellent cooperating speaker. Gayingcairong was born in Laos in 1972. Due to the war, Gayingcairong ran away to the refugee camp in Loei Province of Thailand when he was three, and then escaped to the refugee camp in Nan Province of Thailand when he was seven, and he lived there until he was 20, In 1992, he came to live in Chiang Rai Province of Thailand. In his adolescence, Gayingcairong lived as a refugee, suffering from the pain of homelessness and the fear caused by the war. Gayingcairong witnessed the flight of the Hmong people in Laos due to the warfare in the 1970s and 1980s. His life experiences are very common in the Thai-Lao border villages in northern Thailand. Warfare and refuge have become their indelible life memories.

The original audio and video materials were transcribed into IPA and translated into Chinese by Wu Jinbiao. Then Professor Yu Jinzhi and Wu Jinbiao reviewed the Chinese transcription word by word and sentence by sentence. Then, with continued involvement of Prof. Yu and Wu Jinbiao, the discourse materials were handed over to the American linguist Dr. Cathryn Yang and Zhao Ge, a graduate student in Translation and Interpretation of Yunnan Minzu University, to translate into English. After the completion of all the work, the manuscript was cross-checked by Professor Yu Jinzhi, Dr. Cathryn Yang, Wu Jinbiao and Zhao Ge again and again. Although the four of them tried their best to avoid mistakes, it is still difficult to guarantee that there are no more omissions.

Texts of Thailand's White Hmong, with grammatical annotation in Chinese and English is the first overseas Hmong language material written by domestic scholars and also the first attempt for domestic Hmong-Mien language scholars to collect overseas Hmong-Mien language corpus using the methods of documentary linguistics. The highlights of this book are, from the perspective of methodology, this book uses authentic texts as corpus, based on the concept of providing materials for in-depth study of Hmong-Mien language; it also supplies support for the study of linguistic typology and provides a platform with a high standing point for readers to read the Hmong-Mien language corpus.

The population of overseas Hmong people is about 2 million, which is distributed in Thailand, Laos, Vietnam, Burma, other Southeast Asian countries, Europe and America. The publication of *Texts of Thailand's White Hmong, with grammatical annotation in Chinese and English* means that our domestic scholars have stepped into the field of overseas oral Hmong language corpus collection, and there will be more and more grammatically annotated discourse materials of overseas Hmong language coming out. We sincerely hope that the publication of *Texts of Thailand's White Hmong, with grammatical annotation in Chinese and English* can inspire more and better achievements to come to the public.

Yu Jinzhi
May 30, 2019

缩略语对照表

Abbreviation 缩略语	Labeled Item 分析的词	Grammatical Term	语法术语
CL	Various 多种	classifier	量词
CL.PL	tɕɔ³⁵	collective (plural) classifier	量词"群"
IP	Various 多种	illocutionary particle	语气词
DM	tsaɯ²¹	development marker	发展标记
INT	Various 多种	interjection	感叹词
Q	Various 多种	question	疑问词
QUOT	tia³³	quotation marker	引语标记
COMP		complementizer	宾语从句标记
RECP	ʂi⁵⁵	reciprocal marker	相互标记
P	ʈau⁴⁴	preposition 'to/LOC'	介词
PASS	mɦa³¹	passive	被动
PRF	laɯ²¹	perfect aspect	完成体
PRT	li⁴⁴	particle	助词
PT	mua⁵⁵	pretransitive marker	处置标记
COP	ʑɦɔ³¹	copula	系词
REL	ʔua³³	relative marker	定标
NEG	tʂi³³	negative	否定助词
IRR.NEG	tsʰɔ⁵⁵	irrealis negative	否定助词"别"
RDUP	多种	reduplication	重叠
DIST	pɦua³¹	distal demonstrative	远指

说明：
文中的英文缩略术语参见 Jarkey, Nerida. 2015. *Serial verbs in White Hmong*. Leiden: Brill.

目录/Contents

(1) qa³⁵ 青蛙 ··· 1
　　青蛙 ··· 14
　　The Frogs ··· 15
(2) qai⁵⁵ tʰia⁵⁵ mpua⁴⁴ tʰia⁵⁵ n̠u⁵² 鸡、猪和牛 ·························· 16
　　鸡、猪和牛 ··· 31
　　The Chicken, the Pig and the Ox ······································· 33
(3) ʂa⁵⁵ te³³ 手 ·· 35
　　手 ··· 41
　　The Hand ·· 42
(4) tu⁵⁵ ɳtʂɦua³¹ tʰia⁵⁵ lia⁵⁵ 孤儿和猴子 ··································· 43
　　孤儿和猴子 ··· 53
　　Orphans and Monkeys ·· 54
(5) ntaɯ³⁵ m̠uŋ⁵⁵ lu³³ m̠uŋ⁵⁵ 苗语苗文 ····································· 56
　　苗语苗文 ··· 71
　　Hmong Language and Hmong Writing ······························· 72
(6) pe⁵⁵ m̠uŋ⁵⁵ tɕɔ³⁵ ka⁵⁵li³³ke³⁵tɕai⁴⁴ 苗族的文化习俗 ··············· 74
　　苗族的文化习俗 ·· 91
　　Hmong Cultural Customs ·· 93
(7) ʔua⁴⁴nen⁵⁵ 跳神 ··· 95
　　跳神 ·· 108
　　The Shaman's Dance ·· 109
(8) ke³⁵ pa²¹ tɦua³¹ 丧俗 ·· 111
　　丧俗 ·· 127
　　Funeral Customs ·· 129
(9) tu⁵⁵ʔdeʂ²nu²¹ nɔ⁵⁵tau⁴⁴ xau³⁵ ke³⁵ʔua⁴⁴tʂʰuŋ⁵⁵ 婚事人员 ······ 131
　　办婚事所需要的人员 ·· 142
　　Marriage customs ··· 143
(10) ken⁵⁵kɯ²¹ 经历 ·· 144
　　经历 ·· 185
　　Personal Experience ··· 188

（11）ke⁴⁴ ʔua⁴⁴nen⁵² 生活之道···192

    生活之道···203

    How to Live a Good Life ···204

（12）ka⁵⁵ ke³⁵ ʔua⁴⁴ nɔ²¹ 为官之道··205

    为官之道···224

    How to be an Official ···226

（13）lu⁵⁵nen⁵²lia²¹ 糟糕的生活···228

    糟糕的生活··239

    A Warning Against Ruining Your Life ···240

附录　清莱白苗话语音系统···241

（1）qa³⁵青蛙

青蛙
frogs

1 pua⁵⁵ thau²¹ ʔu⁵⁵, mua⁵² ʔi⁵⁵ pa⁵⁵ qa³⁵ tɕɯŋ⁵⁵ tɕɯŋ⁵⁵ ŋɔ⁵⁵ ʔua⁴⁴ke⁴⁴,
很　　时候　以前　有　　一　　群　青蛙　多　　　　多　　　住　一起
very time ago   have one group frog RDUP~many   live together

很久很久以前，有一大群青蛙住在一起，
Once upon a time, there were a large group of frogs living together,

2 tɕe³³ pa⁵⁵ qa³⁵ ntaɯ²¹ tɕe³³ ʔi⁵⁵ tɕɔ³⁵ lɔ⁵² ʔi⁵⁵ tɕɔ³⁵ me⁴⁴ , tɕe³³
　这样　群　青蛙　那　　这样　一　　些　　大　一　　些　　小　　这样
this way group frog that this way one CL.PL big one CL.PL small this way

这群青蛙有的大有的小，
there were both big and small frogs among them,

3 ʂi⁵⁵ tɕʰɔ³¹ ta³³zɔ⁵²ta³³zɔ³³ , tu³³ tɔ²¹ nɔ⁴⁴ tɔ²¹ tu³³ tɔ²¹ ,
(相互缀) 吵　　没完没了　　　　只　头　这　咬　只　那
RECP   quarrel endlessly   CL CL this bite CL that

它们没完没了地争吵和打斗。这只咬那只，
They kept quarreling with each other endlessly. This one bit that one,

4 tu³³ nɔ⁴⁴ tɔ²¹ tu³³ pe²¹ , tu³³ pe²¹ tɔ²¹ tu³³ ɲta³³ .
　只　这　咬　只　上面　　只　上面　咬　只　下面
CL this bite CL above   CL above bite CL below

这只咬上面那只，上面那只咬下面那只。
this one bit the one up above and the one above bit the one down below,

5 ʂi⁵⁵ tɕɕie³¹ ʂi⁵⁵ tɕɕie³¹ , ʂi⁵⁵ tɕɕie³¹ mu³³ ʂi⁵⁵ tɕɕie³¹ lɔ³³ ,
(相互缀) 吵　(相互缀) 吵　　(相互缀) 吵　去　(相互缀) 吵　来
RECP   quarrel RECP quarrel RECP   quarrel go RECP   quarrel come

吵来吵去，
They quarreled and fought,

6 ʂiɔ⁵⁵　　　tɬʰɔ³¹　　ʂi⁵⁵　　　tɬʰɔ³¹　　tɕe³³　　,　pa⁵⁵　qa³⁵　ni⁴⁴　nɯ³³　xai³³　tʂi³³
　(相互缀)　　吵　　　(相互缀)　　吵　　　这样　　　群　　青蛙　这　　它　　说　　不
　RECP　　　quarrel　RECP　　　quarrel　this way　　group frog this　it　say　NEG

ʂi⁵⁵
(相互缀)
RECP

吵吵闹闹，这样这群青蛙就不能和谐相处了。
quarreled and fought, so they could not get along well with each other.

7 xau³¹　　　　laɯ²¹　ni⁴⁴ lu²¹　.　tɕe³³　　tɕɔ³⁵　qa³⁵　nɔ⁴⁴　nɯ³³　xai³³　tia³³　:
　和睦　　　　　了　　　呢咯　　　这样　　　些　　青蛙　这　　它　　说　　道
　harmoniously　PRF　IP　　　　this way　CL.PL　frog　this　it　say　QUOT

这样，这些青蛙就说道：
Thus, the frogs said:

8 "zua³⁵　ʔua⁴⁴li⁴⁴tɕa³³　?　pe⁵⁵　tɕɔ³⁵　qa³⁵　nɔ⁴⁴　xai³³　tʂi³³　ʂi⁵⁵　　xau³¹
　　要　　　怎么办　　　　　我们　　些　　青蛙　这　　说　　不　　(相互缀)　和睦
　　should　what to do　　　1PL　CL.PL　frog　this　say　NEG　RECP　　harmoniously

"要怎么办？我们这群青蛙不能和谐相处，
"What should we do? We frogs can't get along with each other harmoniously.

9 li⁴⁴　,　pe⁵⁵　zua³⁵　ʔua⁴⁴li⁴⁴tɕa³³　ne⁵²　?　"　tɕɔ³⁵　qa³⁵　nɔ⁴⁴　thia⁵²li⁴⁴　sa³⁵
　的　　　我们　要　　　怎么办　　　　呢　　　　　些　　青蛙　这　　才　　　　　想
　PRT　　1PL　should　what to do　　Q　　　　CL.PL frog　this　just　　　　think

我们要怎么办呢？"这些青蛙才开始思考，
What should we do?" After thinking carefully

10 sa³⁵　tɕe³³　,　tɕɔ³⁵　qa³⁵　nɔ⁴⁴　xai³³　tia³³　:　"ʔɔ⁵⁵　,　mua⁵⁵　tu³³　tɔ³¹　nɔ⁴⁴　lɔ³³
　　想　　这样　　些　　青蛙　这　　说　　道　　　　啊　　　　拿　　只　　头　　这　　来
　　think this way　CL.PL frog this say QUOT　　INT　　take　CL　head this　come

这些青蛙说道："啊，让这只来
the frogs said: "Ah, this one

(1) qa³⁵ 青蛙　　　3

11 ʔua⁴⁴　tu³³　tɕɔ⁵²　lɔ³³　tʂi³³　ʐuŋ⁴⁴ ,　mua⁵⁵　tu³³　tɔ³¹　lɔ³³　ʔua⁴⁴
　　当　　个　　带　　也　　不　　好　　　拿　　个　　那　　来　　当
　　be　　CL　lead　CONJ　NEG　good　take　CL　that　come　be

当首领也不好,

is also not fit to be the leader,

12 tu³³　tɕɔ⁵²　lɔ³³　ntʂhai⁴⁴　tʂi³³　ʐuŋ⁴⁴ ,　pe⁵⁵　tʂi³³　zua³⁵ .　pe⁵⁵　mu³³
　　个　　带　　也　　怕　　　不　　好　　　我们　不　　要　　　我们　去
　　CL　lead　CONJ　worry　NEG　good　1PL　NEG　want　1PL　go

让那只来当首领恐怕也不好,我们不要。

we are afraid that that one is also not fit to be our leader. We don't want that.

13 zua³⁵　ʔi⁵⁵　tu³³　ʔɔ³³　tua⁵²　ʔua⁴⁴　tu³³　ʂai⁵⁵　pe⁵⁵ .　tu³³　ʔɔ³³　ma³³
　　要　　一　　只　　鸭子　来　　当　　　只　　看　　我们　只　鸭子　嘛
　　want　one　CL　duck　come　be　　CL　govern　1PL　CL　duck　IP

我们去请一只鸭子来领导我们。

We want to call a duck to govern us.

14 nɯ³³　tʂi³³　zɦɔ³¹　qa³⁵　ma³³ ,　nɯ³³　xai³³　pe⁵⁵　thia⁵²　mlɦiuŋ³¹ ."
　　它　　不　　是　　青蛙　嘛　　它　　说　　我们　才　　听
　　it　　NEG　be　frog　IP　　it　say　1PL　just　listen

鸭子嘛,它不是青蛙,它说话我们才听。"

It's only his words that we are willing to obey, because a duck is not a frog.

15 mu³³　xai³³　tau⁴⁴　ʔi⁵⁵　tu³³　ʔɔ³³　tua⁵² ."kɔ⁵²　tua⁵²　ʂai⁵⁵　pe⁵⁵　lu⁵² ,
　　去　　说　　得　　一　　只　　鸭子　来　　　你　　来　　看　　我们　咯
　　go　say　get　one　CL　duck　come　2S　come　govern　1PL　IP

去请来了一只鸭子。"你来领导我们吧,

The frogs called a duck. "Come and govern us,

16 kɔ⁵²　tua⁵²　ʂai⁵⁵　pe⁵⁵　lu⁵² .
　　你　　来　　看　　我们　咯
　　2S　come　govern　1PL　IP

你来领导我们吧。

come and govern us.

17 pe⁵⁵ tɕɔ³⁵ qa³⁵ nɔ⁴⁴ ʔi⁵⁵ tu³³ xai³³ ʔi⁵⁵ tu³³ tʂi³³ mlɦuŋ³¹ li⁴⁴ ,
   我们 些 青蛙 这 一 只 说 一 只 不 听 的
   1PL CL.PL frog this one CL say one CL NEG listen PRT

我们这群青蛙谁都不听谁的，
We frogs don't listen to each other,

pe⁵⁵ ma³³ nia⁵² n̪u⁵⁵ ɕi⁵⁵ tɕɦɔ³¹ ta³³ za⁵² ta³³ zɔ³³ li⁴⁴ ,
我们 嘛 年 天 (相互缀) 吵 没完没了 的
1PL IP year day RECP quarrel endlessly PRT

我们嘛，天天没完没了地争吵，
We keep quarreling all the time,

18 xai³³ tʂi³³ ɕi⁵⁵ xau²¹ li⁴⁴ ." tɕe³³ tu³³ ʔɔ³³ tua⁵²
   说 不 (相互缀) 和睦 的 这样 只 鸭子 来
   say NEG RECP harmoniously PRT this way CL duck come

不能和睦相处。"
We can't stick together."

19 ʔua⁴⁴ tu³³ tɕɔ⁵² tau⁴⁴ pa⁵⁵ qa³⁵ ntau²¹ lu⁵² , tu³³ ʔɔ³³ tua⁵² zɔ³⁵ tɕɔ³⁵ qa³⁵ .
   当 个 带 给 群 青蛙 那 咯 只 鸭子 来 守 些 青蛙
   be CL lead P group frog that IP CL duck come guard CL.PL frog

这样，鸭子就来当那群青蛙的首领了，鸭子来看守这群青蛙。
Thus the duck became the leader of the frogs.

20 tua⁵² ʔua⁴⁴ tu³³ tɕɔ⁵² , tu³³ ʔɔ³³ tua⁵² ŋɔ⁵⁵ nte³⁵ nte³⁵ tɕe³³ .
   来 当 只 带 只 鸭子 来 住 久 久 这样
   come be CL lead CL duck come live RDUP~long this way

来当头领，鸭子来住了很长时间。
The duck was the guardian of the frogs for a long time.

21 tu³³ ʔɔ³³ tua⁵² ɕai⁵⁵ tɕɔ³⁵ qa³⁵ nɔ⁴⁴ na³⁵ , tʂi³³ pu⁵⁵ ɕi⁵⁵ tɕɦe³¹ ,
   只 鸭子 来 看 些 青蛙 这 哪 不 让 (相互缀) 吵
   CL duck come govern CL.PL frog this which NEG allow RECP quarrel

鸭子来看着这群青蛙，不让争吵，
The duck guarded the frogs and didn't allow them to quarrel with each other.

(1) qa³⁵ 青蛙

22 len⁵² tɕʰɯ³¹ tha⁵⁵ plau⁵⁵ tɕe³³   tu³³ ʔɔ³³ mua⁵⁵ tu³³ nɔ⁴⁴ nɔ⁵² kɦia³¹ ,
   位   哪   惹   事   这样   只   鸭子 把   只   这   吃   (干脆状)
   CL who make trouble this way CL duck PT CL this eat just

谁惹事的话鸭子就干脆把它给吃了，

The duck would just eat any one who made trouble,

23 tu³³ tɔ²¹ nɔ⁴⁴ tha⁵⁵ plau⁵⁵ tɕe³³   tu³³ ʔɔ³³ mua⁵⁵ tu³³ tɔ²¹ nɔ⁴⁴ nɔ⁵² kɦia³¹ .
   只   那   这   惹   事   这样   只   鸭子 把   只   那   这   吃   (干脆状)
   CL that this make trouble this way CL duck PT CL that this eat just

那只青蛙惹事的话，鸭子就把那只吃掉。

the duck would just eat any one who made trouble.

24 tɕe³³   tɕɔ³⁵ qa³⁵ ntaɯ²¹ nɯ³³ tsi³³ ka²¹ tha⁵⁵ plau⁵⁵ li⁴⁴lu⁵² ,
   这样   些   青蛙 那   它   不   敢   惹   事   嘞咯
   this way CL.PL frog that it   NEG dare make trouble IP

这样，那些青蛙不敢惹是生非了，

Thus none of the frogs dared to make any trouble.

25 ɳtʂhai⁴⁴ ɳtʂhai⁴⁴ ʔɔ³³ nɔ⁵² lu⁵² . ʔu³⁵ , tu³³ ʔɔ³³
   怕   怕   鸭子 吃   咯   哦   只   鸭子
   afraid afraid duck eat IP   INT   CL duck

很害怕被鸭子吃。哦，

They were afraid of being eaten by the duck.

26 tua⁵² nte³⁵   nte³⁵ tɕe³³ , nu³³ tshai⁵⁵   tshai⁵⁵ pla⁵⁵ ,
   来   长   长   这样   它   饿   饿   肚子
   come RDUP~long   this way 3S   RDUP~hungry   belly

鸭子来住了很长时间，它很饿，

The duck had been living there for a very long time; it was very hungry,

27 tshai⁵⁵   tshai⁵⁵ pla⁵⁵ tɕe³³, mua⁵⁵ tɕɔ³⁵ qa³⁵ ntaɯ²¹ nɔ⁵² . ŋɔ⁵⁵   ŋɔ⁵⁵
   饿   饿   肚子   这样   拿   些   青蛙 那   吃   住   住
   RDUP~hungry   belly this way take CL.PL frog that   eat   RDUP~live

很饿，就抓那些青蛙来吃。

the duck would eat frogs when it was hungry.

28 ʔɔ⁵⁵ pe⁵⁵ ņu⁵⁵ tʂhai⁵⁵ pla⁵⁵ nɔ⁵² ʔi⁵⁵ tu³³ , ŋɔ⁵⁵   ŋɔ⁵⁵ ʔɔ⁵⁵ pe⁵⁵ ņu⁵⁵
两 三 天 饿 肚子 吃 一 只 住   住 两 三 天
two three day hungry belly eat one CL RDUP~live   two three day

住两三天饿了就吃一只，

It would eat a frog every two or three days when it felt hungry,

29 tʂhai⁵⁵   tʂhai⁵⁵ pla⁵⁵ tɕe³³ nɔ⁵² ʔi⁵⁵ tu³³ . mua⁵⁵ tɕɔ³⁵ qa³⁵ nɔ⁵² nɔ⁵²
饿   饿 肚子 这样 吃 一 只 拿 些 青蛙 吃 吃
RDUP~hungry   belly this way eat one CL take CL.PL frog RDUP~eat

住两三天饿了就吃一只。

It would eat a frog every two or three days when it felt hungry.

30 tɕe³³ ʐua³⁵ ta³⁵ lu⁵² , tɕɔ³⁵ qa³⁵ ʐua³⁵ tu⁴⁴ nuŋ⁵⁵ lu⁵² , ʐau²¹
这样 要 完 咯 些 青蛙 要 断 种子 咯 次
this way will finish IP CL.PL frog will disrupt species IP time

这样的话，青蛙要被吃光了，这些青蛙要绝种了，

Thus frogs were about to be eaten up and become extinct.

31 nɔ⁴⁴ tɕɔ³⁵ qa³⁵ ʐua³⁵ tu⁴⁴ nuŋ⁵⁵ tɦia³¹   tɦia³¹ li⁴⁴lu⁵² . tɕɔ³⁵ qa³⁵
这 些 青蛙 要 断 种子 真   真 的咯 些 青蛙
this CL.PL frog will disrupt species RDUP~really   IP CL.PL frog

这次，这些青蛙真的要绝种了呀。

This time, the frogs were really going to die out.

32 ntaɯ²¹ ma²¹li⁴⁴ lɔ³³ mu³³ ʂai⁵⁵la⁵² ʔdua⁴⁴ , tia³³: "ʔɔ³⁵ pe⁵⁵ ʐua³⁵ ʔua⁴⁴
那 才 来 去 商量 过 道 哦 我们 要 做
that just come go discuss again QUOT INT 1PL should be

这些青蛙才再一次来商量，说道："啊，我们要怎么办？

The frogs gathered together again and said: "What should we do?

33 li⁴⁴tɕa³³ ? ta²¹ʂi²¹nɔ⁴⁴ pe⁵⁵ mua⁵⁵ tu⁵⁵ ʔɔ³³ ntaɯ²¹ᐟ³⁵ tua⁵² ʂai⁵⁵ pe⁵⁵ ,
怎么 现在 我们 拿 只 鸭子 那 来 看 我们
how now 1PL take CL duck that come govern 1PL

现在我们请那只鸭子来管理我们，

Now we called the duck to govern us,

34 tua⁵² ʔua⁴⁴ tu³³ tɕɔ⁵² pe⁵⁵, tu³³ ʔɔ³³ nɔ⁴⁴ mua⁵⁵ pe⁵⁵ nɔ⁵² nɔ⁵²
来　当　个　带　我们　只　鸭子　这　把　我们　吃　吃
come be CL lead 1PL CL duck this PT 1PL RDUP~eat

来当我们的领导，这只鸭子吃啊吃啊，要把我们吃光了。
to be our leader; this duck is eating us all up.

35 nɔ⁵² zua³⁵ ta³³ le³⁵. zua³⁵ ʔua⁴⁴tɕa³³ ? ʔɔ⁵², zɦɔ³¹ pe⁵⁵ tɕia⁴⁴ nɯ³³
吃　要　完　嘞　要　怎么　啊　是　我们　让　它
eat will finish IP will how INT be 1PL let it

要怎么办呢？
What should we do?

36 ŋɔ⁵⁵ ntsi³⁵ ma³³ pe⁵⁵ zua³⁵ mɦa³¹ nɔ⁵² ta³³ lu³⁵. ʔɔ⁵⁵, zua³⁵
住　再　嘛　我们　要　被　吃　完　咯　啊　要
live again IP 1PL will PASS eat finish IP INT will

啊，要是我们让它跟我们住下去的话，我们要被吃光咯。啊，要怎么办呢？"
We will be eaten up if it stays here. Ah! What should we do?"

37 ʔua⁴⁴li⁴⁴tɕa³³ ni³³ ?" zau²¹ nɔ⁴⁴ tɕo³⁵ qa³⁵ ntaɯ²¹ ma²¹li³³ lɔ³³ mu³³
怎么办　呢　次　这些　青蛙　那　才　来　去
what to do Q time this CL.PL frog that just come go

这次那些青蛙才来商量，
This time, the frogs began discussing it.

38 ʂai⁵⁵la⁵², lɔ³³ taɯ²¹ tsɯ³⁵zi²¹. xai³³ tia³³ : "ʔɔ⁵⁵, pe⁵⁵ tʂi³³ zua³⁵ nɯ³³
商量　来　出　主意　说　道　啊　我们　不　要　它
discuss come out idea say QUOT INT 1PL NEG want it

最后商量来出主意，说道："啊，我们不要它来领导我们了啦，
They worked out an idea and said: "Ah, we no longer want it to be our leader.

39 tua⁵² ʂai⁵⁵ pe⁵⁵ laɯ²¹ lɔ³³. zɦɔ³¹ nɯ³³ tua⁵² ʂai⁵⁵ pe⁵⁵ nte³⁵ nte³⁵
来　看　我们　了　啦　是　它　来　看　我们　久　久
come govern 1PL PRF IP be it come govern 1PL RDUP~long

要是它长时间领导我们。要是它长久地领导我们的话，
If it continues to lead us a long time,

40 tɕe³³ , ŋtʂhai⁴⁴ pe⁵⁵ zua³⁵ tu⁴⁴ nuŋ⁵⁵ sɯ⁵⁵ , pe⁵⁵ zua³⁵ mɦa³¹ nɯ³³
   这样   怕   我们 要   断   种子 仅仅   我们 要   被   它
   this way afraid 1PL will disrupt species only 1PL will PASS 3S
恐怕我们要绝种了，我们要被它吃光咯。
We are afraid that we will be eaten up by him and become extinct.

41 nɔ⁵² ta³³ lu⁵² . tsua³³ ntsi³⁵ mu³³ nɔ⁴⁴ , pe⁵⁵ zua³⁵tʂu²¹ ʔi⁵⁵ tu³³
   吃   完   咯   接   再   去   这   我们 要得   一   只
   eat finish IP next again go this   1PL should   one   CL
从此以后，我们得一个听一个的，
Next, we have to listen to each other,

42 mlɦuŋ³¹ ʔi⁵⁵ tu³³ xai³³ , ʔe³³ pe⁵⁵ mua⁵⁵ pe⁵⁵ tɕɔ³⁵ nɔ⁴⁴ lɔ³³ mu³³ ʔua⁴⁴
   听   一   只   说   那么 我们   拿   我们   些   这   来   去   当
   listen one CL say   then 1PL take 1PL CL.PL this come go be
那么我们只能选自己人做首领，
then we choose the leader among ourselves.

43 tɕɔ³⁵ tɕɔ⁵² sɯ³⁵ ʔɔ³³ , pe⁵⁵ tɔ³⁵qa⁵⁵ ʂai⁵⁵ pe⁵⁵ sɯ⁵⁵ ʔɔ³³ .
   些   带   仅仅   啊   我们   又   看   我们 仅仅   啊
   CL.PL lead only IP   1PL again govern 1PL only IP
我们要自己管理自己啊。
We will again govern ourselves.

44 zɦɔ³¹ pe⁵⁵ tɕia⁴⁴ tu³³ ʔɔ³³ nɔ⁴⁴ tua⁵² ʂai⁵⁵ pe⁵⁵ tɕe³³ ,
   是   我们   让   只   鸭子   这   来   看   我们   这样
   be   1PL   let   CL duck this come govern 1PL this way
要是我们让那只鸭子继续来领导我们的话，
If we let the duck be our leader,

45 pe⁵⁵ zua³⁵ kɦaɯ³¹ tu⁴⁴ nuŋ⁵⁵ sɯ⁵⁵ lu⁵² ." tɕe³³ tɕɔ³⁵ qa³⁵
   我们 要   结束   断   种子   仅仅   咯   这样   些   青蛙
   1PL will finish disrupt species only IP   this way CL.PL frog
我们只会绝种咯。"
we will become extinct."

46 ntaɯ²¹ tua⁵² ʂai⁵⁵ la⁵² tɕe³³ , laɯ³⁵ pɔ²¹ ʐuŋ⁴⁴ xai³³ tia³³ :
那   来   商量   这样   他们 见 好   说 道
that   come discuss this way   3PL see good say QUOT

那么那些青蛙来商量，他们一致认为：
The frogs discussed and agreed:

47 "ʔau⁵⁵ , tʂi³³ zua³⁵ tu³³ ʔɔ³³ ntaɯ²¹ tua⁵² ʂai⁵⁵ pe⁵⁵ laɯ²¹ lɔ⁵² ."
   哦   不   要   只 鸭子 那   来   看   我们   了   啦
   INT   NEG want CL duck that come govern 1PL   PRF   IP

"哦，不要那只鸭子来领导我们了啦。"
"We don't want that duck to govern us anymore."

48 tɕɔ³⁵ qa³⁵ ntaɯ²¹ thia⁵² xai³³ tau⁴⁴ tu³³ ʔɔ³³ tia³³ :
   些   青蛙 那   才   说   给   只   鸭子   道
   CL.PL frog that   just say   P   CL   duck QUOT

那些青蛙才对那只鸭子说道：
Then the frogs told the duck:

49 "pe⁵⁵ tʂi³³ zua³⁵ kɔ⁵² laɯ²¹ lɔ⁵² , kɔ⁵² mu³³ lɔ⁵² , kɔ⁵² mu³³ tau⁴⁴
   我们 不   要   你   了   啦   你   去   啦   你   去   得
   1PL NEG need 2S   PRF   IP   2S   go   IP   2S   go   should

"我们不要你了，你走吧，你可以走啦，
"We do not need you; you should leave;

50 laɯ²¹ lɔ⁵² , pe⁵⁵ tʂi³³ zua³⁵ kɔ⁵² ʂai⁵⁵ pe⁵⁵ laɯ²¹ ."
   了   啦   我们 不   要   你   看   我们   了
   PRF   IP   1PL NEG want 2S   govern 1PL   PRF

我们不要你领导我们了。"
we do not want you to govern us anymore."

51 tsi⁵²li⁴⁴ n̩u⁵⁵ ntaɯ²¹ lɔ³³ tɕe³³ , tɕɔ³⁵ qa³⁵ mua⁵⁵ tu³³ ʔɔ³³ lai⁵² mu³³
   自从   天   那   来   这样   些   青蛙 把   只   鸭子   赶   去
   since   day that come this way CL.PL frog PT   CL   duck drive go

自从那天以后，那些青蛙就把那只鸭子赶回家了，
From that day, the frogs drove the duck back to its home;

52 tse³⁵ , tʂi³³ zua³⁵ tu³³ ʔɔ³³ lau̵²¹ . zɦɔ³¹ tu³³ ʔɔ³³ ntau̵²¹ ŋɔ⁵⁵ tɕe³³ ,
　　家　　不　　要　　只　　鸭子　了　　　是　　只　　鸭子　那　　在　　这样
　　home NEG want CL duck PRF　　be　CL duck that　stay this way
不要那只鸭子了。如果那只鸭子还在的话，
they didn't want the duck. If the duck were still there,

53 nu̵³³ zua³⁵ mua⁵⁵ tɕɔ³⁵ qa³⁵ nɔ⁵² nɔ⁵² , thau²¹ kɦau̵³¹ tɕe³³ ta³³ .
　　它　　要　　拿　　些　　青蛙　吃　　吃　　　时候　结束　则　完
　　it　will take CL.PL frog RDUP~eat　time end　then finish
它还要继续抓这些青蛙吃，最后青蛙就全都完了。
it would continue to eat these frogs until they were no more.

54 tsi⁵²li⁴⁴ ɲu⁵⁵ ʔua³³ tɕɔ³⁵ qa³⁵ mua⁵⁵ tu³³ ʔɔ³³
　　自从　　　天　　(定标) 些　青蛙　把　　只　鸭子
　　since　　day　REL CL.PL frog PT CL duck
自从那些青蛙把那只鸭子赶回家的那天起，
Since that day, that duck was driven back to its home,

55 ntau̵²¹ ntia⁵⁵ khia³⁵ mu³³ tʂe³⁵ lau̵²¹ , tʂi³³ zua³⁵ tu³³ ʔɔ³³ ntau̵²¹ lɔ³³ ʂai⁵⁵ .
　　那　　赶　　跑　　去　　家　　了　　不　　要　　只　鸭子　那　　来　　看
　　that drive run　go home PRF NEG want CL duck that come govern
不要那只鸭子来领导。
they didn't want that duck to be their leader.

56 tɕe³³ tɕɔ³⁵ qa³⁵ ma²¹li⁴⁴ lɔ³³ ʂai⁵⁵la⁵² ,
　　这样　些　青蛙　才　　来　　商量
　　this way CL.PL frog just come discuss
这些青蛙们才来商量，
The frogs started to discuss,

57 zua³⁵ mua⁵⁵ len⁵² tɕɦu̵³¹ lɔ³³ ʔua⁴⁴ tu³³ tɕɔ⁵² . tɕɔ³⁵
　　要　　拿　　位　　哪　　来　　当　　只　　带　　　些
　　should take CL who come be CL lead CL.PL
要让谁来做首领。
who should be the new leader.

58 qa³⁵　　ntaɯ²¹　ma²¹　ʂai⁵⁵la⁵²　tia³³　　 : "mua⁵⁵　len⁵²　tɕhɯ³¹　lɔ³³　ku⁵²　tau⁴⁴ ,
　　青蛙　　那　　　才　　商量　　　道　　　拿　　位　　谁　　来　　都　　得
　　frog　　that　　just　　discuss　　QUOT　take　　CL　who　come　all　okay

那些青蛙才商量说："让谁当首领都可以,

They discussed and said: "Anyone can be the leader,

59 mua⁵⁵　tu³³　lɔ⁵²　lɔ³³　ʔua⁴⁴　tu³³　thaɯ⁵²　ku⁵²　tau⁴⁴ ,
　　拿　　只　　大　　来　　当　　只　　头领　　都　　得
　　take　CL　big　come　be　CL　leader　all　okay

让大的青蛙来当首领可以,

a big one can be the leader,

60 mua⁵⁵　tu³³　me⁴⁴　lɔ³³　ʔua⁴⁴　tu³³　thaɯ⁵²　ku⁵²　tau⁴⁴ ,
　　拿　　只　　小　　来　　当　　只　　头领　　也　　得
　　take　CL　small　come　be　CL　leader　CONJ　okay

让小的青蛙当首领也可以,

a small one can also be the leader.

61 pe⁵⁵　ʂai⁵⁵　pe⁵⁵　sɯ⁵⁵　la³³ .
　　我们　看　　我们　仅仅　啦
　　1PL　see　1PL　only　IP

我们自己领导自己吧。

We can govern ourselves.

62 tsi⁵²li⁴⁴　no⁴⁴　laɯ²¹　tɔ²¹/³⁵　ma³³,　pe⁵⁵　tɕi³³　tshɔ⁵⁵　ʂi⁵⁵　ʂi⁵⁵　tɕhie³¹　laɯ²¹ ,
　　自从　　这　　了　　那　　　嘛　　我们　不　　别　　(相互缀)　(相互缀)　吵　　了
　　since　this　PRF　that　IP　1PL　NEG　IRR.NEG　RECP　RECP　quarrel　PRF

从此以后,我们不要再争吵了,

From now on, we should no longer fight with each other.

63 pe⁵⁵　tshɔ⁵⁵　ʂi⁵⁵　ʂi⁵⁵　tɕhie³¹　ten⁵⁵　men²¹　laɯ²¹ ."
　　我们　别　　(相互缀)　(相互缀)　吵　　矛盾　　　了
　　1PL　IRR.NEG　RECP　RECP　quarrel　conflict　PRF

我们不要再闹矛盾了。"

We should no longer quarrel with each other."

64 tsi⁵²li⁴⁴ ŋɯ⁵⁵ ntaɯ²¹ lɔ³³ tɕe³³, tɕɔ³⁵ qa³⁵ tʂi³³ tɬʰau³¹ nɔ⁵² li⁴⁴ laɯ²¹.
自从　　天　那　　来　这样　些　青蛙　不　被　吃　的　了
since　　day　that　come this way CL.PL frog NEG PASS eat IP PRF

从那天以后，青蛙再也没有被吃了，
Since then, there were no more frogs being eaten up.

65 tɕe³³ tɕɔ³⁵ qa³⁵ ntaɯ²¹ ma²¹li⁴⁴ xua²¹wa²¹,
　这样　些　青蛙　那　才　　繁衍
　this way CL.PL frog that just reproduce

这样青蛙才渐渐繁衍，
Thus, frogs gradually began to reproduce;

66 tɕuŋ⁵⁵ zu³³　tɕuŋ⁵⁵ zu³³ tua⁵²,
　多　渐渐　多　渐渐　来
　many gradually many gradually come

慢慢多起来，
the number of frogs gradually increased,

67 tʰia⁵⁵ tɕɔ³⁵ qa³⁵ nɔ⁴⁴ tʂi³³ tɬʰau³¹ nɔ⁵² laɯ²¹.
　和　些　青蛙　这　不　被　吃　了
　and CL.PL frog this NEG PASS eat PRF

还有这些青蛙不再被吃了。
and no more frogs were eaten.

68 ʔda⁵⁵nɦien³¹ lɔ³³ sau³³ ni⁴⁴nɔ⁴⁴. za⁵² ʔda⁵⁵nɦien³¹
　故事　　来　结束　这样　　个　故事
　story　　come end this way　CL story

故事到此结束了。
This is the end of the story.

69 nɔ⁴⁴ nɯ³³ qhia⁴⁴ tau⁴⁴ xai³³ tia³³ : pe⁵⁵ ʔua⁴⁴ ʔi⁵⁵
　这　它　教　得　说　道　　我们　做　一
　this it teach get say COMP 1PL be one

这个故事，它启示了：
This story teaches us:

70 xai⁴⁴ nɦen³¹ lɔ³³ɕi³³ pe⁵⁵ ʔi⁵⁵ paɯ³⁵ ti⁵⁵nɦen³¹ ,
  种类 人 或者 我们 一 群 人
  kind human or 1PL one group human

我们作为一个民族或者一个群体，

As a nationality or a group,

71 pe⁵⁵ tʂi³³ tshɔ⁵⁵ tɕia⁴⁴ lɯ²¹ tu³³ tua⁵² tʂɯ⁵² pe⁵⁵ ,
  我们 不 别 让 另外 个 来 管理 我们
  1PL NEG IRR.NEG let other CL come govern 1PL

我们不能让外人来管理我们，

We can't let outsiders govern us

72 lɔ³³ zɦɔ³¹ tua⁵² tɕɔ⁵² pe⁵⁵ , pe⁵⁵ zua³⁵tʂu²¹ lɔ³³ ʂi⁵⁵ tɕɔ⁵² pe⁵⁵ ,
  也 是 来 带 我们 我们 要得 来 (相互缀) 领 我们
  CONJ be come lead 1PL 1PL should come RECP lead 1PL

或者来领导我们，我们得自己领导自己，

or lead us. We should lead each other,

73 pe⁵⁵ zua³⁵tʂu²¹ ʔi⁵⁵ tu³³ mlɦɯŋ³¹ ʔi⁵⁵ tu³³ xai³³ ,
  我们 要得 一 只 听 一 只 说
  1PL should one CL listen one CL say

我们得一个听一个的，

we should listen to each other,

74 pe⁵⁵ thia⁵²li⁴⁴ tʂi³³ mua⁵² ten⁵⁵men²¹ , pe⁵⁵ thia⁵²li⁴⁴ tʂi³³ tu⁴⁴ nuŋ⁵⁵ .
  我们 才 不 有 矛盾 我们 才 不 断 种子
  1PL just NEG have conflict 1PL just NEG disrupt species

我们才没有矛盾，我们才会不断延续下去。

so that we will not have conflicts, and we will never die out.

青蛙

　　很久很久以前,有一群青蛙住在一起,这群青蛙有的大有的小。它们整天没完没了地争吵打斗。这一只咬上面那一只,上面那只又咬下面那只,吵来吵去,这样这群青蛙就不能和谐地相处了。

　　"怎么办呢?我们这群青蛙不能和谐相处了。"这些青蛙说,"怎么办?"这群这些青蛙想啊想说:"啊,谁来当首领都不好,谁来做头领大家都不服,我们谁也不要青蛙来当首领,我们去请一只鸭子来领导我们。鸭子不是青蛙,他说的话我们才听。"这些青蛙请来了一只鸭子。"你来领导我们吧,你来领导我们吧,我们谁也不服谁,一天就知道没完没了地争吵,不能和睦相处了。"

　　这样,鸭子就来当青蛙的首领。鸭子来看守这群这些青蛙,不让他们争吵,这只青蛙惹事了就把这只吃掉,那只惹事就把那只吃掉,这样这些青蛙谁也不敢惹是生非,都担心被鸭子吃了。鸭子来住了很长时间,它很饿,饿了就吃青蛙。两三天饿了吃一只,两三天饿了吃一只,这样,这些青蛙就要被吃光了,要绝种了。

　　这次青蛙真的要绝种了。这些青蛙再一次来商量:"该怎么办呢?我们请鸭子来管理我们,来领导我们,这只鸭子都要把我们吃光了,要怎么办呢?要是它一直住下去的话,我们非被吃光不可。啊,要怎么办?"这次,这些青蛙开始商量,出主意说:"啊,我们不要它来领导了。要是它长久领导我们,恐怕我们要绝种,要被它吃光了。接下来,我们得一个听一个说,我们选自己人做首领,以后我们自己管理自己,要是我们还让鸭子来领导我们,我们只会绝种。"

　　这些青蛙一致认为:不要鸭子来领导他们了。这些青蛙就去告诉鸭子说:"我们不需要你了,你走吧,我们不要你领导我们了。"从那以后,这些青蛙就把那只鸭子赶走了。如果那只鸭子还在的话,它会把这些青蛙吃光。

　　自从把鸭子赶走、不要鸭子来领导以后,这些青蛙开始来商量,要选谁做首领。他们说道:"谁当首领都可以,大的当首领可以,小的当首领也可以,我们自己管理自己了。从现在开始,我们不要再争吵了,我们不要再闹矛盾了。"鸭子们说。从那以后,这些青蛙再也没有被吃了,青蛙又渐渐繁衍,慢慢多起来了。

　　故事到此就结束了。这个故事告诉我们:任何一个民族,只有互相团结、互相支持、没有矛盾,我们的种族才会延续下去。

The Frogs

Once upon a time, there were a large group of frogs living together. There were both big and small frogs among them. They kept quarreling with each other endlessly all day. This one bit the one up above and the one above bit the one down below. They quarreled and fought, so they could not get along well with each other.

"What should we do? We frogs can't get along with each other harmoniously" the frogs said. "What should we do?" After thinking carefully, the frogs said: "Ah, no one is fit to be our leader. Whoever becomes the leader, nobody submits to him. None of us want a frog to be our leader, so let's call a duck to govern us. It is only his words that we are willing to obey, because a duck isn't a frog." Thus the frogs called a duck. "Come and govern us, come and govern us. We frogs don't listen to each other. We keep quarreling all the time and can't get along with each other harmoniously."

Thus, the duck became the leader of the frogs. It guarded the group of frogs and didn't allow them to quarrel with each other. The duck would eat any one who made trouble. Therefore, none of the frogs dared to make any trouble out of the fear of being eaten by the duck. The duck had been living with the frogs for a long time and it was very hungry. The duck would eat frogs once it felt hungry. It would eat a frog every two or three days when it was hungry. For this reason, the frogs were about to be eaten up and become extinct.

This time the frogs were really going to die out, so the frogs gathered together again to discuss: "What should we do? We called the duck to govern us but it is going to eat us all up. What should we do? We will be eaten up if it stays here. Ah, what should we do?" This time, the frogs began discussing it and worked out an idea: "Ah, we no longer want it to be our leader. We're afraid that we will be eaten up by it and become extinct if it continues to lead us. Next, we have to listen to each other. We will choose a leader among ourselves and govern ourselves again from now on. We will become extinct if we let the duck be our leader. "

The frogs all agreed that they did not want the duck to lead them anymore. Then the frogs told the duck: "We do not need you. You should leave. We do not want you to lead us anymore." Since then, the frogs drove the duck back to its home. If the duck were still with them, it would have eaten up all the frogs.

Since the duck was driven away and the duck was no longer their leader, the frogs started to discuss the problem that who should be the new leader. They said: "Anyone could be the leader, a big one can be the leader and a small one can also be the leader. We can govern ourselves. From now on, we should no longer fight and have trouble with each other." After that, there were no frogs been eaten up anymore. Thus, the frogs began to reproduce again and the number of frog increased gradually.

This is the end of the story. This story tells us that any nationality should unit together and should help with each other so that we can coexist without conflicts and keep our species going.

（2）qai⁵⁵ thia⁵⁵ mpua⁴⁴ thia⁵⁵ ɲu⁵² 鸡、猪和牛

鸡　　和　　猪　　　和　　牛
chicken and pig and ox

1 pua⁵⁵　thau²¹　ʔu⁵⁵　,　mua⁵²　ʔi⁵⁵　ŋkaɯ²¹　nia²¹tsi³⁵　m̥uŋ⁵⁵　ŋɔ⁵⁵　tau⁴⁴　　tɔ⁵²　ʂia⁵⁵ .
　 很　　时候　 以前　　 有　　 一　　　对　　　 夫妻　　 苗族　 住　　在　　　 坡　　 高
　 very　time　ago　　have　one　CL　　couple　Hmong　live　be.located　slope　high
很久以前，有一对夫妻生活在高山上。
A long time ago, a couple lived high in the mountains.

2 ŋɔ⁵⁵　　　　ŋɔ⁵⁵　mua⁵²　ʔi⁵⁵　ɲu⁵⁵　tɕe³³　　,　tu³³　tsi³⁵　　mɔ⁵⁵　mɔ⁵⁵　tau⁵⁵xau⁴⁴　,
　 住　　　　 住　　 有　　 一　　 天　　 这样　　 个　　丈夫　　 痛　　疼痛　 头
　　RDUP~live　　have　one　day　this way　CL　husband　hurt　pain　head
住着住着有一天，丈夫头很痛，
While they were living there, one day the husband had a headache.

3 tʂi³³tshua⁴⁴　ʂi³³nen⁵²　,　tu³³　nia²¹　tsaɯ²¹
　 不　太　舒服　　　　 个　 妻子　 就
　 NEG very　comfortable　CL　wife　DM
不太舒服,妻子就对丈夫说道：
The husband didn't feel comfortable, so the wife said to him:

4 xai³³　tau⁴⁴　tu³³　tsi³⁵　　xai³³　tia³³　　:　"kɔ⁵²　tsi³⁵　　kɔ⁵²　tʂi³³　tshua⁴⁴
　 说　　给　　个　 丈夫　　 说　　道　　　　 你　　父亲　 你　　 不　　 全
　 say　P　　CL　husband　say　QUOT　　2S　father　2S　NEG　completely
"孩子他爸，你不太舒服的话，
"Father of my child, if you're not feeling completely well,

5 ʂi³³nen⁵²　　　tɕe³³　,　ʔɯ⁴⁴　　mu³³　mua⁵⁵　tu³³　qai⁵⁵　　tɕɔ⁵²　lɔ³³　xu⁴⁴　kɔ⁵²
　 舒服　　　　 的话　　 我俩　　 去　　 拿　　 只　　 鸡　　　 带　　来　　叫　 你
　 comfortable　if　　　we two　go　　take　CL　chicken　bring　come　call　2S

(2) qai⁵⁵ thia⁵⁵ mpua⁴⁴ thia⁵⁵ ɲu⁵² 鸡、猪和牛 17

我俩去拿那只鸡来给你叫魂吧。"
Let's go get a chicken to call back your soul."

6 plɦi³¹ sɯ⁵⁵ lɔ³³ma⁵² ." nɔ³⁵ , tɕe³³ tu³³ qai⁵⁵ ŋɔ³⁵ lai³³ , tu³³
  魂   仅仅 啦嘛   这样   那么 只 鸡   听见 嘞   只
  soul only IP   this way   then CL chicken hear IP CL

这样，那么鸡就听见了，
Thus, the chicken heard them.

7 qai⁵⁵ mu³³ tha²¹ ʈau⁴⁴ tu³³ mpua⁴⁴ tia³³ : "ʔɔ⁵⁵ mpua⁴⁴ ,
  鸡   去   讲   给   头   猪   道   啊   猪
  chicken go tell P   CL pig   QUOT   INT   pig

鸡就去告诉猪说："啊，猪啊，
The chicken told the pig: "Ah, pig,

8 tɦai³¹ki³³ nɔ³⁵/⁴⁴ na³⁵ , pe⁵⁵ nia²¹ thia⁵⁵ pe⁵⁵ tsi³⁵ ŋkaɯ²¹ ʂai⁵⁵la⁵² ,
  早上   这   呐   我们 母亲 和   我们 父亲 对   商量
  morning   this   IP   1PL mother and   1PL father pair   discuss

今早上啊，我们爸妈两个商量，
this morning, our two parents discussed that

9 ŋkaɯ²¹ zua³⁵ mua⁵⁵ ku³⁵ tɕɔ⁵² mu³³ xu⁴⁴ plɦi³¹ nɔ³⁵/⁴⁴ sa³³ .
  对   要   拿   我   带   去   叫   魂   这   啊
  pair   will take 1S   take.along go call soul   this   IP

他俩要把我拿去叫魂啊。
they are going to take me to call back the father's soul.

10 kɔ⁵² zɦo³¹ mpua⁴⁴ , kɔ⁵² lɔ⁵² mi⁴⁴ ntʂi³³ , kɔ⁵² xɔ⁴⁴ pa⁵⁵
   你   是   猪   你   大   小   些   你   再   帮忙
   2S   be   pig   2S   big small CL.PL   2S   again help

你是猪，你大一些，你帮忙给我想想办法，
You are a pig and a little bit bigger than me; help me with some ideas

11 sa³⁵ tʂu³⁵zi²¹ ʈau⁴⁴ ku³⁵ , ʂai⁵⁵ zua³⁵ ʔua⁴⁴li⁴⁴tɕa³³ .
   想   主意   给   我   看   要   怎么办
   think idea   P   1S   see   should what to do

看看该怎么办。
to find out what to do.

12 ʔu⁵⁵ ， zɦɔ³¹ lau³⁵ mua⁵⁵ ku³⁵ tɕɔ⁵² mu³³ xɯ⁴⁴ plɦi³¹ ma³³ ， lau³⁵ mua⁵⁵ ku³⁵
   哦   是   他们   拿   我   带   去   叫   魂   嘛   他们   拿   我
   INT   be   3PL   take 1S   take.along go   call soul IP   3PL take 1S

哦，要是他们把我拿去叫魂的话，
Oh, if they take me to call back the soul,

13 tɕɔ⁵²   mu³³ tua⁴⁴ nɔ⁵² ma³³ ŋtʂhai⁴⁴ xen³⁵ na³⁵ ."
   带   去   杀   吃   嘛   怕   很   啊
   take.along   go   kill eat IP   afraid   very   IP

他们把我拿去杀拿去吃呀，我太害怕了啊。"
I am so scared they will kill and eat me."

14 tɕe³³   tu³³ mpua⁴⁴ xai³³ tia³³   : "ʔau³⁵zau³⁵ ， tua⁴⁴ lɔ³³ zɦɔ³¹ tua⁴⁴ kɔ⁵² sɯ⁵⁵
   这样   头   猪   说   道   噢哟   杀   也   是   杀   你   仅仅
   this way CL pig   say   QUOT   INT   kill CONJ be   kill 2S   only

这样猪说道："噢哟，杀也只是杀你而已，
So the pig said: "Oh, they are going to kill you only;

15 ʔɔ³³ ， tɯ⁵⁵ tɕi³³ zɦɔ³¹ tua⁴⁴ ku³⁵ ʔɔ⁵² ， lau³⁵ tua⁴⁴ lɔ³³ lau³⁵ tua⁴⁴ lau³⁵.
   啊   都   不   是   杀   我   啊   他们   杀   啦   他们   杀   他们
   INT   all NEG   be   kill 1S   IP   3PL   kill IP   3PL   kill 3PL

啊，都不是杀我啊，他们要杀就杀吧。
ah, it's not me that going to be killed. They can go ahead and kill you.

16 ka³⁵tɕi³⁵ mu³³ ʔɔ⁵² ， ku³⁵ tɕi³³ mlɦiuŋ³¹ ʔɔ⁵² ， ka³⁵lia²¹   kɔ⁵² ."
   赶紧   去   啊   我   不   听   啊   随便   你
   hurry   go   IP   1S   NEG listen   IP   according to 2S

赶紧走啊，我不想听啊，随便你。"
You'd better go, I don't want to listen. Do as you please."

17 "ʔu⁵⁵ mpua⁴⁴ ， kɔ⁵² tsau²¹ zua³⁵ tɕi³³ pa⁵⁵ ku³⁵ thia³¹   thia³¹ li⁴⁴ ?"
   哦   猪   你   就   要   不   帮忙 我   真   真   的
   INT   pig   2S   DM   need NEG help 1S   RDUP~really   IP

(2) qai⁵⁵ thia⁵⁵ mpua⁴⁴ thia⁵⁵ ȵu⁵² 鸡、猪和牛   19

"哦！猪，你就真的不帮我的忙吗？"
"Oh! Pig, you are really not willing to help me？"

18 "ʔu³⁵zu³⁵,   mu³³ mu³³ mu³³, tshɔ⁵⁵   tua⁵² xai³³   xai³³ ʔɔ³³,
   哦哟   去   去   去   别   来   说   说   啊
   INT   go   go   go   IRR.NEG   come RDUP~say   IP

"哦哟，走走走，别再来说了，
"Oh, go quickly! Don't come back and say that anymore;

19 la⁵²   la⁵² mlɦuŋ³¹ ni⁴⁴ ʔɔ³³, lauɯ³⁵ tua⁴⁴ lɔ³³ lauɯ³⁵ tua⁴⁴ kɔ⁵² sɯ⁵⁵ ʔɔ³³,
   难   难   听   的   啊   他们   杀   啦   他们   杀   你   仅仅 啊
   hard hard listen   IP   IP   3PL   kill IP   3PL   kill 2S   only IP

太难听了呀，他们要杀也只是杀你啊，
That's a terrible thing to hear; they are going to kill you only,

20 tɯ⁵⁵   tʂi³³   zɦo³¹   tua⁴⁴ ku³⁵ ʔɔ³³, ka³⁵ tɕi³⁵ mu³³."
   都   不   是   杀   我   啊   赶紧   去
   all   NEG   be   kill 1S   IP   hurry   go

又不是杀我，赶紧走。"
not me, quickly go."

21 tu³³ qai⁵⁵   tʂi³³ pɔ²¹qa⁵⁵ mu³³ ʂai⁵⁵la⁵² tau⁴⁴ len⁵² tɕhiɯ³¹.
   只   鸡   不   知道   去   商量   给   位   哪
   CL chicken NEG   know   go   discuss   P   CL   who

鸡不知道要去找谁商量。
The chicken didn't know who to discuss with,

22 zua³⁵ ʔua⁴⁴tɕa³³ ni⁵² ? ntʂhai⁴⁴ zua³⁵ mɦa³¹ tua⁴⁴ pɔ⁵² ? .
   要   怎么   呢   怕   要   被   杀   吧
   should how   Q   afraid will PASS kill   Q

要怎么办呢？恐怕要被杀吧。
What should it do? It may get killed.

23 ʔua⁴⁴tɕa³³ ? ʔau⁵⁵, ŋɔ⁵⁵   ŋɔ⁵⁵ tɦai³¹ki³³   lu⁵², tɕe³³ tu³³
   怎么   哦   住   住   明早   咯   这样   个
   how   INT   RDUP~live   tomorrow morning IP   this way CL

怎么办？哦，不知不觉就到了第二天早上了，
What to do? Oh, it came to the next morning,

24 nia²¹   tsaɯ²¹   mu³³   mua⁵⁵   tu³³   qai⁵⁵   tɕɔ⁵²   lɔ³³   xu⁴⁴
   妻子   就   去   拿   只   鸡   带   来   叫
   wife   DM   go   take   CL   chicken   bring come   call

这样，妻子就去把鸡抓来给丈夫叫魂，
Thus, the wife went to catch the chicken to call back her husband's soul;

25 tu³³   tsi³⁵   plʑi³¹   le³⁵ ，mu³³   nte³³   tu³³   qai⁵⁵   tɕɔ⁵²   lɔ³³   xu⁴⁴
   个   丈夫   魂   嘞   去   抓   个   鸡   带   来   叫
   CL   husband soul   IP   go   catch   CL   chicken   bring come call

去抓那只鸡来给丈夫叫魂，
she caught the chicken to call back the husband's soul.

26 tu³³   tsi³⁵   plʑi³¹ ，tɕɔ⁵²   lɔ³³   xu⁴⁴   plʑi³¹   tɕɔ⁵²   lɔ³³   tua⁴⁴   nɔ⁵²   lu⁵² ，
   个   丈夫   魂   带   来   叫   魂   带   来   杀   吃   咯
   CL   husband soul   bring come   call   soul   bring come   kill   eat   IP

抓来叫魂抓来杀吃咯，
She caught the chicken to call the soul back and eat the chicken.

27 tɕɔ⁵²   lɔ³³   xu⁴⁴   plʑi³¹   tua⁴⁴   nɔ⁵² ，mua⁵⁵   ʈau⁴⁴   tu³³   tsi³⁵   nɔ⁵²   tɕʰa³¹ .
   带   来   叫   魂   杀   吃   拿   给   个   父亲   吃   完
   bring come   call   soul   kill   eat   take   P   CL   father   eat   finish

抓来叫魂然后杀了吃，拿给丈夫吃完。
She caught the chicken to call back the soul and brought it to her husband to eat it up.

28 xu⁴⁴   plʑi³¹   ta³³   lɔ³³   ŋɔ⁵⁵   ŋɔ⁵⁵   ʔɔ⁵⁵   pe⁵⁵   ŋu⁵⁵ ，
   叫   魂   完   来   住   住   两   三   天
   call   soul   finish   come   RDUP~live   two   three day

叫魂结束后两三天，
Two or three days after calling the soul,

29 tu³³   tsi³⁵   ku⁵²   tʂi³³   zuŋ⁴⁴   tʰia⁵⁵ ，tu³³   tsi³⁵   mɔ⁵⁵   ȵa³⁵
   个   父亲   也   不   好   也   个   父亲   痛   重
   CL   father   CONJ   NEG   good   too   CL   father   hurt   heavy

(2) qai⁵⁵ thia⁵⁵ mpua⁴⁴ thia⁵⁵ ɳu⁵² 鸡、猪和牛

丈夫还不见好转，
the husband was not getting better,

30 ẓu³³ ɳ̥a³⁵ ẓu³³ tua⁵² lai³⁵ , tu³³ tsi³⁵ ŋken³³ ŋken³³ li⁴⁴
　　渐渐　　重　　渐渐　　来　　嘞　　个　　丈夫　　虚弱　　虚弱　　的
　　gradually heavy gradually come IP CL husband RDUP~weak PRT

laɯ²¹ ,
了
PRF

丈夫的病渐渐加重了，丈夫的身体很虚弱了，
his condition worsened gradually, and he became very weak.

31 tu³³ tsi³⁵ tsaɯ²¹ qɦau³¹tsa⁵² laɯ²¹ lu⁵² , pɯ⁴⁴ tʂi³³ ʂaɯ³⁵ li⁴⁴ lu⁵² ,
　　个　　父亲　　就　　卧床　　了　　咯　　睡　　不　　起　　的　　咯
　　CL father DM stay in bed PRF IP sleep NEG get up PRT IP

丈夫就卧床不起了，躺着就起不来了，
The husband was confined to bed and couldn't get up.

32 nɔ⁵² tʂi³³ tau³³ mɔ³⁵ li⁴⁴ lu⁵² , tu³³ nia²¹
　　吃　　不　　得　　饭　　的　　咯　　个　　妻子
　　eat NEG can meal IP IP CL wife

吃不了饭了，
He wasn't able to have a meal,

33 thia⁵⁵ tu³³ tsi³⁵ tsaɯ²¹ lɔ³³ ʂai⁵⁵la⁵² : "ʔɔ⁵⁵ , kɔ⁵² tsi³⁵ ʔa⁵² ,
　　和　　个　　丈夫　　就　　来　　商量　　啊　　你　　丈夫　　啊
　　and CL husband DM come discuss INT 2S husband IP

妻子就来跟丈夫商量："啊，孩子他爸啊,
so the wife discussed with her husband: "Ah, Father of my child,

34 kɔ⁵² mɔ⁵⁵ mɔ³⁵ kɔ⁵² ʂaɯ³⁵ tʂi³³ tau³³ tɕe³³ , ʔɯ⁵⁵ lɔ³³
　　你　　痛　　痛　　你　　起　　不　　得　　这样　　我俩　　也
　　2S RDUP~hurt 2S get up NEG can this way we two CONJ

你病重起不了床了，
You are so sick that you can't get out of the bed,

35 tsɔ²¹ tsɔ²¹ ɲi²¹ thia⁵⁵ , tʂi³³ mua⁵² ʔda⁵⁵tʂi⁴⁴ tɕe³³ , ʔɯ⁵⁵ mua⁵⁵
   很困难　　　　也　　不　　有　　什么　　　这样　　　我俩　拿
   very hard　　too　NEG　have　anything　this way　we two　take

我们又很困难，又什么都没有，
and we live such a hard life and don't have anything;

36 nɦia³¹ mpua⁴⁴ ntaɯ²¹ ŋkua⁵² tɕo⁵² lɔ³³ tua⁴⁴ ʔua⁴⁴nen⁵⁵ khɔ⁴⁴ kɔ⁵² sɯ⁵⁵ ʔɔ⁵² ."
   那　　　猪　　　那　　　圈　　带　来　　杀　跳神　　　　医　　你　仅仅　吧
   that　pig　　that　　pen　bring come kill　do ritual　heal　2S　only　IP

我们把圈里的那头猪拿来跳神给你治病吧。"
Let's go to bring the pig in the pigpen to perform a ritual to heal your illness.

37 tɕe³³ tu³³ mpua⁴⁴ tsaɯ²¹ n̥ɔ³⁵ laɯ²¹ .
   这样　　　头　　猪　　　就　　　听见　了
   this way　CL　pig　　DM　　hear　PRF

这样，猪就听见了。
Thus the pig heard them,

38 "ʔu⁵⁵ , ʔua⁴⁴li⁴⁴tɕa³³ laɯ³⁵ ʑua³⁵ mua⁵⁵ ku³⁵ tua⁴⁴ le³⁵ ?
   哦　　为什么　　　　　　他们　要　　　把　　我　　杀　　呢
   INT　why　　　　　　　3PL　want　PT　1S　kill　Q

"哦，为什么他们要把我杀了呢？
"Oh, why do they want to kill me?

39 laɯ³⁵ ʑua³⁵ mu³³ xu⁴⁴ nen⁵⁵ tua⁵² ʑua³⁵ ʔua⁴⁴nen⁵⁵ ʔe³³
   他们　　要　　　去　　叫　　巫师　　来　　要　　跳神　　　　　　唉
   3PL　will　go　call　shaman　come　will　do ritual　IP

他们要去请巫师来跳神唉，
They are going to call a shaman to perform the ritual;

40 ʑua³⁵ mua⁵⁵ ku³⁵ tua⁴⁴ thia⁵⁵ nɔ⁵² le³⁵ . ʔɔ⁵⁵ , ʑua³⁵ ʔua⁴⁴tɕa³³ ne⁵² ?
   要　　　把　　　我　　杀　　和　　吃　　　嘞　　啊　　要　　　怎么办　　呢
   will　PT　1S　kill　and　eat　IP　INT　should　what to do　Q

要把我杀吃了。啊，要怎么办呢？
they are going to kill me and eat me. Ah, what should I do?

(2) qai⁵⁵ thia⁵⁵ mpua⁴⁴ thia⁵⁵ ȵu⁵² 鸡、猪和牛

41 sa³⁵ sa³⁵ ʐua³⁵ ʔua⁴⁴tɕa³³ ， mu³³ ʂai⁵⁵la⁵² tau⁴⁴ ȵu⁵² ʂai⁵⁵ ，
 想　　　想　　要　　怎么办　　　去　　商量　　给　牛　看
 RDUP~think　　　should　what to do　go　discuss　P　ox　see
想想办法，去跟牛商量看看，
Think what to do! I'll go to discuss with the ox;

42 ȵu⁵² lɔ⁵² mi⁴⁴ ntʂi³³， te⁵²ʐau²¹ ȵu⁵² mua⁵² tʂɯ³⁵ʑi²¹ ʐua³⁵ pa⁵⁵ tau⁴⁴ ."
 牛　大　小　　些　　有时　　　牛　有　　主意　　要　帮忙　得
 ox　big small CL.PL sometime ox have idea should help can
牛大一些，或许牛有办法帮得上忙。"
the ox is much bigger than me, maybe the ox can help."

43 tɕe³³ tu³³ mpua⁴⁴ tsaɯ²¹ mu³³ ʂai⁵⁵la⁵² tau⁴⁴
 这样　个　　猪　　就　　去　　商量　　给
 thus　CL　pig　　DM　go　discuss　P
这样，猪就去找牛商量。
Therefore, the pig went to consult with the ox.

44 tu³³ ȵu⁵² . mu³³ tsfiɔ³¹ ntaɯ²¹ tu³³ ȵu⁵² : "ʔɔ⁵⁵， ȵu⁵²， tɦai³¹ ki³³ nɔ³⁵/⁴⁴ na³⁵ ，
 头　 牛　　去　　到　　那　　头　牛　啊　牛　　早上　　这　啊
 CL　ox　go　arrive that　CL　ox　INT　ox　morning this　IP
找到牛那里："啊，牛，今天早上啊，
The pig went to the ox and said: "Ah, ox, this morning,

45 nia²¹ thia⁵⁵ tsi³⁵ laɯ³⁵ ʂai⁵⁵la⁵² le³⁵ ， ta²¹ʂi²¹nɔ⁴⁴
 母亲　和　父亲　他们　商量　　嘞　　现在
 mother and father 3PL discuss IP now
父亲和母亲他们商量了，
Our parents discussed that,

46 pe⁵⁵ tsi³⁵ mɔ³⁵ mɔ⁵⁵ ni⁴⁴， nia²¹ thia⁵⁵ tsi³⁵ ŋkaɯ²¹ ʂai⁵⁵la⁵²
 我们　父亲　痛　　痛　呢　　母亲　和　父亲　对　商量
 1PL father RDUP~hurt IP mother and father pair discuss
现在我们父亲病得很重呢，母亲和父亲他俩商量
now because Father is seriously ill, Mother discussed with him that

47 zua³⁵ mu³³ xu⁴⁴ nen⁵⁵ tua⁵² ʔua⁴⁴nen⁵⁵ kʰɔ⁴⁴ pe⁵⁵ tsi³⁵ ,
　　要　去　叫　巫师　来　跳神　　医　我们　父亲
　　will　go　call　shaman　come　do ritual　heal　1PL　father

要去叫巫师来跳神来医治我们的父亲,

they are going to call a shaman to perform a ritual to heal our father's illness;

48 zua³⁵ mua⁵⁵ ku³⁵ tua⁴⁴ nɔ³⁵/⁴⁴ le³⁵ . kɔ⁵² ʔua⁴⁴ ŋu⁵² kɔ⁵² lɔ⁵² mi⁴⁴ ntʂi³³ ,
　　要　把　我　杀　这　嘞　你　当　牛　你　大　小　些
　　will　PT　1PL　kill　this　IP　2S　be　ox　2S　big　small　CL.PL

要把我杀了嘞, 你是牛, 你大一些,

they are going to kill me. You are an ox and bigger than me,

49 kɔ⁵² mua⁵² l̩ɯ⁵⁵ zuŋ⁴⁴ , kɔ⁵² mua⁵² zuŋ⁴⁴ tʂu³⁵zi²¹ , kɔ⁵² s̩i²¹
　　你　有　脑子　好　你　有　好　主意　你　试
　　2S　have　brain　good　2S　have　good　idea　2S　try

你有好脑子, 有好主意,

you are clever and can work out good ideas,

50 pa⁵⁵ ntau²⁵ tʂu³⁵zi²¹ s̩ai⁵⁵ zua³⁵ ʔua⁴⁴li⁴⁴tɕa³³ , lau̯³⁵ li⁴⁴ tʂi³³ tua⁴⁴ ku³⁵ ʔa⁵² ,
　　帮忙　打　主意　看　要　怎么办　他们　才　不　杀　我　呀
　　help　hit　idea　see　should　what to do　3PL　just　NEG　kill　1S　IP

你试着帮忙出主意看要怎么办, 他们才不杀我,

Please try to help me out with ideas, what should I do so they won't kill me.

51 ku³⁵ ntʂhai⁴⁴ tɦua³¹ kɦau³¹ li⁴⁴ʔɔ³³ ."
　　我　怕　死　非常　啊
　　1S　afraid　death　very　IP

我非常害怕死啊。"

I am very afraid of death."

52 tɕe³³ tu³³ ŋu⁵² xai³³ ʈau⁴⁴ tu³³ mpua⁴⁴ tia³³ : "mu³³ mu³³ mu³³ ,
　　这样　头　牛　说　给　头　猪　道　去　去　去
　　thus　CL　ox　say　P　CL　pig　QUOT　go　go　go

这样, 牛对猪说: "走走走,

Thus, the ox said to the pig: "Get out of here,

(2) qai⁵⁵ tʰia⁵⁵ mpua⁴⁴ tʰia⁵⁵ ȵu⁵² 鸡、猪和牛

53 tɕi³³   zɦɔ³¹   kɯ³⁵   ten⁵⁵men²¹ ,   laɯ³⁵   tua⁴⁴   lɔ³³   tua⁴⁴   kɔ⁵²   sɯ⁵⁵   na³⁵ ,
   不   是   我   事情   他们   杀   也   杀   你   仅仅   呢
   NEG   be   1S   matter   3PL   kill   CONJ   kill   2S   only   IP

不是我的事情，他们杀也只是杀你呢，

it's none of my business. It's you that they want to kill,

54 tɯ⁵⁵   tɕi³³   zɦɔ³¹   tua⁴⁴   kɯ³⁵   na³⁵ ,   mu³³   mu³³   mu³³ ."
   都   不   是   杀   我   呢   去   去   去
   all   NEG   be   kill   1S   IP   go   go   go

又不是杀我啊，走走走。"

It's not me, quickly go."

55 "ʔa³⁵   ȵu⁵² ,   laɯ³⁵   zua³⁵   mua⁵⁵   kɯ³⁵   tua⁴⁴   tɦia³¹   tɦia³¹   ʔɔ³³ ,   tɦai³¹ki³³
   啊   牛   他们   要   把   我   杀   真   真   啊   早上
   INT   ox   3PL   will   PT   1S   kill   RDUP~really   IP   morning

"啊，牛，他们真的是要把我杀了啊，今天早上啊，

"Ah, ox, they are really going to kill me; this morning,

56 nɔ³⁵/⁴⁴   na³⁵ ,   nia²¹   tʰia⁵⁵   tsi³⁵   tɯ⁵⁵   mu³³   xu⁴⁴   nen⁵⁵   ta³³   laɯ²¹   le³⁵ ,
   这   啊   母亲   和   父亲   都   去   叫   巫师   完   了   嘞
   this   IP   mother and   father   all   go   call   shaman finish PRF   IP

母亲和父亲都已经去请巫师了呀，

our parents have already gone to call the shaman,

57 ʔi⁵⁵   tʂa²¹   laɯ³⁵   tua⁵²   ʔua⁴⁴nen⁵⁵   tɕe³³ ,   laɯ³⁵   mua⁵⁵   kɯ³⁵   tua⁴⁴ ,
   一   会儿   他们   来   跳神   这样   他们   把   我   杀
   one   moment 3PL   come   do ritual   thus   3PL   PT   1S   kill

一会他们来跳神的话，他们要把我杀了，

In a little while when they come to perform the ritual, I will get killed；

58 kɔ⁵²   ntʰia³⁵   tʂu³⁵zi²¹   pa⁵⁵   kɯ³⁵   na⁵² ."   tu³³   ȵu⁵²   xai³³   li⁴⁴   qu⁵⁵ :
   你   找   主意   帮忙   我   吧   头   牛   说   像   原来
   2S   find   idea   help   1S   IP   CL   ox   say   be.like former

你帮我出主意吧。" 牛还是像原来那样说：

please help me out with ideas." However, the ox sill said as before:

59 "ka³⁵tɕi³⁵ mu³³ , mu³³ mu³³ mu³³ , tʂi³³ zɦɔ³¹ ku³⁵ ten⁵⁵men²¹
　　赶紧　　　去　　去　　去　　去　　不　　是　　我　　事情
　　hurry　　 go　　go　　go　　go　　NEG　be　　1S　　matter

"赶紧走，走走走，这不是我的事情啊，
"Hurry up, quickly leave, it's none of my business;

60 ʔɔ³³ , kɔ⁵² mu³³ kɔ⁵² , lau³⁵ tua⁴⁴ kɔ⁵² sɯ⁵⁵ tɯ⁵⁵ tʂi³³ zɦɔ³¹ tua⁴⁴ ku³⁵ ,
　　啊　　你　去　　你　　他们　杀　 你　　仅仅　都　　不　　是　　杀　　我
　　INT　2S　 go　　2S　　3PL　 kill　2S　 only　all　NEG　be　　kill　1S

你走你的吧，他们只杀你而已，又不是杀我，
just leave; anyway, it's only you, not me, that they want to kill;

61 mu³³ mu³³ mu³³ ." ʔau⁵⁵ , tu³³ mpua⁴⁴ tʂi³³ pɔ²¹qa⁵⁵ ʔua⁴⁴li⁴⁴tɕa³³ .
　　去　　去　　去　　　哦　　头　　猪　　　不　　知道　　　怎么办
　　go　 go　 go　　　 INT　CL　 pig　　 NEG　know　 what to do

走走走。"哦，猪不知道要怎么办了。
quickly leave." The pig didn't know what to do.

62 tɕe³³ tu³³ mpua⁴⁴ tɔ³⁵qa⁵⁵ lɔ³³ ŋɔ⁵⁵ tɯ⁵⁵pɔ⁵⁵ lu⁵² .
　　这样　头　　猪　　　回　　　来　　住　　等死　　　 啦
　　thus　CL　pig　　　return　come　live　wait for death　IP

怎么办？这样，猪只得回来等死了。
What to do? So all the pig could do was return to his pen and wait for death.

63 ʔi⁵⁵ tʂa²¹ tʂau³³ntu⁵² , tu³³ tsi³⁵nen⁵⁵ tua⁵² tsfɔ³¹ ,
　　一　会儿　　天黑　　　　个　　巫师　　　来　到
　　one　moment　get dark　　CL　 shaman　come　arrive

一会儿天黑了，巫师来到，
After a while, it was getting dark. The shaman came,

64 tsau²¹ mu³³ ʔua⁴⁴nen⁵⁵ . ʔua⁴⁴nen⁵⁵ tɕe³³ mua⁵⁵ tu³³ mpua⁴⁴
　　就　　　去　　跳神　　　　跳神　　　　这样　拿　　头　　猪
　　DM　　 go　 do ritual　　 do ritual　　thus　take　CL　 pig

就开始跳神。跳神需要把那头猪拿来医治丈夫，
and started to perform the ritual, using the pig to cure the husband;

（2）qai⁵⁵ tɕʰia⁵⁵ mpua⁴⁴ tɕʰia⁵⁵ ȵu⁵² 鸡、猪和牛

65 tɕɔ⁵² lɔ³³ kʰɔ⁴⁴ tu³³ tsi³⁵ , mua⁵⁵ tua⁴⁴ nɔ⁵² ta³³ lu⁵² ,
带 来 医 个 丈夫 拿 杀 吃 完 咯
bring come heal CL husband take kill eat finish IP

把猪杀了吃完了，拿

the pig was killed and eaten up.

66 mua⁵⁵ ʔi⁵⁵ tɕʰie³¹ ȵtɕʰiə³¹ lu⁵⁵ tau⁵⁵xau⁴⁴ ʈau⁴⁴ tu³³ tsi³⁵nen⁵⁵ ɴqa⁴⁴ mu³³ nɔ⁵²
拿 一 腿 和 个 头 给 个 巫师 带 去 吃
take one leg and CL head give CL shaman take.along go eat

tɕʰia³¹ .
完
finish

一条猪腿肉和猪头给巫师带回去吃。

One leg and the head of the pig were given to the shaman to take home and eat.

67 ŋɔ⁵⁵ ŋɔ⁵⁵ ʔɔ⁵⁵ pe⁵⁵ ȵu⁵⁵ tɔ²¹qa⁵⁵ tu³³ tsi³⁵ ŋken³³ ʐu⁵² ʐu³³ lu³⁵ ,
住 住 两 三 天 后面 个 丈夫 虚弱 渐渐 咯
RDUP~live two three day after CL husband weak gradually IP

两三天之后，丈夫身体越来越虚弱了，

Two or three days later, the husband's body became gradually weaker;

68 tu³³ tsi³⁵ ʔi⁵⁵ ȵu⁵⁵ ŋken³³ ʔdua⁴⁴ ʔi⁵⁵ ȵu⁵⁵ ,
个 丈夫 一 天 虚弱 过 一 天
CL husband one day weak spend one day

丈夫一天比一天虚弱，

his body was getting weaker day by day;

69 tu³³ tsi³⁵ nɔ⁵² tʂi³³ tau³³ mɔ³⁵ ni⁴⁴lu⁵² .
个 丈夫 吃 不 得 饭 了啊
CL husband eat NEG can meal IP

丈夫吃不下饭了。

he was so sick that he was unable to eat anything.

70 ŋɔ⁵⁵   ŋɔ⁵⁵ tɕe³³ tu³³ tsi³⁵   tʰua³¹ lauɯ²¹ lu⁵² . tu³³ tsi³⁵   tʰua³¹ lauɯ²¹
   住   住   这样 个   丈夫   死   了   咯   个   丈夫   死   了
   RDUP~live   thus CL husband die   PRF   IP   CL   husband dead PRF

过了不久丈夫就死了。
Soon later, the husband passed away.

71 tʂhua³⁵ tu³³ nia²¹ suɯ⁵⁵ , tu³³ tsi³⁵   tʰua³¹ lauɯ²¹ tʂi³³ mua⁵² ŋia⁵² ni⁴⁴lu⁵² .
   剩   个   妻子 仅仅   个   丈夫   死   了   不   有   钱   了呀
   remain CL wife only   CL husband die   PRF   NEG have money IP

丈夫死后只剩妻子一个人了，丈夫死了之后家里没有钱了呀。
The wife was left alone and the family was out of money after the husband's death.

72 tu³³ nia²¹ tia³³   : "ʔua⁴⁴ ʔi⁵⁵ si²¹   nia²¹ tsi³⁵ suɯ⁵⁵ tɕe³³   ,
   个   妻子 道   做   一   世   夫妻   仅仅 这样
   CL wife QUOT   be   one lifetime couple   only this way

妻子说："好难得做一世夫妻，
The wife said: "It's rare luck to be married for a lifetime,

73 mu³³ mua⁵⁵ ʔɯ⁵⁵ tu³³ ŋu⁵² lɔ³³   tua⁴⁴ ʈau⁴⁴ tu³³ tsi³⁵   lu⁵² ."
   去   拿   我俩 个   牛   来   杀   给   个   丈夫   吧
   go   take 1PL CL ox   come   kill P   CL   husband IP

就去把我俩的牛拿来杀了祭祀丈夫吧。"
let's kill our ox as a memorial for my husband."

74 mua⁵⁵ tɕɔ⁵² lɔ³³   tua⁴⁴ ʈau⁴⁴ tu³³ tsi³⁵ , tɕɔ⁵²
   拿   带   来   杀   给   个   丈夫   带
   take bring come   kill P   CL   husband take.along

拿来杀给丈夫，
The ox was killed for her husband,

75 mu³³ ʐɦu³¹ ʈau⁴⁴ xau³⁵ ʔda⁵⁵ te⁵⁵ lu⁵² .
   去   养   给   里   鬼   地   咯
   go   raise P   inside ghost field IP

让他带到阴间去养咯。
so he could raise the ox in the nether world.

(2) qai⁵⁵ tɕʰia⁵⁵ mpua⁴⁴ tɕʰia⁵⁵ ȵu⁵² 鸡、猪和牛

76 tu³³ qai⁵⁵ lɔ³³ tɕʰua³¹, tu³³ mpua⁴⁴ lɔ³³ tɕʰua³¹, tu³³ ȵu⁵² lɔ³³ tɕʰua³¹,
   只   鸡   也   死   只   猪   也   死   只   牛   也   死
   CL chicken CONJ die   CL pig   CONJ die   CL ox   CONJ die

鸡也死了，猪也死了，牛也死了，

The chicken was dead, the pig was dead, and the ox was also dead.

77 vi²¹ ʑɦɔ³¹ ʂauɯ³⁵ʔdauɯ³³ tʂi³³ ɕi⁵⁵ pa⁵⁵, tʂi³³ ɕi⁵⁵ lu⁵⁵,
   因为   是   大家   不   (相互缀) 帮忙   不 (相互缀) 爱
   because be everyone   NEG RECP   help   NEG RECP love

是因为大家不相互帮助，不相互爱护。

It is because they didn't help and love each other.

78 za⁵² ʔda⁵⁵nɦien³¹ nɔ⁴⁴ qhia⁴⁴ xai³³ tia³³ : pe⁵⁵ ʔua⁴⁴ nɦien³¹ ŋɔ⁵⁵,
   个   故事   这   教   说   道   我们   做   人   在
   CL   story   this teach   say   COMP 1PL   be   human   be.located

这个故事教导我们：我们在人世间，

This story teaches us that living in this world,

79 tʰau²¹ lu⁵⁵ ɕi⁵²xauɯ²¹ lauɯ³⁵ mua⁵² ten⁵⁵men²¹, lauɯ³⁵ tua⁵² pia³⁵,
   时候   个   时候   他们   有   事情   他们   来   摆
   time   CL   time   3PL   have   matter   3PL   come   put

当别人有困难的时候，他们来请教自己，

when other people need help and ask us for assistance;

80 qhia⁴⁴ tau⁴⁴ zu³³, zu³³ zua³⁵tau⁴⁴ ȵtʰia³⁵ ʔi⁵⁵ tsɔ⁵² hau⁴⁴ke³⁵ mu³³ pa⁵⁵ lauɯ³⁵.
   告诉   给   自己   自己 要得   找   一   条   前路   去   帮忙 他们
   tell   P   oneself oneself should   find   one   CL   way   go   help 3PL

我们自己要想一个办法去帮助他们。

we ourselves should find a way to help them.

81 tʰau²¹ tsɦɔ³¹ tu³³ tɔ²¹ mua⁵² ten⁵⁵men²¹,
   时候   到   个   那   有   事情
   time   arrive CL   that have   matter

当那个人有事情的时候，

When one asks us for help,

82 zu³³　　zua³⁵tau⁴⁴　mu³³　pa⁵⁵　tu³³　tɔ²¹　．thau²¹　lu⁵⁵　ʂi⁵²xaɯ²¹
　　自己　　要得　　　去　　帮忙　个　　那　　　时候　　个　　时候
　　oneself　should　　go　　help　CL　that　　time　　CL　time

我们得去帮助那个人。
we should reach out our hand to help him.

83 qhɔ³⁵　ten⁵⁵men²¹　ntaɯ²¹　tsfiɔ³¹　zu³³　，lɔ³³　tɕɔ³⁵　tɔ²¹　thia⁵²li⁴⁴
　　处　　事情　　　　那　　到　　　自己　　也　　些　　那　　才
　　place　matter　　　that　arrive　oneself　CONJ　CL.PL　that　just

当事情落到自己头上的时候，
When troubles happen to us,

84 tua⁵²　pa⁵⁵　zu³³　．za⁵²　ʔda⁵⁵　nfien³¹　nɔ⁴⁴　qhia⁴⁴　tau⁴⁴
　　来　　帮忙　自己　　个　　故事　　　　　　这　　教　　　给
　　come　help　oneself　CL　story　　　　this　teach　P

那些被我们帮助的人才会来帮助我们。
those whom we have helped once will be willing to help us.

85 ti⁵⁵nfien³¹　tia³³　：ʔua⁴⁴　nen⁵²　nɔ⁵⁵，zua³⁵tʂu²¹　ʂi⁵⁵　lu⁵⁵　ʂi⁵⁵　pa⁵⁵，
　　人　　　　道　　　做　　生活　住　　要得　　　　(相互缀) 爱　(相互缀) 帮忙
　　human　COMP　be　life　live　should　　RECP　love　RECP　help

这个故事教导我们：生活中，要互帮互助，
This story tells us: In our life, we should help each other,

86 tʂi³³　tshɔ⁵⁵　xai³³　tia³³　zfiɔ³¹　kɔ⁵²　li⁴⁴　ten⁵⁵men²¹，
　　不　　别　　　说　　道　　是　　　你　　的　　事情
　　NEG　IRR.NEG　say　COMP　be　　2S　PRT　thing

不要说是你的事，不是我的事，
don't say that your business is not my business;

87 tʂi³³　zfiɔ³¹　ku³⁵　li⁴⁴　ten⁵⁵men²¹，pua³⁵　len⁵²　zfiɔ³¹　ʂaɯ³⁵ʔdaɯ³³　li⁴⁴　ten⁵⁵men²¹．
　　不　　是　　　我　　的　　事情　　　　各　　位　　是　　大家　　　　的　　事情
　　NEG　be　　1S　PRT　matter　　each　CL　be　everyone　　PRT　matter

各人的事情就是大家的事情。
the problems of each are the problems of everyone.

(2) qai⁵⁵ thia⁵⁵ mpua⁴⁴ thia⁵⁵ ŋu⁵² 鸡、猪和牛

鸡、猪和牛

很久很久以前，有一对苗族夫妇住在高山上。

有一天，丈夫头痛不舒服，妻子就对丈夫说："孩子他爸，你不舒服，我们把那只鸡用来叫你的魂吧。"

这样，鸡听见了他俩的对话，鸡就去跟猪说："今天早上，我们的父母和母亲商量，他俩要把我拿去叫魂，你是猪，你个头大一点，你帮我想想办法看看要怎么办。要是他们拿我去叫魂，拿我去杀了吃的话，那就太可怕了。"

猪说道："杀也只是杀你啊，又不是杀我。他们要杀就杀，赶紧走开，我不想听，你的死活与我无关。"

鸡说："哦，猪，你真的不帮我呀？"

猪说："哦哟，走走走，别在这里说了，我不想再听了，他们杀也只是杀你，又不是杀我，赶紧走。"

鸡不知道要去跟谁商量，要怎么办呢？怕是要被杀吧，怎么办？

第二天早上，妻子就把鸡抓来给丈夫叫魂。拿鸡来叫丈夫的魂，拿来杀了吃。叫完魂过了几天，丈夫不但没有好转，反而病情还渐渐加重了，丈夫卧床不起了，饭也吃不了。妻子就来和丈夫商量："孩子他爸，你病得起不来了，我们又很困难，就把那头猪用来跳魂医治你吧。"

猪听见了夫妻俩的对话，心里很害怕。"啊，他们为什么要杀我呢？他们要请巫师来跳魂，他们要杀我，啊，怎么办呢？"猪想了想就去跟牛商量，牛个头大一些，或许牛可以有好主意。这样，猪就去跟牛商量。

猪去到牛那里："牛啊，今天早上，父母亲他们在商量嘞，现在父亲病得很重，母亲和父亲商量，要去请巫师来跳魂治父亲的病，要把我杀了吃。你是牛，你大一些，你头脑好使，有好主意，你帮我想想办法，看看要怎么办他们才不杀我啊，我真的很怕死啊。"

牛对猪说："走走走，这不是我的事情，他们要杀也只是杀你，又不杀我，走走走！"

"啊，牛，他们真的要杀我呀。今天早上，母亲和父亲他们都已经去请巫师了，一会儿巫师来跳魂，他们就要杀我了，你快想想办法帮帮我。"猪说。

牛还是那句老话："赶紧走，走走走，这不是我的事情。你走你的，他们要杀的是你，又不是杀我，走走走。"

这下子，猪不知道要怎么办了，他只有回来等死。一会儿，天黑了，巫师来到，开始跳魂。妻子就把猪杀了，用来跳魂医治丈夫的病。他俩还送了巫师一条猪腿和一个猪头带回去吃。

过了几天，丈夫的病又加重了，丈夫的病一天比一天重，已经不能吃饭了。过不久丈夫就去世了，只剩下妻子一个人。丈夫死后家里没有什么钱。妻子说："难得做一世夫妻，你死了，我就把我俩的那头牛杀给你吧。"这样，妻子就把牛杀了给死去的丈夫，让丈夫带到阴间去养。

鸡死了，猪死了，牛也死了，是因为大家不懂得互相帮助。这个故事启示我们："当别

人有困难的时候，他们来求助我们，我们要想办法去帮助他们。当那个人有事的时候，我们得去帮助那个人。当事情降临到我们头上的时候，那些被我们帮助的人才会来帮助我们。"这个故事教导我们："生活中，要互帮互助，不要说是你的事，不关我的事，每个人的事情就是我们大家的事情。"

The Chicken, the Pig and the Ox

A long time ago, a Hmong couple lived high in the mountains.

One day, the husband had a headache and didn't feel comfortable. The wife said to him: "Father of my child, let's go get the chicken to call back your soul if you are not feeling well."

The chicken heard their conversation, so it told the pig: "This morning, our parents discussed that they are going to take me to call back Father's soul. You are a pig and bigger than me. Help me with some ideas to find out what to do. I'm so scared if they take me to call back the soul and eat me."

The pig said: "They are going to kill you only. It's not me who's going to be killed. They can go ahead and kill you. Quickly leave me alone. I don't want to listen. Your life has nothing to do with me."

The chicken said: "Oh, pig, you are really not willing to help me?"

The pig said: "Go quickly! Don't come back and say that again. I'm tired of your words. They are going to kill you only, not me. Leave quickly!"

The chicken didn't know who to discuss with or what to do. It thought, "I may get killed. What should I do?"

Next morning, the wife went to catch the chicken to call back her husband's soul. She caught the chicken to call back the soul and then ate it. A few days later, the husband wasn't getting better; on the contrary, his condition worsened gradually. He was confined to bed and couldn't get up and was unable to have a meal. So, the couple discussed it, and the mother said: "Father of my child, you are so sick that you can't get out of bed. We live such a hard life and don't have anything. Let's go bring the pig to perform a ritual to heal your illness."

The pig heard their conversation and was very afraid. "Ah, why do they want to kill me? They are going to call a shaman to perform the ritual. They are going to kill me. What should I do?" The pig thought carefully and went to discuss with the ox. The ox is bigger, so maybe it could help. Therefore, the pig went to consult with the ox.

The pig went to the ox and said: "Ox, this morning our parents discussed about calling a shaman to perform a ritual to heal Father's illness, and they are going to kill and eat me. You are an ox and bigger than me. You are clever and you can come up with good ideas, so please help me with some ideas about what should I do so that they won't kill me. I'm really afraid of death."

The ox said to the pig: "Quickly leave. It's none of my business. It's you they want to kill, not me. Quickly go!"

"Ah, Ox, they are really going to kill me. Our mother and father have already gone to call the shaman this morning. I will be killed later when the shaman comes to perform the ritual in a little while. Please help me out with some ideas." The pig said.

The ox still said: "Quickly leave! Just go! It's none of my business. Anyway, they want to kill you only, not me. Quickly leave!"

So the pig didn't know what to do but return to its pen and wait for death. After a while, it was getting dark. The shaman came and started to perform the ritual. Therefore the wife killed the pig for the ritual to cure her husband's illness. They also gave one leg and the head of the pig to the shaman to take home and eat.

A few days later, the husband's condition worsened gradually. His body was getting weaker day by day. He was so ill that he was even unable to eat anything. Soon after, the husband passed away, leaving his wife alone. The family was out of money after the husband's death. The wife said: "It's a rare luck to stay married for a lifetime; let me kill our ox for you." Thus, the wife killed the ox for her husband so he could raise it in the nether world.

In the end, the chicken was dead, the pig was dead and the ox was also dead. It is because they didn't help each other. This story tells us that we should reach out our hand to help when other people get into trouble and ask for our assistance. When one asks us for help, we should reach out to help. When trouble happens to us, those whom we have helped once will help us. The story teaches us that in our daily life, we should help each other. Don't think that my business is not your business. Actually, the problems of each are the problems of everyone.

（3）ṣa⁵⁵ te³³ 手

只 手
hand

1 pe⁵⁵ ʔua⁴⁴ nen⁵² ŋɔ⁵⁵ , pe⁵⁵ ṣa⁵⁵ te³³ mua⁵² tṣi⁵⁵ tu³³ nti³⁵ te³³ .
　我们　做　生活　在　　　　我们　只　手　有　五　根　指　手
　　1PL　do　life　be.located　1PL　CL　hand　have　five　CL　finger　hand
在我们的生活中，我们每只手有五根手指。
In our life, we have five fingers on each hand.

2 thau²¹ tɕɔ⁵² lɔ³³ tṣɔ⁴⁴ ʔua⁴⁴ ke⁴⁴ , nɯ³³ zua³⁵ mua⁵² tu³³ ṣia⁵⁵
　时候　带　来　放　一起　　　它　要　有　根　高
　　time　bring　come　put　together　3S　will　have　CL　high
放在一起的时候，有的高有的矮，
When they are put together, some are tall and some short,

3 tu³³ qe³³ , mua⁵² tu³³ lɔ⁵² tu³³ me⁴⁴ , tṣi³³ ṣi⁵⁵ tṣi²¹ . pe⁵⁵ ʔua⁴⁴
　根　矮　有　根　大　根　小　不　相互　齐　我们　做
　　CL　short　have　CL　big　CL　small　NEG　RECP　straight　1PL　do
有的大有的小，不一样。
some big and some small, they are not the same.

4 nen⁵² ŋɔ⁵⁵ mua⁵² tu³³ tsaɯ⁵² tu³³ ntṣe⁴⁴ , mua⁵² tu³³ ʈua²¹ ,
　生活　在　　　　有　个　能干　个　聪明　有　个　蠢
　　life　be.located　have　CL　capable　CL　clever　have　CL　stupid
生活中，有聪明人有蠢人，
In our daily life, there are smart people and stupid people,

5 mua⁵² tu³³ ṣia⁵⁵ tu³³ qe³³ , mua⁵² pɔ⁵² nia²¹ tsi³⁵ nen⁵² .
　有　个　高　个　矮　有　女人　男人
　　have　CL　tall　CL　short　have　woman　man

有高的人有矮的人，有男人有女人。
as well as tall and short people, men and women.

6 ʔi⁵⁵ ʂa⁵⁵ te³³, zɦɔ³¹ xai³³ tia³³　　kɔ⁵² mua⁵⁵ ʔi⁵⁵ tu³³ nti³⁵　te³³
　一　边　手　要是　说　道　　你　拿　一　根　指　手
　one side hand　if　say COMP　2S take one CL finger hand

一只手，要是说你用一根手指去抓饭吃，
If you use only one finger to pick up food,

7 tɛɔ⁵² mu³³ tʂua⁵⁵ mɔ³⁵ lɔ³³　nɔ⁵², zen⁵² tʂua⁵⁵ tʂi³³　tau⁴⁴
　领　去　抓　饭　来　吃　　根本　抓　　不　得
　lead go grasp food come eat　at all grasp　NEG get

什么都抓不了，
it's not possible to eat at all.

8 ʔi⁵⁵ zɦau³¹ pua³³ zɦɔ³¹, zua³⁵tʂu²¹　mua⁵⁵ ʔɔ⁵⁵ tu³³ tɛɔ⁵²
　一　次　　是否　是　　要得　　拿　二　根　带
　one time　Q　COP　should　take two CL take.along

必须得用两根手指去夹，
You must use two fingers

9 mu³³ tʂua⁵⁵, thia⁵² le⁴⁴ tau⁴⁴ ʔi⁵⁵ qhɔ⁴⁴ mɔ³⁵ lɔ³³ zɦɔ³¹ tau⁴⁴
　去　抓　　才　　得　一　处　饭　或　是　得
　go grasp　just　get one thing meal or　COP get

才能夹到一点饭或一点肉来吃；
to grasp some rice or meat to eat.

10 ʔi⁵⁵ qhɔ³⁵ ɴqai⁵² lɔ³³　nɔ⁵²; thau²¹ kua³³　kɔ⁵² mua⁵⁵ pe⁵⁵ tu³³
　一　处　肉　来　吃　　时候 (定标)　你　拿　三　根
　one place meat come eat　time REL　2S take three CL

当你用三根手指去捏的时候，
When you use three fingers,

11 tɛɔ⁵² lɔ³³　tʂua⁵⁵, nuɯ³³ zua³⁵tau⁴⁴ ntau⁴⁴ zɦɔ³¹　　mi⁴⁴ ntʂi³³;
　带　来　抓　它　要得　多　(增多状)　小　些
　bring come grasp 3S should　much increasingly small CL.PL

会抓到多些；
you will get more.

12 thau²¹ kɔ⁵² mua⁵⁵ plau⁵⁵ tu³³ tɕɔ⁵² lɔ³³ tʂua⁵⁵, nɯ³³ ʐua³⁵
   时候   你   拿   四   根   带   来   抓   它   要
   time   2S   take   four   CL   bring   come   grasp   3S   will
当你用四根手指抓的时候，
When you use four fingers,

13 tau⁴⁴ ntau⁴⁴ ʑɦɔ³¹ mi⁴⁴ ntʂi³³; thau²¹ kɔ⁵² mua⁵⁵ tʂi⁵⁵ tɕɦɯ³¹
   得   多   (增多状)   小   点   时候   你   拿   五   根
   get   much   increasingly   small   point   time   2S   take   five   CL
又抓到更多一点；
you will get a little more.

14 tɕɔ⁵² lɔ³³ tʂɔ⁴⁴ ʔua⁴⁴ ke⁴⁴ mu³³ tʂua⁵⁵ mɔ³⁵, nɯ³³ ʐua³⁵tau⁴⁴ ntau⁴⁴ xen³⁵ .
   带   来   让   一起   去   抓   饭   它   要得   多   很
   take   come   let   together   go   grasp   food   3S   should   much   very
当你把五根手指放在一起去抓饭时，抓到很多。
When you use five fingers together, you will get much more.

15 lɔ³³ ɕi³³ thau²¹ kɔ⁵² ʐua³⁵ mu³³ ntau³³ ʔi⁵⁵ tu³³ ti⁵⁵ nɦen³¹ tɕɦɯ³¹,
   或是   时候   你   要   去   打   一   个   人   哪
   or   time   2S   need   go   hit   one   CL   person   which
或者当你要去打哪一个人时，
Or when you're going to beat someone,

16 kɔ⁵² mua⁵⁵ ʔi⁵⁵ tu³³ nti³⁵ te³³ tɕɔ⁵² mu³³ tau²¹,
   你   拿   一   根   指   手   带   去   戳
   2S   take   one   CL   finger   hand   take.along   go   poke
你用一根手指去，
if you use one finger

17 tɕɔ⁵² mu³³ tʃhu²¹ lau³⁵ sɯ⁵⁵, pua³³ mɔ⁵⁵ ? kɔ⁵² pua³³ zen⁵² lau³⁵ ?
   带   去   戳   别人   仅仅   是否   疼   你   是否   赢   别人
   take.along   go   poke   others   only   Q   hurt   2S   Q   win   others

只用一根手指去戳别人，别人会疼吗？你能赢别人吗？
to poke others, will they hurt? Can you beat them with one finger?

18 mua⁵⁵ ʔɔ⁵⁵ tu³³ tshu²¹, pua³³ tau⁴⁴ ? ntau³³ pua³³ zen⁵² lau³⁵ ?
    拿　　两　　根　　戳　　是否　得　　打　　是否　赢　　别人
    take　two　CL　poke　Q　　can　hit　Q　　win　others

拿两根手指戳，行吗？能打赢别人吗？
What if using two fingers? Can you beat them?

19 mua⁵⁵ pe⁵⁵ tu³³, mua⁵⁵ plau⁵⁵ tu³³, mua⁵⁵ tʂi⁵⁵ tɕʰu³¹ tɕɔ⁵² lɔ³³
    拿　　三　　根　　拿　　四　　根　　拿　　五　　根　　带　来
    take　three　CL　take　four　CL　take　five　CL　bring　come

用三根、四根五根来捏成一个拳头，
Only by clenching your fist with three, four or five fingers

20 ŋi²¹ ʔua⁴⁴ ʔi⁵⁵ lu⁵⁵ ɲtɕʰi³¹, tʰia⁵² le⁴⁴ zua³⁵ mua⁵² ʐɦo³¹ ,
    捏　　做　　一　　个　　拳头　　才　　　要　　有　　力气
    clench　make　one　CL　fist　　just　　need　have　strength

才会有力气，
can you have the strength

21 tʰia⁵² le⁴⁴ zua³⁵ mu³³ ntau³³ tau⁴⁴ lau³⁵ . zɦo³¹ le⁴⁴ntau²¹ pe⁵⁵ ʔua⁴⁴ nen⁵²
    才　　　要　　去　　打　　得　　别人　　是　　那样　　我们　做　　生活
    just　want　go　hit　can　others　COP　that way　1PL　do　life

才能打得了别人。因此，在我们的生活中
to fight with others. Therefore, in our life,

22 ŋɔ⁵⁵ , zɦo³¹ xai³³ tia³³ kɔ⁵² ʔi⁵⁵ lɦien³¹ su⁵⁵ , kɔ⁵² ʔua⁴⁴ ʔda⁵⁵ tʂi⁴⁴
    在　　　是　　说　　道　　你　　一　　位　　仅仅　　你　　做　　什么
    be.located　COP　say　COMP　2S　one　CL　only　2S　do　what

要是说只有你一个人，
if it's only you,

23 kɔ⁵² zen⁵² ʔua⁴⁴ tau⁴⁴ tʂi³³ zuŋ⁴⁴ mpau²¹ le⁴⁴ tɕuŋ⁵⁵ tɕuŋ⁵⁵ len⁵² ʔua⁴⁴ .
    你　　根本　做　　得　　不　　好　　一样　像　多　　　多　　位　　做
    2S　at all　do　can　NEG　good　same　look　RDUP~much　CL　do

(3) ṣa⁵⁵ te³³ 手

你做什么都不如很多人一起做。
Whatever you do, it won't be as good as people doing it together.

24 tɕuŋ⁵⁵   tɕuŋ⁵⁵ len⁵² ʔua⁴⁴ tɕɔ⁵² lɔ³³   ŋɔ⁵⁵   ʔua⁴⁴ ke⁴⁴ , tɕɔ⁵² lɔ³³   ɲi²¹
    多   多   位   做   带   来   在   一起   带   来   捏
    RDUP~much   CL   do   bring come be.located   together   bring come clench

很多人团结在一起，攥成一个拳头，
People unite together, clenching into a fist

25 ʔua⁴⁴ ʔi⁵⁵ lu⁵⁵ ɲtɕhi³¹ , thia⁵² le⁴⁴ ʐua³⁵ mua⁵² ʐɦo³¹ ,
   做   一   个   拳头   才   要   有   力气
   make one CL fist   just   will have strength

才有力量，
then they will have the power

26 thia⁵² le⁴⁴ ʐua³⁵ ʔua⁴⁴ tau⁴⁴ ʔi⁵⁵ tsɔ⁵² xau⁵² luɯ²¹ tɕen²¹ tɕen⁵⁵ .
   才   要   做   得   一   条   事情   正经
   just   need do   can   one   CL   matter   serious

才能做成一件正事。
to be able to do serious business.

27 ṣa⁵⁵ te³³ lɔ³³ ʐɦo³¹ ṣa⁵⁵ ɲtɕhi³¹ nɔ⁴⁴ , nɯ³³ qhia⁴⁴ tau⁴⁴ xai³³ tia³³ : kua²¹ ṣaɯ³⁵ ʔdaɯ³³
   只   手   或   是   个   拳头   这   它   告诉   得   说   道   让   大家
   CL hand or   COP   CL   fist   this   3S   tell   can say   COMP   let   people

这只手或这个拳头，它揭示一个道理：让大家
The hand or the fist tells us that

28 tsi³³ xai³³ tu³³   mi⁴⁴   tu³³   lɔ⁵² tu³³ ṣia⁵⁵ tu³³ qe³³ , ṣaɯ³⁵ ʔdaɯ³³
   不   说   个   小   个   大   个   高   个   矮   大家
   NEG say   physique small physique big   hight tall hight short people

不论个儿大个儿小，个儿高个儿矮，
no matter if they're big or small, tall or short,

29 tsi³³ xai³³ pɔ⁵² nia²¹ tsi³⁵ nen⁵² , tu³³   lɔ⁵⁵ tu³³   zau⁴⁴ , ṣaɯ³⁵ ʔdaɯ³³
   不   说   女人   男人   个   大   个   小   大家
   NEG say   woman   man   physique big physique small   people

不论男人女人，年长年幼，
male or female, old or young,

30 ʐua³⁵tʂu²¹　lɔ³³　ʂi⁵⁵　kuŋ²¹ te³³ , ʔua⁴⁴ ʔi⁵⁵ lu⁵⁵ n̩tɕhi³¹ ,
　　要得　　来　相互　携　手　　做　一　个　拳头
　　 should　 come　mutual　join　hand　make　one　CL　fist

大家要携起手来，攥成一个拳头，
people should join their hands, making a fist,

31 thia⁵² le⁴⁴ mua⁵² ʐɦɔ³¹　．！
　　才　　有　　力气
　　 just　　 have　 strength

这样才有力量。
that's how they have power.

手

在我们的生活中，我们每只手都有五根手指。五根手指放在一起的时候，有的高有的矮，有的大有的小，不一样。生活中，有聪明人有蠢人，有高的人有矮的人，有男人有女人。

一只手，要是说你用一根手指去抓饭吃，什么都抓不了，必须得用两根手指去夹，才能夹到一点饭或一点肉来吃；当你用三根手指去捏的时候，会抓到多些；当你用四根手指抓的时候，又抓到更多一点；当你把五根手指放在一起去抓饭时，抓到很多。或者当你要去打哪一个人时，你只用一根手指去戳别人，别人会疼吗？你能赢别人吗？拿两根手指戳，行吗？能打赢别人吗？用三根、四根、五根手指头来攥成一个拳头，才会有力气，才能打得了别人。

因此，在我们的生活中，要是说只有你一个人，你做什么都不如很多人一起做。很多人团结在一起，攥成一个拳头，才有力量，才能做成一件正事。

这只手或这个拳头，它揭示一个道理：让大家不论个儿大个儿小，个儿高个儿矮，不论男人女人，年长年幼，大家要携起手来，攥成一个拳头，这样才有力量。

The Hand

In our life, we have five fingers on each hand. When they are put together, some are tall and some are short, some big and some small; they are not the same. The same way, in our daily life, there are smart people and stupid people, as well as tall people and short people, man and woman.

If you only use one finger to pick up food, it's impossible to eat at all. You must use two fingers to grasp some rice or meat to eat. When you use three fingers, you will get more. When you use four fingers, you will get a little more. When you use five fingers to eat, you will get much more. Or when you're going to beat someone, if you poke others with one finger, will they hurt? Can you beat them with one finger? What if using two fingers? Can you beat them? Only by clenching your fist with three, four or five fingers can you have the strength to fight with others.

Therefore, in our life, if it's only you, whatever you do, won't be good as good as people doing it together. People unite together, clenching into a fist, so that they will have the power to be able to complete a serious business.

The hand or the fist tells us that no matter if they are big or small, tall or short, man and woman, old and young, people should join their hands, making a fist; that's how they have power.

（4）tu⁵⁵ ɳtʂɦua³¹ tʰia⁵⁵ lia⁵⁵ 孤儿和猴子

儿子 孤儿　　和　　猴子
son　orphan　and　monkey

1 tʰau²¹ ʔu⁵⁵ , mua⁵² ʔɔ⁵⁵ kɯ³⁵ ti⁵² nia²¹ tsi³⁵ tɦua³¹ tɕʰa³¹ , tu³³ kɯ³⁵
　时候　很久　　　有　两　兄弟　父母　　死　完　　个　弟弟
　time　very long　have　two　brother　parent　die　finish　CL　younger brother
很久以前，有两兄弟父母都死了，弟弟
Long time ago, there were two brothers and their parents all died; the younger brother

2 tsi³³ mua⁵² po⁵² nia²¹ tʰia⁵² ɳtɕɦɔ³¹ nia²¹ ti⁵² tʰia⁵⁵ ti⁵² lɦau³¹ ʔɔ⁵⁵ tu³³ ŋɔ⁵⁵ sɯ⁵⁵ .
　不　　有　妻子　才　和　　嫂嫂　　和　　哥哥　两　个　在　仅仅
　NEG　have　wife　just　and　sister-in-law　and　brother　two　CL　be　only
没有老婆，弟弟才和嫂嫂和哥哥两个住在一起。
had no wife, so the younger brother lived with his brother and sister-in-law.

3 nia²¹ ti⁵² ʂia⁵⁵ tsi³³ zuŋ⁴⁴ , nia⁵² ɲu⁵⁵ tsi⁵⁵ ɳtʂɦua³¹ ʔua⁴⁴ xau⁵² lɯ²¹
　嫂嫂　　　心　不　好　　年　天　叫　孤儿　　做　　事情
　sister-in-law heart NEG good　year day call orphan do　thing
嫂嫂心肠不好，天天叫弟弟干那些重活。
The sister-in-law was malevolent and always asked her brother to do heavy labor works everyday.

4 n̥a³⁵ n̥a³⁵ sɯ⁵⁵ . mua⁵² ʔi⁵⁵ ɲu⁵⁵ ɳtʂɦua³¹ tʰia⁵² tʰɔ³⁵ nia²¹ ti⁵² li⁴⁴ nuŋ⁵⁵
　重重　　　仅仅　有　一　天　孤儿　才　讨　嫂嫂　　的　种子
　DRUP~heavy only　have one day orphan just ask sister-in-law PRT seed
有一天孤儿跟嫂嫂讨
One day, the orphan ask his sister-in-law for

5 pɔ⁵⁵ kɯ³³ tʰia⁵⁵ nuŋ⁵⁵ tau²¹ mu³³ tɕɔ³¹ ʔua⁴⁴ ŋtʂɦua³¹ li⁴⁴ . nia²¹ ti⁵² ʂia⁵⁵
苞谷　　和　　种子　　豆　去　种植　做　孤儿　　的　嫂嫂　　心
corn　　and　seed　　bean　go　plant　do　orphan　PRT　sister-in-law　heart

苞谷种和豆种去种，去自己单过。嫂嫂心肠

corn and bean seeds to plant and live on his own. The sister-in-law was

6 tʂi³³ ʐuŋ⁴⁴ , tʰau²¹ mua⁵⁵ nuŋ⁵⁵ tau²¹ tʰia⁵⁵ nuŋ⁵⁵ pɔ⁵⁵ kɯ³³ tɕɔ⁵² mu³³ ki⁵⁵ tɕʰa³¹
不　　好　　时候　拿　种子　　豆　和　种子　苞谷　　带　去　炒　完
NEG　good　time　take　seed　bean　and　seed　corn　take　go　fry　finish

不好，拿豆种和苞谷种去炒完

malevolent and gave fried bean and corn seeds

7 tʂɔ⁴⁴ ʔe³³ ma²¹ mua⁵⁵ tau⁴⁴ ŋtʂɦua³¹ tɕɔ⁵² mu³³ tɕɔ³¹ . ŋtʂɦua³¹ tɕɔ³⁵ tau²¹
放　(转折连词)　慢　拿　给　孤儿　　带　去　种植　孤儿　些　豆
put　CONJ　slowly　take　give　orphan　take　go　plant　orphan　CL.PL　bean

才拿给孤儿带去种植。孤儿的豆子

to the orphan for planting. The bean

8 tʰia⁵⁵ pɔ⁵⁵ kɯ³³ tua⁵² ʔua⁴⁴ zɔ⁵² ʔua⁴⁴ zen⁵⁵ tʂi³³ ʐuŋ⁴⁴ li⁴⁴ , tsʰɔ³¹ lu⁵⁵ tɕai⁵²
和　　苞谷　　出芽　　(稀稀疏疏状)　　　不　好　的　到　个　季节
and　corn　budding　sparsely　　　　NEG　good　PRT　arrive　CL　season

和玉米出的稀稀疏疏一点不好，到了

and corn he planted was sparse; it was not good at all; when

9 tau²¹ tʰia⁵⁵ pɔ⁵⁵ kɯ³³ ʂia³⁵ lɔ³³ lia⁵⁵ tʂen²¹ lɔ³³ mua⁵⁵ nɔ⁵² tɕʰa³¹ lau²¹ .
豆　和　苞谷　　熟　也　猴子　还　来　拿　吃　完　了
bean　and　corn　ripe　also　mokey　also　come　take　eat　finish　PRF

丰收的季节猴子还来把豆子和玉米吃光了。

the harvest time came, monkeys came to eat the beans and corns all up.

10 ŋtʂɦua³¹ tʰia⁵² mu³³ nɦuŋ³¹ zaɯ²¹ʂau⁵⁵ . zaɯ²¹ʂau⁵⁵ tʰia⁵² xai³³ tau⁴⁴ ŋtʂɦua³¹
孤儿　才　去　问　菩萨　　　菩萨　　　才　说　给　孤儿
Orphan　just　go　ask　Bodhisattva　Bodhisattva　just　say　give　orphan

孤儿才去问菩萨。菩萨才告诉孤儿说：

So the orphan went to ask the Bodhisattva.The Bodhisattva told the orphan:

(4) tu⁵⁵ ntʂɦua³¹ tʰia⁵⁵ lia⁵⁵ 孤儿和猴子

11 tia³³ : " kɔ⁵² tɔ³⁵ qa⁵⁵ mu³³ tʂe³⁵ ʔe³³ , tua⁴⁴ qai⁵⁵ tʰia⁵⁵ nɔ⁵² mɔ³⁵ kɔ²¹
    道   你   返回 去   家   哎   杀   鸡   和   吃   饭   让
    QUOT   2S   return go home IP   kill chicken and eat meal let

"你回家去，杀鸡做饭吃
"Go back to your home, and kill chickens to cook

12 tʂau⁴⁴tʂau⁴⁴ ʔe³³ , kɔ⁵² mua⁵⁵ mɔ³⁵ ntʂau³³ kɔ⁵² qhɔ³⁵ nteau⁵² qhɔ³⁵ ntʂɦɯ³¹ tʰɦa³¹ ,
    饱饱   哎   你   拿   饭   塞   你   嘴巴   鼻子   完
    DRUP~full   IP   2S take meal stuff   2S mouth   nose   finish

饱饱的，你用饭把你的嘴巴鼻子塞满，
and eat; stuff rice into your mouth and nose,

13 kɔ⁵² mu³³ pɯ⁴⁴ ntaɯ²¹ lia⁵⁵ tsɔ⁵² ke³⁵ ʔu⁴⁴ . " ntʂɦua³¹ tʰia⁵² lɔ³³ ʔua⁴⁴
    你   去   睡   处   猴子 条   路   那   孤儿   才   来   做
    2S go sleep place monkey CL   road there   orphan just come do

你去睡在猴子所经之路。" 孤儿回来才
then sleep on the way that monkeys will pass." The orphan did as

14 li⁴⁴ zaɯ²¹ ʂau⁵⁵ xai³³ . ntʂɦua³¹ tsaɯ²¹ tua⁴⁴ qai⁵⁵ tʰia⁵⁵ nɔ⁵² mɔ³⁵ tʂau⁴⁴tʂau⁴⁴
    像   菩萨   说   孤儿   就   杀   鸡   和   吃   饭   饱饱
    like Bodhisattva say   orphan DM   kill chicken and eat meal DRUP~full

照菩萨所说去做。孤儿就杀鸡做饭并且吃饭饱饱的，
what Bodhisattva said after coming home. The orphan killed chickens to cook and ate his full;

15 ʔe³³ , mua⁵⁵ mɔ³⁵ ntʂau³³ qhɔ³⁵ nteau⁵² qhɔ³⁵ ntʂɦɯ³¹ tʰɦa³¹ , mu³³ pɯ⁴⁴
    (转折连词) 拿 饭   塞   嘴巴   鼻子   完   去   睡
    CONJ   take meal stuff   mouth   nose   finish   go   sleep

用饭把嘴巴和鼻子塞满，去睡
he stuffed his mouth and nose with rice, and went to sleep

16 ntaɯ²¹ lia⁵⁵ tsɔ⁵² ke³⁵ . lia⁵⁵ tua⁵² pɔ²¹ ntʂɦua³¹ pɯ⁴⁴ li⁴⁴ tʰɦua³¹ laɯ²¹ .
    那   猴子 条   路   猴子 来   见   孤儿   睡   像   死   了
    that   monkey CL road   money come see orphan sleep like die   PRF

在猴子所经之路上。猴子来看见孤儿死了似的睡着。
on the way that monkeys would pass. The monkeys came and see the orphan sleeping dead.

17 lia⁵⁵   tsaɯ²¹   xai³³   tia³³   : " nɯ³³ ʔua⁴⁴ te⁵⁵   khɯ³⁵khɯ³⁵ , tɕɦɔ³¹   tau²¹   tɕɦɔ³¹
   猴子   就   说   道   他   做   地   苦苦   种植   豆   种植
   monkey DM   say   QUOT   3S   do   field   DRUP~bitter plant   bean   plant

猴子就说："他种地很辛苦，种豆种

Thus the monkeys said: "He worked hard in the field; he died of planting beans and

18 pɔ⁵⁵kɯ³³   tau⁴⁴   pe⁵⁵   nɔ⁵²   ʔe³³   nɯ³³   thia⁵²   tɕɦua³¹   lau²¹ ."   lia⁵⁵   mu³³
   苞谷   给   我们   吃   (顺承连词)   它   才   死   了   猴子   去
   corn   give   1PL   eat   CONJ   3S   just   die   PRF   monkey   go

苞谷给我们吃他才死了。" 猴子去

corns for us." The monkeys got close

ʂai⁵⁵   ntaɯ²¹   qhɔ³⁵ɳtɕau⁵²   qhɔ³⁵ɳtʂɦɯ³¹   pɔ²¹   mɔ³⁵   ʔdaɯ⁵⁵ʔdaɯ⁵⁵ . lia⁵⁵   tsaɯ²¹   xai³³
看   那   嘴巴   鼻子   见   饭   白白   猴子   就   说
see   that   mouth   nose   see   rice   DRUP~white   monkey   DM   say

看嘴巴和鼻子看见满是白色的饭粒。猴子就说

and noticed that the orphan's mouth and nose were filled with white rice. The monkeys said:

19 tia³³   " tɯ⁵⁵   lɯ⁵²lɯ⁵²   ka³³   ntaɯ²¹   te⁵²   qhɔ³⁵   ɳtɕau⁵²   qhɔ³⁵   ɳtʂɦɯ³¹   lau²¹ ."
    道   都   烂烂   蛆虫   那   些   嘴巴   鼻子   了
    QUOT   all   DRUP~rot maggot that   CL.PL mouth   nose   PRF

"嘴巴鼻子都腐烂出蛆了。"

"The corpse begins to rot and the mouth and nose are full of maggots."

20 thau²¹   ntaɯ²¹   ɳtʂɦua³¹   tsaɯ²¹   tʂɔ⁵⁴   ʔi⁵⁵   lu⁵⁵   pau³³   tʂɯ⁴⁴tʂɯ⁴⁴ .   lia⁵⁵   tsaɯ²¹
    时候   那   孤儿   就   放   一   个   屁   臭臭   猴子   就
    time   that   orphan   DM   release one   CL   fart   smelly   monkey   DM

那时候孤儿就放了一个很臭的屁。猴子就

At that time the orphan farted. The monkeys

21 xai³³   tia³³   " ʂai⁵⁵   tʂɯ⁴⁴tʂɯ⁴⁴   lɯ⁵²   lau²¹   thia⁵⁵ ,   pe⁵⁵   zua³⁵tʂu²¹   mua⁵⁵   nɯ³³
    说   道   看   臭臭   烂   了   也   我们   要得   拿   他
    say   QUOT   look   DRUP~smelly rot   PRF   too   1PL   should   take   3S

说："看也已经很臭了，我们要带他

said: "It's already stunk; we should conduct

(4) tu⁵⁵ ɳtʂɦua³¹ tʰia⁵⁵ lia⁵⁵ 孤儿和猴子

22 tɛɔ⁵² mu³³ pa²¹." lia⁵⁵ tʰia⁵² mua⁵⁵ ɳtʂɦua³¹ kɯ³⁵ tɛɔ⁵² mu³³ pa²¹ .
带　　去　办　猴子　才　拿　孤儿　扛　　带　　去　办
carry go make monkey just take orphan shoulder carry go make

去为他办丧事。"猴子才带孤儿去为他办丧事。
a funeral for him." So the monkeys took the orphan to make a funeral for him.

23 tʰau²¹ kɯ³⁵ mu³³ tsɦɔ³¹ ti²¹ ʔi⁵⁵ nta³⁵ tʂua⁴⁴ , ɳtʂɦua³¹ tsaɯ²¹ ʈua⁴⁴
时候　扛　　去　到　对面　一　半　崖子　孤儿　就　睁
time shoulder go arrive opposite one half cliff orphan DM open

当扛到一个半山崖子的时候，孤儿就睁
When they came to a cliff, the orphan opened

24 mɦua³¹ ʔe³³ xai³³ tia³³ "ʔua⁴⁴ ʐuŋ⁴⁴ tʂa²¹ kɯ³⁵ puŋ⁵⁵ na³⁵ !" lia⁵⁵
眼睛　(顺承连词) 说　道　小心　会儿　我　掉　喃　猴子
eyes CONJ say QUOT be careful while 1S fall IP monkey

眼说道："小心我掉下去哦！"猴子
his eyes and said: "Be careful don't let me fall!" The monkeys

qɯ⁴⁴ ʐɔ²¹ʐaɯ³³ tia³³ " tʂi³³ tau⁴⁴ tɦua³¹ ka⁵² ?" mua⁵² ʔi⁵⁵ tʃʰia⁴⁴ tsaɯ²¹ xai³³ :
叫　(纷纷状)　道　不　得　死　吧　有　一　部分　就　说
cry successively QUOT NEG get die Q have one part DM say

纷纷叫道"没有死吗？"有一部分就说：
all cried: "Didn't he die?" Some monkeys said:

tia³³ " laɯ³⁵ tɕua⁵⁵ mpua⁴⁴ ɳʈa²¹ tia⁵² sɯ⁵⁵ ʔɔ³³ ." mu³³ mu³³ ʔi⁵⁵ plɦia³¹
道　他们　下套　猪　下面　坝子　仅仅　啊　去　去　一　会儿
QUOT 3S trick pig below dam only IP go go one while

"是他们在坝子里给野猪下套。"走走一会
"That's the sound of farmers ware setting trap to hunt wild boars in the dam." After a while

25 ɳtʂɦua³¹ tɔ³⁵ qa⁵⁵ xai³³ li⁴⁴ qu⁵⁵ , lia⁵⁵ kɯ⁵² tɔ³⁵ qa⁵⁵ xai³³ li⁴⁴ qu⁵⁵ tʰia⁵⁵
孤儿　返回　说　像　原来　猴子　也　返回　说　像　原来　也
orphan return say like origin monkey also return say like origin too

孤儿又像原来那样说，猴子也只是像原来那样说。
the orphan said as before again, and the moneys also responded as before.

47

26 suɯ⁵⁵ . lia⁵⁵ mua⁵⁵ ɳtʂɦua³¹ kɯ³⁵ lɔ³³ tsɦɔ³¹ lia⁵⁵ tɕhaɯ⁴⁴ , lia⁵⁵
   仅仅 猴子 把 孤儿 扛 来 到 猴子 处 猴子
   only monkey put orphan shoulder come arrive monkey place monkey

猴子把孤儿扛到猴子窝，猴子

The monkeys carried the orphan back to their home and

27 thia⁵² mua⁵⁵ lia⁵⁵ te⁵² lau⁵² kau⁵⁵ tai³³ ʔdia³⁵ ɲia⁵² tai³³ ʔdia³⁵ ku⁵⁵ tɕɔ⁵²
   才 拿 猴子 些 锅 碗 勺 银 碗 勺 金 带
   just take monkey CL.PL pot bowl spoon silver bowl spoon gold take

才拿猴子的锅、金勺银勺金碗银碗来

took out their pots, golden and silver spoons and bowls to

28 lɔ³³ pa²¹ ɳtʂɦua³¹ . tsɦɔ³¹ n̪u⁵⁵ ʔua³³ zua³⁵ tɕɔ⁵² ɳtʂɦua³¹ mu³³ fau³³ ,
   来 办 孤儿 到 天 (定标) 要 带 孤儿 去 埋
   come conduct orphan arrive day REL should carry orphan go bury

给孤儿办丧。到了要把孤儿抬去埋那天，

conduct funeral for him. It was until the day when the orphan was carried to bury,

29 ɳtʂɦua³¹ thia⁵² li⁴⁴ ʂaɯ³⁵ tʂen³³ lɔ³³ lia⁵⁵ ɳtʂhai⁴⁴ɳtʂhai⁴⁴ lia⁵⁵ thia⁵²
   孤儿 才 起 (迅速状) 来， 猴子 怕怕 猴子 才
   orphan just get up quickly come monkey DRUP~afraid monkey just

孤儿才迅速站起来，猴子很害怕

he get up quickly, the monkeys were so scared

30 ʂaɯ³⁵ khia³⁵ tɦa³¹ mu³³ lau²¹ . ɳtʂɦua³¹ thia⁵² mua⁵⁵ lia⁵⁵ te⁵² lau⁵² kau⁵⁵
   起 跑 完 去 了 孤儿 才 拿 猴子 些 锅
   get run finish go PRF orphan just take monkey CL.PL pot

猴子跑光了。孤儿才拿猴子的锅、

that they ran away. So the orphan took the pots,

31 tai³³ ʔdia³⁵ ɲia⁵² tai³³ ʔdia³⁵ ku⁵⁵ tɕɔ⁵² mu³³ mɦua³¹ , ʔua⁴⁴ tau⁴⁴ ɳtʂɦua³¹
   碗 勺 银 碗 勺 金 带 去 卖 做 给 孤儿
   bowl spoon silver bowl spoon gold carry to sell do P orphan

金勺银勺、金碗银碗去变卖，使孤儿变得

golden and silver spoons and bowls to sell, which made

(4) tu⁵⁵ ntʂɦua³¹ tʰia⁵⁵ lia⁵⁵ 孤儿和猴子

mua⁵² mua⁵² ȵia⁵² li⁴⁴ lauɯ²¹ . ntʂɦua³¹ ti⁵² lɦau³¹ pɔ²¹ ntʂɦua³¹ mua⁵² mua⁵² ȵia⁵²,
有   有   钱   的   了   孤儿   哥哥   见   孤儿   有   有   钱
have have money PRT PRF orphan brother see orphan have have money

很有钱。孤儿哥哥见孤儿很有钱,

the orphan rich. The brother found the orphan become rich,

32 ntʂɦua³¹ ti⁵² lɦau³¹ tʰia⁵² li⁴⁴ mu³³ nɦuŋ³¹ ntʂɦua³¹ tia³³ ʔua⁴⁴ tɕa³³
   孤儿   哥哥   才   去   问   孤儿   道   做   怎么
   orphan brother just go ask orphan COMP do how

孤儿哥哥才去问孤儿说为什么

so he asked the orphan why is

33 ntʂɦua³¹ xɔ⁴⁴ mua⁵² ȵia⁵² . ntʂɦua³¹ tʰia⁵² li⁴⁴ qhia⁴⁴ tau⁴⁴ ntʂɦua³¹ ti⁵² lɦau³¹,
   孤儿   又   有   钱   孤儿   才   告诉   给   孤儿   哥哥
   orphan again have money orphan just tell P orphan brother

孤儿会这么有钱。孤儿才告诉他哥哥,

he so rich. So the orphan told his brother how to do;

34 ntʂɦua³¹ ti⁵² lɦau³¹ tʰia⁵² mu³³ ʔua⁴⁴ tau³³ li⁴⁴ ntʂɦua³¹ xai³³ . ntʂɦua³¹ ti⁵² lɦau³¹
   孤儿   哥哥   才   去   做   跟   的   孤儿   说   孤儿   哥哥
   orphan brother just go do follow PRT orphan say orphan brother

孤儿哥哥才照孤儿说的去做。孤儿哥哥

the brother then did as what the orphan said. The orphan's brother

35 mu³³ zɔ³⁵ pe²¹ te⁵⁵ tɕa³³ pɔ²¹ lia⁵⁵ lɔ³³ nɔ⁵² pɔ⁵⁵ kɯ³³ tʰia³¹ . ntʂɦua³¹
   去   守   上面 地   怎么   见   猴子   来   吃   苞谷   真   孤儿
   go guard above field how see monkey come eat corn real orphan

去地里看守真的看见有猴子来吃苞谷。孤儿

went to guard the field and really saw the monkeys coming to eat corns. So the orphan's

36 ti⁵² lɦau³¹ tʰia⁵² mu³³ nɦuŋ³¹ zauɯ²¹ ʂau⁵⁵, zauɯ²¹ ʂau⁵⁵ xai³³ ʔi⁵⁵ za²¹ li⁴⁴ ʔua³³
   哥哥   才   去   问   菩萨   菩萨   说   一   样   像   (定标)
   brother just go ask Bodhisattva Bodhisattva say one kind like REL

哥哥才去问菩萨,菩萨如对孤儿说一样说给孤儿哥哥。

brother went to ask the Bodhisattva; the Bodhisattva told the brother just as he told to the orphan.

37 xai³³ tau⁴⁴ ntʂɦua³¹ . ntʂɦua³¹ ti⁵² lɦau³¹ thia⁵² li⁴⁴ lɔ³³ tua⁴⁴ qai⁵⁵ nɔ⁵² mɔ³⁵
说　　给　　孤儿　　　　孤儿　　　哥哥　　才　　　来　　杀　　鸡　　吃　　饭
say　　P　　orphan　　　orphan　　brother　just　　come　kill　chicken　eat　meal

孤儿哥哥才来杀鸡做饭吃饱饱的，

So the orphan's brother killed chickens to cook and ate his full;

38 tsau⁴⁴tsau⁴⁴ mua⁵⁵ mɔ³⁵ ntsaɯ³³ qhɔ³⁵ nteau⁵² qhɔ³⁵ ntʂɦɯ³¹ mu³³ pɯ⁴⁴ ntaɯ²¹
　饱　　　　　拿　　饭　　塞　　　嘴巴　　　鼻子　　　　　去　　睡　那
　DRUP~full　take　meal　stuff　mouth　　　nose　　　　　　go　sleep that

用饭把嘴巴鼻子塞满然后去睡在

he stuffed his mouth and nose with rice and then slept

39 lia⁵⁵ tsɔ⁵² ke³⁵ . lia⁵⁵ lɔ³³ pɔ²¹ ntʂɦua³¹ ti⁵² lɦau³¹ lia⁵⁵ xai³³ tia³³ "
　猴子　　条　　路　　猴子　　来　　见　　孤儿　　　哥哥　　　　猴子　　说　　道
　monkey CL　road　monkey　come　see　orphan　brother　　monkey　say　QUOT

猴子经过的路上。猴子来看见孤儿哥哥猴子说：

on the way that monkeys would pass. The monkeys saw the orphan's brother and said:

40 nɯ³³ ʔua⁴⁴ te⁵⁵ khɯ³⁵khɯ³⁵ nɯ³³ thia⁵² tɦua³¹ laɯ²¹, pe⁵⁵ tɕɔ⁵² nɯ³³ mu³³
　他　　做　　地　　苦苦　　　　　他　　才　　死　　了　　　我们　带　　他　　去
　3S　　do　　field　DRUP~bitter　3S　　just　die　　PRF　　1PL　take　3S　　go

"他种地太辛苦他才死了，我们带他去办丧。"

"He worked hard in the field so he died; let's conduct a funeral for him.

41 pa²¹ ." mu³³ ʂai⁵⁵ ntaɯ²¹ qhɔ³⁵ nteau⁵² qhɔ³⁵ ntʂɦɯ³¹ mua⁵² mɔ³⁵ ʔdaɯ⁵⁵ʔdaɯ⁵⁵
　办　　　　去　　看　　那　　嘴巴　　　鼻子　　　　　　有　　饭　　白　　白
　make　　go　look　that　mouth　　　nose　　　　　　have　rice　white white

去看嘴巴鼻子满是白色的饭粒。

The monkeys found his mouth and nose were filled with white rice.

42 ŋɔ⁵⁵ . lia⁵⁵ tsaɯ²¹ xai³³ tia³³ " lɯ⁵²lɯ⁵² ka³³ li⁴⁴ laɯ²¹ ." lia⁵⁵ thia⁵²
　在　　猴子　　就　　说　　道　　烂烂　　　　蛆虫　　的　　了　　　猴子　　才
　be　　monkey　DM　say　QUOT　rot　　　　maggot　PRT　PRF　monkey just

猴子就说"腐烂见蛆了。"猴子才

The monkeys said "The corpse begins to rot and full of maggots." The monkeys

(4) tu⁵⁵ ɳʈʂɦua³¹ tɕʰia⁵⁵ lia⁵⁵ 孤儿和猴子

mua⁵⁵	ɳʈʂɦua³¹	ti⁵² lɦau³¹	kɯ³⁵	mu³³ pa²¹	.	lia⁵⁵	kɯ³⁵	mu³³	tsɦɔ³¹
把	孤儿	哥哥	扛	去 办		猴子	扛	去	到
PT	orphan	brother	shoulder	go make		monkey	shoulder	go	arrive

把孤儿哥哥扛去办丧。猴子扛着孤儿哥哥走到
carried the orphan's brother to conduct a funeral. When the monkeys carried the brother to

ti²¹	ʔi⁵⁵	nta³⁵	tʂua⁴⁴ ,	ɳʈʂɦua³¹	ti⁵² lɦau³¹	tsaɯ²¹	xai³³	tia³³ :	"ʔua⁴⁴	ʐuŋ⁴⁴	kɯ³⁵
对面	一	半	崖子	孤儿	哥哥	就	说	道	小心	我	
opposite	one	half	cliff	orphan	brother	DM	say	QUOT	be careful	1S	

半山崖子上，孤儿哥哥就说："小心我
the cliff, and the brother said: "Be careful and

43	puŋ⁵⁵	ʔɔ³⁵ . "	qen⁴⁴	tu³³	lia⁵⁵	tsaɯ²¹	xai³³	tia³³	" vua³⁵ ,	tɕen²¹	tɕi³³	tau⁴⁴
	掉	啊	部分	个	猴子	就	说	道	哇	还	不	得
	fall	IP	part	CL	monkey	DM	say	QUOT	INT	still	NEG	should

掉下去啊。"部分猴子就说"哇，还没有死。"
don't let me fall." Some monkey said: "Wow, he didn't die yet."

44	tɕʰua³¹ . "	mua⁵²	qen⁴⁴	tu³³	lia⁵⁵	tsaɯ²¹	te⁵⁵	xai³³	tia³³	tɕi³³	ʐɦɔ³¹ .
	死	有	部分	个	猴子	就	回答	说	道	不	是
	die	have	part	CL	monkey	DM	anwser	say	QUOT	NEG	be

部分猴子给出了否定的回答。
Some monkeys gave the negative answer.

45	"laɯ³⁵	tɕɯ⁵⁵	mpua⁴⁴	ɳʈa²¹	tia⁵²	sɯ⁵⁵ . "	lia⁵⁵	kɯ³⁵	mu³³	tsɦɔ³¹	pe²¹
	他们	下套	猪	下面	坝子	仅仅	猴子	扛	去	到	上面
	3S	trick	pig	below	dam	only	monkey	shoulder	go	arrive	above

"他们在坝子里给猪下套。"猴子扛着孤儿哥哥走到前面一点
"That's the sound of famers who are setting traps in the dam for hunting boars." The monkeys carried the brother and moved forward a little,

46	nte⁵²	ɳʈʂɦua³¹	ti⁵² lɦau³¹	tsaɯ²¹	tɔ³⁵	qa⁵⁵	xai³³	li⁴⁴	qu⁵⁵ ,	lia⁵⁵	ku⁵²	te⁵⁵
	前面	孤儿	哥哥	就	返回	说	的	原来		猴子	也	回答
	front	orphan	brother	DM	return	say	PRT	origin		monkey	also	answer

孤儿哥哥就又像原来那般说，猴子也只像原来
the brother said that again as before and the monkeys answered

47 li⁴⁴　　qu⁵⁵　　thia⁵⁵　　sɯ⁵⁵　.　lia⁵⁵　　tɔ³⁵　qa⁵⁵　kɯ³⁵　　　mu³³　tsɦɔ³¹　pe²¹　nte⁵²　me⁴⁴
　　像　　原来　　也　　仅仅　　猴子　　返回　扛　　去　　　到　　上面　前面　小
　　　like　origin　also　only　　monkey　return　shoulder　go　arrive　above　front　little
那般回答。猴子继续扛着走到前面一点，
like before as well. The monkeys continued carrying the brother and moving forward a little,

48 ɳtʂi³³　　thia⁵⁵　,　ɳtʂɦua³¹　ti⁵²　lɦau³¹　tsaɯ²¹　tɔ³⁵　qa⁵⁵　xai³³　tia³³　"　ʔua⁴⁴　zuŋ⁴⁴　kɯ³⁵
　　些　　　也　　　孤儿　　　哥哥　　　就　　返回　说　　道　　　小心　　我
　　CL.PL　also　orphan　brother　DM　return　say　QUOT　be careful　1S
孤儿哥哥就又说道"小心我
the orphan's brother said again: "Be careful and

49 puŋ⁵⁵　!"　tɕɔ³⁵　　lia⁵⁵　tɦia³¹　ɳtɦɔ⁴⁴　　tsaɯ²¹　ʔi⁵⁵　tshi⁵²　xai³³　tia³³　"　tʂi³³
　　掉　　　些　　　猴子　　完　　（彻底状）　　就　　一起　　说　　道　　　　不
　　fall　　CL.PL　monkey　finish　completely　DM　together　say　QUOT　　NEG
掉下去！"所有猴子就一起说
don't let me fall!" All the monkeys said together

50 tau⁴⁴　tɦua³¹　tɦia³¹　ʂa³³　!"　lia⁵⁵　　thia⁵²　mua⁵⁵　ɳtʂɦua³¹　ti⁵²　lɦau³¹　tʂɔ⁴⁴　puŋ⁵⁵
　　得　　死　　真　　嘛　　猴子　　才　　把　　孤儿　　哥哥　　　放　　掉
　　get　die　real　IP　　monkey　just　PT　orphan　brother　drop　fall
"真的没有死嘛！"猴子才把孤儿哥哥放下
"He is really not dead yet!" The monkeys threw the orphan's brother off

51 qa⁵⁵　　tʂua³³　tɦua³¹　lau²¹　.　za⁵²　ʔda⁵⁵　nɦien³¹　nɔ⁴⁴　qhia⁴⁴　xai³³　tia³³　nɦien³¹　zuŋ⁴⁴
　　底　　崖子　　死　　了　　个　　故事　　　这　　告诉　说　　道　　人　　　好
　　bottom　cliff　die　PRF　CL　story　this　tell　say　COMP　human　good
山崖死了。这个故事告诉我们好人
the cliff to die. This story tells us that good people

zen⁵²　tau⁴⁴　zuŋ⁴⁴　,　nɦien³¹　phe²¹　zen⁵²　lɔ³³　tau⁴⁴　qhɔ³⁵　phe²¹　.
肯定　得　　好　　　人　　坏　　肯定　也　　得　　处　　坏
must　get　good　　human　bad　must　also　get　place　bad
会有好报，坏人也会食恶果。
will get good gains, and bad people will suffer bad consequences.

（4） tu^{55} ntʂɦua^{31} thia^{55} lia^{55}孤儿和猴子

孤儿和猴子

很久以前，有两兄弟的父母都死了，弟弟没有老婆，弟弟就和嫂嫂和哥哥两个住在一起。

嫂嫂心肠不好，天天叫弟弟干那些重活。有一天孤儿跟嫂嫂讨要苞谷种和豆种去种，去自己单过。嫂嫂心肠不好，拿豆种和苞谷种去炒完才拿给孤儿带去种。孤儿的豆子和玉米出的稀稀疏疏一点不好，到了丰收的季节猴子还来把豆子和玉米吃光了。

孤儿就去问菩萨。菩萨才告诉孤儿说："你回家去，杀鸡做饭吃的饱饱的，你用饭把你的嘴巴鼻子塞满，你去睡在猴子经过的路上。"孤儿回来照菩萨所说去做。孤儿就杀鸡做饭并且吃得饱饱的，用饭把嘴巴和鼻子塞满，去睡在猴子所经之路上。猴子来看见孤儿死了似的睡着了。猴子就说："他种地很辛苦，种豆种苞谷给我们吃他才死了。"猴子去看嘴巴和鼻子里满是白色的饭粒。猴子就说："嘴巴鼻子都腐烂出蛆了。"那时候孤儿就放了一个很臭的屁。猴子就说"看也已经很臭了，我们要带他去为他办丧事。"猴子才带孤儿去为他办丧事。当扛到一个半山崖子的时候，孤儿就睁眼说道："小心我掉下去哦！"猴子纷纷叫道："没有死吗？"有一部分就说"是他们在坝子里给野猪下套。"走了一会孤儿又像原来那样说，猴子也只是像原来那样说。猴子把孤儿扛到猴子窝，猴子才拿猴子的锅、金勺银勺金碗银碗来给孤儿办丧。到了要把孤儿抬去埋那天，孤儿才迅速站起来，猴子很害怕就跑光了。孤儿就拿猴子的锅、金勺银勺、金碗银碗去变卖，他就变得很有钱。

孤儿哥哥看见孤儿很有钱，孤儿哥哥就去问孤儿说为什么孤儿会这么有钱。孤儿告诉他哥哥，孤儿哥哥就照孤儿说的去做。孤儿哥哥去地里看守真的看见有猴子来吃苞谷。孤儿哥哥去问菩萨，菩萨如对孤儿说一样说给孤儿哥哥。孤儿哥哥才来杀鸡做饭吃的饱饱的，用饭把嘴巴鼻子塞满，然后去睡在猴子经过的路上。猴子来看见孤儿哥哥猴子说"他种地太辛苦他才死了，我们带他去办丧。"去看嘴巴鼻子满是白色的饭粒。猴子就说"腐烂见蛆了。"猴子才把孤儿哥哥扛去办丧。猴子扛着孤儿哥哥走到半山崖子上，孤儿哥哥就说"小心我掉下去啊。"部分猴子就说"哇，还没有死。"部分猴子给出了否定的回答。"他们在坝子里给猪下套。"猴子扛着孤儿哥哥走到前面一点，孤儿哥哥就又像原来那般说，猴子也只像原来那般回答。猴子继续扛着走到前面一点，孤儿哥哥就又说道"小心我掉下去！"所有猴子就一起说："真的没有死嘛！"猴子才把孤儿哥哥放下山崖摔死了。

这个故事告诉我们好人会有好报，坏人也会自食恶果。

Orphans and Monkeys

Long time ago, there were two brothers and their parents all died. The younger brother had no wife so he lived together with his brother and sister-in-law.

The sister-in-law was malevolent and always asked her brother to do heavy labor works every day. One day the orphan asked his sister-in-law for corn and bean seeds to live on his own. However the sister-in-law was so mean that she gave fried seeds to the orphan. As the result, the beans and corns he planted were sparse. Even worse, when the harvest time came, monkeys ate the beans and corns all up.

Therefore the orphan went to ask the Bodhisattva. The Bodhisattva told him: "Go back to your home. Kill chickens to cook and eat your full. Then stuff your mouth and nose with rice and sleep on the way that monkeys will pass. " The orphan came back and did as the Bodhisattva told him. He killed chickens to eat his full and stuffed his mouth and nose with rice and went to sleep on the way that monkeys would pass. The monkeys came and see the orphan sleeping dead. The monkeys passed by and said: "He worked hard in the field. He died of planting beans and corns for us." They found his mouth and nose is full of white rice, so they said: "The corpse is already rotted and full of maggots." At that time the orphan farted. The monkeys thus said: "It seems that the corpse has already stunk. We should conduct a funeral for him." So the monkeys carried the orphan to conduct a funeral. When they came to a cliff, the orphan opened his eyes and said "Be careful! Don't let me fall!" The monkeys all shouted "Didn't he die?" Some answered "That's the sound of farmers who are setting traps to hunting wild boars in the dam." After a while, the orphan said as before and the monkeys answer as before as well. The monkeys carried the orphan to their home, and took out pots, golden and silver spoons and bowls to conduct funeral. It was until the day when the orphan was carried to bury, he suddenly get up. The monkeys were so scared that they all run away. So the orphan took the pots, golden and silver spoons and bowls to sell and became rich.

The orphan's brother found his younger brother become rich. So he asked the orphan why he became so rich. The orphan told his brother and the brother did as what he said. The orphan's brother went to guard the field and noticed monkeys would come to eat corns. So he asked the Bodhisattva and got the same answer as his brother. The orphan's brother also killed chickens and ate his full; stuffed his mouth and nose with rice, and then slept on the way that monkeys would pass. The monkeys saw the brother and said "He worked hard in the field so he died. Let's conduct a funeral for him." Then they found his mouth and nose was full of white rice, so they said "The corpse has already rotted and is full of maggots." Then they carried the brother to conduct funeral. The monkeys carried the brother to the cliff; the brother said "Be careful! Don't let me fall." Some monkeys said "Wow, he is not dead yet." But some monkeys gave their negative answer: "That's the sound of farmers who are setting traps for boars in the dam." The monkeys continued carrying the brother and moving forward. The orphan said that again and the monkeys also responded as before. They kept walking and the brother said again "Be careful! Don't let me fall!" All the monkeys said "He is really not dead yet!" So the monkeys threw him off the cliff to die.

This story tells us that good people will get good gains while bad people will suffer from bad consequences.

（5）ntaɯ³⁵ m̥uŋ⁵⁵ lu³³　m̥uŋ⁵⁵ 苗语苗文
　　　书　　苗族　　话　　　苗族
　　　book　Hmong　language　Hmong

1 ŋu⁵⁵ nɔ⁴⁴, ku³⁵ sa³⁵ lɔ³³ tha²¹ tsɦɔ³¹ mi⁴⁴ ntʂi³³ pe⁵⁵ tɕɔ³⁵ ntaɯ³⁵
  天　　这　　我　　想　来　讲　　到　　小　　些　　我们　些　　书
  day　this　1S　want come talk about small CL.PL 1PL CL.PL book

今天，我想谈谈苗语和苗文。
Today I want to talk about Hmong language or Hmong writing.

2 m̥uŋ⁵⁵ lɔ³³ zɦɔ³¹ lu³³ m̥uŋ⁵⁵ . vi²¹ li⁴⁴ tɕa³³ xɔ⁴⁴ zua³⁵ mua⁵⁵ tɕɔ⁵²
  苗族　　或　是　话　　苗族　　　为什么　　　又　　要　拿　带
  Hmong　or　COP language Hmong　why　　again should take bring

为什么要说苗语苗文呢？
Why the Hmong language and writing?

3 lɔ³³ tha²¹ ? vi²¹ zɦɔ³¹ ta²¹ ɕi²¹ nɔ⁴⁴ pɔ²¹ tau⁴⁴ xai³³ tia³³ : pe⁵⁵ tɕɔ³⁵
  来　讲　　因为　　是　　现在　　　见　得　说　道　我们 些
  come talk because COP now　　　see get say COMP 1PL CL.PL

因为现在看到了一些现象：
It is because that I observed some phenomena.

4 tu⁵⁵ tɕɔ³⁵ ntshai³³ ŋɔ⁵⁵ ʈau⁴⁴ tshen⁵² ta²¹ ɕi²¹ nɔ⁴⁴ , tʂi³³ pau⁵⁵ lu³³
  儿子　些　　女儿　　在　　给　　代　　现在　　　　不　知道　话
  son CL.PL daughter be.located P generation now　　NEG know language

现在这一代的青少年
Youths of the contemporary generation

5 m̥uŋ⁵⁵ , xai²¹ lu³³ m̥uŋ⁵⁵ tʂi³³ men⁵² , zɦɔ³¹ li⁴⁴ ntaɯ²¹ ku³⁵ thia⁵² li⁴⁴
  苗族　　说　话　　苗族　　不　清晰　　是　　那样　　　我　才
  Hmong say language Hmong NEG clear COP that way 1S just

不会说苗语，说苗语说不准确，
can't speak Hmong language, or they speak non-standard language.

6 ʐua³⁵ mua⁵⁵ lɔ³³ tʰa²¹ , kɔ²¹ pe⁵⁵ tɕɔ³⁵ nia²¹ tɕɔ³⁵ tsi³⁵ ʂaɯ³⁵ ʔdaɯ³³
　要　　拿　　来　　讲　　让　我们　些　母亲　些　父亲　大家
　will　take　come　talk　let　1PL　CL.PL　mother　CL.PL　father　all

因此，我才要来谈苗语苗文，
Therefore, that's why I am going to talk about Hmong language and writing,

7 mɔ⁵⁵ ʂia⁵⁵ qʰia⁴⁴ lu³³ m̥uŋ⁵⁵ tau⁴⁴ pe⁵⁵ tɕɔ³⁵ mi⁴⁴ ɳua²¹ .
　重视　教　话　苗族　给　我们　些　小　孩子
　value　teach　language　Hmong　P　1PL　CL.PL　small　children

使长辈们重视教孩子说苗语。
hoping it can make elders pay attention to teach their children speak Hmong language.

8 len⁵² tʰɯ³¹ xɔ⁴⁴ pau⁵⁵ ntaɯ³⁵ m̥uŋ⁵⁵ , ku⁵² pa⁵⁵ qʰia⁴⁴ ntaɯ³⁵ m̥uŋ⁵⁵
　位　　哪　又　知道　书　苗族　可以　帮　教　书　苗族
　CL　who　again　know　book　Hmong　can　help　teach　book　Hmong

谁还懂苗文的，可以给大家教苗文。
Those who understand Hmong writing can teach us about it.

9 tau⁴⁴ . len⁵² tʰɯ³¹ tʂi³³ pau⁵⁵ ntaɯ³⁵ m̥uŋ⁵⁵ , tu³³ ntaɯ²¹ ʐua³⁵ xai³³
　给　位　哪　不　知道　书　苗族　个　那　要　说
　P　CL　who　NEG　know　book　Hmong　CL　that　will　say

谁不懂苗文，谁就说不准苗语。
Those who don't know about Hmong writing do not speak it clearly.

10 lu³³ m̥uŋ⁵⁵ tʂi³³ men⁵² . pe⁵⁵ tɕɔ³⁵ ŋɔ⁵⁵ tau⁴⁴ ʂa⁵⁵ tʰai⁵⁵ te⁵⁵ , tɕɔ³⁵
　话　苗族　不　清晰　我们　些　在　给　边　泰国　地　些
　language　Hmong　NEG　clear　1PL　CL.PL　be.located　P　side　Thailand　land　CL.PL

我们泰国这里，
Here in Thailand,

11 me⁴⁴ tu⁵⁵ me⁴⁴ ɳua²¹ mu³³ kaɯ²¹ ntaɯ³⁵ tʰai⁵⁵ ʐɦo³¹ fen²¹ tɕuŋ⁵⁵ ,
　小　儿子　小　孩子　去　读　书　泰国　是　份　多
　little　son　little　children　go　read　book　Thailand　COP　part　much

多数孩子都去学习泰文。
most children are learning Thai language.

12 thau²¹ mu³³ kaɯ²¹ ntaɯ³⁵ thai⁵⁵ ntau⁴⁴ ntau⁴⁴ laɯ²¹ , nɯ³³ tʂi³³ ŋtɛɔ⁴⁴ qa⁵⁵
   时候 去 读   书   泰国   多   多   了   他   不   记得
   time go read book Thailand RDUP~much   PRF   3S NEG remember

他们长时间去学习泰文之后，就会渐渐不记得他自己的苗语了。
After spending a long time studying the Thai language, they will gradually forget their Hmong.

13 nɯ³³ tɛɔ³⁵ lu³³ m̥uŋ⁵⁵ laɯ²¹ . lɔ³³ zɦɔ³¹ nɯ³³ tʂi³³ pau⁵⁵ ntaɯ³⁵ m̥uŋ⁵⁵ ,
   他   些   话   苗族   了   或 是   他   不   知道   书   苗族
   3S CL.PL language Hmong PRF or COP 3S   NEG know book   Hmong

他不懂苗文，
If one can't understand Hmong writing,

14 nɯ³³ pau⁵⁵ ntaɯ³⁵ thai⁵⁵ , nɯ³³ lu⁵⁵ ʂua⁵⁵ zen⁵⁵ ntaɯ²¹ nɯ³³ zua³⁵
   他   知道   书   泰国   他   个   声音   那   他   要
   3S   know book   Thailand 3S   CL   voice   that   3S   will

但他懂泰文，
but he knows Thai writing,

15 xai³³ mu³³ tau³³ tɛɔ³⁵ lu³³ thai⁵⁵ , tɛai³³ zua³⁵ ʔua⁴⁴ tau⁴⁴ nɯ³³ xai³³
   说   去   跟   些   话   泰国   那么   要   使   给   他   说
   say   go follow CL.PL language Thailand thus will cause P   3S   say

他的口音就会像泰语的口音，
he will have Thai accent,

16 lu³³ m̥uŋ⁵⁵ tʂi³³ men⁵² . tɛɔ³⁵ ŋɔ⁵⁵ tau⁴⁴ ʂa⁵⁵ ʂua³⁵ te⁵⁵ lɔ³³ ʔi⁵⁵
   话   苗族   不   清晰   些   在   给   边   汉族 地   也   一
   language Hmong NEG clear CL.PL be.located P side Han land CONJ one

za²¹ ,
样
way

那么就会使他说苗语不准确。这种情况中国苗族也一样，
which makes his Hmong language incorrect. The same is true among Chinese Hmong,

17 tɕɔ³⁵   ŋɔ⁵⁵   ʂa⁵⁵   mplfiɔ³¹   te⁵⁵   lɔ³³   ʔi⁵⁵   za²¹ ,   tɕɔ³⁵   ʂa⁵⁵   ŋa⁵⁵   la⁵²   te⁵⁵   lɔ³³
   些   在   边   老挝   地   也   一   样   些   边   越南   地   也
   CL.PL be.located side Laos   land CONJ   one   way   CL.PL side   Laos   land   CONJ
老挝苗族也一样，越南苗族也一样，
also Laotian Hmong, Vietnamese Hmong

18 ʔi⁵⁵   za²¹ ,   tɕɔ³⁵   ŋɔ⁵⁵   tau⁴⁴   me³³   ka³³   te⁵⁵   lɔ³³   ʔi⁵⁵   za²¹ .   thau²¹   lu⁵⁵
    一   样   些   在   给   美国   地   也   一   样   时候   个
   one   way   CL.PL be.located P   America land CONJ   one   way   time   CL

ʂi⁵²   xaɯ²¹
时候
 time
美国苗族也一样。
and American Hmong.

19 nɯ³³   mu³³   kaɯ²¹   tɕɔ³⁵   ntaɯ³⁵   me³³   ka³³ ,   nɯ³³   tʂi³³   ȵtɕɔ⁴⁴   qa⁵⁵
    他   去   读   些   书   美国   他   不   记得
    3S   go   read   CL.PL   book   America   3S   NEG   remember
他去学习英语的时候，
When he's learning English,

20 lɔ³³   kaɯ²¹   nɯ³³   tɕɔ³⁵   lu³³   m̥uŋ⁵⁵   laɯ²¹ .   xai³³   lu³³   me³³   ka³³   ma³³ , nɯ³³
    来   读   他   些   话   苗族   了   说   话   美国   嘛   他
  come read   3S   CL.PL words   Hmong PRF   say   words America IP   3S
他不记得说他的苗语了。
he will forget to speak Hmong language.

21 xai³³   tau⁴⁴   ʐuŋ⁴⁴   xen³⁵ ,   ta⁵⁵   ʂi³³   nɯ³³   xai³³   lu³³   m̥uŋ⁵⁵   tʂi³³   tau⁴⁴   laɯ²¹ ,
   说   得   好   很   但是   他   说   话   苗族   不   得   了
  speak   can   good   very   but   3S   say   language Hmong NEG   can   PRF
说英语嘛，他说得很好，但是他说苗语却不行了。
He performs well when it comes to English, instead of Hmong language.

22 tɕɔ³⁵　　ŋɔ⁵⁵　　　 tau⁴⁴ ʂua³⁵ te⁵⁵ , nɯ³³ xai³³ tau⁴⁴ lu³³　　ʂua³⁵ ʐuŋ⁴⁴ xen³⁵ ,
　　些　　　在　　　　给　汉族　地　　他　说　　得　话　　　汉　　好　　很
　　CL.PL　be.located　P　Han　land　3S　say　can　language　Han　good　very
在中国的苗族，他说汉语说得很好，
The Hmong people in China can speak Chinese fluently,

23 ta⁵⁵ ʂi³³ thau²¹ tɦi³¹　 kɦia³¹　　 mu³³ tau⁴⁴ lu³³　　m̥uŋ⁵⁵ , tɕai³³ nɯ³³ xai³³ tɕi³³
　　但是　时候　转　　（干脆状）　去　给　　话　　　苗族　　那么　他　说　不
　　but　　time　switch　simply　　go　P　language　Hmong　thus　3S　speak　NEG
但是当马上转说苗语时，他就不会说了。
But when they switch to Hmong language, they're not able to speak.

24 tau⁴⁴ lauɯ²¹ . qhɔ³⁵ nɔ³⁵　　 nɯ³³ ʐɦo³¹ ʔi⁵⁵ qhɔ⁴⁴ ten⁵⁵ men²¹ ʔua³³ nɯ³³ ŋɔ⁵⁵
　　得　　了　　　处　这样　　　它　　是　　一　处　　问题　　（定标）　它　在
　　can　PRF　place　this way　3S　COP　one　place　problem　REL　3S　be.located
这种情况是
This situation

25 ṭau⁴⁴ ta²¹ ʂi²¹ nɔ⁴⁴ ta⁵⁵ tɔ²¹ tɕhi²¹ ɕi²¹ ŋɔ⁵⁵　　　tau⁴⁴ tshua⁴⁴ lu⁵⁵ te⁵⁵ tɕhaɯ³³ .
　　给　　现在　　　正当　　　出现　　　在　　　给　　全　　个　地方
　　P　　now　　just when　　appear　be.located　P　　all　　CL　place
现在各地普遍出现的问题。
occurs universally in all areas.

26 ʐɦo³¹ li⁴⁴ ntaɯ²¹, ku³⁵ sa³⁵ kɔ²¹ pe⁵⁵ tɕɔ³⁵　　nia²¹　tɕɔ³⁵　tsi³⁵　ʐua³⁵tʂu²¹
　　是　　那样　　　我　想　让　我们　些　　母亲　　些　　父亲　要得
　　COP　that way　1S　want　let　1PL　CL.PL　mother　CL.PL　father　should
因此，我想我们这些长辈得传承我们的苗语，
Therefore, I think our elders have to pass down our Hmong language.

27 tau⁴⁴　khaɯ³³　pe⁵⁵　tɕɔ³⁵　lu³³　　m̥uŋ⁵⁵ , ne⁵² ŋtɕɔ⁴⁴ ŋtʂuŋ³⁵ naɯ³⁵ ,
　　得　　传承　　我们　些　　话　　　苗族　　你们　记住　（牢记状）　啊
　　should　pass.on　1PL　CL.PL　language　Hmong　2PL　remember　firmly　IP

thaɯ²¹ lu⁵⁵
时候　个
　time　CL

你们要牢牢记住啊，
Please bear this in mind firmly.

28 ʂi⁵² xaɯ²¹ laɯ³⁵ nɦiuŋ³¹ xai³³ tia³³ ：" ne⁵² zɦɔ³¹ nɦien³¹ ʔɖa⁵⁵tʂi⁴⁴ ？" pe⁵⁵ thia⁵² li⁴⁴
　时候　别人　问　　说　　道　　　你们　是　人　　什么　　　我们　才
　time　others ask　say　QUOT 2PL COP human what　　　1PL　just

当别人问："你们是什么民族？"
When people ask, "What's your nationality?"

29 zua³⁵ qhia⁴⁴ ʈau⁴⁴ laɯ³⁵ xai³³ tia³³：" pe⁵⁵ zɦɔ³¹ nɦien³¹ m̥uŋ⁵⁵ ."
　要　　告诉　给　　他们　说　　道　　我们　是　　人　　　苗族
　should tell　P　　3PL　say　QUOT 1PL COP human Hmong

我们才好告诉人家："我们是苗族。"
We are able to say "We are Hmong".

30 thaɯ²¹ ntaɯ²¹, laɯ³⁵ xɔ⁴⁴ zua³⁵ nɦiuŋ³¹ ntsi³⁵ xai³³ tia³³ ：" m̥uŋ⁵⁵ zɦɔ³¹
　时候　那　　别人　又　要　　问　　补充　说　道　　苗族　是
　time　that　others again will　ask　supply say QUOT Hmong he

那时候，他们又追问："苗族是谁？
Then if they question closely, "Who are the Hmong?

31 len⁵² tɕhɯ³¹ ？ pe⁵⁵ tʂi³³ pau⁵⁵ m̥uŋ⁵⁵ ʔai³³ ." ne⁵² zua³⁵tau⁴⁴ te⁵⁵ ʈau⁴⁴ laɯ³⁵
　位　哪　　我们　不　知道　苗族　哎　　你们　要得　　回答　给　别人
　CL　who　1PL NEG know Hmong M　2PL should　answer P others

我们不认识苗族哎。"你们要这样回答别人：
We don't know about Hmong." You should answer like this:

32 ʈau³³ li⁴⁴ ntaɯ²¹ nɔ⁴⁴ ：" m̥uŋ⁵⁵ zɦɔ³¹ len⁵² tɕhɯ³¹ ？ m̥uŋ⁵⁵ zɦɔ³¹ ʔi⁵⁵ xai³⁵
　跟　像　　那　　　　苗族　是　位　哪　　苗族　是　一　种
　follow be.like that　　Hmong COP CL who　Hmong COP one kind

"苗族是谁？
"Who are the Hmong?

33 nɦen³¹ ʔua³³ zu³³ mua⁵² zu³³ lu³³ , zu³³ tʂi³³ xai³³ len⁵² tɕʰɯ³¹ lu³³
　　人　（定标）自己　有　自己　话　　　自己　不　说　位　哪　话
　　human REL self have self language self NEG say CL who language
苗族是一个有自己语言、不说别人语言的民族。
Hmong is a nationality which has its own language and people, not another nationality's language,

34 ɴqe⁴⁴ ʔɔ⁵⁵ , m̥uŋ⁵⁵ zɦɔ³¹ ʔi⁵⁵ xai³⁵ nɦen³¹ ʔua³³ zu³³ mua⁵² zu³³ ntaɯ³⁵ .
　　第二　　　苗族　　是　一　种　人　（定标）自己　有　自己　书
　　secondly Hmong COP one kind human REL self have self book
第二，苗族是一个有自己文字的民族。
secondly, a nationality with its own writing,

35 ɴqe⁴⁴ pe⁵⁵ , m̥uŋ⁵⁵ zɦɔ³¹ ʔi⁵⁵ xai³⁵ nɦen³¹ ʔua³³ zu³³ mua⁵² zu³³ tʂuŋ³³ tʂʰɔ⁴⁴
　　条　三　苗族　　是　一　种　人　（定标）自己　有　自己　服饰
　　CL three Hmong COP one kind human REL own have own costume
第三，苗族是一个有自己独特服饰的民族。
and thirdly, a nationality with its own unique costumes.

36 tɕi³³ zuŋ⁴⁴ li⁴⁴ len⁵² tɕʰɯ³¹ . ɴqe⁴⁴ plau⁵⁵ , m̥uŋ⁵⁵ zɦɔ³¹ ʔi⁵⁵ xai³⁵
　　不　像　　位　哪　　条　四　苗族　　是　一　种
　　NEG be.like CL who CL four Hmong COP one kind
第四，苗族是一个
Fourthly, Hmong is a

37 nɦen³¹ ʔua³³ zu³³ mua⁵² zu³³ ka⁵⁵ li³³ ke³⁵ tɕai⁴⁴ tɕi³³ zuŋ⁴⁴ li⁴⁴ len⁵²
　　人　（定标）自己　有　自己　风俗习惯　　　不　像　　位
　　human REL self have self customs NEG be.like CL
有自己独特风俗习惯的民族。
nationality which has unique manners and customs.

38 tɕʰɯ³¹ . zɦɔ³¹ xai³³ tia³³　　len⁵² tɕʰɯ³¹ mua⁵² plau⁵⁵ za²¹ nɔ⁴⁴ , tu³³ ntaɯ²¹
　　哪　　　是　说　道　　位　哪　　有　四　样　　这　个　那
　　who COP say COMP CL who have four style this CL that
要是谁满足以上四条，那这个人就是苗族。
People who fulfill those four things above are Hmong people.

(5) ntaɯ³⁵ m̥uŋ⁵⁵ lu³³ m̥uŋ⁵⁵ 苗语苗文

39 zɦɔ³¹ m̥uŋ⁵⁵ . zɦɔ³¹ li⁴⁴ ntaɯ²¹, pe⁵⁵ zua³⁵tau⁴⁴ khaɯ³³ pe⁵⁵ tɕɔ³⁵ lu³³ ,
　　是　　苗族　　是　那样　　我们　要得　　传承　　我们　些　　话
　　COP Hmong　COP that way　1PL should　pass.on 1PL CL.PL language
因此，我们得好好传承我们的语言，
Thus, we should pass on our language properly.

40 pe⁵⁵ zua³⁵tau⁴⁴ khaɯ³³ pe⁵⁵ tɕɔ³⁵ ntaɯ³⁵ , pe⁵⁵ zua³⁵tau⁴⁴ khaɯ³³ pe⁵⁵
　　我们　要得　　传承　　我们　些　　书　　　我们　要得　　传承　　我们
　　1PL should　pass.on 1PL CL.PL book　　1PL should　pass.on 1PL
我们得传承我们的文字，我们得传承我们的服饰，
We need to pass down our characters and costumes.

41 tɕɔ³⁵ tʂuŋ³³ tʂʰo⁴⁴ , pe⁵⁵ zua³⁵tau⁴⁴ khaɯ³³ pe⁵⁵ tɕɔ³⁵ ka⁵⁵ li³³ ke³⁵ tɕai⁴⁴ .
　　些　　服饰　　　　我们　要得　　传承　　我们　些　　风俗习惯
　　CL.PL costume　　1PL should　　pass.on 1PL CL.PL custom
我们得传承我们的风俗习惯。
We need to pass down our customs.

42 pe⁵⁵ tʰia⁵² li⁴⁴ te⁵⁵ tau⁴⁴ ʈau⁴⁴ lɦua³¹ lɯ²¹ xai³⁵ nɦien³¹ xai³³ tia³³ : "pe⁵⁵
　　我们　才　　回答　得　给　别人　　　另外　种　　人　　说　道　　　我们
　　1PL just　answer can P others moreover kind human say QUOT 1PL
我们才能回答其他民族的人："我们是苗族"。
So we can respond people of other nationalities that "we are Hmong".

43 zɦɔ³¹ m̥uŋ⁵⁵ ." tʰɔ³⁵ tsi²¹ naɯ³⁵ , n̥u⁵⁵ nɔ⁴⁴ ku³⁵ tʂi⁵⁵ tau⁴⁴ ŋa³⁵
　　是　　苗族　　对不起　啊　　天　这　我　不　得　穿
　　COP Hmong sorry　IP　day this 1S NEG can wear
对不起，今天我没有穿苗族服装来，
Sorry, I'm not wearing my Hmong costume,

44 khaɯ⁵⁵ ɳtɕaɯ³³ m̥uŋ⁵⁵ , vi²¹ zɦɔ³¹ tʂi³³ tau⁴⁴ mpa⁵² tua⁵² . n̥u⁵⁵ nɔ⁴⁴ mua⁵²
　　衣服　　　　　苗族　　因为　是　不　得　准备　　来　　天　这　有
　　cloth　　　Hmong because COP NEG can prepare come day this have
因为没有准备。
for that I didn't prepare.

45 tɕɔ³⁵   tu⁵⁵   tɕɔ³⁵   ntshai³³   kaɯ²¹   ntaɯ³⁵   ŋɔ⁵⁵   ʈau⁴⁴   ʂa⁵⁵   ʂua³⁵   te⁵⁵ ,   tua⁵²
些   儿子   些   女儿   读   书   在   给   边   汉族   地   来
CL.PL   son   CL.PL   daughter   read   book   be.located P   side   Han   land   come

今天有中国的苗族学生来,
Today here comes Chinese Hmong students

46 tshaɯ⁵⁵   faɯ⁵⁵   tsfiɔ³¹   tɕɔ³⁵   lu³³   m̥uŋ⁵⁵   ŋɔ⁵⁵   ʈau⁴⁴   ʂa⁵⁵   thai⁵⁵   te⁵⁵ ,
分析   到   些   话   苗族   在   给   边   泰国   地
analyze   about   CL.PL   language Hmong   be.located P   side   Thailand land

ku³⁵
我
1S

来调查泰国苗语,
to investigate Hmong language in Thailand,

47 tau⁴⁴   mua⁵²   xɯ³⁵   tʂa²¹   tua⁵²   kuŋ²¹ .   zfiɔ³¹   li⁴⁴   ntaɯ²¹ ,   thia⁵²   li⁴⁴   mua⁵⁵
得   有   机会   来   参与   是   那样   才   拿
get   have   chance   come   participate   COP   that way   just   take

我才有机会参与。因此,
so I get the opportunity to participate in. Thus,

48 tɕɔ³⁵   lu³³   nɔ⁴⁴   tɕɔ⁵²   lɔ³³   tha²¹   pu⁵⁵   tau⁴⁴   tɕɔ³⁵   tu⁵⁵   ntshai³³   kaɯ²¹   ntaɯ³⁵
些   话   这   带   来   讲   送   给   些   儿子   女儿   读   书
CL.PL words this   bring   come speak   send   P   CL.PL   son   daughter   read   book

我才把这些话拿来讲给中国的苗族学生,
I want to deliver these words to Chinese Hmong students,

49 ŋɔ⁵⁵   ʈau⁴⁴   ʂa³⁵   ʂua³⁵   te⁵⁵ ,   tɕai³³   ku⁵²   zfiɔ³¹   ʔi⁵⁵   qhɔ³⁵   xɯ³⁵   tʂa²¹   ʔua³³
在   给   边   汉族   地   那么   也   是   一   处   机会   (定标)
be.located P side   Han   land   so that CONJ COP   one   place   chance   REL

这也是一个
this is also

(5) ntaɯ³⁵ m̥uŋ⁵⁵ lu³³ m̥uŋ⁵⁵ 苗语苗文

50 mua⁵⁵ tɕo⁵² lɔ³³ nthua³⁵ qhia⁴⁴ ʈau⁴⁴ pe⁵⁵ tɕo³⁵ kɯ³⁵ ti⁵² m̥uŋ⁵⁵
   拿   带   来   打开   告诉   给   我们 些   兄弟   苗族
   take bring come open tell   P   1PL CL.PL brother Hmong

向中国多位苗族兄弟展示的机会，
an opportunity to show our Chinese Hmong brothers these words

51 tɕuŋ⁵⁵   tɕuŋ⁵⁵ len⁵²， kɔ²¹ ne⁵² tau⁴⁴ tɕo⁵²   mu³³ nthua³⁵ qhia⁴⁴ ʈau⁴⁴ ne⁵²
   多   多位   让   你们 得   带   去   打开   告诉   给   你们
   RDUP~much CL   let   2PL can take.along   go   open   tell   P   2PL

tɕo³⁵
些
CL.PL

让你们把这些话带去告诉你们的孩子，
which you can tell to your children.

52 me⁴⁴ tu⁵⁵ me⁴⁴ ɲua²¹   tsua³³ ntsi³⁵， ʑɦo³¹ li⁴⁴ ntaɯ²¹， sa³⁵ kɔ²¹ ne⁵² mɔ⁵⁵ ʂia⁵⁵
   小   儿子 小   孩子   接着   是   那样   想   让   你们 重视
   little son little children next   COP that way   think let 2PL value

因此，想让你们
Thus, we want you

53 ʈau⁴⁴ qhia⁴⁴ lu³³   m̥uŋ⁵⁵ ʈau⁴⁴ ne⁵² tɕo³⁵ tu⁵⁵ tɕo³⁵ ntshai³³， ne⁵²
   给   教   话   苗族   给   你们 些   儿子 些   女儿   你们
   P   teach language Hmong P   2PL CL.PL son CL.PL daughter   2PL

mɔ⁵⁵ ʂia⁵⁵
重视
value

重视给你们的孩子教苗语，
to value teaching your children Hmong language

54 qhia⁴⁴ ntaɯ³⁵ m̥uŋ⁵⁵ ʈau⁴⁴ ne⁵² tɕo³⁵ tu⁵⁵ tɕo³⁵ ntshai³³ tɕo³⁵ me⁴⁴
   教   书   苗族   给   你们 些   儿子 些   女儿   些   小
   teach book   Hmong P   2PL CL.PL son CL.PL daughter CL.PL little

让你们重视给你们的孩子教苗文。

and teach your children how to write Hmong writing.

55 ɲua²¹ . thau²¹ ne⁵² tɕɔ³⁵ mi⁴⁴ ɲua²¹ pau⁵⁵ ntaɯ³⁵ m̥uŋ⁵⁵ lauɯ²¹ ,
孩子　　时候　　你们　　些　　小　　孩子　　懂　　书　　苗族　　了
children　time　　2PL　CL.PL　little　children　understand　book　Hmong　PRF

laɯ³⁵
他们
3PL

当你们的小孩懂苗文了,
If your children can understand Hmong writing,

56 zua³⁵ xai³³ lu³³ m̥uŋ⁵⁵ men⁵² . mua⁵² tɕuŋ⁵⁵ len⁵² ntau⁴⁴ tu³³ xai³³ tia³³
要　　说　　话　　苗族　　准确　　有　　多位　　　　　说　　道
will　say　language　Hmong　accurate　have　many　CL　　　say　COMP

他们说苗语就会准确。
they will be able to speak Hmong language accurately.

57 kaɯ²¹ ntaɯ³⁵ m̥uŋ⁵⁵ tsaɯ⁵² lɔ³³ mu³³ ɲthia³⁵ tʂi³³ tau⁴⁴ nɔ⁵² , tʂi³³ mua⁵²
读　　书　　苗族　　会　　也　　去　　找　　不　　得　　吃　　不　　有
read　book　Hmong　know.how　CONJ　go　find　NEG　get　eat　NEG　have

有很多人都说懂苗文也挣不了饭吃,找不到事情做,
Many people say that understanding Hmong language can't feed us or give us a job

58 xau⁵² lɯ²¹ ʔua⁴⁴ , tʂi³³ tau⁴⁴ ɲia⁵² tsɦia³¹ . ta⁵⁵ ʂi³³ ne⁵² ntɕɔ⁴⁴ ntʂuŋ³⁵
事情　　做　　不　　得　　钱　　钱　　但是　　你们　　记住　　(牢记状)
matter　do　NEG　get　money　money　but　2PL　remember　firmly

naɯ³⁵ ,
啊
IP

挣不了钱。但是你们记住了啊,
and earn money. But, remember that

59 zɦɔ³¹ len⁵² tɦɯ³¹ xai³³ tʂi³³ tau⁴⁴ lu³³ m̥uŋ⁵⁵ men⁵² , nɯ³³ tsaɯ²¹ ʐua³⁵
是　　位　　哪　　说　　不　　得　　话　　苗族　　准确　　他　　就　　要
COP　CL　who　say　NEG　can　language　Hmong　accurately　3S　DM　will

(5) ntaɯ³⁵ m̥uŋ⁵⁵ lu³³ m̥uŋ⁵⁵ 苗语苗文

要是谁说苗语不准确，即使他再怎么帅，
no matter how handsome those who speak non-standard Hmong language are,

60 zuŋ⁴⁴ ɳtɕʰau³¹ mpau²¹ tɕa³³ , nɯ³³ ʑen⁵² tʂi³³ mua⁵² n̥u⁵⁵ zua³⁵ tau⁴⁴ ʔua⁴⁴
   帅   多么   他 根本 不 有 天 要 得 做
   handsome how much 3S at all NEG have day will get do

他根本不会有机会
they won't get the chance

61 pe⁵⁵ tu³³ tu⁵⁵ ɳtɕʰau³¹na⁵⁵ ʔi⁵⁵ zɦau³¹ , nɯ³³ tʂi³³ mua⁵² n̥u⁵⁵ zua³⁵ tau⁴⁴
   我们 个 儿子 郎蛇   一 次   他 不 有 天 要 得
   1PL CL son snake-husband one time 3S NEG have day will get

选为美男子，他也不会有机会
to be Prince Charming at all and won't get the opportunity

62 ʔua⁴⁴ pe⁵⁵ tu³³ pʰe⁵² ʔe⁵² mɯ³⁵ vi²¹ ʔi⁵⁵ zau³³ . tu³³ ntshai³³ tɕʰɯ³¹ nɯ³³
   做 我们 个 男主角   电影 一 次   个 女儿 哪 她
   do 1PL CL hero   movie one time CL daughter who 3S

当电影的男主角。哪一个女孩子
to be the hero of movie. No matter how beautiful a girl

63 tsau²¹ zua³⁵ zuŋ⁴⁴ ŋkau⁵² mpau²¹ li⁴⁴ tɕa³³ , zɦo³¹ xai³³ tia³³ nɯ³³ xai³³
   就   要   漂亮   多么   是   说 道 她 说
   even will beautiful how much   COP say COMP 3S say

就算再怎么漂亮，要是她说苗语不准确，
who speak Hmong language inaccurately is,

64 lu³³ m̥uŋ⁵⁵ tʂi³³ men⁵² , tʂi³³ mua⁵² ʔi⁵⁵ n̥u⁵⁵ ʔua⁴⁴ nɯ³³ zua³⁵ tau⁴⁴
   话 苗族 不 准确 不 有 一 天 (定标) 她 要 得
   language Hmong NEG accurate NEG have one day REL 3S need get

她永远不会有机会
she will never get the chance

65 lɔ³³ ʔua⁴⁴ pe⁵⁵ tu³³ ntshai³³ ŋkau⁵² ntʂhua⁵⁵ ʔi⁵⁵ zau³³ .
   来 做 我们 个 女儿 女孩 绿 一 次
   come do 1PL CL daughter girl green one time

选为苗族美女，
to be elected as the beauty of Hmong.

66 nɯ³³   zua³⁵   tṣi³³   mua⁵²   ṇu⁵⁵   tau⁴⁴   lɔ³³   ʔua⁴⁴   pe⁵⁵
    她   要   不   有   天   得   来   做   我们
    3S   will   NEG   have   day   get   come   do   1PL

她永远不会有机会做电影的女主角。
She will never get the opportunity to the heroine of a movie.

67 tu³³   na⁴⁴   ʔe⁵²   mɯ³⁵   vi²¹   ʔi⁵⁵   zau³³ . ŋtɕɔ⁴⁴   ŋtʂuŋ³⁵   li⁴⁴ nɔ⁴⁴ . zɦɔ³¹   li⁴⁴ nɔ⁴⁴ ,
    个   女主角 电影   一   次   记住   (牢记状)   这样   因此
    CL   heroine movie   one   time   remember firmly   this way   thus

你要牢记这些话。因此，
You need to keep these words in mind firmly. Thus,

68 qhɔ³⁵   nɔ⁴⁴   zɦɔ³¹   ʔi⁵⁵   qhɔ³⁵   ke³⁵   tshɯ⁵⁵ ʂia⁵⁵   tau⁴⁴   pe⁵⁵   tɕɔ³⁵   ntshai³³
    处   这   是   一   处   路   举   心   给   我们   些   女儿
    place   this   COP   one   place   road   raise   heart   P   1PL   CL.PL   daughter

这是我对我们的子女的一点劝勉，
this is my advice for our children,

69 tɕɔ³⁵   tu⁵⁵   ,   kɔ²¹   ne⁵²   lɔ³³   mɔ⁵⁵   ʂia⁵⁵   mu³³   kaɯ²¹ntau⁵⁵ kaɯ²¹ntaɯ³⁵ ,
    些   儿子   让   你们   来   疼   心   去   读   布   读   书
    CL.PL   son   let   2PL   come   hurt   heart   go   read   fabric   read book

让你们重视读书，
to make you value reading,

70 lɯ²¹ za²¹   ntaɯ³⁵   thia⁵⁵   ŋtɕɔ⁴⁴   ŋtʂuŋ³⁵   lɔ³³   kaɯ²¹   pe⁵⁵   tɕɔ³⁵   ntaɯ³⁵
    另外   书   和   记住   (牢记状)   来   读   我们   些   书
    in addition   book   and   remember firmly   come   read   1PL   CL.PL   book

m̥uŋ⁵⁵,
苗族
Hmong

读别的书和我们的苗文书，
to read other kinds of books and Hmong books,

（5）ntaɯ³⁵ m̥uŋ⁵⁵ lu³³ m̥uŋ⁵⁵ 苗语苗文

71 kaɯ²¹　pe⁵⁵　tɕɔ³⁵　lu³³　　m̥uŋ⁵⁵．ʐɦɔ³¹ tʰau²¹ ne⁵² tʂi³³ pau⁵⁵　ntaɯ³⁵
　 读　 我们　些　 话　　 苗族　 是　 时候　你们　不　 懂　　 书
　 read　1PL　CL.PL　language　Hmong　COP　time　2PL　NEG　understand　book

m̥uŋ⁵⁵
苗族
Hmong

读我们的苗语。当你们不懂苗文

read our Hmong writing. If you don't know Hmong writing,

72 ne⁵²　tʂi³³　pau⁵⁵　　lu³³　　　m̥uŋ⁵⁵，tɕai³³　pe⁵⁵　m̥uŋ⁵⁵　tɕɔ³⁵　tsu⁵² tɕi⁴⁴　lɔ³³
　 你们　不　　懂　　　话　　　苗族　　那么　　我们　苗族　　些　　文化　　　或
　 2PL　NEG　understand　language　Hmong　so that　1PL　Hmong　CL.PL　culture　or

ʐɦɔ³¹
是
COP

不懂苗语的时候，那么我们苗族的文化或

or Hmong language, then our Hmong culture

73 pe⁵⁵　m̥uŋ⁵⁵　tɕɔ³⁵　　ka⁵⁵li³³ke³⁵tɕai⁴⁴，sɯ³³ li⁴⁴ ke³⁵ pa²¹ tʰua³¹，tʂʰuŋ⁵⁵ kɔ³³，
　 我们　苗族　 些　　 风俗习惯　　　　 比如　 　丧葬　　　　　婚事
　 1PL　Hmong　CL.PL　custom　　　　　such as　　funeral　　　wedding

我们苗族的风俗习惯，例如丧葬、婚礼

or our Hmong customs such as funeral and wedding

74 lɔ³³　ʐɦɔ³¹ tʂʰua⁵⁵ qen⁵²　，tʂʰua⁵⁵ ta⁵²　，tʂʰua⁵⁵ ŋtɕa³³　，xai³³ kɯ³³tsʰia⁵²，
　 或　　是　　吹　 芦笙　　 吹　　笛子　　吹　 口弦　　　 说　　山歌
　 or　COP　blow　reed pipe　blow　flute　blow　buccal reed　say　folk song

或吹芦笙、吹笛子、吹口弦、唱山歌、

or reed pipe playing, flute and buccal reed playing, folk song singing,

75 lu³³tau²¹，pa⁵² xua²¹　，nɯ³³ zua³⁵ puŋ⁵⁵ tʰia⁵⁵ zua³⁵ plɔ⁵² mu³³ ta³³ ŋtʰɔ⁴⁴，
　 谜语　　说唱　　　它　要　丢　和　要　消失　去　完　（彻底状）
　 riddle　oral literature　3S　will　lost　and　will　vanish　go　finish completely

猜谜语、说唱，它们将要彻底地丢失和失传。

riddles guessing and oral literature will be totally lost.

76 zɦɔ³¹ thau²¹ ne⁵² pau⁵⁵ ntaɯ³⁵ m̥uŋ⁵⁵ pau⁵⁵ lu³³ m̥uŋ⁵⁵ laɯ²¹ , ne⁵²
　　是　　时候　你们　懂　　书　　苗族　懂　　话　　苗族　了　你们
　　COP　time　2PL　understand　book　Hmong　understand　language　Hmong　PRF　2PL

ʐua³⁵
要
should

如果你们懂苗语苗文了，
If you understand Hmong language and writing,

77 ʔua⁴⁴ tau⁴⁴ tshua⁴⁴ ʐa²¹ ʔua³³ ŋɔ⁵⁵ tau⁴⁴ xau³⁵ m̥uŋ⁵⁵ lu⁵⁵ nen⁵² .
　　做　　得　　全　　样　(定标)　在　　给　　里　苗族　个　生活
　　do　can　all　way　REL　be.located　P　inside　Hmong　CL　life

你们能在苗族的生活中做很多事情。
you can accomplish a lot in the life of the Hmong.

苗语苗文

今天，我想谈谈苗语和苗文。

为什么要说苗语苗文呢？因为现在看到了一些现象：现在这一代的青少年不会说苗语，说苗语说不准确，因此，我才要来谈苗语苗文，使长辈们重视教孩子说苗语。谁还懂苗文的，可以给大家教苗文。

谁不懂苗文，谁就说不准苗语。在我们泰国这里，多数孩子都去学习泰文，他们长时间去学习泰文之后，就会渐渐不记得他自己的苗语了。他不懂苗文，但他懂泰文，他的口音就会像泰语的口音，那么就会使他说苗语不准确。这种情况中国苗族也一样，老挝苗族也一样，越南苗族也一样，美国苗族也一样。他去学习英语的时候，他不记得说他的苗语了。说英语嘛，他说得很好，但是他说苗语却不行了。在中国的苗族，他说汉语说得很好，但是当马上转说苗语时，他就不会说了。这种情况是现在各地普遍出现的问题。因此，我想我们这些长辈就要传承我们的苗语。

当别人问："你们是什么民族？"我们才好告诉人家："我们是苗族。"那时候，他们又追问："苗族是谁？我们不认识苗族哎。"你要这样回答别人："苗族是谁，苗族是一个有自己语言、不说别人语言的民族。第二，苗族是一个有自己文字的民族。第三，苗族是一个有自己独特服饰的民族。第四，苗族是一个有自己独特风俗习惯的民族。要是谁满足以上四条，那这个人就是苗族。因此，我们得好好传承我们的语言，我们得传承我们的文字，我们得传承我们的服饰，我们得传承我们的风俗习惯。我们才能回答其他民族的人："我们是苗族"。对不起，今天我没有穿苗族服装来，因为没有准备。今天有中国的苗族学生来，来调查泰国苗语，我才有机会参与。因此，我才把这些话讲给中国的苗族学生听，这也是一个向中国多位苗族兄弟展示的机会，让你们接着把这些话告诉你们的孩子。让你们重视教你们自己的孩子学苗语，让你们重视教你们自己的孩子学苗文。

当你们的小孩懂苗文了，他们说苗语就会准确。有很多人都说懂苗文也挣不了饭吃，找不到事情做，挣不了钱，但是你们要记住了啊，要是谁说苗语不准确，即使他再怎么帅，他根本不会有机会选为美男子，他也不会有机会当电影的男主角。哪一个女孩子，就算再怎么漂亮，要是她说苗语不准确，她永远不会有机会选为苗族美女，她永远不会有机会当电影的女主角。你要牢记这些话。因此，这是我对我们的子女的一点劝勉，让你们重视读书，读别的书和我们的苗文书，说我们的苗语。当你们不懂苗文不懂苗语的时候，那么我们苗族的文化或我们苗族的风俗习惯，例如丧葬、婚礼或吹芦笙、吹笛子、吹口弦、唱山歌、猜谜语、说唱，它们将要彻底地丢失和失传。

如果你们懂苗语苗文了，你们能在苗族的生活中做很多事情。

Hmong Language and Hmong Writing

Today, I want to talk about Hmong language and Hmong writing.

Why the Hmong language and writing? It is because I've observed a phenomenon that the youth of the contemporary generation can't speak the Hmong language, or they speak non-standard Hmong language. Therefore, that's why I am going to talk about Hmong language and writing, hoping it can make elders pay attention to teaching their children to speak Hmong language. Those who can understand Hmong writing can teach us about it.

People who don't understand Hmong writing cannot be able to speak it clearly. Here in Thailand, most children are learning Thai language. After spending long time studying Thai language, they will gradually forget their Hmong language. If one can't understand Hmong writing, but he knows Thai language, he will have Thai accent, which will make his Hmong language incorrect. The same is true among Chinese Hmong, Laotian Hmong, Vietnamese Hmong and American Hmong. When one is learning English, he will forget to speak his Hmong language. He performs well when it comes to English, instead of Hmong language. The Hmong people in China can speak Chinese fluently; however, they are not able to speak when they switch to Hmong language. This kind of situation occurs universally in all areas. Therefore, I wish our elders could pass down our Hmong language.

When people ask, "What's your nationality?" We are able to say, "We are the Hmong". Then if they question closely, "Who are the Hmong? We don't know about the Hmong." You should answer them like this: "Who are the Hmong? The Hmong is a nationality which has its own language and speaks no other language. Secondly, Hmong is a nationality with its own writing. Thirdly, Hmong is a nationality with its own unique costumes. Fourthly, Hmong is also a nationality which has its unique manners and customs. People who fulfill the four things above are the Hmong people." Thus, we should pass down our own characters, costumes and customs, so that can we respond people of other nationalities that "we are Hmong". I'm so sorry that I'm not wearing my Hmong costumes, because I didn't prepare. Today, here come Chinese Hmong students to investigate Hmong language in Thailand, so I could have the chance to participate. I want to deliver these words to Chinese Hmong students. This is also an opportunity to show our Chinese Hmong brothers these words, which you can tell your children. Thus, we want you to value teaching your children with Hmong language and teach your children how to write Hmong writing.

If your children can understand Hmong writing, they will be able to speak Hmong language accurately. Many people say that understanding Hmong language cannot feed us or give us a job and earn money. But remember that no matter how handsome those who speak non-standard Hmong language are, they won't get the chance to be Prince Charming at all or get the chance to be the hero of movie. Likewise, no matter how beautiful a girl who speaks Hmong language inaccurately is, she would never get the opportunity to be elected as the Beauty of Hmong, and she will never get the chance to be the heroine of a movie. You should keep these words firmly in your mind. Therefore, this is my advice for our children, to make you value reading, to read other kinds of books and Hmong books, and to speak Hmong language. If you don't understand Hmong language or writing, then our culture and customs like funeral, wedding and reed pipe playing, flute and buccal reed playing, folk song singing, riddle guessing and oral literature will be completely lost.

If you can understand Hmong language and writing, you can accomplish a lot in the life of the Hmong.

(6) pe⁵⁵ m̥uŋ⁵⁵ tɕɔ³⁵ ka⁵⁵li³³ke³⁵tɕai⁴⁴ 苗族的文化习俗

我们 苗族　些　　传统习俗
1PL　Hmong CL.PL traditional customs

1 m̥uŋ⁵⁵　tɕɔ³⁵　ka⁵⁵　li³³　　ke³⁵　tɕai⁴⁴,　sɯ³³le⁴⁴　zɦɔ³¹　ke³⁵　plɔ⁵²　tɦua³¹ ,
　苗族　些　　路　理　　路　理　　像　　是　　路　消失　死
　Hmong CL.PL road reason road reason be.like COP road vanish die
苗族的风俗习惯，如葬礼、
The customs of Hmong such as funeral,

2 ke³⁵tʂhuŋ⁵⁵kɔ³³ , ke³⁵　tʂo⁴⁴　plɦi³¹ , ke³⁵　ʔua⁴⁴　ɳu⁵² ʔda⁵⁵ ,
　路　婚礼　　　路　放　　魂　　路　做　　牛　鬼
　road wedding　road release soul　road make ox ghost
婚嫁、放魂、做牛鬼、
wedding, releasing soul ritual, ox ghost ritual,

3 ke³⁵ʔua⁴⁴mpua⁴⁴tai⁴⁴ , ke³⁵　ʔua⁴⁴　mpua⁴⁴ʔda⁵⁵　tɦuŋ³¹ ,
　路　做　猪　□　　　路　做　　猪　　鬼　　桌子
　road make pig　　　road make pig ghost table
做猪鬼、做祭门猪、
pig ghost ritual, making pig sacrifice,

4 nɔ⁵²mɔ³⁵mple⁵²tʂhia⁵⁵ , nɔ⁵²　tʂia⁵⁵　pe⁵⁵　tɕɦau³¹　lɔ³³　zɦɔ³¹
　吃　饭　米　新　　　吃　　新年　　三　　十　　　或　　是
　eat food rice new　　eat newyear three ten　or　COP
新米节、新年或花山节。
New Rice Festival, New Year or Flower Festival.

5 ɴqau³³tɔ⁵². pe⁵⁵　mua⁵²　ntau⁴⁴　za²¹　ntau⁴⁴　tʂa³⁵　ŋɔ⁵⁵　tau⁴⁴　xau³⁵
　赶　坡　　我们　有　　多　　样　　多　　种　　在　　给　　里
　drive hillside 1PL have much style much kind be.located P inside

(6) pe⁵⁵ m̥uŋ⁵⁵ tɕɔ³⁵ ka⁵⁵li³³ke³⁵tɕai⁴⁴ 苗族的文化习俗

在苗族的生活中有各种各样的习俗，
There are all kinds of customs in the life of the Hmong people.

6 m̥uŋ⁵⁵ lu⁵⁵ nen⁵² , pe⁵⁵ m̥uŋ⁵⁵ tɕɔ³⁵ lau³³ ʔi⁵⁵tʂɯ²¹ xai³³ tia³³ :
   苗族　个　生活　我们　苗族　些　老　一直　说　道
   Hmong CL life　1PL Hmong CL.PL old always say COMP

苗族祖先有句话流传至今：
An ancient Hmong saying has been passed down till now:

7 ʔi⁵⁵ tʂa⁵⁵ te⁵⁵ ʔi⁵⁵ tʂa³⁵ tsu⁵² , ʔi⁵⁵ tʂa⁵⁵ te⁵⁵ ʔua⁴⁴ tɕi³³ zuŋ⁴⁴le⁴⁴
   一　个　地　一　种　文化　一　个　地　做　不　像
   one CL place one CL kind culture one CL place do NEG be.like

一个地方一种文化，一个地方不同于一个地方，
Each place has its own culture; culture differs in different places,

8 ʔi⁵⁵ tʂa⁵⁵ te⁵⁵ , ʔi⁵⁵ lu⁵⁵ zɔ³³ ʔua⁴⁴ tɕi³³ zuŋ⁴⁴le⁴⁴ ʔi⁵⁵ lu⁵⁵ zɔ³³ ,
   一　个　地　一　个　村子　做　不　像　一　个　村子
   one CL place one CL village do NEG be.like one CL village

一个村子不同于一个村子，
and differs in different villages.

9 pe⁵⁵ ʔi⁵⁵ tʂɯ²¹ zen⁵² mua⁵² lɔ⁴⁴ lu³³ nɔ⁴⁴ . ta⁵⁵ʂi³³ ʈaɯ³³le⁴⁴
   我们　一直　确实　有　句　话　这　但是　根据
   1PL always indeed have CL words this but according to

我们的确一直有这句话。
We indeed have always had this saying.

10 qho³⁵ ku³⁵ lɔ³³ mu³³ tɕhaɯ⁵⁵faɯ⁵⁵ tau⁴⁴ , ʔi⁵⁵ tʂa⁵⁵ te⁵⁵ nɯ³³
   处　我　来　去　分析　得　一　个　地　它
   place 1S come go analyze get one CL land 3S

但是，根据我的分析，
However, according to my analysis,

11 mua⁵² ʔɔ⁵⁵ pe⁵⁵ tʂa³⁵ tsu⁵² . vi²¹ le⁴⁴ tɕa³³ xɔ⁴⁴ xai³³ le⁴⁴ nɔ⁴⁴ ?
   有　两　三　种　文化　为什么　又　说　像　这
   have two three kind culture why again say be.like this

一个地方有两三种文化。为什么又这样说呢？
one place has two or three kinds of culture. Why would I say that?

12 ʔi⁵⁵ lu⁵⁵ zɔ³³ tʰɯ³¹ nɯ³³ mua⁵² m̥uŋ⁵⁵ ʔdaɯ⁵⁵, m̥uŋ⁵⁵ ntʂua⁵⁵,
　　一　个　村子　哪　它　有　苗族　白　　苗族　绿
　　one CL village where 3S have Hmong white Hmong green

一个村子如果它有白苗、绿苗，
If one village has both White Hmong and Green Hmong,

13 nɯ³³ tɯ⁵⁵ mua⁵² ʔɔ⁵⁵ tʂa³⁵ tsu⁵² laɯ²¹, ʑɦɔ³¹ xai³³ tia³³ lu⁵⁵ zɔ³³
　　它　都　有　两　种　文化　了　　是　说　道　个　村子
　　3S both have two kind culture PRF COP say COMP CL village

那么它就有两种文化了，
there are two kinds of culture in this village.

14 ntaɯ²¹ nɯ³³ mua⁵² m̥uŋ⁵⁵ ʔdu⁵⁵, nɯ³³ mua⁵² m̥uŋ⁵⁵ lia⁵⁵, mua⁵²
　　那　它　有　苗族　黑　　它　有　苗族　红　　有
　　that 3S have Hmong black 3S have Hmong red have

如果说那个村子还有黑苗、红苗、
If there are also Black Hmong, Red Hmong,

15 m̥uŋ⁵⁵ ʔda⁵², mua⁵² m̥uŋ⁵⁵ ʂua⁴⁴, tɕai³³ lu⁵⁵ zɔ³³ ntaɯ²¹ nɯ³³ mua⁵²
　　苗族　黄　　有　苗族　汉　　那么　个　村子　那　它　有
　　Hmong yellow have Hmong Han so CL village that 3S have

黄苗、汉苗，
Yellow Hmong and Han Hmong in the village,

16 tsɦɔ³¹ plau⁵⁵ tʂi⁵⁵ tʂa³⁵ tsu⁵². kɔ⁵² mu³³ kaɯ²¹ ʔi⁵⁵ tu³³ kɯ³³ lɔ³³,
　　到　四　五　种　文化　你　去　读　一　个　师傅　来
　　about four five kind culture 2S go read one CL master come

那么这个村子就有四五种文化了。
then there are four or five kinds of culture in the village.

17 ku³⁵ mu³³ kaɯ²¹ ʔi⁵⁵ tu³³ kɯ³³ lɔ³³, tu³³ tɔ²¹ mu³³ kaɯ²¹ ʔi⁵⁵ tu³³
　　我　去　读　一　个　师傅　来　　个　那　去　读　一　个
　　1S go read one CL master come CL that go read one CL

你去跟一个师傅学，我去跟另一个师傅学，他又去跟其他的师傅学，
You learn from one master; I learn from one master and he goes to learn from another master;

18 kɯ³³   lɔ³³   , pe⁵⁵ ʂaɯ³⁵ʔɖaɯ³³ lɔ³³   mu³³ ʔua⁴⁴ ʔi⁵⁵ za²¹ ʔɖe⁵²nu²¹ ,
   师傅   来   我们   大家   来   去   做   一   样   事情
   teacher come   1PL   all   come go   do   one style thing

然后我们大家共同做一件事，
then we all do something together.

19 pi³⁵tsɯ³⁵ pe⁵⁵ lɔ³³   mu³³ taɯ⁴⁴ ke³⁵ , ɲia³³ xai³³ ɲia³³. zɦɔ³¹ le⁴⁴ntaɯ²¹
   比如   我们   来   去   指   路   各   说   各   是   那样
   such as   1PL   come   go   point road   each say   each   COP that

比如我们去指路，各说各的。
For example, when we give directions, each will say it in their own way.

20 pe⁵⁵ tɕɔ³⁵ lau³³ xai³³ tia³³ : ʔi⁵⁵ tʂa⁵⁵ te⁵⁵ ʔi⁵⁵ tʂa³⁵ tsu⁵² , ta⁵⁵ ʂi³³
   我们 些   老   说   道   一   个   地   一   种   文化   但是
   1PL   CL.PL old   say   COMP   one   CL   place one   kind culture but

因此，我们的老一辈说：一个地方一种文化，
Therefore, our old generation says: there's one culture in one place,

21 tʂi³³ zɦɔ³¹. ʔi⁵⁵ tʂa⁵⁵ te⁵⁵ ʔɔ⁵⁵ pe⁵⁵ tʂa³⁵ tsu⁵² , qhɔ³⁵ ʔua³³ pe⁵⁵ m̥uŋ⁵⁵
   不   是   一   个   地   两   三   种   文化   处   (定标) 我们 苗族
   NEG   COP   one   CL   place two   three kind   culture place REL   1PL   Hmong

其实不是这样的。一个地方两三种文化，
but it's not true. With two or three different kinds of culture in one place,

22 phen⁵²   tʂi³³ ʂi⁵⁵ xau²¹ , ku³⁵ xai³³ kɔ⁵² tʂi³³ mlɦiuŋ³¹ , kɔ⁵² xai³³ ku³⁵
   硬是   不   相互 和   我   说   你   不   听   你   说   我
   obstinately NEG RECP harmony 1S   say   2S   NEG   listen   2S   say   1S

这些不同的文化会让我们不团结，我说你不听，你说我不听，
we Hmong will not be harmonious. I can't convince you and you can't convince me.

23 tʂi³³ mlɦiuŋ³¹ , vi²¹   zɦɔ³¹ ʔi⁵⁵ tʂa⁵⁵ te⁵⁵ mua⁵² ʔɔ⁵⁵ pe⁵⁵ tʂa³⁵ tsu⁵² ,
   不   听   因为   是   一   个   地   有   两   三   种   文化
   NEG   listen   because COP   one   CL   place have   two   three kind culture

因为一个地方有两三种文化，
It is because that there are two or three kinds of culture in one place.

24 pe⁵⁵　mɯŋ⁵⁵　tɕɔ³⁵　lau³³　thia⁵²　le⁴⁴　xai³³　tia³³　：pe⁵⁵　tɕɔ³⁵　ke³⁵　tɕai⁴⁴
　　我们　苗族　些　老　才　才　说　道　　我们　些　　道理
　　1PL　Hmong CL.PL old　just　just　say　COMP　1PL　CL.PL truth

我们苗族老人才说道：我们的道理是猪狗道理，
Thus the Hmong elders said: our principles are animal-like,

25 ʑɦo³¹　ʔde³⁵　mpua⁴⁴　tɕai⁴⁴，pe⁵⁵　ʔua⁴⁴　le⁴⁴　　ʔde³⁵　mpua⁴⁴　ʔua⁴⁴，pe⁵⁵
　　是　狗　猪　　道理　我们　做　像　　狗　猪　　做　　我们
　　COP dog　pig　　truth　1PL　do　be.like　dog　pig　　do　　1PL

我们做的事像猪狗做的事，
so that things we do are animal-like,

26 tʂi³³　ʔua⁴⁴　le⁴⁴　nɦien³¹　ʔua⁴⁴. vi²¹ le⁴⁴ tɕa³³ lau³⁵　lɯ²¹　　xai³⁵　nɦien³¹
　　不　做　像　　人　做　　为什么　　他们　另外　种　人
　　NEG do　be.like human do　why　　　3PL　in addition kind human

我们做的事不像人做的事。为什么别的民族他们却能团结起来？
and aren't like what people can do. Why can people of other nationalities stick together?

27 lau³⁵　xɔ⁴⁴　xai³³　ʂi⁵⁵　xau²¹　? vi²¹　ʑɦo³¹　lau³⁵　ʔua⁴⁴　zuŋ⁴⁴　ʔi⁵⁵　za²¹，
　　他们　又　说　相互　和　　因为　是　他们　做　好　一　样
　　3PL　again say mutual harmony　because COP 3PL　do　good one style

是因为他们做法一致，
That's because they do things in harmony,

28 lau³⁵　ʔua⁴⁴　ʔi⁵⁵　ke⁴⁴，pe⁵⁵　ɲia³³　ʔua⁴⁴　ɲia³³. vi²¹ le⁴⁴ tɕa³³ xɔ⁴⁴　xai³³
　　他们　做　一　路　　我们　各　做　各　　为什么　又　说
　　3PL　do　one road　1PL　each do　each　why　　again say

因为他们齐心，而我们却各做各的。
and they are united, while we only do our own things.

29 tia³³　ɲia³³　ʔua⁴⁴　ɲia³³　? mɯŋ⁵⁵　va⁵²　lɔ³³　ʑɦo³¹　va⁵²　ŋtɕua⁵⁵，mua⁵²　va⁵²
　　道　各　做　各　　苗族　王　或　是　王　家　　有　王
　　COMP each do　each　Hmong Wang or　COP Wang home　have　Wang

为什么说是各做各的呢？比如，苗族的王姓或王氏家族，
Why would I say that? For example, there are people named Wang

30 ʂua³⁵, va⁵² ma⁵⁵, va⁵² tʂaɯ⁵⁵, nɯ³³ mua⁵² ntau⁴⁴ ntau⁴⁴.
　　汉　　王　彝　　王　周　　它　　有　　多　　多
　　Han　Wang Yi　Wang Zhou　3S　have　RDUP~many

有叫"王汉、王彝、王周"等多个名字。
such as "Wang Han", "Wang Yi", "Wang Zhou" and many more in the Wang family.

31 zɦɔ³¹ le⁴⁴ntaɯ²¹, nɯ³³ zɦɔ³¹ va⁵² ɳtɕua⁵⁵ ʔi⁵⁵ za²¹, ta⁵⁵ ʂi³³ nɯ³³
　　是　　那样　　　它　　是　　王　家　　一　　样　　但是　　它
　　COP　that　　　3S　COP Wang family one style　but　　3S

因此，虽然他们同是王家，
Therefore, although they are all members of the Wang family,

32 khia³⁵ʔda⁵⁵khia³⁵qhua⁴⁴ tɯ⁵⁵ tʂi³³ zuŋ⁴⁴ ʔi⁵⁵za²¹. ʔɔ⁵⁵ tu³³ kɯ³⁵ ti⁵²
　　跑　　鬼　　跑　　客人　　都　　不　　好　　一样　　两　个　弟　兄
　　run ghost run guest　　　all　NEG good the same　two CL brother

但是他们祭祀的祖宗都不一样。
they worship different ancestors.

33 nia²¹ tsi³⁵ ʔi⁵⁵ pla⁵⁵ zɦiu³¹ tɯ⁵⁵ ʔua⁴⁴ tʂi³³ zuŋ⁴⁴ ʔi⁵⁵za²¹, ʔi⁵⁵ lɦien³¹
　　母亲父亲　一　　肚子　养　　都　做　　不　　好　　一　样　　一　位
　　parents　 one belly raise all do　NEG good one style　one CL

同父同母同一个肚子生的俩兄弟做法都不相同，
Born in the same womb, two brothers with the same parents also do things differently;

34 ʔua⁴⁴ ʔi⁵⁵ za²¹, xai³³ zuŋ⁵²zuŋ⁵²zi²¹, kɔ⁵² mu³³ ʂai⁵⁵ ku³⁵ ʔdai²¹
　　做　　一　样　　说　容容易　　　　你　去　看　我　块
　　do　one kind　say easy　　　　　 2S　go look 1S piece

一个做一样，说得很容易，
Everyone does things differently, that's easy to say;

35 si²¹ka⁵⁵ tɯ⁵⁵ tʂi³³ zuŋ⁴⁴le⁴⁴ tu³³ kɯ³⁵ tɔ²¹ ʔdai²¹ si²¹ka⁵⁵. ʔɔ⁵⁵
　　神位　　都　　不　　像　　　个　弟弟　那　块　　神位　　　两
　memorial tablet all NEG be.like CL brother that piece memorial tablet two

你看我家的灵位和弟弟家的都不一样。
you can see, the memorial tablets in my house and in my brother's house are not the same.

36 tu³³ tsi³⁵   tu⁵⁵ ; tu³³ tu⁵⁵   ʔdai²¹ si²¹ka⁵⁵   tɯ⁵⁵ tʂi³³ ʐuŋ⁴⁴le⁴⁴ tu³³ tsi³⁵
   个 父亲 儿子   个 儿子   块   神位   都   不 像   个 父亲
   CL father son CL son   piece memorial tablet all NEG be.like CL father

俩父子，儿子家的灵位和他父亲家的都不一样，
Also, the tablets in the son's house are different from that in the father's house;

37 ʔdai²¹ si²¹ ka⁵⁵   , tu³³ tu⁵⁵   tu³³ tsi³⁵ ʔɔ⁵⁵ lɦien³¹ ʔua⁴⁴ si²¹ka⁵⁵   tɯ⁵⁵ tʂi³³
   块   神位   个 儿子   个 父亲   两   位   做   神位   都   不
   piece memorial tablet   CL son   CL father two CL   make memorial tablet both NEG

父子俩做的灵位都不相同。
father and son make different memorial tablets.

38 ʐuŋ⁴⁴ ʔi⁵⁵ za²¹ . zɦɔ³¹ le⁴⁴ntɯ²¹ pe⁵⁵ tsɔ⁵² ke³⁵ sa³⁵ ʔi⁵⁵ lɦien³¹
   好   一   样   是   那样   我们 条   路 想   一 位
   good one style COP that way   1PL CL road think one CL

因此，我们才各想各的，
Therefore, we only mind our own business,

39 thia⁵²le⁴⁴ sa³⁵ ʔi⁵⁵ za²¹ , ʔua⁴⁴ tau⁴⁴ pe⁵⁵ tʂi³³ ʂi⁵⁵   xau²¹   . mua⁵⁵
   才   想   一 样   做   给   我们 不   (相互缀) 和   拿
   just   think one style do   P   1PL NEG RECP   harmony take.along

这使我们不和睦。
which results in our lack of harmony.

40 pi³⁵tsɯ³⁵ ʔi⁵⁵ qhɔ⁴⁴ , ʐuŋ⁴⁴ ŋkau³³ le⁴⁴ thau²¹ mua⁵² ʔi⁵⁵ tu³³ lau³³
   比喻   一   处   好   正好   的   时候   有   一 个   老
   metaphor one place good just   PRT time   have one CL old

打一个比方，当有个老人去世的时候，
For an analogy, when an elder passed away,

41 tau⁴⁴ ta³³   tsɔ⁵² ʂia⁴⁴ ʔi⁵⁵ tu³³ ʐua³⁵ kua²¹ tɕɔ⁵²   mu³³ tsɔ⁴⁴ ti²¹ tuŋ⁵⁵ ,
   得   完   条   命   一   个 要   让   带   去   让   那   山
   get finish CL   life one CL want let take.along go   let that hill

(6) pe⁵⁵ m̥uŋ⁵⁵ tɕɔ³⁵ ka⁵⁵li³³ke³⁵tɕai⁴⁴ 苗族的文化习俗　　81

一个说要抬到山上去埋，

one says he would carry the corpse up to the hill and bury him,

42 ʔi⁵⁵　tu³³　ʐua³⁵　kua²¹　tɛɔ⁵²　mu³³　tɕia⁴⁴　n̥ṭa²¹　te⁵⁵　,
　　一　　个　　要　　让　　带　　去　　放　　下面　地
　　one　CL　want　let　carry　go　drop　below　place

一个说要抬到地里去埋，

one says he would bury the corpse in the ground,

43 ʔi⁵⁵　tu³³　ʐua³⁵　kua²¹　tɛɔ⁵²　mu³³　tɕia⁴⁴　n̥ṭa²¹　kɯ⁵²　xa⁴⁴　.
　　一　　个　　要　　让　　带　　去　　放　　下面　沟　　山谷
　　one　CL　want　let　carry　go　drop　below　ravine　valley

一个要让抬到山沟里去埋。

another one says he would carry the corpse to the ravine to bury.

44 pe⁵⁵　ʔua⁴⁴　nen⁵²　ŋɔ⁵⁵　,　　pe⁵⁵　mua⁵⁵　ʔi⁵⁵　tu³³　tɛɔ⁵²　mu³³　tɕia⁴⁴　ti²¹　ṭuŋ⁵⁵　,
　　我们　做　　生活　在　　　我们　拿　　一　　个　　带　　去　　放　　那　　山
　　1PL　do　life　be.located　1PL　take　one　CL　carry　go　drop　that　hill

我们活着的人，我们把一个死者抬到山上去埋，

We the living carry one dead up to the hill to bury,

45 mua⁵⁵　ʔi⁵⁵　tu³³　tɛɔ⁵²　mu³³　tɕia⁴⁴　n̥ṭa²¹　kɯ⁵²　xa⁴⁴　.　ŋɔ⁵⁵　ʂau²¹
　　拿　　一　　个　　带　　去　　放　　下面　沟　　山谷　　在　　上面
　　take　one　CL　carry　go　drop　below　ravine　valley　be.located　above

把另一个死者抬到山沟里去埋。

and carry another dead down to the ravine to bury.

46 nen⁵²　,　ʔi⁵⁵　tu³³　ŋɔ⁵⁵　　n̥ṭa²¹　kɯ⁵²　xa⁴⁴　,　ʔi⁵⁵　tu³³　ŋɔ⁵⁵　　tɔ²¹　te⁵⁵　,　ʔi⁵⁵
　　生活　　一　　个　　在　　下面　沟　　谷　　一　　个　　在　　那　　地　　一
　　life　one　CL　be.located　below　ravine　valley　one　CL　be.located　that　place　one

在世的时候，也是一个住在山沟里，一个住在地里，

When we are alive, one lives in the ravine, one lives in the field,

47 tu³³　ŋɔ⁵⁵　　pɦua³¹　pe²¹　ṭuŋ⁵⁵　,　thau²¹　ta³³　tsɔ⁵²　ʂia⁴⁴　mu³³　ʔua⁴⁴　ʔda⁵⁵　lau²¹　lɔ³³,
　　个　　在　　那　　上面　山　　时候　　完　　条　　命　　去　　做　　鬼　　了　　啦
　　CL　be.located　that　up　hill　time　finish　CL　life　go　do　ghost　PRF　IP

一个住在山上，当我们死去做鬼的时候，

and one lives in the mountains, so when we die,

48 ʔi⁵⁵ tu³³ tʂen²¹ mu³³ ŋɔ⁵⁵   ʔi⁵⁵ qhɔ⁴⁴ thia⁵⁵ , pe⁵⁵ tsɔ⁵² ke³⁵
    一   个 还   去   在   一   处   和   我们 条   路
   one CL again go be.located one place and   us   CL road

我们还是一个住一处，

we still live separately;

49 sa³⁵ ɲia³³ thia⁵²le⁴⁴ zua³⁵ sa³⁵ mu³³ ɲia³³ , pe⁵⁵ tʂi³³ lɔ³³ kuŋ²¹
   想   各   才   才   要   想   去   各   我们 不   来   共
  think each just just want think go   each   1PL NEG come together

所以我们才各想各的，我们不在一起共事。

that's why we only mind our own business and do not work together.

50 ʔua⁴⁴ke⁴⁴ . qhɔ³⁵ ntaɯ²¹ zfiɔ³¹ qhɔ³⁵ ʔua³³ ʔua⁴⁴ tau⁴⁴ pe⁵⁵ tʂi³³ ʂi⁵⁵ xau²¹ .
    一起   处   那   是   处   (定标) 让   给   我们 不   相互 和
  together   place that   COP   part   REL   let   P   1PL NEG RECP harmony

那就是我们不和睦的原因。

That's why we are inharmonious.

51 ʔi⁵⁵ qhɔ⁴⁴ ntsi³⁵ , pe⁵⁵ tɕɔ³⁵ ka⁵⁵ lfii³¹ ke³⁵ tɕai⁴⁴ zfiɔ³¹ ʔi⁵⁵ tɕɔ³⁵ ʔua³³
   一   处   补   我们 些   路   理   路   理   是   一   些   (定标)
  one place supplement 1PL CL.PL road reason road reason COP   one CL.PL REL

再者，我们的风俗习惯是很有价值的，

Moreover, our customs are of great value.

52 zuŋ⁴⁴ xen³⁵ , zuŋ⁴⁴le⁴⁴ zfiɔ³¹ tɕɔ³⁵ za⁵² tʂhuŋ⁵⁵ , tsi³⁵sai³⁵ , za⁵²
    好   很   像   是   些   曲   婚宴   丧礼歌   曲
   good very   be.like   COP CL.PL tune wedding party funeral song   tune

qen⁵²   ,
芦笙
lusheng (a kind of reed-pipe instrument)

比如婚礼歌、丧礼歌、芦笙曲、山歌和谜语，

For example, wedding song, funeral song, *lusheng* tune, folk song and riddle,

53 kɯ³³tshia⁵², lu³³tau²¹, tɕɔ³⁵ nɔ⁴⁴ ʑɦɔ³¹ ʔi⁵⁵ tɕɔ³⁵ khaɯ³³ m̥uŋ⁵⁵ lu⁵⁵ nen⁵²,
山歌　　谜语　　些　这　是　一　些　传承　苗族　个　生活
folk song　riddle　CL.PL　this　COP　one　CL.PL　pass on　Hmong　CL　life

这些是记录苗族生活、传承苗族历史的文化。

All of these are the culture that records the life of Hmong and pass on the history of Hmong.

54 khaɯ³³ m̥uŋ⁵⁵ ken⁵⁵kɯ²¹. pɦua³¹ thau²¹ ntu⁵² tʂi²¹ te⁵⁵ tɕɦau³¹,
传承　苗族　历史　　那　时候　天　造　地　裂
pass on　Hmong　history　that　time　heaven　create　earth　crack

开天辟地的时候,

When the heaven was separated from the earth,

55 pɦua³¹ thau²¹ tʂi³³ tau⁴⁴ mua⁵² lu⁵⁵ ntia⁵²te⁵⁵, ʐaɯ²¹ʂau⁵⁵, ti⁵⁵nɦien³¹, tsia⁵²,
那　时候　不　得　有　个　世界　　神　　　人　　　兽
that　time　NEG　get　have　CL　world　god　human　animal

还没有世界，神、人、兽、

the world had not been created yet and gods, humans, animals,

56 ɕuŋ⁵⁵ntuŋ⁴⁴, ʔda⁵⁵, ʂaɯ³⁵ʔdaɯ³³ tʂen²¹ ŋɔ⁵⁵ ʔua⁴⁴ke⁴⁴. nɯ³³ xai³³ tsfɦɔ³¹
竹子　树　　鬼　　大家　　　还　在　一起　它　说　到
bamboo tree　ghost　people　still　be.located　together　3S　say　about

草木、鬼，大家还生活在一起。

plants and ghosts were all living together.

57 pɦua³¹ thau²¹ tʂi³³ pau⁵⁵ xai³³ tia³³ ʔthau⁴⁴ pe³³tʂɦau³¹ tshia⁵⁵ ɕuŋ⁴⁴ lɔ³³ laɯ²¹,
那　时候　不　知道　说　道　过　多少　　　千　　年　来　了
that　time　NEG　know　say　COMP　pass　how much　thousand　year　come　PRF

这些文化反映了几千年来的历史，

This culture reflects the history of thousands of years,

58 tɕɔ³⁵ nɔ⁴⁴ ʑɦɔ³¹ ʔi⁵⁵ tɕɔ³⁵ khaɯ³³ ken⁵⁵kɯ²¹ ʐuŋ⁵⁵ xen³⁵.
些　这　是　一　些　传承　历史　好　很
CL.PL　this　COP　one　CL.PL　pass on　history　good　very

这些文化很好地传承了一些历史。

and some of this culture passes on history very well.

59 pe⁵⁵ tṣi³³ tsaɯ⁵² ntau⁵⁵ tṣi³³ tsaɯ⁵² ntaɯ³⁵ ， pe⁵⁵ tṣi³³ tau⁴⁴ mua⁵⁵ tɕɔ⁵² lɔ³³
　 我们　不　会　布　不　会　书　　我们　不　得　拿　带　来
　 1PL　NEG　can　fabric　NEG　can　book　1PL　NEG　get　take　bring　come

但我们不懂文字，我们没能记录保存下来，
However, we don't know how to write it down, so we failed to keep the record

60 ʂau⁴⁴ tɕia⁴⁴ ， ʔi⁵⁵ phau²¹ xai³³ ʔthau⁴⁴ ʔi⁵⁵ phau²¹ ， ʔi⁵⁵ tia²¹ qhia⁴⁴
　 写　保存　一　辈　说　过　一　辈　一　代　告诉
　 write　preserve　one　generation　say　pass　one　generation　one　generation　tell

一辈教给一辈，一代传给一代，
to pass it down from generation to generation,

61 ʔthau⁴⁴ ʔi⁵⁵ tia²¹ ， tʂɔ⁴⁴ tau⁴⁴ xau³⁵ pe⁵⁵ lu⁵⁵ l̥ɯ⁵⁵ sɯ⁵⁵ . tu³³ kaɯ²¹
　 过　一　代　放　给　里　我们　个　脑子　仅仅　个　读
　 pass　one generation　drop　P　inside　1PL　CL　brain　only　CL　study

只能留在我们的脑子里。
by only keeping it in our mind.

62 tau⁴⁴ ntau⁴⁴, tɕai³³ nɯ³³ tau⁴⁴ ntau⁴⁴, tu³³ kaɯ²¹ tau⁴⁴ tʂɦau³¹ , tɕai³³ nɯ³³
　 得　多　那么　他　得　多　个　读　得　少　那么　他
　 get　much　so that　3S　get　much　CL　study　get　few　so that　3S

学得多的，他就记得多；学到少的，他就记得少，
The more one learns, the more he will remember; the less he learns, the less he will remember.

63 tau⁴⁴ tʂɦau³¹ , qhɔ³⁵ nɔ⁴⁴ zɦo³¹ ʔi⁵⁵ qhɔ³⁵ ʔua³³ vi²¹ pe⁵⁵ tṣi³³ mua⁵²
　 得　少　处　这　是　一　处　(定标)　因为　我们　不　有
　 get　less　place　this　COP　one　place　REL　because　1PL　NEG　have

这是因为我们没有文字记录下来。
This is because that we don't have characters of ours to keep a record.

64 ntau⁵⁵ ntaɯ³⁵ khaɯ³³ tɕia⁴⁴ . pe⁵⁵ tɕɔ³⁵ ka⁵⁵ lɦi³¹ ke³⁵ tɕai⁴⁴ nɔ⁴⁴ zɦo³¹ ʔi⁵⁵
　 布　书　传承　保存　我们　些　路　理　路　理　这　是　一
　 fabric　book　pass on　preserve　1PL　CL.PL　road　reason　road　reason　this　COP　one

我们的风俗习惯是很好的，
We have excellent customs,

(6) pe⁵⁵ m̪uŋ⁵⁵ tɕɔ³⁵ ka⁵⁵li³³ke³⁵tɕai⁴⁴ 苗族的文化习俗

65 tɕɔ³⁵   zuŋ⁴⁴   xen³⁵ ,   nɯ³³   khaɯ³³   tsfiɔ³¹   ken⁵⁵   kɯ²¹   lu⁵⁵   ntia⁵²te⁵⁵ ,   ti⁵⁵nfien³¹   lɔ³³
些   好   很   它   传承   到   历史   个   世界   人   来
CL.PL good very 3S pass on about history CL world human come

它说到世界历史,

which covers the world's history,

66 mu³³   tɕhi²¹ɕi²¹   ʔua⁴⁴   nen⁵²   ʈau⁴⁴   xau³⁵   lu⁵⁵   ntia⁵²te⁵⁵   nɔ⁴⁴ .   ta⁵⁵   ɕi³³
去   出世   做   生活   给   里   个   世界   这   但是
go born do life P inside CL world this but

说到人类是怎么出现在这个世界上。

and how human beings came into this world.

67 pe⁵⁵   tʂi³³   tsaɯ⁵²   ɕi³⁵ ,   thau²¹   lu⁵⁵   ɕi⁵²   xaɯ²¹   pe⁵⁵   tɕɔ⁵²   lɔ³³   ɕi³⁵ ,   pe⁵⁵   tɕɔ⁵²
我们 不 会 用   时候 个 时候   我们 带 来 用   我们 带
1PL NEG can use time CL time 1PL bring come use 1PL bring

但是我们不会使用我们的文化,当我们拿来使用的时候,

But we are incapable of using our culture; when we put it into use,

68 lɔ³³   ɕi³⁵   ʈau⁴⁴   tɕɔ³⁵   tshen⁵²   tshen²¹   tʂi³³   zuŋ⁴⁴   ʔi⁵⁵   za²¹ ,   tɕɔ³⁵   ntsia⁵⁵   lu³³
来 用 给 些   尺寸   不 好 一 样   些 意思 话
come use P CL.PL size NEG good one style CL.PL meaning words

我们对我们文化的理解不一样,

each of us understands our culture in different way,

69 pe⁵⁵   tɕɔ⁵²   lɔ³³   qhia⁴⁴   lɔ³³   qhia⁵⁵   tʂi³³   zuŋ⁴⁴   ʔi⁵⁵   za²¹ .   thau²¹   lu⁵⁵
我们 带 来 告诉 也 告诉 不 好 一 样   时候 个
1PL bring come tell CONJ tell NEG good one style time CL

我们传授的也不一样。

so what we pass on differs.

70 ɕi⁵²   xaɯ²¹   pe⁵⁵   tɕɔ⁵²   lɔ³³   ɕi³⁵   ʈau⁴⁴   m̪uŋ⁵⁵   lu⁵⁵   nen⁵² ,   thau²¹   ʔua⁴⁴   nen⁵²
时候 我们 带 来 用 给 苗族 个 生活   时候 做 生活
time 1PL bring come use P Hmong CL life time drop life

当我们把这些文化用在苗族生活中的时候,

When we apply these cultures to our life as Hmong,

71 ŋɔ⁵⁵ pe⁵⁵ tɯ⁵⁵ tʂi³³ ʂi⁵⁵ l̪u⁵⁵ le⁴⁴ , tʰau²¹ tɕʰua³¹ mu³³ ʔua⁴⁴ ʔda⁵⁵ lɔ³³ ,
　　在　　我们　都　不　(相互缀)　爱　的　时候　死　去　做　鬼　啦
　　be.located 1PL all NEG RECP love IP time die go do ghost IP
活着的时候我们都不相爱，当死去变鬼的时候，
we don't love each other even if when we're alive, and when we're dead and become ghosts,

72 tʂen²¹ mu³³ ɳʈʰia³⁵ ten⁵⁵ men²¹ tʰia⁵⁵ . ku³⁵ mua⁵⁵ pi³⁵ tsɯ³⁵ , ʔɔ⁵⁵ tu³³
　　还　去　找　问题　也　．　我　拿　比方　　两　个
　　still go find problem too 1S take analogy two CL
还要去找对方的麻烦。 我打个比方，
we will still make troubles for each other. For an analogy,

73 nu³³mɦua³¹ ʂi⁵⁵ l̪u⁵⁵ xen³⁵ , kuŋ²¹ ʔi⁵⁵ lu⁵⁵ qʰɔ³⁵ ɴqe³³ , ta⁵⁵ ʂi³³ ,
　　兄妹　　相互　爱　很　共　一　个　处　生下　但是
　　sibling RECP love very together one CL place deliver but
两个兄妹很团结，同父同母，
there are two siblings with the same parents, who are united with each other;

74 tʰau²¹ tɕʰɯ³¹ zɦɔ³¹ ʔi⁵⁵ tu³³ tɕʰɯ³¹ tau⁴⁴ ɳtɕai²¹ lu⁵⁵ ntia⁵² te⁵⁵ lau²¹ ,
　　时候　哪　是　一　个　哪　得　离开　个　世界　了
　　time where COP one CL where get leave CL world PRF
但是当其中一个去世了，
however, one of them passed away,

75 pi³⁵ tsɯ³⁵ tu³³ nu³³ tau⁴⁴ ɳtɕai²¹ lu⁵⁵ ntia⁵² te⁵⁵ lau²¹ , tua⁵² xu⁴⁴ tu³³ mua²¹
　　比喻　个　哥哥　得　离开　个　世界　了　　来　叫　个　妹妹
　　metaphor CL brother get leave CL world PRF come call CL sister
比如哥哥去世了，哥哥家的人来请妹妹去奔丧。
for instance, the brother died and his families invite the sister to the funeral.

76 mu³³ ʔua⁴⁴ mua²¹ pʰau⁵² . ʔɔ⁵⁵ tu³³ nɔ⁴⁴ tɯ⁵⁵ zɦɔ³¹ kuŋ²¹ ʔi⁵⁵ lu⁵⁵
　　去　做　妹妹　姑姑　两　个　这　都　是　共　一　个
　　go do sister anut two CL this both COP together one CL
这兄妹俩是吃同一个奶头长大的，
The two siblings suckled at the same breast,

77 mi³³ no⁵² l̥ɔ⁵⁵ , ta⁵⁵ ʂi³³ thau²¹ tu³³ nu³³ ȵtɕai²¹ ntia⁵² te⁵⁵ lauɯ²¹ ,
　　奶　吃　大　　但是　时候　个　哥哥　离开　世界　了
　　milk eat big　but　time CL brother leave world PRF
但是当哥哥去世时，
but when the brother died,

78 tu³³ mua²¹ mu³³ tsfiɔ³¹ . qhɔ³⁵ tʂen⁵⁵ tfiia³¹ , thau²¹ tu³³ nu³³ ȵtɕai²¹ lauɯ²¹ ,
　　个　妹妹　去　到　　处　真　真　　时候　个　哥哥　离开　了
　　CL sister go arrive place real real time CL brother leave PRF
妹妹来到了。按理说，哥哥去世时，
his sister comes. By rights, if brother dies,

79 tu³³ mua²¹ zua³⁵ tʂu²¹ mu³³ pa⁵⁵ thia⁵² le⁴⁴ zfiɔ³¹ .
　　个　妹妹　要得　得　去　帮忙　才　才　是
　　CL sister need should go help just just COP
妹妹应该帮忙处理后事才是。
his sister should help with the funeral treatment.

80 ta⁵⁵ ʂi³³ , thau²¹ tu³³ mua²¹ mu³³ tsfiɔ³¹ tʂen²¹ mu³³ ȵthia³⁵ ten⁵⁵ men²¹
　　但是　　时候　个　妹妹　去　到　　还　去　找　　问题
　　but　 time CL sister go arrive still go find problem
但是，妹妹来奔丧时反而要去找哥哥的妻子和儿女的麻烦，
However, on the contrary, the sister would find troubles with her brother's wife and children when she attends the funeral,

81 tau⁴⁴ tu³³ nu³³ tɕɔ³⁵ pɔ⁵² nia²¹ me⁴⁴ ȵua²¹ , ʔua⁴⁴ tau⁴⁴ zua³⁵tʂu²¹ tau⁴⁴
　　给　个　哥哥　些　女人　小　孩子　　做　给　要得　　得
　　P CL brother CL.PL woman little children do P should should
使得他们跪拜祈求妹妹的原谅
which makes them kneel down and beg for the sister's forgiveness,

82 lɔ³³ pe⁴⁴ lɔ³³ thɔ³⁵ , lɔ³³ the²¹ ȵia⁵² . qhɔ³⁵ no⁴⁴ zfiɔ³¹ ʔi⁵⁵ qhɔ³⁵
　　来　拜　来　讨　　或　支付　钱　　处　这　是　一　处
　　come implore come ask or pay money place this COP one place

ten⁵⁵ men²¹

问题

 problem

或赔钱。

or indemnify her with money.

83 ʔua³³ ẓuŋ⁴⁴ ŋkau³³ ni⁴⁴ tuŋ⁵² ntʂia⁵⁵ pe⁵⁵ mua⁵⁵ tʂau³³ tɕia⁴⁴ . mua⁵² ʔi⁵⁵
   (定标) 好 （恰好状） 这 桌 米 我们 拿 放 保存 有 一
   REL good exactly this table rice 1PL take drop preserve have one

这个问题就像一箩筐米一样先放着不说。
This issue is like a basket of rice. Let's leave it aside temporarily.

84 ṇu⁵⁵ tɕʰɯ³¹ tsɦɔ³¹ tu³³ mua²¹ , ẓua³⁵tau⁴⁴ mu³³ xu⁴⁴ tu³³ nu³³ tɕɔ³⁵
   天 哪 到 个 妹妹 要得 去 叫 个 哥哥 些
   day where arrive CL sister should go call CL brother CL.PL

有一天妹妹去世了，妹妹的家人得去把哥哥的儿子叫来。
One day when the sister passed away, her families invite her brother's sons to the funeral.

85 tu⁵⁵ tua⁵² . pe⁵⁵ m̥uŋ⁵⁵ xai³³ tia³³ ŋu⁵² tɕʰua³¹ tʂʰua³⁵ ku⁵⁵ , tsi³⁵ tɕʰua³¹
   儿子 来 我们 苗族 说 道 牛 死 剩 角 父亲 死
   son come 1PL Hmong say QUOT ox die remain horn father die

我们苗族有句老话叫"牛死留角，爹死留子"。
There's an old saying of Hmong goes: "The ox dies leaving its horn, a father dies leaving his son."

86 tʂʰua³⁵ tu⁵⁵ . tʰau²¹ mu³³ xu⁴⁴ tɕɔ³⁵ tu⁵⁵ tua⁵² , tɕɔ³⁵ tu⁵⁵ ẓua³⁵ tua⁵²
   剩 儿子 时候 去 叫 些 儿子 来 些 儿子 要 来
   remain son time go call CL.PL son come CL.PL son will come

当哥哥的儿子来到时，
When sons of the brother come,

87 nṭʰia³⁵ ten⁵⁵ men²¹ tau⁴⁴ tu³³ phau⁵² tɕɔ³⁵ mi⁴⁴ tu⁵⁵ mi⁴⁴ ŋua²¹ , ʔi⁵⁵ ẓa²¹
   找 问题 给 个 姑姑 些 小 儿子 小 孩子 一 样
   find problem P CL aunt CL.PL little son little children one style

他们又找姑姑的子女的麻烦，
they would also find troubles with children of their aunt,

88 ŋkau³³ le⁴⁴ thau²¹ tɕɔ³⁵ tɔ²¹ nɔ⁴⁴ mu³³ ɲthia³⁵ ten⁵⁵ men²¹ tau⁴⁴ tɕɔ³⁵
正好 的 时候 些 那 这 去 找 矛盾 给 些
exactly PRT time CL.PL that this go find conflict P CL.PL

正如姑姑以前去找他们的麻烦一样。
just like the way their aunt did to them.

89 tɔ²¹ ʔi⁵⁵ za²¹ thia⁵⁵ . pe⁵⁵ m̥uŋ⁵⁵ thia⁵² le⁴⁴ mua⁵² lɔ⁴⁴ lu³³ xai³³ tia³³ :
那 一 样 和 我们 苗族 才 才 有 句 话 说 道
that one style and 1PL Hmong just just have CL words say QUOT

因此，我们苗族才有句老话说：
Thus, there's an old saying of Hmong people:

90 pau⁵² kua⁴⁴ ẓau⁵⁵ ŋtʂua⁵⁵ . pau⁵² mu³³ pau⁵² lɔ³³ , ʔua⁴⁴ lɔ³³ tsfiɔ³¹ tau⁴⁴
还 汤 菜 绿 还 去 还 来 做 来 到 给
return soup vegetable green return go return come do come arrive P

还青菜汤。还来还去，矛盾延续至今。
Returning the vegetable soup, which only results in endless conflicts.

91 nia⁵² n̥u⁵⁵ nɔ⁴⁴ . qhɔ³⁵ nɔ⁴⁴ zfiɔ³¹ ʔi⁵⁵ qhɔ³⁵ ten⁵⁵ men²¹ ŋɔ⁵⁵ tau⁴⁴ xau³⁵
年 天 这 处 这 是 一 处 问题 在 给 里
year day this place this COP one place problem be.located P inside

这就是我们苗族生活中的一个问题，
This is one of the problems in our life as Hmong;

92 pe⁵⁵ m̥uŋ⁵⁵ lu⁵⁵ nen⁵² , zfiɔ³¹ ʐua³⁵ mua⁵⁵ tha²¹ tsfiɔ³¹ qhɔ³⁵ ke³⁵ mu³³ khɔ⁴⁴
我们 苗族 个 生活 是 要 拿 讲 到 处 路 去 医治
1PL Hmong CL life COP want take speak about place road go heal

如果要说解决这个问题的办法嘛，
there are lots of ways

93 qhɔ³⁵ nɔ⁴⁴ ma³³, nɯ³³ mua⁵² ntau⁴⁴ xen³⁵ . ta⁵⁵ ʂi³³ ku³⁵ mua⁵⁵ pi³⁵ tsɯ³⁵
处 这 嘛 它 有 多 很 但是 我 拿 比喻
place this IP 3S have many very but 1S take metaphor

它有很多。但是上面的这些事只是我打的小小比方，
to solve this problem. Nonetheless, examples above are only my analogies,

94 me⁴⁴　　　me⁴⁴　ţau⁴⁴　pe⁵⁵　kua²¹　pe⁵⁵　tɕɔ⁵²　mu³³　sa³⁵　, thia⁵⁵　tɕɔ⁵²
　　小　　　　小　　给　　我们　让　我们　带　　去　　想　　　和　　带
　　RDUP~little　　　P　　1PL　let　1PL　carry　go　　think　and　take.along
让我们大家去思考
to make us think,

95 mu³³　tshaɯ⁵⁵　ɳʈhia³⁵　xai³³　tia³³　　nia⁵²　ŋu⁵⁵　nɔ⁴⁴　qhɔ³⁵　pe⁵⁵　xai³³　tʂi³³
　　去　　支持　　寻找　　说　　道　　　年　　天　　这　　处　　　我们　说　　不
　　go　support　find　say　COMP　year　day　this　place　1PL　say　NEG
和去寻找我们苗族至今不团结的原因是什么。
and find out the reason why we Hmong people can't stick together up to now.

96 ʂi⁵⁵　　　xau²¹　　zɦɔ³¹　ʔda⁵⁵ tʂi⁴⁴ .
　　(相互缀)　和睦　　是　　什么
　　 RECP　　harmony　COP　what

苗族的文化习俗

　　苗族的风俗习惯，如葬礼、婚嫁、放魂、做牛鬼、做猪鬼、做祭门猪、新米节、新年或花山节。苗族祖先有句话流传至今：一个地方一种文化，一个地方不同于一个地方，一个村子不同于一个村子，我们的确一直有这句话。

　　但是，根据我的分析，一个地方有两三种文化。为什么又这样说呢？一个村子如果它有白苗、绿苗，那么它就有两种文化了，如果说那个村子还有黑苗、红苗、黄苗、汉苗，那么这个村子就有四五种文化了。

　　你去跟一个师傅学，我去跟另一个师傅学，他又去跟其他的师傅学，然后我们大家共同做一件事，比如我们去指路，各说各的。因此，我们的老一辈说：一个地方一种文化，其实不是这样的。

　　一个地方两三种文化，这些不同的文化会让我们不团结，我说你不听，你说我不听，因为一个地方有两三种文化，我们苗族老人才说道：我们的道理是猪狗道理，我们做的事像猪狗做的事，我们做的事不像人做的事。

　　为什么别的民族他们却能团结起来？是因为他们做法一致，因为他们齐心，而我们却各做各的。为什么说是各做各的呢？比如，苗族的王姓或王氏家族，有叫"王汉、王彝、王周"等多个名字。因此，虽然他们同是王家，但是他们祭祀的祖宗都不一样。同父同母同一个肚子生的俩兄弟做法都不相同，一个做一样，说得很容易，你看我家的灵位和弟弟家的都不一样。俩父子，儿子家的灵位和他父亲家的都不一样，父子俩做的灵位都不相同。因此，我们才各想各的，这使我们不和睦。

　　打一个比方，当有个老人去世的时候，一个说要抬到山上去埋，一个说要抬到地里去埋，一个要让抬到山沟里去埋。我们活着的人，我们把一个死者抬到山上去埋，把另一个死者抬到山沟里去埋。在世的时候，也是一个住在山沟里，一个住在地里，一个住在山上，当我们死去做鬼的时候，我们还是一个住一处，所以我们才各想各的，我们不在一起共事。那就是我们不和睦的原因。

　　再者，我们的风俗习惯是很有价值的，比如婚礼歌、丧礼歌、芦笙曲、山歌和谜语，这些是记录苗族生活、传承苗族历史的文化。开天辟地的时候，还没有世界，神、人、兽、草木、鬼，大家还生活在一起。这些文化反映了几千年来的历史，这些文化很好地传承了一些历史。但我们不懂文字，我们没能记录保存下来，一辈教给一辈，一代传给一代，只能留在我们的脑子里。学得多的，他就记得多；学到少的，他就记得少，这是因为我们没有文字记录下来。

　　我们的风俗习惯是很好的，它说到世界历史，说到人类是怎么出现在这个世界上。但是我们不会使用我们的文化，当我们拿来使用的时候，我们对我们文化的理解不一样，我们传授的也不一样。当我们把这些文化用在苗族生活中的时候，活着的时候我们都不相爱，当死去变鬼的时候，还要去找对方的麻烦。我打个比方，两个兄妹很团结，同父同母，但是当其中一个去世了，比如哥哥去世了，哥哥家的人来请妹妹去奔丧。这兄妹俩是吃同一个奶头长大的，但是当哥哥去世时，妹妹来到了。按理说，哥哥去世时，妹妹应该帮忙处理后事才是。但是，妹妹来奔丧时反而要去找哥哥的妻子和儿女的麻烦，使得他们跪拜祈求妹妹的原谅或赔钱。这个问题就像一箩筐米一样先放着不说。有一天妹妹去世了，妹妹家的人得去把哥哥的儿子叫来。我们苗族有句老话叫"牛死留角，爹死留子"。当哥哥的儿子来到时，他们又找姑姑的子女的麻烦，正如姑姑以前去找他们的麻烦一样。因此，我们苗族才有句老话说：还青菜汤。还来还去，矛盾延续至今。

这就是我们苗族生活中的一个问题，如果要说解决这个问题的办法嘛，它有很多。但是上面的这些事只是我打的小小比方，让我们大家去思考和去寻找我们苗族至今不团结的原因是什么。

Hmong Cultural Customs

There are lots of customs of Hmong such as funeral, wedding, releasing soul ritual, ox ghost ritual, pig ghost ritual, making pig sacrifice, New Rice Festival, New Year and Flower Festival. An ancient saying of Hmong has been passed down till now: Each place has its own culture; culture differs in different places and different villages.

However, according to my analysis, one place has two or three kinds of culture. Why would I say that? If one village has both White Hmong and Green Hmong, then there are two kinds of culture in this village. If there are also Black Hmong, Red Hmong, and Yellow Hmong and Han Hmong in the village, then there're four or five kinds of culture in this village.

You learn from one master; I learn from one master and he goes to learn from another master; then we all do something together. For instance, when we give directions, each will say it in their own way. Therefore, our old saying that "There's one culture in one place" is actually not true.

With two or three different kinds of culture in one place, we Hmong people will not be harmonious. I can't convince you and you can't convince me. It is because there are two or three kinds of culture in one place. Thus the Hmong elders said: "Our principles are animal-like, so the things we do are also animal-like and aren't like what people can do.

Why can people of other nationalities stick together? That's because of that they do things in harmony and they are united, while we only do our own things. Why would I say so? For example, there are people named "Wang Han", "Wang Yi", and "Wang Zhou" and many more in the Wang family of Hmong. Although they are all members of Wang family, they worship different ancestors. Born in the same womb, two brothers with same parents also do things differently; everyone does things differently, it's easy to say. You see the memorial tablets in my house are different from that in my brother's house. Furthermore, even the tablets in the son's house and in the father's house are different. Father and son make different memorial tablets. Therefore, we only mind our own business, which results in our lack of harmony.

For an analogy, when an old man passed away, one says he would carry the corpse up the hill to bury him; one says he would bury the corpse in the ground; another one says he would carry the corpse to the ravine to bury. As living people, we carry one dead up to the hill to bury, and then carry another dead down to the ravine to bury. When we are alive, one lives in ravine, one lives in the field and one lives in the mountains, so when we die and become ghosts, we still live separately. So that's why we only mind our own business and do not work together. This is the reason why we are inharmonious.

Moreover, our customs are of great value, such as wedding song, funeral song, *lusheng* (a kind of reed-pipe instrument) tune, folk song and riddle. All those are cultures that record the life of the Hmong people and pass on the history of the Hmong. When the heaven was separated from the earth and the world hadn't been created yet, gods, humans, animals, plants and ghost were all living together. These cultures reflect the history of thousands of years and some of them pass on history very well. However, we don't know how to write it down, so that we failed to keep the records to pass it down from generation to generation, but only keeping in our own mind. The more one learns, the more he will remember; and the less he learns, the less he will remember. It is because we don't have characters of ours to keep a record.

We have excellent customs which cover world's history and how human beings came into this world. Nonetheless we are incapable of using our culture. When we put it into use, each of us understands our culture in different ways, so what we pass on differs. We don't love each other even if when we're alive; when we're dead and become ghosts, we will still make trouble for each other. For an analogy, there are two siblings with the same parents, a brother and a sister, who are united. However, one of them passed away. For instance, the brother was dead, and his family invites the sister to his funeral. The two siblings suckled at the same breast, but when the brother dies, his sister comes. By rights, his sister should help with the funeral treatment. However, on the contrary, the sister would find troubles with her brother's wife and children when she attends the funeral, which makes them kneel down and beg for sister's forgiveness or indemnify her with money. This issue is like a basket of rice, so we just leave it aside temporarily. One day when the sister passed away and her family also invites her brother's sons to the funeral. There's an old saying of Hmong goes: "The ox dies leaving its horns, a father dies leaving his sons". So when sons of the brother come, they would also find troubles with their aunt's children, just like the way their aunt did to them. Therefore, there's an old saying of Hmong people: "Returning vegetable soup, which only results in endless conflicts."

This is one of the problems in our life as Hmong. Of course there are lots of ways to solve it. Nonetheless, examples above are only my analogies, which could make us think and find out the reason why we Hmong people can't stick together all the time until now.

(7) ʔua⁴⁴nen⁵⁵ 跳神

做　巫师
make shaman

1 m̥uŋ⁵⁵　tɕɔ³⁵　tu⁵⁵　ʔdе⁵²nu²¹ , lɔ³³　zɦɔ³¹　tɕɔ³⁵　tu⁵⁵　ʂi³⁵　ŋɔ⁵⁵　tau⁴⁴
　苗族　　些　　儿子　事情　　　或　　是　　 些　　儿子　用　 在　　 给
　Hmong CL.PL son　thing 　　or 　COP　CL.PL son　use be.located P

苗族跳神的人，或跳神时所用的物品，
What people carry out shaman's dance, and what things do they need to do so

2 xau³⁵　tsɔ⁵²　ke³⁵　ʔua⁴⁴nen⁵⁵　, ŋɔ⁵⁵　　tau⁴⁴　ʂa⁵⁵　thai⁵⁵　te⁵⁵　mua⁵²　ʔda⁵⁵tʂi⁴⁴ ?
　里　　 条　　路　　做巫师　　　 在　　　 给　　 边　　泰国　　 地　　有　　　 什么
　inside CL　road make shaman　be.located P　side Thailand land　have　what

在泰国这边有什么？
in Thailand?

3 qhɔ³⁵　ʔi⁵⁵　ntaɯ²¹　nɔ⁴⁴ , zɦɔ³¹　tu³³　tsi³⁵　nen⁵⁵ 　. tu³³　tsi³⁵　nen⁵⁵
　处　　 一　　那　　　这　　是　　 个　　(雄性缀) 巫师　　个　　(雄性缀) 巫师
　place　one that　this　COP　CL　　　　shaman　　CL　　　　　shaman

第一个人，是巫师。
The first one is shaman,

4 zɦɔ³¹　tu³³　ʔua⁴⁴nen⁵⁵ 　, la³³　zɦɔ³¹　ʂi³⁵zɦi³¹ .
　是　　 个　　跳巫师　　　　也　　是　　　师爷
　COP　CL　dance shaman　CONJ COP　advisor

这个巫师是跳神的人，也是师爷。
who performs shaman's dance, he is also the advisor.

5 tu³³　ʔɔ⁵⁵ , zɦɔ³¹　tu³³　xɯ⁵²ʂau³⁵ . zua³⁵tʂu²¹　tau⁴⁴　mua⁵²　tu³³　xɯ⁵²ʂau³⁵ ,
　个　　 二　　是　　 个　　服侍　　　　要得　　　　得　　 有　　 个　　服侍
　CL　two　COP　CL　serve　　　should　　　should have　CL　serve

第二个人，是侍者。必须得有侍者，
The second one is the servants, who are indispensible.

6 zɦɔ³¹ tu³³ mu³³ ʂai⁵⁵ tu³³ tsi³⁵ nen⁵⁵ ʔua⁴⁴nen⁵⁵ , ŋɔ⁵⁵ tau⁴⁴
　是　个　去　看　个　(雄性缀) 巫师 做 巫师　　在　　给
　COP CL go look CL shaman　　make shaman　be.located P

侍者是照看巫师跳神的人，
Servants are responsible for take caring of the shaman when he performs the dance.

7 xɔ³⁵ ʔi⁵⁵ tha⁵² nen⁵⁵ la³³ zɦɔ³¹ ʔi⁵⁵ tu³³ tsi³⁵ nen⁵⁵ ʔua³³ nɯ³³
　里　一　神坛 巫师　或　是　一　个　(雄性缀) 巫师 (定标) 他
　inside one altar shaman or COP one CL　　shaman REL 3S

在一场跳神仪式里或巫师
In a shaman's dance ritual or when

8 zua³⁵ ʔua⁴⁴nen⁵⁵ ntaɯ²¹ . nɯ³³ mua⁵² tɛɔ³⁵ tɯ⁵² ʂi³⁵
　要　做 巫师　　那　　他　有　些　　物品 用
　need make shaman that　　3S have CL.PL articles use

要去跳神时。巫师有
shaman is about to dance, there are

9 ntau⁴⁴ za²¹ ntau⁴⁴ tʂa³⁵ ŋɔ⁵⁵ tau⁴⁴ xɔ³⁵ , ʔi⁵⁵ tshia⁴⁴ ku⁵² pau⁵⁵ laɯ²¹ ,
　多　样　多　种　在　　给　里　一　部分　也　知道 了
　many style many kind be.located P inside one part CONJ know PRF

多种多样的跳神用品，有些已经知道了，
variety of articles for a shaman's dance, some of which are already known

10 ʔi⁵⁵ tshia⁴⁴ pau⁵⁵ tʂi³³ tau⁴⁴ tsɦɔ³¹ . qhɔ³⁵ ʔi⁵⁵ ntaɯ²¹ nɔ⁴⁴ , zɦɔ³¹
　一　部分　知道 不　得　到　　处　一　那　这　是
　one part know NEG get reach place one that this COP

有些还不完全知道。第一，是
but some are yet unknown. Firstly, there's

11 lu⁵⁵ tha⁵² nen⁵⁵ . lu⁵⁵ tha⁵² nen⁵⁵ zɦɔ³¹ lu⁵⁵ qhɔ³⁵tɕhaɯ⁴⁴ ʔua³³
　个　神坛 巫师　个　神坛 巫师　是　个　地方　　　(定标)
　CL altar shaman CL altar shaman COP CL place REL

神坛。神坛是巫师的神兵神将所在的地方，
an altar, a place where the divine troops of shaman stay

12 ʔda⁵⁵nen⁵⁵   ŋɔ⁵⁵   , qhɔ³⁵tɕhaɯ⁴⁴ ʔua³³   lɔ³³   mu³³ ten³⁵tia²¹ tɕɔ³⁵
   鬼 巫师   在   地方   （定标） 来   去   招待   些
   ghost shaman be.located place   REL   come   go   entertain   CL.PL

是招待巫师的神兵神将的地方。
and a place for serving them.

13 ʔda⁵⁵nen⁵⁵   . qhɔ³⁵ tsua³³ ntsi³⁵ mu³³, zɦɔ³¹ lu⁵⁵ ʈuŋ⁵² nen⁵⁵ . lu⁵⁵
   鬼 巫师   处   接   接   去   是   个   桌子   巫师   个
   ghost shaman   place next   next   go   COP   CL table shaman CL

下一种，是"神桌"。
Next, there's a "gods' table",

14 ʈuŋ⁵² nen⁵⁵   zɦɔ³¹ tu³³ nen³³xua⁵⁵tɕua⁴⁴ , la³³
   桌子 巫师   是   个   马   云   风   或
   table shaman COP   CL horse cloud wind   or

"神桌"是能呼风唤雨的马，
which is a horse that can control the forces of nature.

15 zɦɔ³¹ ŋɔ⁵⁵   ʈau⁴⁴ xau³⁵ tɕɔ³⁵ lu³³ nen⁵⁵ xu⁴⁴ ua⁴⁴ kau⁵⁵lu⁵²kau⁵⁵mua²¹ .
   是   在   给   里   些   话   巫师   叫   做   □   骡 □   马
   COP   be.located P   inside CL.PL words shaman call make   mule horse

跳神时也被巫师称作"神骡神马"。
It's also called "holy mule and holy horse".

16 tsua³³ ntsi³⁵   mu³³ , zɦɔ³¹ ɳʈɦua³¹nen⁵⁵ . ɳʈɦua³¹nen⁵⁵
   接   补   去   是   鼓   巫师   鼓   巫师
   next supplement go   COP   drum shaman   drum shaman

下一种，是"神鼓"。"神鼓"
Next is the "gods' drum", a drum

17 zɦɔ³¹ ɳʈɦua³¹ tshi⁵⁵ qhua⁴⁴ , ɳʈɦua³¹ tshi⁵⁵ tu⁵⁵ tʂɦɔ³¹ .
   是   鼓   使唤   客人   鼓   使唤   儿子 士兵
   COP   drum   order guest   drum   order son   soldier

是使唤神兵神将的鼓，是使唤巫师的士兵的鼓。
which can summon and order divine troops and soldiers of shaman.

18 thau²¹ lu⁵⁵ ɕi⁵²xaɯ²¹ ʔi⁵⁵ tɛɔ³⁵ tu⁵⁵ tʃɦɔ³¹ zua³⁵ mu³³
   时候 个   时候   一   些   儿子 士兵   要 去
   time CL time   one CL.PL son soldier need go

ɕi⁵⁵   ntau³³ ɕi⁵⁵ tua⁴⁴,
(相互缀)   打   (相互缀) 打
 RECP   beat   RECP beat

当这些士兵要去打仗时,
When these soldiers are going to enter the field,

19 zua³⁵tau⁴⁴ ntau³³ ɲtɦua³¹ . ntau³³ ɲtɦua³¹ tshi⁵⁵ tu⁵⁵ tʃɦɔ³¹ ,
    要得   打   鼓   打   鼓   使唤 儿子 兵
    should   beat drum   beat   drum   order son soldier

要得打鼓。打鼓使唤士兵,
drums should be played. It's necessary to play the drum to summon and order soldiers

20 kua²¹ tɛɔ³⁵ tu⁵⁵ tʃɦɔ³¹ ntaɯ²¹ thia⁵² li⁴⁴ mua⁵² ɕia⁵⁵
    让   些   儿子 兵   那   才   才   有   心
    let   CL.PL son soldier that just just have hear

才能让那些士兵有信心
so that can they be encouraged and keep high morale

21 mu³³ ɕi⁵⁵ ntau³³ ɕi⁵⁵ tua⁴⁴ . qhɔ³⁵ tsua³³ ntsi³⁵ mu³³ , zɦɔ³¹ ɕa⁵⁵ .
    去 (相互缀) 打 (相互缀) 打   处   接   补   去   是   香
    go RECP beat RECP   beat place next supplement go COP incense

去打仗。下一种,是香。
to fight. Next is incense,

22 ɕa⁵⁵ zɦɔ³¹ i⁵⁵ tɛɔ⁴⁴ tɛɔ⁵² lɔ³³ ɭaɯ³⁵ tau⁴⁴ kua²¹ nɯ³³ ɲtɕhɔ⁴⁴
    香   是   一   些   带   来   烧   给   让   它   冒烟
   incense COP one CL.PL bring come burn P let 3S smoking

香用来烧,让巫师的神兵神将
which is used for burning for divine troops and soldiers

(7) ʔua⁴⁴nen⁵⁵ 跳神

23 pa⁴⁴ tṣɯ⁴⁴qa⁵⁵ tau⁴⁴ tɕɔ³⁵ ʔda⁵⁵nen⁵⁵, kua²¹ nɯ³³ thia⁵² li⁴⁴
气味 臭香 给 些 鬼神 让 它 才 才
smell stink fragrant P CL.PL ghost god let 3S just just

闻到香的烟味，让神兵神将

to smell, so that can they

24 mua⁵² ʂia⁵⁵ mu³³ ua⁴⁴ xau⁵²lɯ²¹ . tsua³³ ntsi³⁵ mu³³, zɦɔ³¹ qe⁴⁴ .
有 心 去 做 事情 接 补 去 是 蛋
have heart go do thing next supplement go COP egg

有心思去做事情。下一种，是鸡蛋。

concentrate on their work. Next is chicken egg,

25 lu⁵⁵ qe⁴⁴ zɦɔ³¹ ʔi⁵⁵ qhɔ³⁵ khuŋ²¹plɦi³¹ , la³³ zɦɔ³¹ ʔi⁵⁵ qhɔ³⁵
个 蛋 是 一 处 东西 魂魄 也 是 一 处
CL egg COP one place thing soul CONJ COP one place

鸡蛋是用来叫魂的东西，也是一点

which is also an article for the shaman's dance and a small way of saying

26 ʔde⁵²ʂia⁵⁵ . lau³⁵ tɕɔ³⁵ lau³³ xai³³ tia³³ : "lau³³ ntʂhaɯ⁴⁴ pe⁴⁴ ,
水 心 他们 些 老 说 道 老 羡慕 拜
water heart 3PL CL.PL old say QUOT old admire worship

心意。老人说道："老人想要被尊重，

thanks. Elders always say that "old people want be to respected

27 mi⁴⁴ ȵua²¹ zau⁴⁴ ntʂhaɯ⁴⁴ qe⁴⁴ ." qe⁴⁴ zɦɔ³¹ ʔi⁵⁵ qhɔ⁴⁴ khuŋ²¹plɦi³¹
小 孩子 小 羡慕 蛋 蛋 是 一 处 东西 魂魄
little children little admire egg edd COP one place thing soul

小孩想要鸡蛋。"鸡蛋是一种礼品，

and children want eggs." An egg is a kind of gift

28 tɕɔ⁵² lɔ³³ tau⁴⁴ tɕɔ³⁵ ʔda⁵⁵nen⁵⁵ , kua²¹ ʔda⁵⁵nen⁵⁵ thia⁵² li⁴⁴
带 来 给 些 神兵神将 让 神兵神将 才 才
bring come P CL.PL divine troops let divine troops just just

拿给巫师的神兵神将，让神兵神将

for divine troops and soldiers of shaman to drive them

29 ɴqɦua³¹ mu³³ tɕau²¹ɳʈu⁵²tɕau²¹plɦi³¹ . tsua³³ ntsi³⁵ mu³³ , zɦɔ³¹
　　勤奋　　去　　追赶　魂魄　追赶　魂魄　　接　　补　　去　　是
　　diligent　go　chase　soul　chase soul　next supplement　go　COP

奋力追赶魂魄。下一种，是

to spare no effort to chase after spirits and souls. Next,

30 mua³³lɔ²¹ . la³³ zɦɔ³¹ tɛɔ³⁵ pa⁵²mplɦɛ³¹ . tɛɔ³⁵ pa⁵²mplɦɛ³¹ ku⁵²
　　马料　　也　　是　　些　　花　稻谷　　些　　花　稻谷　　也
　　horse feed　CONJ COP CL.PL flower grain　CL.PL flower grain CONJ

马料。马料就是米花。这些米花

there's horse feed, which are rice flowers,

31 zɦɔ³¹ i⁵⁵ qhɔ⁴⁴ khuŋ²¹plɦi³¹ , la³³ zɦɔ³¹ ʔdɛ⁵²ʂia⁵⁵ tau⁴⁴ tɛɔ³⁵ ʔda⁵⁵nen⁵⁵
　　是　　一　　处　　礼品　　也　　是　　水　心　给　　些　　神兵神将
　　COP one place gift　　CONJ COP water heart P CL.PL divine troop

也是一种礼品，祭献给神兵神将。

another kind of sacrificial gift for divine troops.

32 ʔi⁵⁵ za²¹ ŋkau³³ thia⁵⁵ . tsua³³ ntsi³⁵ mu³³ , zɦɔ³¹ ʔdɛ⁵² tʂhua⁵² .
　　一　样　正好　也　　接　补　　去　是　　水　药
　　one style exactly too　next supplement go COP water medicine

下一种，是药水。

The next is liquid medicine,

33 la³³ zɦɔ³¹ ʔdɛ⁵² tɕauɹ²¹ ʂia³⁵ , la³³ zɦɔ³¹ pe⁵⁵ mua⁵² ʔi⁵⁵ qhɔ³⁵ ŋɔ⁵⁵
　　也　　是　　水　　救　　命　　也　　是　　我们　有　　一　　处　　在
　　CONJ COP water save life　CONJ COP 1PL have one place be.located

药水也是救命水，也是我们在

which is also the water of life and

34 ʈau⁴⁴ xau³⁵ ʔda⁵⁵nɦen³¹ xai³³ tia³³ "kua⁵⁵mua⁵²tʂua²¹" . kua⁵⁵mua⁵²tʂua²¹
　　给　　里　　故事　　说　　道　　药　□　□　　药　□　□
　　P inside story say COMP medicine　　medicine

民间故事里所说的"瓜马爪"。

what we call "Guamazhua" in folk stories,

35 la³³ zɦɔ³¹ tɕɔ³⁵ ʔd̪e⁵² tʂhua⁵² .
也   是   些   水   药
CONJ COP   CL.PL water medicine

"瓜马爪"也是药水。
which is also a kind of liquid medicine.

36 thau²¹ ʔi⁵⁵ tu³³ ti⁵⁵nɦen³¹ tɦɯ³¹ nɯ³³ mɔ⁵⁵ mɔ⁵⁵tɦua³¹ lau²¹,
时候   一   个   哪   他   病   病死   了
time   one CL person   where 3S RDUP~illness die PRF

当有人病死的时候，
When someone dies of illness,

37 tɕɔ⁵²   mu³³ tʂhua³¹ tau⁴⁴, kua²¹ tu³³ ti⁵⁵nɦen³¹ ntaɯ²¹ nɯ³³ tɔ³⁵qa⁵⁵
带   去   喷   给   让   个   人   那   他   回
take.along go sprinkle P   let   CL person   that   3S   back

拿去给他喷，使他复活。
the liquid medicine can bring him back to life.

38 tɕia⁵² ʂaɯ³⁵ lɔ³³ . tsua³³ ntsi³⁵ mu³³, zɦɔ³¹ nti²¹ ʔd̪e⁵²zɦa³¹ .
活   起来   来   接   接   去   是   碗   水 □
live   get up come   next   next   go   COP   bowl water

下一种，是神水。
Next is the holy water.

39 nti²¹ ʔd̪e⁵²zɦa³¹ zɦɔ³¹ nti²¹ ʔd̪e⁵² xɯ⁵²xua⁵², nti²¹ ʔd̪e⁵² tɕɔ⁵² lɔ³³
   碗   水 □   是   碗   水   武功   碗   水   带   来
   bowl water   COP   bowl water kongfu   bowl water bring come

神水是武功水，用来洗去人身上的病，
It's kongfu water that is used to get rid of illnesses for people.

40 ntsua³⁵mɔ⁵⁵ ntsua³⁵ntʂa⁵², zɦɔ³¹ ʔi⁵⁵ nti²¹ ʔd̪e⁵² ʔua³³ nɯ³³ mua⁵² xɯ⁵² xua⁵²
   洗病   洗病   是   一   碗   水   (定标) 它   有   武功
   wash illness wash illness   COP   one bowl water REL   3S   have   kongfu

是一种有功力
It's a kind of powerful water

41 tɕɔ⁵² lɔ³³ ntsua³⁵mɔ⁵⁵ ntsua³⁵ ɳtʂa⁵² . nuu³³ mua⁵² ntʂi³³ zua³⁵ zuŋ⁴⁴
　　带　　来　　　洗　病　　　洗　　病　　　它　　有　　点　　要　　好
　　bring come wash illness wash illness 3S   have bit will good

能洗去疾病的水。它也有点像
that can wash illness away and is also similar to

42 i⁵⁵za²¹ li⁴⁴ nti²¹ ʔd̠e⁵² tʂhua⁵² thia⁵⁵ . tsua³³ ntsi³⁵ mu³³, zɦɔ³¹
　　一样　　像　　碗　　水　　药　　也　　　接　　补　　去　　是
　　the same be.like bowl water medicine too next supplement go COP

"瓜马爪"那种药水。下一种，是
the "Guamazhua". The next is

43 nta⁵² nen⁵⁵ . nta⁵² nen⁵⁵ la³³ ʔi⁵⁵ tsha⁴⁴ xu⁴⁴ ua⁴⁴ ta⁵⁵ tia²¹ nen⁵⁵ . tia²¹
　　剑　　巫师　　剑　　巫师　　也　　一　　部分　　叫　　做　　把　　刀　　巫师　　刀
　　sword shaman sword shaman CONJ one part call make CL knife shaman knife

"神剑"。"神剑"有部分人也把它叫作"神刀"。
divine sword. There are also some people calling it "divine blade".

44 nen⁵⁵ , nta⁵² nen⁵⁵ nuu³³ zuŋ⁴⁴ ʔi⁵⁵za²¹ . ʔi⁵⁵ tshia⁴⁴ zɦɔ³¹ ta⁵⁵ tia²¹ ,
　　巫师　　剑　　巫师　　它　　好　　一样　　　一　　部分　　是　　把　　刀
　　shaman sword shaman 3S good the same one part COP CL knife

"神刀"和"神剑"作用是一样的。有一部分巫师用刀，
"Divine blade" has the same function as "divine sword". Some shamans use a blade

45 ʔi⁵⁵ tshia⁴⁴ zɦɔ³¹ ta⁵⁵ nta⁵² . ta⁵⁵ nta⁵² nen⁵⁵ la³³ zɦɔ³¹ tia²¹ nen⁵⁵ , tɯ⁵⁵
　　一　　部分　　是　　把　　剑　　把　　剑　　巫师　　或　　是　　刀　　巫师　　铃
　　one part COP CL sword CL sword shaman or COP blade shaman bell

有一部分巫师用剑。"神剑"或"神刀"，
and some shamans use a sword. "Divine sword", "divine blade",

46 nen⁵⁵ , tsia⁵⁵ nen⁵⁵ , tɕɔ³⁵ no⁴⁴ zɦɔ³¹ tɕɔ³⁵ tia²¹ tɕɔ³⁵ phɔ²¹ la³³ zɦɔ³¹
　　巫师　　剪刀　　巫师　　些　　这　　是　　些　　刀　　些　　枪　　或　　是
　　shaman shears shaman CL.PL this COP CL.PL knife CL.PL spear or COP

巫师铃、巫师剪，这些都是刀枪，
"shaman's bell" and "shaman's shears" are sword and spear,

(7) ʔua⁴⁴nen⁵⁵ 跳神

47 lu³³　　thai⁵⁵　　xai³³　tia³³　　ʔa²¹wu³⁵ .　tɕɔ³⁵　　nɔ³⁵　　zɦɔ³¹　tɕɔ³⁵　　zua³⁵　tɕɔ⁵²　　　　mu³³
　　来　　　泰国　　　说　　道　　　武器　　　些　　　这样　　是　　　些　　　要　　　带　　　　　去
　　come　thailand　say　COMP　weapon　CL.PL　this　COP　CL.PL　need　take.along　go
在泰语称作武器。这些武器要拿去
all called weapons in Thai language, which are used to

48 ɳtɕɦɔ³¹　ʔda⁵⁵　　ʂi⁵⁵　　ntau³³　ʂi⁵⁵　　tua⁴⁴ 　． mua⁵⁵　tsia⁵⁵　nen⁵⁵　　mu³³　tua⁴⁴ ,
　　和　　　　鬼　　(相互缀)　打　　(相互缀)　杀　　　　拿　　　剪刀　　巫师　　　去　　　杀
　　and　　ghost　RECP　　beat　RECP　　kill　　take　shears　shaman　go　　kill
和鬼厮杀。拿巫师剪去杀鬼，
fight with ghosts. If the ghost cannot be defeated and killed by shaman's shears,

49 tua⁴⁴　tʂi³³　zen⁵²,　zua³⁵tau⁴⁴　mua⁵⁵　nta⁵²　nen⁵⁵　　mu³³　tua⁴⁴ .
　　杀　　　不　　赢　　要得　　　　拿　　　剑　　　巫师　　　去　　杀
　　kill　NEG　win　　should　　take　sword　shaman　go　　kill
打不赢，就要拿神剑去杀鬼。
shaman would use the divine sword to kill them.

50 mua⁵⁵　nta⁵²　nen⁵⁵ ,　tsia⁵⁵　nen⁵⁵ ,　　tɯ⁵⁵　nen⁵⁵ ,　　mu³³　ɳtɕɦɔ³¹
　　拿　　　剑　　　巫师　　剪刀　　巫师　　　铃　　巫师　　　去　　　和
　　take　sword　shaman　shears　shaman　bell　shaman　go　　and
拿神剑、巫师剪、巫师铃，去和
Shamans would use divine sword, shaman's shears and shaman's bell

51 ʔda⁵⁵　　ʂi⁵⁵　　ntau³³　ʂi⁵⁵　　tua⁴⁴ ,　kua²¹　ʔda⁵⁵　ɳtʂhai⁴⁴　ʔda⁵⁵　khia³⁵ . tsua³³
　　鬼　　(相互缀)　打　　(相互缀)　杀　　　让　　　鬼　　怕　　　　鬼　　跑　　　　接
　　ghost　RECP　beat　RECP　　kill　　let　ghost　afraid　ghost　run　　next
鬼厮杀，让鬼害怕、让鬼逃跑。
to fight with ghosts and make them afraid and run away.

52 ntsi³⁵　　　mu³³,　zɦɔ³¹　thi³⁵xau³⁵　　,ʔdai²¹　thi³⁵ xau³⁵　　ʔua³³　tɕɔ⁵²　lɔ³³
　　补　　　　去　　是　　　遮　额头　　　　块　　　遮　额头　　　(定标)　带　　来
　　supplement　go　COP　cover forehead　CL　　cover forehead　REL　bring come

mpɦɔ³¹
遮
cover

下一种，是"巫师帕"，用于遮盖巫师的面部。
Next is "shaman's bandanna", which is used to cover shaman's face.

53 ntaɯ²¹ tu³³ tsi³⁵ nen⁵⁵ . ʔdai²¹ thi³⁵xau³⁵ nɔ⁴⁴ zɦɔ³¹ ʔi⁵⁵ tshia⁴⁴
　　那　　个　巫师　　块　　遮额头　　　这　是　一　部分
　　that　CL　sorcercer　CL　cover forehead　this　COP　one　part

这种头帕有一部分人
Some people call this bandanna

54 laɯ³⁵ xu⁴⁴ ʔua⁴⁴ phua²¹ nen⁵⁵ . phua²¹ nen⁵⁵ la³³ zɦɔ³¹ ntaɯ³⁵ nen⁵⁵
　　他们　叫　做　　帕　　巫师　　帕　　巫师　也　是　纸　　巫师
　　3S　call　make　bandanna　shaman　bandanna　shaman　CONJ　COP　paper　shaman

他们把它叫做"巫师帕"。"巫师帕"也有用纸做的。
"the shaman's bandanna". There are also bandannas made of paper.

55 thau²¹ lu⁵⁵ ʂi⁵²xaɯ²¹ nɯ³³ mu³³ ɳʈɦɔ³¹ ʔda⁵⁵ ʂi⁵⁵ ntau³³
　　时候　个　时候　　他　去　　和　　鬼　(相互缀)　打
　　time　CL　time　　3S　go　　and　ghost　RECP　beat

当巫师去打鬼的时候，
When shaman exorcises demons,

56 ʂi⁵⁵ tua⁴⁴ , nɯ³³ zua³⁵tau⁴⁴ mua⁵² phua²¹ . mua⁵² ntaɯ³⁵ ɳʈɦɔ³¹ nɯ³³
　(相互缀)　杀　他　　要得　　　有　　帕　　　有　　纸　　和　　他
　RECP　kill　3S　should　　have　bandanna　have　paper　and　3S

ʔua⁴⁴ ke⁴⁴,
一起
together

他要有巫师帕。戴上巫师帕，
he should have bandanna. Wearing the shaman's bandanna,

57 nɯ³³ tɕɔ⁵² lɔ³³ thai³⁵ ntaɯ²¹ lu⁵⁵ ɳʈʂe⁵² mɦua³¹ ,
　　它　　带　来　　遮　　那　　个　耳朵　眼睛
　　3S　bring　come　cover　that　CL　ear　eye

巫师帕遮住巫师的面部，
having the face covered by the bandanna,

58 nɯ³³ pɔ²¹ ʂa⁵⁵ za⁵² , pɔ²¹ ʂa⁵⁵ ʐen⁵⁵ . tsua³³ ntsi³⁵
 他 见 边 阳间 见 边 阴间 接 接
 3S see side the upper world see side the nether world next next

巫师就能看见阳间，看见阴间。
the shaman can see through the upper world and the nether world.

59 mu³³, ʐɦɔ³¹ tʉ²¹tɕia⁵⁵ . tʉ²¹tɕia⁵⁵ ʐɦɔ³¹ ʔi⁵⁵ tu³³ tʉ²¹tɕia⁵⁵ ʔua³³ tɛɔ⁵²
 去 是 烛蜡 烛蜡 是 一 个 烛蜡 (定标) 带
 go COP candle wax candle wax COP one CL candle wax REL take.along

下一种，是蜡烛。蜡烛用来
Next is candle. Candle is used

60 mu³³ tau³³ kua²¹ tɕɦi³¹ pɔ²¹ ke³⁵ , la³³ ʐɦɔ³¹ ŋɔ⁵⁵ tau⁴⁴ xau³⁵ lu³³
 去 点 让 燃 见 路 也 是 在 给 里 话
 go ignite let flaming see road CONJ COP be.located P inside word

点燃照明，在巫师用语里
for illumination. In shaman's language,

61 nen⁵⁵ xai³³ tia³³ ten⁵⁵luŋ⁵² ten⁵⁵tʂa³⁵ , la³³ ʐɦɔ³¹ ʔi⁵⁵ lɔ⁴⁴ lu³³ xai³³
 巫师 说 道 灯笼 灯盏 也 是 一 句 话 说
 shaman say COMP light cage light cup CONJ COP one CL word say

也叫作灯具，也叫作
it's also called lamps and

62 tia³³ ʐen⁵⁵ za⁵² tɔ²¹ , tɛɔ⁵² lɔ³³ tɔ²¹ kua²¹ pɔ²¹ tɕi⁴⁴ ,
 道 阴间 阳间 镜子 带 来 照 让 见 亮
 COMP the nether world the upper world mirror bring come reflect let see bright

kua²¹ pɔ²¹ mu³³
让 见 去
let see go

"阴阳镜"，让巫师看见
"Mirror of Yin and Yang" and can help the shaman find out

63 tsɦɔ³¹ tau⁴⁴ xɔ³⁵ ʔua³³ tu³³ mɔ⁵⁵ ntau²¹ ʂai⁵⁵ nɯ³³ ŋɔ⁵⁵ tau⁴⁴ xɔ³⁵ tɦɯ³¹ ,
 到 给 哪 (定标) 个 病 那 看 他 在 给 处 哪
 reach P where REL CL illness that look 3S be.located P place where

病人在哪里，
where the patient is,

64 kua²¹ pɔ²¹ ke³⁵ ṭau⁴⁴ thaɯ²¹ lu⁵⁵ ʂi⁵² xaɯ²¹ tu³³ tsi³⁵nen⁵⁵ ntaɯ²¹ mu³³
　　让　见　路　给　时候　个　时候　　个　(雄性缀)巫师　那　去
　　let　see　road　P　time　CL　time　　CL　　　shaman　that　go

让巫师看得见路去寻找病人的魂魄。
to make the road visible for shaman to find the spirit of the patient.

65 nʈhia³⁵ tu³³ nʈu⁵² plɦi³¹ . tsua³³ ntsi³⁵ mu³³ , zɦɔ³¹ tu³³ tɕhɔ⁵² nen⁵⁵ .
　　找　　个　魂　魂　　接　补　　去　　是　个　桥　巫师
　　find　CL　soul soul　next supplement go　COP CL bridge shaman

下一种，是巫师桥。
The next is shaman's bridge.

66 tu³³ tɕhɔ⁵² nen⁵⁵ zɦɔ³¹ ʔi⁵⁵ tsɔ⁵² ke³⁵ tɦau³¹ , ʔua³³ tɕɔ³⁵ ʔda⁵⁵nen⁵⁵
　　个　桥　　巫师　是　一　条　路　走　　(定标) 些　鬼　巫师
　　CL bridge shaman COP one CL road walk REL CL.PL ghost shaman

巫师桥是一条路，巫师的神兵神将
Shaman's bridge is a road for divine troops and soldiers

67 ntaɯ²¹ nɯ³³ zua³⁵ tɦau³¹ mu³³ tɦau³¹ lɔ³³ . tu³³ tɕhɔ⁵² nen⁵⁵ thia⁵⁵
　　那　　他　要　走　去　走　来　　个　桥　　巫师　和
　　that　3S need walk go walk come　CL bridge shaman and

要在上面走来走去。
to walk back and forth.

68 tsɔ⁵² ʂa⁵⁵ nen⁵⁵ nɯ³³ zuŋ⁴⁴ ʔi⁵⁵ za²¹ . nɯ³³ zɦɔ³¹ ʔi⁵⁵ tsɔ⁵² ke³⁵ ṭau⁴⁴
　　条　路　巫师　它　好　一　样　　它　是　一　条　路　给
　　CL road shaman 3S good one style　3S COP one CL road P

巫师桥和巫师路是一样的。这条路
The shaman's bridge is the same as the shaman's road. On this road,

69 tɕɔ³⁵ ʔda⁵⁵ tɦau³¹ mu³³ tɕau²¹ tu³³ nʈu⁵² plɦi³¹ tɔ³⁵qa⁵⁵ lɔ³³
　　些　　鬼　　走　去　追赶　个　魂　　魂　　回　　来
　　CL.PL ghost walk go chase CL soul soul back come

让神兵神将走下去把病人的魂魄带回
divine troops and soldiers will bring back the spirit of the patient

70 ʈau⁴⁴ ʂau⁴⁴ lu⁵⁵ tha⁵² .
　　给　　上　　个　　神坛
　　P　　up　　CL　　altar
神坛。
to the altar.

跳神

苗族跳神的人，或跳神时所用的物品，在泰国这边有什么？

第一个人，是巫师。这个巫师是跳神的人，也称师爷。

第二个人，是侍者。必须得有侍者，侍者是在一场跳神仪式里或巫师要去跳神时照看巫师跳神的人。

巫师有多种多样的跳神用品，有些人已经知道了，有些人还不完全知道。

第一，是神坛。神坛是巫师的神兵神将所在的地方，是招待巫师的神兵神将的地方。

下一种，是"神桌"。"神桌"是能呼风唤雨的马，跳神时也被巫师称作"神骡神马"。

下一种，是"神鼓"。"神鼓"是使唤神兵神将的鼓，是使唤巫师的士兵的鼓。当这些士兵要去打仗时，要得打鼓。打鼓使唤士兵，才能让那些士兵有信心去打仗。

下一种，是香。香用来烧，让巫师的神兵神将闻到香的烟味，让神兵神将有心思去做事情。

下一种，是鸡蛋。鸡蛋是用来叫魂的东西，也是一点心意。老人说："老人想要被尊重，小孩想要鸡蛋。"鸡蛋是一种礼品，拿给巫师的神兵神将，让神兵神将奋力追赶魂魄。

下一种，是马料。马料就是米花。这些米花也是一种礼品，祭献给神兵神将。

下一种，是药水。药水也是救命水，也是我们在民间故事里所说的"瓜马爪"。"瓜马爪"也是药水。当有人病死的时候，拿去给他喷，使他复活。

下一种，是神水。神水是武功水，用来洗去人身上的病，是一种有功力能洗去疾病的水。它也有点像"瓜马爪"那种药水。

下一种，是"神剑"。"神剑"有部分人也把它叫作"神刀"。"神刀"和"神剑"作用是一样的。有一部分巫师用刀，有一部分巫师用剑。"神剑"或"神刀"，巫师铃、巫师剪，这些都是刀枪，在泰语称作武器。这些武器要拿去和鬼厮杀。拿巫师剪去杀鬼，打不赢，就要拿神剑去杀鬼。拿神剑、巫师剪、巫师铃，去和鬼厮杀，让鬼害怕、让鬼逃跑。

下一种，是"巫师帕"，用于遮盖巫师的面部。这种头帕有一部分人他们把它叫作"巫师帕"。"巫师帕"也有用纸做的。当巫师去打鬼的时候，他要有巫师帕。戴上巫师帕，巫师帕遮住巫师的面部，巫师就能看见阳间，看见阴间。

下一种，是蜡烛。蜡烛用来点燃照明，在巫师用语里也叫作灯具，也叫作"阴阳镜"，让巫师看见病人在哪里，让巫师看得见路去寻找病人的魂魄。

下一种，是巫师桥。巫师桥是一条路，巫师的神兵神将要在上面走来走去。巫师桥和巫师路是一样的。这条路让神兵神将走下去把病人的魂魄带回神坛。

The Shaman's Dance

What people carry out the shaman's dance, and what things do they need to do so in Thailand?

The first person is the shaman, who performs the shaman's dance; he is also the advisor.

The second person is the servant, who is indispensable. Servants are responsible for taking care of the shaman when he performs the ritual.

In a shaman's dance ritual or when shaman is about to dance, there is a variety of articles for the shaman's dance, some of which are already known but some are yet unknown.

Firstly, there's an altar, a place where the divine troops of shaman stay and a place for serving them.

Next is the "gods' table", which is a horse that can control the forces of nature. It's also called "holy mule and holy horse".

Next is the "gods' drum", which can summon and order divine troops and soldiers of shaman. When these soldiers are going to enter the battlefield, drums should be played. It's necessary to play the drum to summon and order soldiers so that can they be encouraged and keep high morale to fight.

Next is the incense, which is used to burning for divine troops and soldiers to smell, so that they can concentrate on their work.

Next is the chicken egg, which is also an article for the shaman's dance and a small way of saying thanks. Elders always say, "Old people want to be respected and children want eggs." Eggs are a kind of gift for divine troops and soldiers of shaman to drive them to spare no effort to chase after spirits and souls.

Next, there's horse feed, which are rice flowers, another kind of sacrificial gift for divine troops.

Next is liquid medicine, which is also the water of life and what we call "Guamazhua" in folk stories, which is also a kind of liquid medicine. When someone dies of illness, the liquid medicine can bring him come back to life.

Next is the holy water. It's kongfu water that is used to get rid of illnesses for people. It's a kind of powerful water that can wash illness away and is also similar to the "Guamazhua".

Next is the divine sword. There are also some people calling it "divine blade". "Divine blade" has the same function as "divine sword". Some shamans use a blade and some shamans use a sword. "Divine sword", "divine blade", "shaman's bell" and "shaman's shears" are all swords and spears, which are called weapons in Thai language. These weapons are used to fight with ghosts. If the ghost cannot be defeated and killed by shaman's shears, shaman would use the divine sword to kill them. They would use divine sword, shaman's shears and shaman's bell to fight with ghosts and make them afraid and run away.

Next is "shaman's bandanna", which is used to cover shaman's face. Some people call this bandanna "the shaman's bandanna". There are also bandannas made of paper. It's necessary for the shaman to have a bandanna when he exorcises demons. Having the face covered by the bandanna, the shaman can see through the upper world and the nether world.

 Next is the candle, which is used for illumination. In shaman's language, it's also called lamp and "Mirror of Yin and Yang". It can help shaman find out where the patient is, to make the road visible for shaman to find the spirit of patient.

 Next is the shaman's bridge, a road for divine troops and soldiers to walk back and forth. The shaman's bridge is the same as shaman's road. On this road, divine troops and soldiers will bring back the spirit of patient to the altar.

（8）ke³⁵ pa²¹ tɕhua³¹ 丧俗

路　办　死
road　handle　death

1 m̥uŋ⁵⁵　tɕɔ³⁵　tu⁵⁵　ʔde⁵²nu²¹　ŋɔ⁵⁵　　tau⁴⁴ ke³⁵pa²¹tɕhua³¹ ， ŋɔ⁵⁵　　tau⁴⁴
　苗族　　些　　人　　事情　　　在　　　给　路办死　　　在　　　给
　Hmong CL.PL person matter　be.located P　road handle die　be.located P

苗族办丧事中的人，
In Thailand, the people conducting funerals of the Hmong

2 ʂa⁵⁵　thai⁵⁵　　te⁵⁵　mua⁵²　tau³³　li⁴⁴　　ntau²¹nɔ⁴⁴ . tu³³　ʔi⁵⁵, zɦɔ³¹
　边　　泰国　　地　　有　　跟　　像　　　处　　这　　个　一　是
　side Thailand land have follow be.like place this　CL one COP

在泰国是这样的。第一个人，
are as follows. The first person

3 ka³⁵　ʂɯ²¹ . tu³³　ka³⁵　ʂɯ²¹　zɦɔ³¹　tu³³　lɔ³³　mu³³　tua³⁵　ʔde⁵²nu²¹
　管事　　个　管事　　是　　个　来　　去　　抓　　事情
　steward　CL steward　COP CL come go catch matter

是管事。管事就是负责
is the steward, who is responsible for

4 tɕha³¹　ntho⁴⁴　　ntau²¹　ʔi⁵⁵　nten³³　tɕhua³¹ . tu³³　ʔɔ⁵⁵, tu³³　thau⁵²　ɕɔ²¹
　完　　（彻底状） 处　　一　　场　　　死　　个　两　　个　头　　孝
　finish completely place one CL　die　　CL two　CL head filiality

整个丧事全部事宜的人。第二个人，
all the matters of the whole funeral. The second person

5 tɕua⁵⁵ . pe⁵⁵　zua³⁵tau⁴⁴　mua⁵²　ʔi⁵⁵　tu³³　thau⁵²　ɕɔ²¹　tɕua⁵⁵
　家　　我们　　要得　　　　有　　一　　个　　头　　孝　家
　home 1PL　should　　　have one　CL head filiality home

是孝家的头儿。我们得有一个孝家的头儿,
is the leader of the family of deceased. It is necessary for us to select a leader

6 tua⁵² ŋɔ⁵⁵ ţau⁴⁴ xau³⁵ lu⁵⁵ tʂe³⁵ tua⁵² qhia⁴⁴ ʔua⁴⁴ʔdeֽ⁵²ʔua⁴⁴nu²¹ .
  来 在   给 里 个 家 来 教 做 水 做 事情
  come be.located P inside CL home come teach make water do matter

来死者家里教大家做事情。
to come to the family of the deceased and teach them how to deal with the funeral affairs.

7 thau²¹ lu⁵⁵ ʂi⁵² xauŋ²¹ ka³⁵ ʂɯ²¹ lɔ³³ zɦɔ³¹ tɕɔ³⁵ tu⁵⁵ qa⁵⁵ tu⁵⁵ nu²¹
  时候 个 时候   管事 或 是 些   儿子 后面 儿子 事情
  time CL time   steward or COP CL.PL son behind son matter

当管事或办丧事的人
When the steward or people who conduct the funeral

8 ntaɯ²¹ zua³⁵ zua³⁵ ʔda⁵⁵tʂi⁴⁴, tu³³ thau⁵² ɕɔ²¹ tɕua⁵⁵ nɔ⁴⁴
  那 要 需要 什么   个 头 孝   家 这
  that need need what   CL head filiality home this

有什么需要的时候,这个孝家的头儿
need, something the leader

9 zɦɔ³¹ tu³³ zua³⁵ mu³³ mpa⁵²ʔdeֽ⁵²mpa⁵²tɕaɯ³⁵ , mpa⁵²qai⁵⁵mpa⁵²mpua⁴⁴,
  是 个 要 去 准备水准备酒   准备鸡 准备猪
  COP CL need go prepare water prepare wine prepare chicken prepare pork

要去准备酒水,准备食材,
is supposed to prepare alcohol and food,

10 mpa⁵²ŋu⁵²mpa⁵²tɯ²¹, tɕɔ⁵² lɔ³³ ţau⁴⁴ tɕɔ³⁵ tu⁵⁵qa⁵⁵tu⁵⁵nu²¹
  准备牛 准备 水牛   带 来 给 些   劳务人员
  prepare ox prepare buffalo bring come P CL.PL working personnel

猪肉,准备祭品,拿来给那些办丧事的人用。
pork and sacrificial offerings for them.

11 ntaɯ²¹ ʂi³⁵ . ʔthau⁴⁴ ntaɯ²¹ , tu³³ tɕua⁵⁵tʂa³⁵ .
  那 用 过   那   个 家长
  that use pass that CL patriarch

下一个人,是家长。
Next is the patriarch,

12 tu³³ tɕua⁵⁵tʂa³⁵ zɦo³¹ tu³³ ʔua³³ zua³⁵tau⁴⁴ lo³³ lɦai³¹ ʔda⁵⁵ lo³³ zɦo³¹
   个   家长   是   个 (定标) 要得   来   祭献   鬼   或 是
   CL patriarch   COP CL REL   should   come sacrifice ghost or COP

家长是祭鬼或者说

who is responsible for conducting sacrifice to the ghost or

13 pu⁵⁵ ʐau⁵⁵ pu⁵⁵ mo³⁵ tau⁴⁴ tu³³ tɕʰua³¹ ntaɯ²¹ tau⁴⁴ no⁵² .
   喂   菜   喂   饭   给   个   死   那   得   吃
   feed dish feed rice give CL dead that can eat

是给死者祭献饭菜的人。

rather sacrifice food to the deceased.

14 tu³³ tsua³³ ntsi³⁵ mu³³, zɦo³¹ tu³³ taɯ⁴⁴ ke³⁵ . tu³³ taɯ⁴⁴ ke³⁵ zɦo³¹
   个   接   补   去   是   个   指   路   个   指   路   是
   CL next supplement go   COP CL point road   CL point road COP

下一个人，是指路人。指路人是

The next person is the guide, who is in charge of

15 tu³³ zua³⁵ qhia⁴⁴ ke³⁵ tau⁴⁴ tu³³ tɕʰua³¹ mu³³ tɕɦua³¹pɦo³¹ tɕɦua³¹zɦaɯ³¹.
   个   要   告诉   路   给   个   死   去   见   奶奶   见   爷爷
   CL need tell   road give CL die   go   see grandma see grandpa

给死者指路让他去见祖宗的那个人。

showing the way for the deceased to go to his ancestors.

16 ʔtʰau⁴⁴ ntaɯ²¹ , tu³³ xia⁵⁵ khau⁴⁴ŋtʂɯ³¹nen³³ . tu³³ xia⁵⁵
   过   那   个   编   鞋子   木马   个   编
   pass that   CL weave shoe wooden horse   CL weave

下一个人，是编木马鞋的人。

The next one is the person who makes wooden horse shoes.

17 khau⁴⁴ ŋtʂɯ³¹ nen³³ zɦo³¹ tu³³ ʔua³³ mu³³ tsia³⁵ ʔo⁵⁵ tu³³ ntuŋ⁴⁴
   鞋子   木马   是   个   (定标) 去   砍   两   根   树
   shoe wooden horse COP CL REL   go   chop   two CL tree

编木马鞋的人是去砍两根树

He would cut down some trees

18 tɕɔ⁵² lɔ³³ xia⁵⁵ tu³³ nen³³ thia⁵⁵ lɔ³³ xia⁵⁵ ŋkaɯ²¹
   带   来   编   匹   马   和   来   编   对
   bring come weave CL horse and come weave pair

拿来做木马和编一双

to make a wooden horse and a pair of

19 khau⁴⁴ma⁵²khau⁴⁴ntɦua³¹ ʈau⁴⁴ tu³³ tɦua³¹ ntaɯ²¹ . tu³³ tsua³³ ntsi³⁵ mu³³ ,
   鞋子 麻 鞋子 麻   给   个   死   那   个   接   补   去
   show hemp shoe hemp P CL die that CL next supplement go

麻鞋给死者的那个人。下一个人，

hemp shoes for the deceased. The next person

20 zɦɔ³¹ tsi³⁵qen⁵² . ŋɔ⁵⁵ ʈau⁴⁴ te⁵² nten³³ lɔ⁵² , zua³⁵tau⁴⁴ thɔ³⁵
   是   父亲芦笙   在   给   些   场   大   要得   讨
   COP father lusheng be.located P CL.PL CL big should ask

是芦笙师。丧事办得隆重，要得请

is the *lusheng* (a kind of reed-pipe instrument) performer. If people want a solemn funeral,

21 le⁴⁴ pe⁵⁵ lɦien³¹ tsi³⁵qen⁵² . tɕɔ³⁵ nten³³ me⁴⁴ , zua³⁵ tau⁴⁴ thɔ³⁵
   像   三   位   父亲芦笙   些   场   小   要   得   讨
   be.like three CL father *lusheng* CL.PL field small should get ask

三个芦笙师。丧事办得简单，要请

they should invite three *lusheng* performers. If people want a simple funeral,

22 li⁴⁴ ʔɔ⁵⁵ tu³³ tsi³⁵qen⁵² . tu³³ tsua³³ ntsi³⁵ mu³³, zɦɔ³¹ tsi³⁵nʈua³³ .
   像   两   个   父亲芦笙   个   接   补   去   是   父亲鼓
   be.like two CL father *lusheng* CL connect supplement go COP father drum

两个芦笙师。下一个人，是鼓师。

they should invite two *lusheng* performers. The next one is the drummer.

23 fen²¹ ntau⁴⁴ pe⁵⁵ thɔ³⁵ ʔɔ⁵⁵ lɦien³¹ tsi³⁵qen⁵² . ʔi⁵⁵ lɦien³¹ lɔ³³ tʂhua⁵⁵
   份   多   我们   讨   两   位   父亲芦笙   一   位   来   吹
   part much 1PL ask two CL father *lusheng* one CL come blow

多数情况下，我们请两位芦笙师。

In most cases, we would invite two *lusheng* performers,

(8) ke³⁵ pa²¹ tɕʰua³¹ 丧俗

24 qen⁵² , ʔi⁵⁵ lɦien³¹ ʐua³⁵tau⁴⁴ lɔ³³ ntau³³ ɳʈua³³ . tu³³ ntsi³⁵ mu³³ ,
芦笙　　一　　位　　　要得　　来　　打　　鼓　　　个　　补　　　　去
lusheng　one　CL　　should　　come　beat　drum　CL　supplement　go

一位来吹芦笙，一位来打鼓。下一个人，

one of whom plays the *lusheng* and the other plays the drum. The next one

25 zɦɔ³¹ tsʰɯ⁵²ka⁵⁵ . tsʰɯ⁵² ka⁵⁵ zɦɔ³¹ tu³³ lɔ³³ mu³³ ʔua⁴⁴ ʐau⁵⁵ .
　　是　　厨官　　　　厨官　　　　是　　个　来　去　　做　　菜
　　COP　kitchen official　kitchen official　COP　CL　come　go　make　dish

是厨官。厨官是来做菜的人。

is the kitchen official, the one who cooks.

26 tu³³ tsua³³ ntsi³⁵ mu³³ , zɦɔ³¹ tu³³ tʂa³⁵ pʰɔ²¹ . tu³³ tʂa³⁵ pʰɔ²¹ ntaɯ²¹ ,
　个　　接　　补　　　去　　　是　　个　　掌　　枪　　　个　　掌　　枪　　那
　CL　next　supplement　go　COP　CL　hold　gun　CL　hold　gun　that

下一个人，是掌枪的人。那个掌枪的人，

The next one is the gun owner.

27 nɯ³³ zɦɔ³¹ tu³³ ʔua³³ tʰau²¹ tu³³ tʰɯ³¹ tau⁴⁴ ta³³ tsɔ⁵² ɕia⁴⁴ laɯ²¹ ,
　他　　是　　个　(定标)　时候　　个　　哪　　得　　完　　条　　命　　了
　3S　COP　CL　REL　time　CL　who　can　finish　CL　life　PRF

当有人去世的时候，

When someone is dead,

28 tu³³ tʂa³⁵ pʰɔ²¹ ntaɯ²¹ ʐua³⁵ zɦɔ³¹ tu³³ tua⁵² tua⁴⁴ pe⁵⁵ pʰɔ²¹ ʔua⁴⁴ nte⁵² .
　个　　掌　　枪　　那　　要　　是　　个　　来　　杀　　三　　枪　　做　　前面
　CL　hold　gun　that　need　COP　CL　come　kill　three　gun　make　front

那个掌枪的人要先来打三枪。

the gun owner would shoot three times first.

29 lɔ³³ zɦɔ³¹ nɯ³³ tsaɯ²¹ tʂi³³ zɦɔ³¹ tu³³ tua⁵² tua⁴⁴ pe⁵⁵ pʰɔ²¹
　或　　是　　他　　就　　不　　是　　个　　来　　杀　　三　　枪
　or　COP　3S　just　NEG　COP　CL　come　kill　three　gun

或者即使他不是打前面三枪的人，

Or even if he isn't the man who does the three shots,

30 ʔua⁴⁴ nte⁵², lɔ³³   nɯ³³ zɦɔ³¹ tu³³ tua⁵² tua⁴⁴ phɔ²¹ ʂaɯ³⁵ntsɔ³⁵, ta³⁵ʂu⁴⁴ ,
   做   前面 也   他   是   个   来   杀   枪   起早   中午
   make front CONJ 3S COP CL come kill gun get up early noon

他也是早上、中午、

he should be the one who comes to fire a gun in the morning, noon,

31 tʂau³³ntu⁵², ʔi⁵⁵ tɕɦa³¹ m̥ɔ⁴⁴ thau²¹ zua³⁵ ka⁵² ntɕɦu³¹ . lu⁵⁵ ʂi⁵² xaɯ²¹
   天黑   一   半   晚上 时候 要   亮   天   个   时候
   dark   one half night time need light day   CL time

晚上、黎明来打枪的人。

evening and at dawn.

32 thau²¹ laɯ³⁵ ntau³³tɕɦɔ³¹ , nɯ³³ zɦɔ³¹ tu³³ ʔua³³ zua³⁵ tua⁵²
   时候 他们   打   士兵   他   是   个 (定标) 要   来
   time 3PL beat soldier 3S   COP CL REL need come

当他们要打鬼的时候，他要来

When people come to exorcise, he would come to

33 tua⁴⁴ phɔ²¹ thia⁵⁵ thau²¹ ʔua³³ n̥u⁵⁵ qhua⁴⁴tsɯ³³   , mua⁵² xau³⁵
   杀   枪   和   时候 (定标) 天   大葬夜   有   户
   kill gun and   time   REL   day burial day evening have family

打枪，大葬夜那天有丧客来时，

fire the gun. If there are guests coming in the evening of the burial day,

34 qhua⁴⁴ tua⁵² , nɯ³³ zɦɔ³¹ tu³³ ʔua³³ zua³⁵ lɔ³³ tua⁴⁴ phɔ²¹ tɔ³³ tsai³³
   客人   来   他   是   个   (定标) 要   来   杀   枪   等   接
   guest come 3S COP CL   REL need come kill gun wait next

他是要打枪迎接

the gun owner should fire a gun to

35 tɕɛ³⁵ ʔua³³ ʔua⁴⁴ qhua⁴⁴ tua⁵² . ˀthau⁴⁴ ntaɯ²¹ zɦɔ³¹ tu³³ tsi³⁵ tsɦia³¹ .
   些   (定标) 做   客人   来   那   是   个   父亲 棺材
   CL.PL REL do guest   come pass that   COP   CL father coffin

丧客的那个人。下一个人，是做棺材的人。

welcome guests. The next one is the person who makes the coffin.

（8）ke³⁵ pa²¹ tɕʰua³¹ 丧俗

36 tu³³ tsi³⁵ tsʰia³¹ ʐɦɔ³¹ tu³³ ʐua³⁵ mu³³ kaɯ⁴⁴ ntuŋ⁴⁴ lɔ³³ ʐɦɔ³¹ ʐua³⁵
   个 父亲 棺材 是 个 要 去 锯 树 或 是 要
   CL father coffin COP CL need go saw tree or COP should

做棺材的人是要去锯树或是

He would saw trees or

37 mu³³ pʰua⁴⁴ ntuŋ⁴⁴ ʔua⁴⁴ xɯ²¹ l̪e⁵⁵ tɕɔ⁵² lɔ³³ ȶau⁴⁴ tu³³ tɕʰua³¹ .
   去 劈 树 做 棺材 带 来 给 个 死
   go chop tree make coffin bring come P CL die

要去劈树拿来给死者做棺材的人。

cut down trees to make coffin for the deceased.

38 ʔtʰau⁴⁴ ntaɯ²¹ ʐɦɔ³¹ tu³³ xau⁴⁴tɦɔ³¹ . mua⁵² te⁵² qhɔ³⁵tɕhaɯ⁴⁴,
   过 那 是 个 头 士兵 有 些 地方
   pass that COP CL head soldier have CL.PL place

下一个人，是打鬼的领头人。有些地方，

The next one is the leader of the exorcism ritual. At some places

39 nɯ³³ mua⁵² tu³³ xau⁴⁴tɦɔ³¹ . mua⁵² te⁵² qhɔ³⁵tɕhaɯ⁴⁴,
   它 有 个 头 士兵 有 些 地方
   3S have CL head soldier have CL.PL place

它有打鬼的领头人。有些地方，

there are leaders of exorcism and some places

40 nɯ³³ tʂi³³ mua⁵² . lu⁵⁵ ʂi⁵² xaɯ²¹ ʐua³⁵ taɯ²¹tɦɔ³¹ ,
   它 不 有 个 时候 要 出 兵
   3S NEG have CL time need out soldier

它没有。打鬼的时候，

there are not. When the exorcism is conducted,

41 ʔi⁵⁵ tu³³ ŋɔ⁵⁵ xau³⁵ tʂe³⁵ , ʔi⁵⁵ mpɔ⁵² ŋɔ⁵⁵ n̪tau²¹ ʐuŋ³⁵. tu³³ xau⁴⁴
   一 个 在 里 家 一 群 在 外面 个 头
   one CL be.located inside home CL CL.PL be.located outside CL dead

一个人在家里，一群人在外面。

one stays at home and a group of people stay outside.

42 tɕɦɔ³¹ ntaɯ²¹ zɦɔ³¹ tu³³ ʔua³³ nɯ³³ zua³⁵tau⁴⁴ ɳtɕɦi³¹   lu⁵⁵ tʂe³⁵ ,
    兵   那   是   个   (定标)   他   要得   转   个   家
    soldier that   COP   CL   REL   3S   should   turn around CL   home

打鬼的领头人是带着大家围着房子转的人。

The leader of exorcism is the one who leads people to walk around the house.

43 pɔ⁵² nia²¹ ɳtɕɦi³¹   ɕa⁴⁴ lɯ²¹ , tsi³⁵ nen⁵² ɳtɕɦi³¹   tɕua⁵² lɯ²¹ .
   女人   转   七   次   男人   转   九   次
   woman   turn around seven time   man   turn around nine   time

妇女要转七圈，男子转九圈。

A woman should walk around seven times and a man nine times.

44 zɦɔ³¹ pɔ⁵² nia²¹ ɳtɕɦi³¹   ɕa⁴⁴ lɯ²¹ , ɳtɕɦi³¹   plau⁵⁵ lɯ²¹ mu³³ ɳtɕɦi³¹
   是   女人   转   七   次   转   四   次   去   转
   COP   woman   turn around seven time   turn around four time go turn around

妇女七圈，顺转四圈，逆转三圈。

A woman should go seven rounds of which four rounds are clockwise and three rounds are counterclockwise.

45 pe⁵⁵ lɯ²¹ lɔ³³ . zɦɔ³¹ tsi³⁵ nen⁵² ɳtɕɦi³¹   tʂi⁵⁵ lɯ²¹ mu³³ ɳtɕɦi³¹   plau⁵⁵
   三   次   来   是   男人   转   五   次   去   转   四
   three time come COP man   turn around five time go turn around four

男子顺转五圈，逆转四圈。

A man should go five rounds clockwise and four rounds counterclockwise.

46 lɯ²¹ tɔ³⁵qa⁵⁵ lɔ³³ . ta⁵⁵ ɕi³³ mua⁵² qen⁴⁴ pua³⁵ nɦien³¹ tʂi³³ mua⁵² tu³³
   次   回   来   但是 有   份   个把   人   不   有   个
   time back   come   but   have part   CL   person NEG   have CL

但是，有部分人没有领头打鬼的人,

However, some people don't have the leader to lead them,

47 xau⁴⁴ tɕɦɔ³¹ , mua⁵² qen⁴⁴ pɦaɯ³¹ mua⁵². ʔɦaɯ⁴⁴ ntaɯ²¹, tɛɔ³⁵
   头   兵   有   份   堆   有   过   那   些
   head soldier have part   pile   have   pass   that   CL.PL

有部分人有。下一个,

but some have. The next is

(8) ke³⁵ pa²¹ tɕʰua³¹ 丧俗

48 tʂu³⁵tʂe³⁵ . tɕɔ³⁵ ntaɯ²¹ pe⁵⁵ xu⁴⁴ ʔua⁴⁴ ɕɔ²¹ tɕua⁵⁵ . tɕɔ³⁵ ɕɔ²¹ tɕua⁵⁵
　主　家　　些　　那　　我们　叫　做　　孝　　家　　些　孝　家
　host family　CL.PL　that　1PL　call　make filiality home　CL.PL　filiality home
是主人家。主人家我们叫作孝家。
the host family, which we call them "filial family" (the family of the deceased).

49 nɔ⁴⁴ tʂua³⁵ zɦɔ³¹ nɯ³³ lu⁵⁵ sen²¹　lɔ³³ zɦɔ³¹ mpɔ⁵² kɯ³⁵ ti⁵² ntaɯ²¹
　这　只　是　他　个　姓　　或　是　群　兄弟　那
　this CL COP 3S CL last name　or COP CL.PL brother　that
这些孝家包括跟死者同姓或者跟死者
This family includes all the people who have the same last name with the deceased

50 tɕai³³ zɦɔ³¹ ɕɔ²¹ tɕua⁵⁵ ta³³ ɳtʰɔ⁴⁴. tu³³ tsua³³ ntsi³⁵ mu³³ , zɦɔ³¹
　那么　是　孝　家　完　(完全状)　个　接　补　去　是
　so that COP filiality home finish completely CL connect supplement go COP
是兄弟的所有人。下一个，是柴头。
or are brothers of the deceased. The next one is the firewood chief,

51 tu³³ tsʰai⁵²tʰaɯ⁵² . tu³³ tsʰai⁵² tʰaɯ⁵² zɦɔ³¹ tu³³ tsia³⁵ taɯ³³.
　个　柴　头　个　柴　头　是　个　砍　柴
　CL firewood head CL firewood head COP CL chop firewood
柴头是砍柴的人。
who cuts the firewood.

52 zua³⁵tʂu²¹ mua⁵² tu³³ tsia³⁵ taɯ³³, pe⁵⁵ tʰia⁵² mua⁵² taɯ³³ lɔ³³ ʔua⁴⁴ zau⁵⁵
　要得　有　个　砍　柴　我们　才　有　柴　来　做　菜
　should have CL chop firewood 1PL just have firewood come make dish
要有砍柴的人，我们才有柴来做菜
There are people who cut firewood so that we can use the wood

53 ʔua⁴⁴ mo³⁵ nɔ⁵² . tu³³ tsua³³ ntsi³⁵　mu³³, zɦɔ³¹ tu³³ ʂi³⁵tʰaɯ⁵² . tu³³
　做　饭　吃　个　接　补　去　是　个　汤头　个
　make rice eat CL connect supplement go COP CL soup head CL
做饭吃。下一个，是汤头。
to cook. The next one is the water chief,

54 ʂi³⁵tʰaɯ⁵² zɦɔ³¹ tu³³ kɯ³⁵ ʔḍe⁵² . ʐua³⁵tʂu²¹ mua⁵² tu³³ ʂi³⁵tʰaɯ⁵²
   汤头   是   个   挑   水   要得   有   个   汤头
   soup head COP CL carry water should   have CL soup head

汤头是挑水的人。要有汤头

who takes charge of carrying water. With them

55 lɔ³³ ʂi³³ tu³³ kɯ³⁵ ʔḍe⁵² mu³³ kɯ³⁵ ʔḍe⁵² lɔ³³ , tɕʰia⁵² le⁴⁴ tau⁴⁴ ʔḍe⁵²
   或是   个   挑   水   去   挑   水   来   才   才   得   水
   or   CL carry water go carry water come just just get water

或是挑水的人去挑水，才有水

carrying water for us, we are be able to use water

56 tɕɔ⁵² lɔ³³ ʔua⁴⁴ ʐau⁵⁵ ʔua⁴⁴ mɔ³⁵ nɔ⁵² . tsua³³ ntsi³⁵   mu³³, zɦɔ³¹ xau³⁵
   带   来   做   菜   做   饭   吃   接   补   去   是   户
   bring come make dish make rice eat connect supplement go   COP family

拿来做菜做饭吃。下一个，是丧客。

to cook. The next one is the guest.

57 qhua⁴⁴ . tʰau²¹ mua⁵² ʔi⁵⁵ tu³³ tɕʰiɯ³¹ ta³³ ʂi²¹ nen⁵², pe⁵⁵ ʐua³⁵tau⁴⁴
   客人   时候   有   一   个   哪   完   世   生活   我们 要得
   guest   time have one CL who finish world life 1PL should

当有人去世时，

When someone passes away,

58 mu³³ xu⁴⁴ ʔi⁵⁵ tɕɔ³⁵ tʂʰen⁵⁵ʐe⁴⁴ , mua²¹pʰau⁵² tsi³⁵ʔḍa⁵⁵lɦiau³¹
   去   叫   一   些   亲戚   姑姑   舅舅
   go call one CL.PL relative   aunt   uncle

我们得去告诉亲戚，姑姑舅舅

we have to inform our relatives such as aunts and uncles

59 lɔ³³ zɦɔ³¹ ntʂʰai³³ vau³⁵ , tɕɔ³⁵ ʔua³³ tʂʰen⁵⁵ʐe⁴⁴ tu³³ tɕʰua³¹ ntaɯ²¹ ,
   或   是   女儿   女婿   些   (定标) 亲   近   个   死   那
   or   COP daughter son-in-law CL.PL REL close near CL die that

或者女儿女婿，以及跟死者亲近的那些人，

or daughters and sons-in-law, and those who were close to the deceased

(8) ke³⁵ pa²¹ tɕʰua³¹ 丧俗

60 xu⁴⁴ ʂaɯ³⁵ʔɖaɯ³³ tua⁵² ʔua⁴⁴ qhua⁴⁴ . tɕɔ³⁵ ntaɯ²¹ pe⁵⁵ xu⁴⁴ xau³⁵ qhua⁴⁴ .
叫　大家　　　来　做　客人　些　那　我们　叫　户　客人
call people come do guest CL.PL that 1PL call family guest

叫大家来奔丧。这些人我们叫作丧客。

to hasten home for the funeral. Those are the ones we call guests.

61 tʰau²¹ lu⁵⁵ ʂi⁵²xaɯ²¹ , tɕɔ³⁵ xau³⁵ qhua⁴⁴ tua⁵² mua⁵² ʔi⁵⁵ tu³³ tʂen²¹ tɕen⁵⁵
时候　个　时候　　　些　户　客人　来　有　一　个　正经
time CL time CL.PL family guest come have one CL decent

当丧客来奔丧时，那些丧客中有一个

When they come to our home, one of these guests

62 ntaɯ²¹ tɕɔ³⁵ xau³⁵ qhua⁴⁴ ntaɯ²¹, ʑɦɔ³¹ ki³³ . tu³³ ki³³ ntaɯ²¹
处　些　户　客人　那　是　交礼人　个　交礼人　那
place CL.PL family guest that COP etiquette person CL etiquette person that

正式的代表，是交礼人。那个交礼人

would be the formal representative, who is the so-called etiquette person.

63 ʑɦɔ³¹ ʔi⁵⁵ tu³³ tʂen²¹ tɕen⁵⁵ ʔua³³ mua⁵⁵ ʐau⁵⁵ mua⁵⁵ mɔ³⁵ tɕɔ⁵² lɔ³³
是　一　个　正式　(定标)　拿　菜　拿　饭　带　来
COP one CL formal REL take dish take rice bring come

代表丧客拿出丧客带来的菜和饭

He would sacrifice the food that guests bring

64 ʈau⁴⁴ tu³³ tɕʰua³¹ nɔ⁵², ʐua³⁵ mua⁵⁵ ȵia⁵²tʂʰa³⁵ntu⁵² tɕɔ⁵² lɔ³³ tɕɔ⁵⁵
给　个　死　吃　要　拿　钱　阳光　带　来　交
P CL die eat want take money sunlight bring come hand over

祭献给死者吃，要把丧客带来的礼金

to the deceased, and hand over the cash gift that guests bring

65 ʈau⁴⁴ ɕɔ²¹ tɕua⁵⁵, tɕɔ⁵² lɔ³³ tɕɔ⁵⁵ ʈau⁴⁴ ka³⁵ ʂi²¹. ʔtʰau⁴⁴ ntaɯ²¹, mua⁵²
给　孝　家　带　来　交　给　管事　过　那　有
P filiality home bring come hand over P steward pass that have

交给孝家，交给管事。下一个人，

to the filial family or the steward. The next one,

66 ʔi⁵⁵ tɕɔ³⁵ ŋɔ⁵⁵ ŋɔ⁵⁵ pe⁵⁵ tʂi³³ pau⁵⁵ xai³³ tia³³ nɯ³³ ʑɦɔ³¹ len⁵²
一 些 在 在 我们 不 知道 说 道 他 是 位
one CL.PL RDUP~be.located 1PL NEG know say COMP 3S COP CL

tɕɦɯ³¹ .
哪
who

我们不知道他是谁。
we don't know who he is.

67 nɯ³³ sa³⁵ tua⁵² tʂhua⁵⁵ qen⁵² ʔua⁴⁴ ke³⁵ ɳtɕɔ⁴⁴ tsɦɔ³¹ tu³³ tɕɦua³¹ ntaɯ²¹ .
他 想 来 吹 芦笙 做 路 思念 到 个 死 那
3S want come blow lusheng make road miss about CL die that

他想来吹芦笙表达对死者的思念。
He would like to express that he misses the deceased by playing the *lusheng*.

68 tɕɔ³⁵ nɔ⁴⁴ pe⁵⁵ xu⁴⁴ ʔua⁴⁴ ʂau⁴⁴ . ʂau⁴⁴ ʑɦɔ³¹ ʔi⁵⁵ tɕɔ³⁵ ʔua³³ nɯ³³
些 这 我们 叫 做 朋友 朋友 是 一 些 (定标) 他
CL.PL this 1PL call make friend friend COP one CL.PL REL 3S

ŋɔ⁵⁵ ŋɔ⁵⁵
在 在
RDUP~be.located

这种人我们叫作"朋友"。这种朋友他们自己带芦笙来，
We call these people "friends". They would bring *lusheng* here on their own,

69 nɯ³³ tɕia⁴⁴ni⁴⁴ tɦɔ⁴⁴ qen⁵² tua⁵² , tua⁵² ʔthia⁴⁴ qen⁵² , tua⁵² ʔua⁴⁴
他 就 拔 芦笙 来 来 跳 芦笙 来 做
3S just pull lusheng come come dance lusheng come make

来跳芦笙舞，来凑热闹，
perform *lusheng* dance, offer support,

70 ke³⁵lɔ²¹ʑe²¹ , tʂhua⁵⁵ qen⁵² tau⁴⁴ tu³³ tɕɦua³¹ ntaɯ²¹ . tɕɔ³⁵ nɔ⁴⁴
路 热闹 吹 芦笙 给 个 死 那 些 这
road jollification blow lusheng P CL die that CL.PL this

给死者吹芦笙。
and play the *lusheng* for the deceased.

(8) ke³⁵ pa²¹ tɕʰua³¹ 丧俗

71 zɕɔ³¹ ʂau⁴⁴ . tʰau²¹ lu⁵⁵ ʂi⁵²xaɯ²¹ ʔua³³ pe⁵⁵ zua³⁵ lɔ³³ mu³³ xai³³
    是   友人   时候 个 时候   （定标） 我们   要   来   去   说
    COP friend time CL time   REL   1PL   need come go say

这种人是"朋友"。当我们要来唱丧歌的时候，
These people are friends. When we are going to sing dirges,

72 tsi³⁵sai³⁵, pe⁵⁵ zua³⁵ mua⁵² ʔi⁵⁵ ŋkaɯ²¹ tsi³⁵sai³⁵ .
    丧歌   我们   要   有   一   对   丧歌师
    dirges   1PL   need have one   CL   dirge singer

我们需要有一对丧歌师。
we need a couple of dirge singers.

73 tɕɔ⁵² lɔ³³ tsʰen⁵⁵ tsɦɔ³¹ nɯ³³ lu⁵⁵ nen⁵² xai³³ tia³³ : tʰau²¹ nɯ³³ ŋɔ⁵⁵   ,
    带   来   清理   到   他   个   生活   说   道   时候   他   在
    bring come clean about 3S   CL   life say QUOT   time   3S   be.located

这对歌师要用歌声细数死者生前的功德：死者在世时，
They would count merits and virtues that the deceased made by singing: when he/she was alive,

74 nɯ³³ mua⁵² pe³³ tʂɦaɯ³¹ len⁵² mi⁴⁴ ɲua²¹ , tʂɦaɯ³¹ len⁵² tu⁵⁵ ,
    他   有   多少   位   小孩子   少   位   儿子
    3S   have how many CL   little children few   CL   son

他有多少个孩子，多少个儿子，
how many children he had, how many sons or

75 tʂɦaɯ³¹ len⁵² ntshai³³ , nɯ³³ kʰɯ³⁵ mua⁵² ʔda⁵⁵tsi⁴⁴ , mua⁵² ɲia⁵² ntau⁴⁴
    少   位   女儿   他   苦   有   什么   有   银   多
    few   CL   daughter 3S   bitter have   what   have   silver much

多少个女儿，他挣到什么，有多少钱，
daughters he had, how much he earned, how much money

76 mpau²¹li⁴⁴tɕa³³ , nɯ³³ mua⁵² lia⁵² mua⁵² te⁵⁵ ntau⁴⁴ mpau²¹li⁴⁴tɕa³³ .
    怎样   他   有   田   有   地   多   怎样
    how   3S   have field have   land much   how

有多少土地；
and land he owned;

77 thau²¹ nɯ³³ xɔ⁴⁴ tau⁴⁴ ta³³ ʂi²¹ nen⁵² laɯ²¹, zua³⁵ mua⁵⁵ fai⁵⁵ ʈau⁴⁴
   时候 他 又 得 完 世 生活 了 要 拿 分开 给
   time 3S again get finish world life PRF need take separate P
当他去世了，要把财产分给谁；
when he passed away, who will inherit his fortune;

78 len⁵² tɕʰɯ³¹, zua³⁵ lɔ³³ mu³³ tshen⁵⁵ te⁵² kʰuŋ²¹ ʂi³⁵ nɔ⁴⁴, tshen⁵⁵ tsfiɔ³¹
   位 哪 要 来 去 清点 些 东西 用 这 清点 到
   CL who need come go check CL.PL thing use this check about
要来清点家产，清点他的生活。
We need to check his property and his life experiences.

79 nɯ³³ lu⁵⁵ nen⁵². zua³⁵ lɔ³³ mu³³ qhua⁵⁵kɔ²¹fuŋ²¹kɔ²¹. zfiɔ³¹ni⁴⁴ntaɯ²¹,
   他 个 生活 要 来 去 孝顺教育 是 这样
   3S CL life need come go filial education COP this style
要来进行孝顺教育。因此，这对歌师，
We need to carry out filial education. Therefore, this pair of singers

80 tu³³ nɔ⁴⁴ zfiɔ³¹ ŋkaɯ²¹ tsi³⁵sai³⁵, lɔ³³ zfiɔ³¹ ŋkaɯ²¹ tu⁵⁵
   个 这 是 对 丧歌师 或 是 对 儿子
   CL this COP pair dirge singer or COP pair son
这就是丧歌师，或者是一对唱丧歌的人。
is the dirge singer, or a pair of dirge singers.

81 xai³³ sai³⁵. ʔi⁵⁵ tu³³ tsua³³ ntsi³⁵ mu³³, zfiɔ³¹ tu³³ tsɯ⁵²lɦau³¹.
   说 丧歌 一 个 接 补 去 是 个 祖 老
   say dirges one CL connect supplement go COP CL ancestor old
下一个人，是老祖。
The next one is the elder,

82 tu³³ tsɯ⁵²lɦau³¹ zfiɔ³¹ tu³³ ʔua³³ zua³⁵ tua⁵² tshen⁵⁵nu⁵²tshen⁵⁵ɴqe⁴⁴,
   个 祖 老 是 个 (定标) 要 来 清 债务 清 债务
   CL ancestor old COP CL REL need come clean debt clean debt
老祖是一个要来清算债务，
a person who is in charge of counting debt

(8) ke³⁵ pa²¹ tɕʰua³¹ 丧俗   125

83 lɔ³³ zɦɔ³¹ te⁵² za²¹ pʰe²¹ za²¹ tʂi³³ ʐuŋ⁴⁴ mua⁵⁵ tʂɦe³¹ tau²¹ mu³³.
　 或　是　些　样　丑　样　不　好　拿　撤　出　去
　 or　COP　CL.PL　style　ugly　style　NEG　good　take　withdraw　out　go
或者是把不好的东西撤出去的人。
or cleaning out the bad things.

84 qʰɔ³⁵ kɦaɯ³¹ tɔ²¹qa⁵⁵ nɔ⁴⁴, zɦɔ³¹
　 处　末尾　后面　这　是
　 place　end　behind　this　COP
最后一个人，是磕头迎接客人的孝子。
The last person is the filial son who kowtows to welcome guests.

85 tɕɔ³⁵ tu⁵⁵ se²¹ɕɔ²¹. tɕɔ³⁵ ɕɔ²¹tɕua⁵⁵ ntaɯ²¹, nɯ³³ mua⁵² tɕɔ³⁵ tu⁵⁵
　 些　儿子　睡孝　些　孝家　那　他　有　些　儿子
　 CL.PL　son　sleep filiality　CL.PL　filiality family　that　3S　have　CL.PL　son
那些孝子，有男的
Among them, there are both men

86 tɕɔ³⁵ ntshai³³ ʔua³³ nɯ³³ nia²¹ nɯ³³ tsi³⁵ tau⁴⁴ ta³³ ɕi²¹ nen⁵² laɯ²¹.
　 些　女儿　(定标)　他　母亲　他　父亲　得　完　世　生活　了
　 CL.PL　daughter　REL　3S　mother　3S　father　get　finish　world　life　PRF
有女的，他的父亲母亲过世了。
and women. When their parents die,

87 tʰaɯ²¹ ŋkaɯ²¹ tsi³⁵sai³⁵ ntaɯ²¹ lɔ³³ qʰua⁵⁵kɔ²¹fuŋ²¹kɔ²¹, tɕɔ³⁵
　 时候　对　丧歌师　那　来　孝顺教育　些
　 time　toward　funeral song singer　that　come　filial education　CL.PL
当丧歌师来进行孝顺教育的时候，
and the dirge singers come to carry out filial education,

88 tu⁵⁵ tɕɔ³⁵ ntshai³³ ntaɯ²¹ lɔ³³ ɕɔ²¹, lɔ³³ tsai³³ kuŋ⁵⁵ tsai³³ m̥uŋ⁴⁴.
　 儿子　些　女儿　那　来　孝　来　接　功德　接　命运
　 son　CL.PL　daughter　that　come　filiality　come　recieve　merits　recieve　fate
这些孝子孝女们要来跪拜，来接受死者赐给的功德和运气。
those filial sons and daughters should worship on bended knees to receive the merits and virtues that the deceased bestows.

89 tɕɔ³⁵　　nɔ⁴⁴　pe⁵⁵　xu⁴⁴　ʔua⁴⁴　tu⁵⁵　se²¹ ɕɔ²¹
　　些　　　这　　我们　叫　　做　　儿子　睡孝
　　CL.PL　this　1PL　call　make　son　sleep filiality

这些人我们叫做孝子。
We call them filial sons.

丧俗

苗族办丧事的人员，在泰国是这样的。

第一个人，是管事。管事就是负责整个丧事全部事宜的人。

第二个人，是主人家的头儿。我们得有一个主人家的头儿，来死者家里教大家做事情。当管事或办丧事的人有什么需要的时候，这个主人家的头儿要去准备酒水，准备食材，猪肉，准备祭品，拿来给那些办丧事的人用。

下一个人，是家长。家长是祭鬼或者是给死者祭献饭菜的人。

下一个人，是指路人。指路人是给死者指路让他去见祖宗的那个人。

下一个人，是编木马鞋的人。编木马鞋的人是去砍两根树拿来做木马和编一双麻鞋给死者的那个人。

下一个人，是芦笙师。丧事办得隆重，要得请三个芦笙师。丧事办得简单，要请两个芦笙师。

下一个人，是鼓师。多数情况下，我们请两位芦笙师。一位来吹芦笙，一位来打鼓。

下一个人，是厨官。厨官是来做菜的人。

下一个人，是掌枪的人。那个掌枪的人，当有人去世的时候，那个掌枪的人要先来打三枪。或者即使他不是打前面三枪的人，他也是早上、中午、晚上、黎明来打枪的人。当他们要打鬼的时候，他要来打枪，大葬夜那天有客人来时，他要来打枪迎接客人。

下一个人，是做棺材的人。做棺材的人是要去锯树或是要去劈树拿来给死者做棺材的人。

下一个人，是打鬼的领头人。有些地方，它有打鬼的领头人。有些地方，它没有。打鬼的时候，一个人在家里，一群人在外面。打鬼的领头人是带着大家围着房子转的人。妇女要转七圈，男子转九圈。妇女七圈，顺转四圈，逆转三圈。男子顺转五圈，逆转四圈。但是，有部分人没有领头打鬼的人，有部分人有。

下一个人，是主人家。主人家我们叫做孝家。这些主人家包括跟死者同姓或者跟死者是兄弟的所有人。

下一个人，是柴头。柴头是砍柴的人。要有砍柴的人，我们才有柴来做菜做饭吃。

下一个人，是汤头。汤头是挑水的人。要有汤头或是挑水的人去挑水，才有水拿来做菜做饭吃。

下一个人，是丧客。当有人去世时，我们得去告诉亲戚，姑姑舅舅或者女儿女婿，以及跟死者亲近的那些人，叫大家来奔丧。这些人我们叫做丧客。当丧客来奔丧时，那些丧客中有一个正式的代表，这个代表叫"交礼人"。那个交礼人代表丧客拿出丧客带来的菜和饭祭献给死者吃，要把丧客带来的礼金交给主人家，交给管事。

下一个人，我们不知道他是谁。他想来吹芦笙表达对死者的思念。这种人我们叫作"朋友"。这种朋友他们自己带芦笙来，来跳芦笙舞，来凑热闹，给死者吹芦笙。这种人是"朋友"。

下一个人，当我们要来唱丧歌的时候，我们需要有一对丧歌师。这对歌师要用歌声细数死者生前的功德：死者在世时，他有多少个孩子，多少个儿子，多少个女儿，他挣到什么，有多少钱，有多少土地；当他去世了，要把财产分给谁；要来清点家产，清点他的生活。要来进行孝顺教育。因此，这对歌师，就是丧歌师，或者是一对唱丧歌的人。

　　下一个人，是老祖。老祖是一个要来清算债务，或者是把不好的东西撤出去的人。

　　下一个人，是磕头迎接客人的孝子。那些孝子，有男有女，他们的父亲母亲过世了。当丧歌师来进行孝顺教育的时候，这些孝子孝女们要来跪拜，来接受死者赐给的功德和运气。这些人我们叫做孝子。

Funeral Customs

In Thailand, the people conducting funerals of Hmong people are as follows.

The first person is the steward, who is responsible for all the matters of the whole funeral.

The second person is the leader of the family of deceased. It is necessary for us to select a leader to come to the family of the deceased to teach people how to deal with funeral affairs. When there's something the steward or people who conduct the funeral need, the leader is supposed to prepare alcohol and food, pork and sacrificial offering for them.

The next person is patriarch, who is responsible for conducting sacrifice to the ghost or rather sacrifice food to the deceased.

The next person is the guide, who would show the way for deceased to go to his ancestors.

The next one is person who makes wooden horse shoes. He would cut down some trees to make wooden horse and a pair of hemp shoes for the deceased.

The next person is the *lusheng* (a kind of reed-pipe instrument) performer. If people want a solemn funeral, they should invite three *lusheng* performers. If people want a simple one, they should invite two *lusheng* performers.

The next person is the drummer. In most cases, we would invite two *lusheng* performers, one of whom plays the *lusheng* and the other plays the drum.

The next one is the kitchen official, the one who cooks.

The next one is the gun owner. When someone passes away, the gun owner would come to shoot three times first. Or even if he isn't the man who does the three shots, he should be the one who comes to fire a gun in the morning, noon, evening and at dawn. When people come to exorcise, he would come to fire the gun. If there are guests coming in the evening of the burial day, the gun owner should fire a gun to welcome guests.

The next one is person who makes the coffin. He would saw trees to make the coffin for the deceased.

The next one is the leader of the exorcism ritual. At some places, there are leaders of exorcism, and at some places there aren't. When exorcism is conducted, one stays at home and a group of people stay outside. The leader of exorcism is the one who leads people to walk around the house. A woman should walk around seven times and a man nine times. A woman should go seven rounds, of which four rounds are clockwise, and three rounds are counterclockwise. A man should go nine rounds, of which five rounds are clockwise, and four rounds are counterclockwise. However, some people don't have a leader to lead them.

The next is the host family, which we call them "filial family" (the family of the deceased). This family includes all the people who have the same last name with the deceased or are brothers of the deceased.

The next person is the firewood chief, who cuts the firewood. There are people who cut firewood so that we can use the wood to cook.

The next person is the water chief, who takes charge of carrying water. With them carrying water for us, we are able to use the water to cook.

The next is the guest. When someone passes away, we have to inform our relatives such as aunts and uncles or daughters and son-in-law, and those who were closed to the deceased to hasten home for the funeral. Those people are ones who we call guests. When they come, one of these guests would be the formal representative, who is the so-called "etiquette person". He would sacrifice the food that guests bring to the deceased on behalf of all the guests and hand over the cash gift that all the guests bring to the host family or the steward.

The next one, we don't know who he is. He expresses that he misses the deceased by playing the *lusheng*. We call them "friends". They would bring their own *lusheng* here and perform *lusheng* dance to offer support and play the *lusheng* for the deceased. These people are friends.

Next, when we are going to sing dirges, we need a couple of dirge singers. They would count the merits and virtues that the deceased made by singing about the following: when he was living, how many children he had, how many sons or daughters he had, how much he earned, how much money and land he owned; when he passed away, who will inherit his fortune. We need to check his property and his life experiences. We need to carry out filial education. Therefore, this pair of singers is the dirge singer, or a pair of dirge singers.

The next person is the elder, the one who's in charge of counting debt or cleaning out the bad things.

The last person is the filial son who kowtows to welcome guests. Among them, there are both men and women. When their parents passed away, and the dirge singers come to carry out filial education, those filial sons should worship on bended knee to receive the merits and virtues that the deceased bestows. We call them filial sons.

（9）tu⁵⁵ʔɖe⁵²nu²¹ ɳɔ⁵⁵ʈau⁴⁴xau³⁵ ke³⁵ʔua⁴⁴tʂhuŋ⁵⁵
婚事人员

人	事情	在	给	里	路	做	婚事
person	thing	at	P	inside	road	do	marriage

1 m̩uŋ⁵⁵ tɕɔ³⁵ tu⁵⁵ ʔɖe⁵²nu²¹ ɳɔ⁵⁵   ʈau⁴⁴ xau³⁵ ke³⁵ʔua⁴⁴tʂhuŋ⁵⁵,
  苗族   些   儿子 事情   在   给   里 路 做 婚事
  Hmong CL.PL son matter be.located P inside road make marriage
办婚事所需要的人员，
In Thailand, personnel needed for marriage

2 ɳɔ⁵⁵   ʈau⁴⁴ ʂa⁵⁵ thai⁵⁵ te⁵⁵, mua⁵² ʈau³³ li⁴⁴ ɳta²¹ nɔ⁴⁴.
  在   给   边   泰国   地   有   跟   像   下面   这
  be.located P   side Thailand land have follow be.like below this

tua²¹men⁵²kuŋ⁵⁵,
大媒公
 big matchmaker

在泰国这边，有下面这些。大媒公，
are as follows. First is the big matchmaker,

3 ʑɦo³¹ tu³³ ʐua³⁵ lɔ³³ mu³³ xai³³ ʐa⁵² xai³³ tshen⁵²tshen²¹ tʂhuŋ⁵⁵,
  是   个   要   来   去   说   曲   说   步骤   婚事
  COP   CL will come go   say tune say   procedure   marriage
是要去唱婚嫁歌谈婚事、
the one who sings wedding songs and negotiates about marriage affairs

4 xai³³ ɴqe⁴⁴mi³³ɴqe⁴⁴nɔ⁴⁴. tua²¹men⁵²kuŋ⁵⁵
  说   价格奶 价格 饭   大媒公
  say   price milk price rice big matchmaker

谈聘金聘礼的人。
and the bride price.

5 ʑɦɔ³¹ tu³³ ʔua³³ ʑua³⁵ lɔ³³ mu³³ ŋtɦɔ³¹ tu³³ ŋtɦiau³¹vau³⁵ mu³³
  是   个   (定标) 要   来   去   和   个   男郎 女婿   去
  COP   CL   REL   will come go   and   CL   man   son-in-law go

大媒公要陪新郎去
The matchmaker would accompany the bridegroom

6 xai³³ nɯ³³ tu³³ pɔ⁵²nia²¹ , tʂɔ⁴⁴ ɴqe⁴⁴mi³³ɴqe⁴⁴ŋɔ⁴⁴ lɔ³³ ʑɦɔ³¹
  说   他   个   妻子   放   价格 奶 价格 饭   或者   是
  say   3S   CL   wife   put   price milk price rice or   COP

他的未婚妻家，商量聘金聘礼或是
to his fiancée's house to discuss the bride price or

7 mu³³ tʂhen⁵⁵ tɕɔ³⁵ tʂhen⁵²tʂhen²¹ tʂhua⁴⁴ tʂhua⁴⁴ za²¹ ŋɔ⁵⁵ tau⁴⁴ xau³⁵
  去   清理   些   步骤   全   全   样   在   给   里
  go   clean   CL.PL procedure   RDUP~all   style be.located P inside

去落实举办婚礼各种事宜。
conduct all kinds of wedding matters.

8 tuŋ⁵² tʂhuŋ⁵⁵ ntaɯ²¹ . tu³³ tsua³³ ntsi³⁵ mu³³, ʑɦɔ³¹ tu³³ lɯ²¹men⁵²kuŋ⁵⁵
  桌   婚事   那   个   接   接   去   是   个   二媒公
  table marriage that   CL   connect connect go   COP   CL   second matchmaker

下一个人，是二媒公。
Next is the second matchmaker,

9 tu³³ lɯ²¹men⁵²kuŋ⁵⁵   ʑɦɔ³¹ tu³³ lɔ³³ pa⁵⁵ tu³³ tua²¹men⁵²kuŋ⁵⁵ tʂhua⁴⁴ tʂhua⁴⁴
  个   二媒公   是   个   来   帮忙   个   大媒公   全   全
  CL   second matchmaker   COP   CL   come help   CL   big matchmaker RDUP~all

二媒公是来协助大媒公完成婚礼所有事情的人。
who gives assistance to the big matchmaker to handle all wedding matters.

10 za²¹ ʔde⁵²nu²¹ tɕɦa³¹ ŋtɦo⁴⁴   . tu³³ tsua³³ ntsi³⁵ mu³³
   样   事情   完   (完全状)   个   接   接   去
   style matter   finish completely   CL   next   next   go

(9) tu⁵⁵ʔdҽ⁵²nu²¹ nɔ⁵⁵ʈau⁴⁴xau³⁵ke³⁵ʔua⁴⁴tʂhuŋ⁵⁵婚事人员

下一个人，是婚事主管。
The next one is the marriage supervisor,

11 zɦo³¹   tu³³   tsi³⁵tshia⁵²tɕɔ²¹ . tu³³   tsi³⁵tshia⁵²tɕɔ²¹   zɦo³¹   tu³³   ka³⁵sɯ²¹   tʂhuŋ⁵⁵ .
    是   个   (雄性缀)婚事   个   (雄性缀)婚事   是   个   管事   婚事
    COP   CL   marriage   CL   marriage   COP   CL   supervisor marriage

这个婚事主管是婚事的管事。
who is the manager of wedding affairs.

12 tu³³   ka³⁵sɯ²¹   tʂhuŋ⁵⁵   nɔ⁴⁴, nɯ³³   zɦo³¹   tu³³   lɔ³³   mu³³   ʂai⁵⁵   ɕua³³
    个   管事   婚事   这   他   是   个   来   去   看   看
    CL   supervisor marriage   this 3S   COP   CL   come   go   look   look

这个婚事管事，他要去要监督
He manages

13 ʔdҽ⁵²nu²¹   tshua⁴⁴   za²¹   ŋɔ⁵⁵   xau³⁵   , lɔ³³   mu³³   tu⁵⁵tu²¹   ʈau⁴⁴   tɕɔ³⁵
    事情   全   样   在   里   来   去   督促   给   些
    matter   all   style   be.located   inside   come   go   supervise P   CL.PL

婚事中的各种事宜，督促
all the wedding affairs and supervises

14 men⁵²kuŋ⁵⁵   lɔ³³   mu³³   xai³³   ɴqe⁴⁴mi³³ɴqe⁴⁴ŋɔ⁴⁴,   lɔ³³   mu³³
    媒公   来   去   说   费用奶费用饭   来   去
    matchmaker   come   go   say   fee milk fee rice   come   go

    tɕɔ⁵²   ma⁵²   tɕɔ⁵²   ʔua⁴⁴
    带   忙   带   做
    take.along   busy   take.along   do

媒公去商量聘礼聘金，去带领大家做事，
the matchmaker in discussing the bride price, and leads people to do the work

15 lɔ³³   mu³³   qhia⁴⁴   tɕɔ³⁵   tu⁵⁵   qhe³⁵   tu⁵⁵   nu²¹   ʔua⁴⁴   ɴqai⁵²   ʔua⁴⁴
    来   去   教   些   人   奴隶   人   事情   做   肉   做
    come   go   teach   CL.PL   person   slave   person   matter   make   meat   make

去安排打杂的人做饭做菜
and arranges people who do odd jobs to cook

16 zau⁵⁵ ʔua⁴⁴ mɔ³⁵ tau⁴⁴ ʂauɯ³⁵ʔdauɯ³³ nɔ⁵². tu³³ nɔ⁴⁴ zɦɔ³¹ tu³³ ka³⁵sɯ²¹ .
菜　做　饭　给　大家　　　吃　个　这　是　个　管事
dish　make　rice　give　all　　　eat　CL　this　COP　CL　supervisor

给大家吃。管这些事情的这个人就是管事。
for everyone. The one who is responsible for these things is the supervisor.

17 thau²¹ lu⁵⁵ ʂi⁵²xauɯ²¹ ʔde⁵²nu²¹ ta³³ , nɯ³³ zua³⁵ lɔ³³ mu³³ tʂɦie³¹ɴqai⁵²tʂɦie³¹ta³⁵ ,
时候　个　时候　　事情　　完　　他　要　来　去　留　肉　留　肋骨
time　CL　time　　matter　　finish　3S　will　come　go　leave meat leave rib

当婚礼结束的时候，他要去预备肉和肋骨，
When the wedding is over, he should go to prepare some meat and ribs

18 lɔ³³ mu³³ tʂɦie³¹ tʂhua⁴⁴ za²¹ , tɕɔ⁵² lɔ³³ mu³³ ten³⁵tia²¹
来　去　留　全　样　带　来　去　招待
come　go　leave　all　style　bring　come　go　treat

去预备各种物品，拿去答谢
and other things to acknowledge people

19 tɕɔ³⁵ tu⁵⁵ ʔde⁵² tu⁵⁵ nu²¹ ʔua³³ mu³³ pa⁵⁵ tuŋ⁵² tʂhuŋ⁵⁵ ntaɯ²¹ .
些　人　事情　人　事情　(定标)　去　帮忙　桌　婚事　那
CL.PL　person matter person matter　REL　go　help　table marriage that

帮忙办婚事的这些人。
who helped the marriage.

20 ɲtɕɦiau³¹vau³⁵ , ɲtɕɦiau³¹vau³⁵ zɦɔ³¹ tu³³ ʔua³³ nɯ³³ zua³⁵
男郎　女婿　　男郎　女婿　　是　个　(定标)　他　娶
man son-in-law　man son-in-law　COP　CL　REL　3S　marry

新郎，新郎是娶妻子的人。
The bridegroom is the man who will marry the wife.

21 pɔ⁵²nia²¹ . ŋkau⁵²ŋa⁵⁵ , ŋkau⁵²ŋa⁵⁵ zɦɔ³¹ tu³³ ntshai³³ ʔua³³
妻子　　女郎　儿媳　　女郎　儿媳　　是　个　女儿　(定标)
wife　　woman daughter-in-law　woman daughter-in-law　COP　CL　daughter　REL

nɯ³³ mu³³ zua³⁵
她　去　嫁
3S　go　marry

(9) tu⁵⁵ʔdʑe⁵²nu²¹ ŋɔ⁵⁵ʈau⁴⁴xau³⁵ ke³⁵ʔua⁴⁴tʂhuŋ⁵⁵婚事人员

新娘，新娘是在婚礼中要
The bride is the girl who

22 tsi³⁵ ŋɔ⁵⁵ ʈau⁴⁴ ʈuŋ⁵² tʂhuŋ⁵⁵ ntauɯ²¹ . tu³³ tsua³³ ntsi³⁵ mu³³ zɦɔ³¹
   丈夫 在 给 桌 婚事 那 个 接 补 去 是
   husband be.located P table marriage that CL connect supplement go COP

tu³³ phi⁵²la⁵² .
个 陪郎
CL groomsman

出嫁的那个女孩。下一个人，是伴郎。
will get married at the wedding. The next one is the groomsman,

23 tu³³ phi⁵²la⁵² zɦɔ³¹ tu³³ mu³³ ʔua⁴⁴ lɦua³¹ ɳʈɦɔ³¹ ʈau⁴⁴ tu³³ ɳʈɦau³¹vau³⁵ .
   个 陪郎 是 个 去 做 伙伴 和 给 个 男郎女婿
   CL groomsman COP CL go make companion and P CL man son-in-law

伴郎是去给新郎做伴的人。
who will accompany the bridegroom at the wedding.

24 tu³³ ɳʈɦau³¹vau³⁵ nɯ³³ pe⁴⁴, phi⁵²la⁵² zua³⁵ ɳʈɦɔ³¹ pe⁴⁴ . tu³³
   个 男郎女婿 他 拜 陪郎 要 和 拜 个
   CL man son-in-law 3S worship groomsman will and worship CL

ɳʈɦau³¹vau³⁵ mu³³
男郎女婿 去
man son-in-law go

新郎叩拜，伴郎要跟着叩拜。新郎去杀猪，
The groomsman also should follow alongside the bridegroom as he worships. If the bridegroom goes to butcher pigs,

25 tʂen³⁵ mpua⁴⁴, lɔ³³ tu³³ phi⁵²la⁵² zua³⁵ ʈau⁴⁴ mu³³ pa⁵⁵ tʂen³⁵ mpua⁴⁴ . tu³³
   杀 猪 也 个 伴郎 要 得 去 帮忙 杀 猪 个
   kill pig CONJ CL groomsman will get go help kill pig CL

伴郎也要跟着去帮忙杀猪。
the groomsman should also offer to help.

136　　　　　　　　　　　　泰国白苗话语法标注文本

26 tsua³³　　ntsi³⁵　　　　mu³³　zɦɔ³¹　tu³³　nia²¹tai³³ntʂhua⁵⁵ .　tu³³　nia²¹tai³³ntʂhua⁵⁵　lɔ³³
　　接　　　补　　　　　　去　　是　　个　　姨妈　　绿色　　　个　　姨妈　　绿色　　也
　　connect　supplement　go　COP　CL　aunt　green　　CL　aunt　green　CONJ

下一个人，是伴娘。伴娘
The next is the bridesmaid,

27 zɦɔ³¹　tu³³　nia²¹　ʔua⁴⁴　lɦua³¹　 .　tu³³　nɔ⁴⁴　zɦɔ³¹　zua³⁵　mu³³　ʔua⁴⁴　lɦua³¹
　　是　　个　　母亲　　做　　伙伴　　　个　　这　　是　　要　　去　　做　　伙伴
　　COP　CL　mother　make　companion　CL　this　COP　will　go　make　companion

ntɕɦɔ³¹
和
and

也是做伴的姑娘。这个人要去陪伴
who will be the companion of the

28 tu³³　ŋkau⁵²ŋa⁵⁵　　　　ʔua⁴⁴ke⁴⁴ .　tu³³　ŋkau⁵²ŋa⁵⁵　　　tsɦɔ³¹　tɦɯ³¹ ,　tu³³
　　个　　女郎儿媳　　　　一起　　　　个　　女郎儿媳　　　　到　　哪　　　个
　　CL　woman daughter-in-law　together　CL　woman son-in-law　arrive　where　CL

nia²¹tai³³ntʂhuŋ⁵⁵
姨妈　婚事
aunt　marriage

新娘。新娘到哪里，这个伴娘
bride. The bridesmaid would go

29 nɔ⁴⁴　nɯ³³　zua³⁵tau⁴⁴　ntɕɦɔ³¹　tu³³　ŋkau⁵²ŋa⁵⁵　　　tsɦɔ³¹　tɦɯ³¹ .　tu³³
　　这　　她　　要得　　　　和　　　个　　女郎儿媳　　　　到　　　哪　　　个
　　this　3S　should　　　and　　CL　woman daughter-in-law　arrive　where　CL

ŋkau⁵²ŋa⁵⁵
女郎 儿媳
woman daughter-in-law

她要跟着到哪里。新娘
everywhere the bride goes. The bridesmaid would also sleep

(9) tu⁵⁵ʔd̠e⁵²nu²¹ n̠ɔ⁵⁵ʈau⁴⁴ xau³⁵ ke³⁵ʔua⁴⁴tʂhuŋ⁵⁵ 婚事人员

30 pɯ⁴⁴ xɔ³⁵ tɕhɯ³¹, tu³³ nia²¹tai³³ŋtʂhuŋ⁵⁵ nɔ⁴⁴ ʐua³⁵tau⁴⁴ ŋtɕhiɔ³¹ tu³³
　　睡　　哪　　哪　　个　姨妈　　　　婚事　　这　　要得　　　和　　个
　　sleep where where CL aunt marriage this should and CL

ŋkau⁵²ŋa⁵⁵
女郎 儿媳
woman daughter-in-law

睡哪里，这个伴娘要跟着新娘
wherever the bride sleeps.

31 ntaɯ²¹ pɯ⁴⁴ xɔ³⁵ tɕhɯ³¹ . tsfiɔ³¹ thau²¹ mu³³ ʔua⁴⁴ ʈuŋ⁵² tʂhuŋ⁵⁵ ntaɯ²¹ tia³⁵
　　那　　睡　　哪　　哪　　　到　　时候　　去　　做　　桌　　婚事　　那　　完成
　　that sleep where where arrive time go make table marriage that complete

睡哪里。直到整个婚礼结束
The bridesmaid should always follow the bride till the wedding ends and

32 tɔ³⁵qa⁵⁵ lɔ³³ tsfiɔ³¹ tʂe³⁵ . tu³³ tsua³³ ntsi³⁵ mu³³, ʐfiɔ³¹ tu³³ tu⁵⁵ tua³⁵
　回　　　来　　到　　家　　　个　　接　　补　　去　　是　　个　儿子　抓
　back come arrive home CL connect supplement go COP CL son grab

tsia⁵² .
钱
money

新娘回到新郎家里。下一个人，是管钱的人。
the bride gets back to the bridegroom's house. Next is the one who manages money.

33 tu³³ tu⁵⁵ tua³⁵ tsia⁵² lɔ³³ ʐfiɔ³¹ tu³³ ʔua³³ pe⁵⁵ xu⁴⁴ ʔua⁴⁴ tu³³ tu⁵⁵ tɕe³⁵
　个　儿子　抓　钱　　也　　是　　个　(定标) 我们 叫　　做　　个　儿子　递
　CL son grab money CONJ COP CL REL 1PL call do CL son deliver

管钱的人也是倒酒给男女双方媒公的人。
He is also the one who serves alcohol for the matchmakers of both two parties.

34 tɕaɯ³⁵ . tu³³ tu⁵⁵ tua³⁵ tsia⁵² nɔ⁴⁴ ʐfiɔ³¹ tu³³ ua³³ thau²¹ lu⁵⁵ ɕi⁵² xaɯ²¹ mu³³
　酒　　个　儿子　抓　钱　　这　　是　　个　(定标) 时候　个　时候　去
　alcohol CL son grab money this COP CL REL time CL time go

这个管钱的人，当婚礼中饭菜上齐
When all the dishes are served at the wedding feast

35 ʔua⁴⁴ tʂhuŋ⁵⁵ ʈau⁴⁴ ʐau⁵⁵ ʈau⁴⁴ mɔ³⁵ tʂhi⁵² tɕha³¹ ʐua³⁵ nɔ⁵² ʐua³⁵ xau³³, nɯ³³
做　　婚事　　摆　　菜　　摆　　饭　　齐　　完　　要　　吃　　要　　喝　　他
make marriage place dish place rice together finish will eat will drink 3S
要吃饭的时候，他
and people are about to eat, he

36 ʐɦɔ³¹ tu³³ ʐua³⁵ lɔ³¹ mu³³ tɕe³⁵ tɕaɯ³⁵ ʈau⁴⁴ tɕɔ³⁵ qhua⁴⁴ ʔua³³ tua⁵² kuŋ²¹
是　　个　　要　　来　　去　　递　　酒　　给　　些　　客人　 (定标)　来　　拱
COP CL will come go deliver wine give CL.PL guest REL come hump
要去给客人倒酒。
should serve guests alcohol.

37 nɔ⁵² kuŋ²¹ xau³³ ŋɔ⁵⁵ ʈuŋ⁵² tʂhuŋ⁵⁵ ntaɯ²¹. tu³³ nɔ⁴⁴ ʐɦɔ³¹ tu³³ tu⁵⁵ tua³⁵
吃　拱　　喝　　在　　桌　　婚事　　那　　个　　这　　是　　个　　儿子　抓
eat hump drink be.located table marriage that CL this COP CL son grab
做上面这些事的人就是管钱的人。
The person who does the things above is the one who manages the money.

38 tsia⁵² . tu³³ tsua³³ ntsi³⁵ mu³³, ʐɦɔ³¹ tu³³ tu⁵⁵ tʂhua⁵²pha⁵² . tu³³ tu⁵⁵
钱　　个　接　　补　　去　是　　个　儿子　茶　　盘　　个　儿子
money CL next supplement go COP CL son tea tray CL son
下一个人，是端茶盘的人。
Next is the person who carries the tea tray

39 tʂhua⁵²pha⁵² nɔ⁴⁴ ʐɦɔ³¹ tu³³ tsha⁵⁵ ʐau⁵⁵ . thau²¹ lu⁵⁵ ʂi⁵²xaɯ²¹ mu³³ ʔua⁴⁴
茶　　盘　　这　是　　个　添　　菜　　时候　个　　时候　　去　　做
tea tray this COP CL add dish time CL time go make
端茶盘的人是添菜的人。办婚礼的时候，
and who serves dishes. At the wedding,

40 tʂhuŋ⁵⁵ , mua⁵² ʔi⁵⁵ tɕɔ³⁵ kɯ³⁵ti⁵²nen⁵²tʂa⁴⁴ mua⁵² tɕɔ³⁵ qhua⁴⁴ tua⁵² ʐau²¹
婚事　　有　　一　　些　　弟兄亲戚　　　　有　　些　　客人　　来　　坐
marriage have one CL.PL brother relative have CL.PL guest come sit
有一些亲戚和一些客人
when a table is exactly full of

(9) tu⁵⁵ʔdẹ⁵²nu²¹ nɔ⁵⁵ʈau⁴⁴ xau³⁵ ke³⁵ʔua⁴⁴tʂhuŋ⁵⁵婚事人员

41 ʂau⁴⁴ lu⁵⁵ ʈuŋ⁵² pu³⁵ ŋkau³³, tu³³ tu⁵⁵ tʂhua⁵² pha⁵² nɔ⁴⁴ zɦɔ³¹ tu³³
上 个 桌 满 正好 个 儿子 茶 盘子 这 是 个
up CL table full exactly CL son tea tray this COP CL

正好坐满一桌，这个端茶盘的人

relatives and guests, the one who carries the tea tray

42 zua³⁵ lɔ³³ mu³³ tsha⁵⁵ zau⁵⁵ tau⁴⁴ ʂau²¹, kua²¹ zau⁵⁵ tɕi³³ tu⁴⁴ ŋtɕua⁴⁴,
要 来 去 添 菜 给 上面 让 菜 不 断 间隙
will come go add dish give above let dish NEG break gap

要去给这桌人上菜，让菜碗不空，

should serve dishes for them and don't let the dishes be empty

43 kua²¹ ʂaɯ³⁵ʔdɯ³³ mua⁵² ntsɦua³¹, mua⁵² nɔ⁵² mua⁵² xau³³.
让 大家 有 下饭 有 吃 有 喝
let all have eat food have eat have drink

让大家有菜下饭、有吃有喝。

so everyone has enough to eat and drink.

44 tu³³ tsua³³ ntsi³⁵ mu³³, zɦɔ³¹ tʂhu²¹. tʂhu²¹ zɦɔ³¹ tu³³ ʔua⁴⁴ mɔ³⁵.
个 接 补 去 是 厨 厨 是 个 做 饭
CL connect supplement go COP cook cook COP CL make meal

下一个人，是厨子。厨子是做饭的人。

Next is the cook, who cooks the meal

45 zua³⁵tʂu²¹ mua⁵² tu³³ nɔ⁴⁴ mu³³ ʔua⁴⁴ mɔ³⁵, ʂaɯ³⁵ʔdɯ³³ thia⁵² li⁴⁴ zua³⁵tau⁴⁴ zau⁵⁵
要得 有 个 这 去 做 饭 大家 才 才 要得 菜
should have CL this go make meal people just just should dish

得要有厨子去做饭，大家才有菜有饭吃。

so that people have something to eat.

46 tau⁴⁴ mɔ³⁵ nɔ⁵². ŋtɦɔ³¹ ntaɯ²¹, mua⁵² nia²¹tai³³ zaɯ²¹tsi³⁵ .
得 饭 吃 和 那 有 岳母 岳父
get meal eat and that have mother-in-law father-in-law

接着，有岳母岳父。

Next are the mother-in-law and father-in-law.

47 nia⁵²tai³³   zaɯ²¹tsi³⁵ , ʑɦɔ³¹ tu³³ ntʂhai³³ ʔua³³ mu³³ ʐua³⁵ tsi³⁵
   岳母   岳父   是   个   女儿   (定标) 去   嫁   丈夫
   mother-in-law father-in-law COP CL daughter REL   go marry husband

岳母岳父是这个要出嫁的
They are the parents of

48 ntaɯ²¹ nɯ³³ nia²¹ thia⁵⁵ nɯ³³ tsi³⁵ . ɳtʃɦɔ³¹ ntaɯ²¹ , ʐua³⁵ mua⁵² nia²¹lɔ⁵⁵
   那   她   母亲 和   她   父亲   和   那   要   有   伯母
   that   3S mother and 3S father and   that   will have aunt

女儿的母亲和父亲。接着，要有伯母、
the girl who will get married. Then her aunts and

49 tsi³⁵lɔ⁵⁵ , nia²¹ntsaɯ²¹ tsi³⁵ntsaɯ²¹ , ʐua³⁵ tua⁵² kuŋ²¹ lu⁵⁵ tʂhuŋ⁵⁵ ntaɯ²¹ .
   伯父   姆姆   叔叔   要   来   共   个   婚事   那
   uncle   aunt   uncle   will come together CL marriage that

大伯、姆姆、叔叔，要来参加婚礼。
uncles will come to attend the wedding,

50 ʐua³⁵ mua⁵² nu³³ti⁵²nu³³kɯ³⁵ , mua⁵² nu³³mpaɯ³³ . nu³³mpaɯ³³ ʑɦɔ³¹
   要   有   兄弟哥兄弟弟   有   兄弟表   兄弟表   是
   will have brother   have brother cousin brother cousin COP

要有哥哥弟弟和堂哥堂弟，有表哥表弟。
as well as her brothers and cousins.

51 ʔi⁵⁵ tu³³ tʂen²¹tɕen³⁵ ŋɔ⁵⁵ tau⁴⁴ xɔ³⁵ ʔi⁵⁵ tuŋ⁵² tʂhuŋ⁵⁵ . ʐua³⁵tʂu²¹ mua⁵²
   一   个   正经   在   给   里   一   桌   婚事   要得   有
   one CL decent   be.located P   inside one table marriage should   have

表哥表弟是婚礼中的一个重要角色。
Cousins play important roles at wedding,

52 nu³³mpaɯ³³nu³³ti⁵² tɕɔ⁵² lɔ³³ phi²¹   tu³³ ɳtʃɦau³¹vau³⁵ , phi²¹   tu³³
   兄弟表兄弟哥   带   来   搭伴   个   男郎女婿   搭伴   个
   brother cousin brother bring come accompany CL man son-in-law accompany CL

tu⁵⁵ phi⁵²la⁵² ,
儿子 陪郎
son groomsman

（9）tu⁵⁵ʔd̪e⁵²nu²¹ n̪ɔ⁵⁵tau⁴⁴ xau³⁵ ke³⁵ʔua⁴⁴tʂhuŋ⁵⁵ 婚事人员

因为要有表哥表弟来和新郎搭伴，和伴郎搭伴，
because cousins accompany the bridegroom

53 ʐua³⁵tau⁴⁴ lɔ³³ mu³³ ʂi⁵⁵ ʐen²¹ ʔua⁴⁴ ʑaɯ²¹zi⁵² ʑaɯ²¹ʔd̪a⁵⁵ .
　　要得　　　来　　去　（相互缀）　认　　做　　姐夫/妹夫　　舅舅
　　should　　come　go　　RECP　　recognize make brother-in-law uncle

双方才能去认姐夫、妹夫、舅舅。
so that the bride and the bridegroom can confirm their kin relationships with brother-in-laws and uncles.

办婚事所需要的人员

办婚事所需要的人员，在泰国这边，有下面这些。

大媒公，是要去唱婚嫁歌谈婚事、谈聘金聘礼的人。大媒公要陪新郎去他的未婚妻家，商量聘金聘礼或是去落实举办婚礼各种事宜。

下一个人，是二媒公。二媒公是来协助大媒公完成婚礼所有事情的人。

下一个人，是婚事主管。这个婚事主管是婚事的管事。这个婚事管事，他要去要监督婚事中的各种事宜，督促媒公去商量聘礼聘金，去带领大家做事，去安排打杂的人做饭做菜给大家吃。管这些事情的这个人就是管事。当婚礼结束的时候，他要去预备肉和肋骨，去预备各种物品，拿去答谢帮忙办婚事的这些人。

新郎，新郎是娶妻子的人。

新娘，新娘是在婚礼中要出嫁的那个女孩。

下一个人，是伴郎。伴郎是去给新郎做伴的人。新郎叩拜，伴郎要跟着叩拜。新郎去杀猪，伴郎也要跟着去帮忙杀猪。

下一个人，是伴娘。伴娘也是做伴的人。这个人要去陪伴新娘。新娘到哪里，这个伴娘她要跟着到哪里。新娘睡哪里，这个伴娘要跟着新娘睡哪里。直到整个婚礼结束新娘回到新郎家里。

下一个人，是管钱的人。管钱的人也是倒酒给男女双方媒公的人。这个管钱的人，当婚礼中饭菜上齐要吃饭的时候，他要去给客人倒酒。做上面这些事的人就是管钱的人。

下一个人，是端茶盘的人。端茶盘的人是添菜的人。办婚礼的时候，有一些亲戚和一些客人正好坐满一桌，这个端茶盘的人要去给这桌人上菜，让菜碗不空，让大家有菜下饭、有吃有喝。

下一个人，是厨子。厨子是做饭的人。得要有厨子去做饭，大家才有菜有饭吃。

接着，有岳母岳父。岳母岳父是这个要出嫁的女儿的母亲和父亲。

接着，要有伯母、大伯、婶婶、叔叔，要来参加婚礼。

要有哥哥弟弟和堂哥堂弟，有表哥表弟。表哥表弟是婚礼中的一个重要角色。因为要有表哥表弟来和新郎搭伴，和伴郎搭伴，双方才能去认姐夫、妹夫、舅舅。

Marriage customs

In Thailand, personnel needed for marriage are as follows.

First is the big matchmaker, the one who sings wedding songs and negotiates about marriage affairs and the bride price. The matchmaker would accompany the bridegroom to his fiancée's house to discuss about the bride price or conduct all kinds of wedding matters.

Next is the second matchmaker, who gives assistance to the big matchmaker to handle all wedding matters.

Next one is the marriage supervisor, who is the manager of wedding affairs. He manages all the marriage affairs and supervises the matchmaker in discussing the bride price, and leads people to do their work and arranges people who do odd jobs to cook for all. The one who is responsible for these things is the supervisor. When the wedding is over, he should go to prepare some meat, ribs and other things to acknowledge the people who helped with the wedding.

The bridegroom is the one who marries the wife.

The bride is the girl who will get married at wedding.

Next is the groomsman, who will accompany the bridegroom at the wedding. He should also follow alongside the bridegroom as he worships. If the bridegroom goes to butcher pigs, the groomsman should also offer help.

Next is the bridesmaid, who will accompany the bride at the wedding. She would go everywhere the bride goes. She would also sleep where the bride sleep. The bridesmaid should always follow the bride till the wedding ends and the bride gets back to bridegroom's house.

Next is the person who manages the money. He is also the one who serves alcohol for the matchmakers of both parties. He will serve guests alcohol when all the dishes are all served at the wedding feast and people are about to eat. The person who does things above is the one who manages money.

Next is the person who carries the tea tray and who serves dishes. At the wedding, when the table is exactly full of relatives and guests, the one who carries tea tray should serve dishes for them and don't let the dishes get empty, so everyone has enough to eat and drink.

Next is the cook, who cooks the meals for all so that people have something to eat.

Next are the mother-in-law and father-in-law. They are the parents of the girl who will get married. Then her aunts and uncles will also come to attend the wedding.

Moreover, there are also brothers and cousins, who play important roles at the wedding. Cousins accompany the bridegroom, so the bride and bridegroom can confirm their kin relationships with brother-in-laws and uncles.

(10) ken⁵⁵kɯ²¹经历

经历
experience

1 ŋɔ⁵⁵ʐuŋ⁴⁴, ku³⁵ zɦɔ³¹ ka⁵⁵ʐen⁵⁵tɕhia⁵²ʐuŋ⁴⁴, sen²¹ m̥uŋ⁵⁵ wa⁵²,
　大家好　　我　是　嘎英才融　　　　姓　苗族　王
　be.good　　1S　COP　Gayingcairong　　last name　Hmong　Wang
大家好，我是嘎英才融，我姓王，
Hello everyone, my name is Gayingcairong; my last name is Wang.

2 lɔ³³ zɦɔ³¹ sen²¹ wa⁵² ŋtɕua⁵⁵. ku³⁵ ŋɔ⁵⁵ tau⁴⁴ thai⁵⁵te⁵⁵, ŋɔ⁵⁵
　也　是　姓　王　家　　我　在　给　泰国　　　在
　CONJ COP last name Wang home　1S be.located P Thailand be.located
也称王姓。我住在泰国，
or my family name is Wang. I live in Thailand,

3 lu⁵⁵ sen³⁵ tɕhin⁴⁴lai⁴⁴. ta²¹ʂi²¹nɔ⁴⁴ ku³⁵ mua⁵² plau⁵⁵ tɕfiau³¹
　个　省　　清莱　　　现在　　　我　有　四　　十
　CL province Chiang Rai now　　1S have four ten
在清莱府。现在我四十五岁，
in Chiang Rai Province. Now I'm forty-five years old,

4 tʂi⁵⁵ ɕuŋ³³, ku³⁵ ʔua⁴⁴ xau⁵²lɯ²¹ tau⁴⁴ xau³⁵ tʂen²¹fɯ³⁵, ŋɔ⁵⁵ tau⁴⁴
　五　年　　我　做　活路　　　给　里　政府　　　在　给
　five year 1S make way to survive P inside government be.located P
我在政府里工作。
I work in the government.

5 xau³⁵ lu⁵⁵ ʐe⁵² ʐɔ³³ zɦɔ³¹ tshi²¹ khɔ⁴⁴ ʐe⁵² ʐɔ³³. ku³⁵ ʐua³⁵ pia³⁵
　里　个　村　村　是　建设　医治　村　村　我　要　摆
　inside CL village village COP construct heal village village 1S should put

(10) ken⁵⁵kɯ²¹ 经历

在村里的工作是管治村庄。
I'm responsible for village management and government.

6 mi⁴⁴　n̥tʂi³³　ku³⁵　le⁴⁴　ken⁵⁵kɯ²¹，xai³³　tia³³　ku³⁵　qɔ³³　tɕʰɯ³¹　lɔ³³，
　 小　　点　　我　 的　 经历　　　说　　道　　 我　 从　　 哪　　 来
　 little bit   1S   PRT experience   say COMP 1S from where come

我要讲一些我的经历，说我从哪里来，
I'm going to talk about my experience, about where I come from;

7 ku³⁵　nia²¹　ku³⁵　tsi³⁵　xu⁴⁴　li⁴⁴tɕa³³，ʂaɯ³⁵　ʔdaɯ³³　ʂɔ⁵²　qa⁵⁵　ʂai⁵⁵　ʂe⁵⁵，
　 我　　母亲　　我　 父亲　 叫　　怎么　　　大家　　　　　 瞧　　后面　 看　　看
　 1S   mother 1S   father call   how   people   look behind see   see

我的父母叫什么，大家看看
what the name of my parents are; you can see

8 ku³⁵　lu⁵⁵　nen⁵²　zuŋ⁴⁴　li⁴⁴tɕa³³．ku³⁵　zɦo³¹　ʔi⁵⁵　tu³³　mi⁴⁴　n̥ua²¹　m̥uŋ⁵⁵，
　 我　 个　 生活　　好　　 怎么　　　我　 是　　一　 个　 小　　 孩子　 苗族
　 1S   CL   life   good   how   1S   COP   one   CL little   kid   Hmong

我的生活怎么样。我是一个苗族孩子，
how's my life. I am a Hmong child;

9 zɦu³¹　ŋɔ⁵⁵　tau⁴⁴　ʂa⁵⁵　lɔ³³tʂua³³　te⁵⁵，ku³⁵　zɦu³¹　tau⁴⁴　tʰau²¹　ɕuŋ⁴⁴　1972．
　 生　　在　　给　　边　　 老挝　　　 地　　我　 生　　给　　 时候　 年　　1972
　 born be.located P   side   Laos   land   1S   born   P   time   year   1972

我出生在老挝那边，我生于1972年。
I was born in Laos in 1972.

10 ku³⁵　mua⁵²　n̥u⁵⁵n̥ɦuŋ³¹　li⁴⁴　pe⁵⁵　ɕuŋ³³，lu⁵⁵　ʂi⁵²　xaɯ²¹　ntaɯ²¹
　 我　　有　　 年龄　　　　像　　三　　 年　　　 个　 时候　　 那
　 1S   have   age   be.like three year   CL   time   that

当我三岁的时候，那个时候在打战，
When I was three years old, it was a time of war;

11 mua⁵²tsɔ³⁵mua⁵²tɕɦɔ³¹．ʔua⁴⁴　tsɔ³⁵　ʔua⁴⁴　tɕɦɔ³¹　ŋɔ⁵⁵　tau⁴⁴　ʂa⁵⁵　lɔ³³　tʂua³³，sɯ³³li⁴⁴
　 有　　老虎　有　　士兵　　　做　　 老虎　 做　　 士兵　　 在　　给　　 边　　老挝　　 像
　 have tiger have soldier   make tiger   make soldier be.located P   side   Laos   be.like

在老挝那边打仗,
Laos was at war;

12 zɦɔ³¹ mua⁵² tɕɔ³⁵ nɦen³¹ ʔa³³ma³³li³³ka³³ , nɦen³¹ faɯ⁵⁵ki³³ ,
   是　　有　　些　　　人　　美国　　　　　　人　　法国
   COP　have　CL.PL　human　America　　　　human　France

有美国人、法国人,
there were Americans and French;

13 laɯ³⁵ tua⁵² ʔua⁴⁴ tsɔ³⁵ ʔua⁴⁴ tɬɔ³¹ ŋɔ⁵⁵ ʈau⁴⁴ ʂa⁵⁵ te⁵⁵tɕɦaɯ³³ lɔ³³tʂua³³ .
   他们　来　　做　　老虎　做　　士兵　在　　　给　　边　　地方　　　　老挝
   3PL　come　make　tiger　make　soldier　be.located　P　side　place　　Laos

他们来老挝打战。
they came to Laos to fight.

14 lu⁵⁵ ʂi⁵²xaɯ²¹ ŋua²¹xua³⁵ zɦu³¹ ku³⁵ ntaɯ²¹ , pe⁵⁵ tɕɔ³⁵ m̥uŋ⁵⁵ fai⁵⁵
   个　　时候　　　刚刚　　　生　　我　　那　　　我们　些　　苗族　　分开
   CL　time　　　just　　　born　1S　that　　1PL　CL.PL　Hmong　separate

我刚出生的那个时候,我们苗族分为两帮。
The time when I was just born, we Hmong people was divided into two groups.

15 ʔɔ⁵⁵ pa⁵⁵ . pe⁵⁵ mua⁵² ʔi⁵⁵ tɕɔ³⁵ m̥uŋ⁵⁵ mu³³ ɳʈɦɔ³¹ ʈau⁴⁴ xua⁵⁵ tai³³
   二　帮　　我们　有　　一　些　　苗族　　去　　和　　给　　皇帝
   two　faction　1PL　have　one　CL.PL　Hmong　go　and　P　emperor

我们有一些苗族加入老挝王国军队,
Some of us Hmong people joined the Lao Royal Army,

16 mplɦɔ³¹ tɬɔ³¹ , tɕɔ³⁵ ɳʈɦɔ³¹ xua⁵⁵ tai³³ mplɦɔ³¹ tɬɔ³¹ ntaɯ²¹ zɦɔ³¹ wa⁵²pɔ³⁵
   老挝　头　　些　　和　　皇帝　　老挝　头　　那　　是　　王宝
   Laos　head　CL.PL　and　emperor　Laos　head　that　COP　Wang Bao

老挝王国军队的领袖是王宝,
of which the leader was Wang Bao,

17 tɕɔ⁵² xau⁴⁴ , ɳʈɦɔ³¹ ʈau⁴⁴ tʂen²¹fu³⁵ ʔa³³ma³³li³³ka³³ . mua⁵² ʔi⁵⁵
   带　　头　　和　　给　　政府　　　美国　　　　　　有　　一
   lead　head　and　P　government　America　　　　have　one

老挝王国军队受美国政府领导。
and the troop was led by the U.S. government.

18 tɕhɔ³¹ tua⁵² kuŋ²¹tʂha²¹ , lɔ³³ zɦɔ³¹ mu³³ ɳʈɦɔ³¹ tɕɔ³⁵ khɔ³³mɔ³³le³⁵si²¹tɔ⁵² ,
   头   来   共产党   也   是   去   和   些   共产党
   head come Communist Party CONJ COP go and CL.PL Communist Party

老挝苗族有一部分加入共产党，也就是跟随共产党，
Part of the Hmong in Laos joined the Communist Party, namely followed the Communist Party;

19 sɯ³³li⁴⁴ zɦɔ³¹ fai³⁵ʔda⁵²lau⁵²mplia⁵²zɔ⁵⁵ ,
   像   是   菲黄罗陪幺
   be.like COP Feihuangluopeiyao

例如菲黄罗陪幺、
such as Feihuangluopeiyao ,

20 za⁵²thɔ⁵²tu⁵⁵ , thia⁵⁵ tɕuŋ⁵⁵ tɕuŋ⁵⁵ len⁵² . lu⁵⁵ ɕi⁵²xaɯ²¹ thau²¹ tɕɔ³⁵
   杨陶朵   和   多   多   位   个   时候   时候   些
   Yang Taoduo and RDUP~many CL CL time time CL.PL

杨陶朵等多位苗族人。那个时候，老挝共产党
Yang Taoduo and many other Hmong people. At that time, the Communist Party of Laos

21 ɳʈɦɔ³¹ ɕi⁵⁵ntau³³ɕi⁵⁵tua⁴⁴ ntaɯ²¹ , tɕɔ³⁵ ʔua³³ ŋ⁵⁵ tau⁴⁴ tɕhɔ³¹
   和   (相互缀)打(相互缀) 杀   那   些   (定标) 在   给   头
   and RECP fight RECP kill   that CL.PL REL be.located P head

xua⁵⁵tai³³
皇帝
 emperor

和老挝王国军队打仗，老挝王国军队
was at war with the Laos Royal Army, and the Royal Army

22 mplɦɔ³¹ ntaɯ²¹ tau⁴⁴ ʂɯ⁴⁴ tɕɔ³⁵ ɳʈɦɔ³¹ kuŋ²¹tʂha²¹ . zɦɔ³¹ li⁴⁴ntaɯ²¹ ,
   老挝   那   得   输   些   和   共产党   是   像那
   Laos   that   get   lose CL.PL and   Communist Party COP be.like that

输给了老挝共产党军队。因此，
lost the war to the troops of the Communist Party of Laos. Therefore,

23 tʂen²¹fɯ³⁵ ʔa³³ma³³li³³ka³³ zua³⁵tau⁴⁴ thi²¹ tɔ³⁵ mu³³ ŋɔ⁵⁵ nɯ³³
   政府   美国   要得   退   回   去   在   它
   government America   should   retreat back go   be.located 3S

美国军队只得撤回自己的国家，
the U.S. military had to retreat back to their country;

24 lu⁵⁵ te⁵⁵tɕhaɯ³³, faɯ⁵⁵ki³³ lɔ³³ zua³⁵tau⁴⁴ thi²¹ tɔ³⁵ mu³³ faɯ⁵⁵ki³³ lu⁵⁵
   个   地方   法国   也   要得   退   回   去   法国   个
   CL   place   France   CONJ should   retreat back go   France   CL

法国军队也只得撤回自己的国家。
the French military also had to retreat back to their country.

25 te⁵⁵tɕhaɯ³³ . lu⁵⁵ tɕai⁵² ntaɯ²¹, ʔa³³ma³³li³³ka³³ thi²¹ tu⁵⁵ŋtfiɔ³¹ xau³⁵
   地方   个   时间   那   美国   退   士兵   里
   place   CL   time   that   America   retreat soldier   inside

那个时候，美国从老挝撤军
At that time, the U.S. millitary retreated from Laos

26 mplfiɔ³¹ tɔ³⁵ qa⁵⁵ mu³³ ʔa³³ma³³li³³ka³³ . thau²¹ pe⁵⁵ tɕɔ³⁵ nia²¹ tɕɔ³⁵ tsi³⁵
   老挝   回   去   美国   时候   我们 些   母亲   些   父亲
   Laos   back go   America   time   1PL   CL.PL mother CL.PL father

回国。在两军打仗的时候，
back to America. When the two sides were fighting,

27 ŋɔ⁵⁵ ʈau⁴⁴ lu⁵⁵ tɕai⁵² ʔua⁴⁴ tʂɔ³⁵ ʔua⁴⁴ tfiɔ³¹ ntaɯ²¹, laɯ³⁵ zua³⁵tau⁴⁴
   在   给   个   时间   做   老虎   做   士兵   那   他们   要得
   be.located P   CL   time   make tiger make   soldier that   3PL   should

我们的父母们，他们只得
our parents had to

28 tau²¹ ntaɯ²¹ tsɔ⁵² ke³⁵ ʔua⁴⁴ tʂɔ³⁵ ʔua⁴⁴ tfiɔ³¹ khia³⁵ lɔ³³ ʈau⁴⁴ thai⁵⁵ te⁵⁵,
   出   那   条   路   做   老虎   做   士兵   跑   来   给   泰国   地
   out that   CL   road   make tiger make   soldier run   come P   Thailand land

从战争国逃往泰国，
run away from the war to Thailand,

(10) ken⁵⁵kɯ²¹经历

29 thia⁵² li⁴⁴ tɕɔ⁵²　　　 pe⁵⁵ tɕɔ³⁵ me⁴⁴ ŋua²¹ me⁴⁴　　 me⁴⁴ lɔ³³ mu³³ ʈau⁴⁴
　　才　 带　　　　　　 我们 些　 小　 孩子　 小　　　 小　 来　 去　 给
　　just　 take.along　 1PL CL.PL little kid　 RDUP~little　 come go　 P

才带着我们这些小孩来泰国。
so they tooks us little kids to Thailand.

30 thai⁵⁵　 te⁵⁵　. ku³⁵ nia²¹　 ku³⁵ tsi³⁵ ʔua⁴⁴ nte⁵² zua³⁵ lɔ³³ ŋɔ⁵⁵
　　泰国　　 地　　 我　 母亲　　 我　 父亲　 做　 前面　 要　 来　 在
　　Thailand land　 1S mother　 1S father make front will come be.located

我们的父母在来
then I will come back to the previous topic. Before my parents

31 ʈau⁴⁴ saɯ³³na⁵²pu³³we³³ ntaɯ²¹ , ku³⁵ nia²¹　 ku³⁵ tsi³⁵　 laɯ³⁵
　　给　 沙耶武里　　　　　　　 那　　 我　 母亲　　 我　 父亲　　 他们
　　P　 Xayaburi　　　　　　　 that　 1S mother　　 1S father　 3PL

老挝沙耶武里省之前，
came to Xayaburi Province of Laos,

32 zɦu³¹ ŋɔ⁵⁵　　 ʈau⁴⁴ ʂa⁵⁵ ʔu⁵⁵lu³³mu³³sai³³ , lɔ³³ zɦɔ³¹ lu⁵⁵ ʈuŋ⁵⁵ laɯ³⁵ xu⁴⁴
　　生　　 在　　　 给　 边　 乌多姆赛　　　　　 也　 是　 个　 山　　 他们 叫
　　born be.located P　 side Oudomxay　　　　 CONJ COP CL mountain 3PL call

我的父母生在老挝乌多姆赛省的一座山上，这座山他们叫作
my parents were born in a mountain in Oudomxay Province of Laos, which was called

33 ʔua⁴⁴ ʈuŋ⁵⁵phɯ³³thu³³ . ŋkaɯ²¹ ŋɔ⁵⁵　 lɔ⁵⁵　 tua⁵² ŋkaɯ²¹ ʂi⁵⁵zua³⁵ , ŋkaɯ²¹
　　做　 山　 普陀　　　　　　 对　 在　　 长大　 来　 对　　 (相互缀)　 要　 对
　　make mountain Putuo　 couple be.located grow up come couple　 RECP will couple

普陀山。他俩在那里长大在那里结婚，
the Putuo Mountain. They grew up and married there,

34 ʂi⁵⁵zua³⁵ ʈau⁴⁴ ntaɯ²¹ lu⁵⁵ sen³⁵　 ʔu⁵⁵lu³³mu³³sai³³ , ma²¹ li⁴⁴ khia³⁵ tʂɔ³⁵tɕɦɔ³¹
　　(相互缀) 要　 给　 那　 个　 省　　 乌多姆赛　　　　　 慢　 才　 跑　　 老虎士兵
　　RECP will P　 that CL province Oudomxay　　　　　 slow just run　 tiger soldier

他俩在乌多姆赛省结婚。后来由于逃避战争
they married in Oudomxay Province. Later, in order to escape from war,

35 lɔ³³ mu³³ ʈau⁴⁴ s̪a⁵⁵ xue⁵⁵sai²¹ , tɔ³⁵ khia³⁵ lɔ³³ mu³³ ʈau⁴⁴ lau⁴⁴phua⁵⁵pa³³ ,
　　来　　去　　给　　边　　会晒　　　回　　跑　　来　　去　　给　　朗勃拉邦
　　come　go　P　side　Houayxay　back　run　come　go　P　Luang Prabang

才来到老挝博胶省会晒市，又跑到琅勃拉邦山，
they came to Houayxay, Bokeo Province of Laos, and then came to Luang Prabang Mountain,

36 lɔ³³ ŋɔ⁵⁵ ʈau⁴⁴ ntaɯ²¹ ʈuŋ⁵⁵ʔdu⁵⁵ . ma²¹ li⁴⁴ khia³⁵
　　来　　在　　给　　那　　山黑　　　　慢　才　跑
　　come　be.located　P　that　mountain black　slow　just　run

住在黑山。
and lived in Black Mountain.

37 ntaɯ²¹ ʈuŋ⁵⁵ ʔdu⁵⁵ lɔ³³ mu³³ ʈau⁴⁴ ntaɯ²¹ saɯ³³na⁵²pu³³we³³ , l̪a⁴⁴
　　那　　山　　黑　　来　　去　　给　　那　　沙耶武里　　　　　　　跨
　　that　mountain　black　come　go　P　that　Xayabori　cross

从黑山跑到沙耶武里省，
Then they migrated to Xayaburi from Black Mountain;

38 ntaɯ²¹ saɯ³³na⁵²pu³³we³³ lɔ³³ ŋɔ⁵⁵ ntaɯ²¹ kia²¹te⁵⁵ , lu⁵⁵ zɔ³³
　　那　　沙耶武里　　　　　来　　在　　那　　界地　　　　个　村子
　　that　Xayaburi　come　be.located　that　boundary land　CL　village

住在沙耶武里省的一个边境村，这个村子
they lived in a border village in Xayaburi, which

39 ŋai⁵²ŋai²¹ . ʔua⁴⁴ nte⁵² ku³⁵ tsi³⁵ laɯ³⁵ lɔ³³ ŋɔ⁵⁵ ʈau⁴⁴ ntaɯ²¹ ʔu⁵⁵lu³³mu³³sai³³
　　岩爱　　　做　前面　我　父亲　他们　来　在　　给　那　乌多姆赛
　　Ngai'ai　make　front　1S　father　3PL　come　be.located　P　that　Oudomxay

叫岩爱村。我祖父母他们来乌多姆赛省之前，
was called Ngai'ai village. Before my grandparents came to Oudmxay Province,

40 ntaɯ²¹ , lɔ³³ ʑɔ³¹ ʑua³⁵ ʑɦu³¹ ku³⁵ nia²¹ thia⁵⁵ ku³⁵ tsi³⁵ ntaɯ²¹ .
　　那　　　也　是　要　生　我　母亲　和　我　父亲　那
　　that　CONJ　COP　will　born　1S　mother　and　1S　father　that

我的父母快要出生了。
my mother and father were almost about to be born.

(10) ken⁵⁵kɯ²¹经历

41 ku³⁵ ʑɦaɯ³¹ xu⁴⁴ ʔua⁴⁴ ʂau⁵⁵len⁵², ku³⁵ ʑɦaɯ³¹ thia⁵⁵ ku³⁵ pɦɔ³¹ laɯ³⁵
　　我　　爷　　叫　　做　　绍楞　　　　我　　爷　　和　　我　　奶奶　　他们
　　1S　grandpa call　do　Shaoleng　 1S　grandpa and　1S　grandma 3PL
我爷爷叫绍楞，我爷爷奶奶他们
My grandpa's name is Shaoleng; my grandparents

42 zɦɔ³¹ tɕɔ³⁵ khia³⁵ ŋɔ⁵⁵ tau⁴⁴ ʂa⁵⁵ phuŋ⁴⁴sa³³li³³, lɔ³³ mu³³ tau⁴⁴
　　是　　些　　跑　　在　　给　　边　　丰沙里　　　　来　　去　　给
　　COP　CL.PL run be.located P side Phongsali　　come go　P
从丰沙里省跑来的，跑到
run away from Phongsali Province to

43 ʂa⁵⁵ ʔu⁵⁵lu³³mu³³sai³³, ma²¹li⁴⁴ lɔ³³ mua⁵² ku³⁵ tsi³⁵. ku³⁵ ʑɦaɯ³¹
　　边　　乌多姆赛　　　　才　　来　　有　　我　　父亲　　我　　爷
　　side Oudomxay　　　　 just　come have　1S　father　1S　grandpa
乌多姆赛省，才生下我父亲。
Oudomxay Province and then gave birth to my father.

44 thia⁵⁵ ku³⁵ pɦɔ³¹ laɯ³⁵ ʔua⁴⁴nte⁵² zua³⁵ khia³⁵ lɔ³³ tʂhɯ²¹ tau⁴⁴
　　和　　我　　奶奶　　他们　做　　前面　　要　　跑　　来　　出　　给
　　and　1S　grandma 3PL do front　 will　run　come out　give
在我祖父母跑到
Before my grandparents came to

45 ntaɯ²¹ ʂa⁵⁵ phuŋ⁴⁴sa³³li³³, pe⁵⁵ tu³³ ʑɦaɯ³¹kuŋ⁵⁵ xu⁴⁴
　　那　　　边　　丰沙里　　　　我们　个　　爷公　　　　　叫
　　that　side Phongsali　　　 1PL　CL grandpa grandpa call
丰沙里省之前，我们的曾祖父
Phongsali Province, our great-grandfather's name

46 ua⁴⁴ ŋa⁵²ʂau³⁵, pe⁵⁵ tu³³ ʑɦaɯ³¹ʂua⁵⁵ xu⁴⁴ ʑɦaɯ³¹ tsuŋ⁵²tsɯ⁵⁵.
　　做　　岩绍　　　我们　个　　爷　　□　　叫　　爷　　棕邹
　　do　Ngashao　1PL　CL grandpa　　call grandpa Zongzou
叫岩绍，我们的高祖父叫棕邹。
was Ngashao; our great-great-grand father's name was Zongzou.

47 ma³³　　　　ku³⁵ tʂi³³ pau⁵⁵ ntaɯ²¹ ʐɦaɯ³¹ tsuŋ⁵²tsɯ⁵⁵ mu³³ tau⁴⁴ ntaɯ²¹
　　(转折连词)　我　不　知道　那　爷　棕邹　去　给　那
　　CONJ　　　1S　NEG　know　that　grandpa Zongzou　go　P　that

但是我不知道从高祖父棕邹到

But I don't know where the two generations of my great-great grand father Zongzou and

48 ʐɦaɯ³¹ ŋa⁵²ʂau³⁵ ʔɔ⁵⁵ tia²¹　　nɦien³¹ nɔ⁴⁴, nɯ³³ ŋɔ⁵⁵　　tau⁴⁴ ʂa⁵⁵ tɦɯ³¹
　爷　岩绍　两　代　人　这　他　在　给　边　哪
　grandpa Ngashao　two generation human this　3S　be.located P　side where

曾祖父岩绍这两代人，他们从哪里来。

great-grand father Ngashao came from.

49 lɔ³³　. ua⁴⁴nte⁵² laɯ³⁵ zua³⁵ kʰia³⁵ lɔ³³　tʂʰɯ²¹ tau⁴⁴ ntaɯ²¹ ʂa⁵⁵
　来　做 前面　他们　要　跑　来　出　给　那　边
　come　do front　3PL　will　run　come out　P　that　side

在他们跑来丰沙里省之前，

Before they came to Phongsali Province,

50 pʰuŋ⁴⁴sa³³li³³ , ma³³　　ku³⁵ ntʂɦien³¹ xai³³ tia³³　ʐɦaɯ³¹ tsuŋ⁵²tsɯ⁵⁵
　丰沙里　　(转折连词)　我　相信　说　道　爷　棕邹
　Phongsali　CONJ　　1S　believe　say　COMP　grandpa Zongzou

我相信高祖棕邹

but I believe that my great-great grandfather Zongzou

51 tʰia⁵⁵ ʐɦaɯ³¹ ŋa⁵²ʂau³⁵ laɯ³⁵ tɕɔ³⁵ , laɯ³⁵ zua³⁵ ŋɔ⁵⁵　tau⁴⁴ ʂa⁵⁵
　和　爷　岩绍　他们　些　他们　要　在　给　边
　and　grandpa Ngashao　3PL　CL.PL　3PL　will　be.located P　side

和曾祖岩绍他们，他们住在

and great-grandfather Ngashao were living in

52 zɯ³³na³³ te⁵⁵tɕɦaɯ³³ , laɯ³⁵ ma²¹ kʰia³⁵ lɔ³³　mu³³ tau⁴⁴ ʂa⁵⁵
　越南　地方　他们　慢　跑　来　去　给　边
　Vietnam　place　3PL　slow　run　come go　P　side

越南那边，后来他们才跑到丰沙里省。

Vietnam; only later did they come to Phongsali Province.

(10) ken⁵⁵kɯ²¹ 经历

53 phuŋ⁴⁴sa³³li³³ . thau²¹ khia³⁵ lɔ³³ mu³³ tau⁴⁴ ʂa⁵⁵ phuŋ⁴⁴sa³³li³³ ,
丰沙里　　　时候　跑　来　去　给　边　丰沙里
Phongsali　　time　run　come　go　P　side　Phongsali
他们跑到丰沙里省的时候，
It was not until they came to Phongsali Province

54 ma²¹li⁴⁴ lɔ³³ zɦu³¹ ku³⁵ zɦaɯ³¹ ʂau⁵⁵len⁵² . ʂa⁵⁵ phuŋ⁴⁴sa³³li³³ ntaɯ²¹
才　　来　生　我　爷　绍楞　　　边　丰沙里　　那
just　come　born　1S　grandpa　Shaoleng　side　Phongsali　that
才生下我爷爷绍楞。丰沙里那边
did they give birth to my grandpa Shaoleng. In Phongsali Province,

55 mua⁵²tʂɔ³⁵mua⁵²tɕɦɔ³¹ , pe⁵⁵ zɦaɯ³¹ ʂau⁵⁵len⁵² ma²¹li⁴⁴ khia³⁵
有 老虎 有 士兵　　我们 爷　　绍楞　　　才　　跑
have tiger have soldier　1PL　grandpa　Shaoleng　just　run
有战事，我们的爷爷绍楞才跑
there was war; therefore our grandpa Shaoleng escaped to

56 lɔ³³ ntaɯ²¹ ʔu⁵⁵lu³³mu³³sai²¹ , ma²¹li⁴⁴ lɔ³³ zɦu³¹ ku³⁵ tsi³⁵ .
来　那　　乌多姆赛　　　　才　　来　生　我　父亲
come that　Oudomxay　　　just　come　born　1S　father
来乌多姆赛省，才生下我爸爸。
Oudomxay, only then could they give birth to my father.

57 ku³⁵ tsi³⁵ xu⁴⁴ ʔua⁴⁴ thai⁵⁵ .
我　父亲　叫　做　泰
1S　father　call　do　Tai
我爸爸叫泰。
My father's name is Tai.

58 thau²¹ zɦu³¹ tau⁴⁴ ku³⁵ tsi³⁵ ntaɯ²¹, nɯ³³ mua⁵² tʂɔ³⁵tɕɦɔ³¹ ʔua⁴⁴
时候　生　得　我　父亲　那　　它　有　老虎士兵　　做
time　born　get　1S　father　that　3S　have　tiger soldier　make
生我父亲的那个时候战事频繁，
It was always war when my father was born,

59 ntu⁴⁴ʐu³³ , ma²¹li⁴⁴ khia³⁵ lɔ³³ mu³³ ʈau⁴⁴ xue⁵⁵sai³³ . xue⁵⁵sai³³ lɔ³³
　(频繁状)　　才　　跑　　来　去　　给　　会晒　　　　会晒　　来
　frequently　just　run　come　go　P　Houayxay　Houayxay　come

才跑到会晒。从会晒
so they escaped to Houayxay. Then they escaped to

60 mu³³ ʈau⁴⁴ lau⁴⁴phua⁵⁵pa³³ , khia³⁵ ntaɯ²¹ lau⁴⁴phua⁵⁵pa³³ lɔ³³
　去　　给　　朗勃拉邦　　　　跑　　那　　朗勃拉邦　　　来
　go　P　Luang Prabang　run　that　Luang Prabang　come

跑来琅勃拉邦山，从琅勃拉邦山
Luang Prabang Mountain from Houayxay, and then

61 mu³³ ʈau⁴⁴ saɯ³³na⁵²pu³³we³³ . lu⁵⁵ ʂi⁵²xaɯ²¹ ntaɯ²¹ ku³⁵ tʂi³³ pau⁵⁵
　去　　给　　沙耶武里　　　　个　时候　　那　　我　　不　　知道
　go　P　Xayaburi　　CL　time　that　1S　NEG　know

跑到沙耶武里省。那个时候我不知道
moved to Xayaburi Province. I didn't know at that time

62 lau³⁵ khia³⁵ ʔi⁵⁵ qhɔ³⁵ mu³³ ʈau⁴⁴ ʔi⁵⁵ qhɔ³⁵ nte³⁵ mpau²¹li⁴⁴tɕa³³ , lɔ³³
　他们　跑　　一　处　　去　给　　一　处　　长　　怎样　　　　或
　3PL　run　one　place　go　P　one　place　long　how　　or

他们在一个地方住了多久才跑到另一个地方，
how long they lived in one place before they moved to another place,

63 zɦo³¹ ŋo⁵⁵ ʔi⁵⁵ qhɔ³⁵ tɕhaɯ⁴⁴ nte³⁵ mpau²¹li⁴⁴tɕa³³ . we²¹ ʈau⁴⁴ qhɔ³⁵
　是　　在　　一　处　地方　长　　怎样　　　因为　给　处
　COP　be.located　one　place　place　long　how　　because　P　place

或者说在一个地方住多久。
or how long they lived in one place.

64 thau²¹ nte⁵² tʂen²¹ tʂi³³ tau⁴⁴ zɦo³¹ ku³⁵ . ta⁵⁵ʂi³³ ʈaɯ³³li⁴⁴ ken⁵⁵kɯ²¹
　时候　前面　还　　不　得　生　我　　但是　　根据　　　历史
　time　before　still　NEG　get　born　1S　but　according to　history

因为在那之前还没有生我。但是，根据
It is because I wasn't born yet at that time. However, according to

(10) ken⁵⁵kɯ²¹经历　　　　155

65 ʔua³³　　ku³⁵　pɦo³¹　sau⁵⁵len⁵²　tau⁴⁴　tha²¹　ṭau⁴⁴　ku³⁵,　nɯ³³　xai³³　li⁴⁴no⁴⁴
　（定标）　我　　奶奶　　绍楞　　　得　　　讲　　给　　我　　她　　说　　像这
　REL　　　1S　grandma　Shaoleng　get　　tell　　P　　1S　　3S　say　be.like this
我的绍楞奶奶给我讲的家史，根据她所讲的事情
the family history, my grandma Shaoleng told me, according to things she said,

66 thia⁵⁵　nɯ³³　tɕo⁵²　　ku³⁵　mu³³　sai⁵⁵　tɕo³⁵　qu⁵⁵te⁵⁵qu⁵⁵tɕhaɯ⁴⁴　ʔua³³　thau²¹
　和　　　她　　带　　　我　　去　　看　　些　　　旧地　旧地方　　　　　（定标）时候
　and　　3S　take.along　1S　　go　　look　CL.PL　old place old place　REL　　time
和她带我去看过的以前他们住过的
and the old places where they once lived, which she showed us,

67 ʔu⁵⁵　　laɯ³⁵　ŋo⁵⁵,　　ku³⁵　ɳʈʂɦien³¹　xai³³　tia³³　ʑɦaɯ³¹　tsuŋ⁵²tsɯ⁵⁵
　以前　　他们　　在　　　我　　　相信　　　说　　道　　　爷　　　　棕邹
　before　3PL　be.located　1S　believe　　say　COMP　grandpa　Zongzou
老地方，我相信高祖棕邹
I believe that my great-great grandfather Zongzou

thia⁵⁵　ʑɦaɯ³¹　ŋa⁵²sau³⁵　laɯ³⁵　thau²¹nte⁵²　ŋo⁵⁵　　tau⁴⁴　sa⁵⁵　zɯ³³na³³　te⁵⁵tɕhaɯ³³.
和　　　爷　　　岩绍　　　　他们　　时候前面　　在　　　给　　边　　越南　　　地方
and　grandpa Ngashao　3PL　time front　be.located　P　side　Vietnam　place
和曾祖岩绍他们以前住在越南。
and my great-grandfather Ngashao lived in Vietnam before.

68 thau²¹　lu⁵⁵　ʂi⁵²xau²¹　ʑɦiu³¹　ku³⁵　ŋo⁵⁵　　tau⁴⁴　ntaɯ²¹　lu⁵⁵　zo³³　ʔdai⁵²na³⁵,
　时候　　个　　时候　　　生　　　我　　在　　　给　　　那　　　个　　村子　奈娘
　time　CL　time　　born　1S　be.located　P　　that　CL　village　Nainiang
我出生在
I was born in

69 lu⁵⁵　maŋ³³phaŋ³³,　sen³⁵　saɯ³³na⁵²pu³³we³³　ntaɯ²¹.
　个　　芒平　　　　　省　　　沙耶武里　　　　　那
　Cl　Mangping　　province　Xayaburi　　　　　that
沙耶武里省芒平县奈娘村。
Nainiang village of Mangping County, Xayaburi Province.

70 ku³⁵ ʐɦu³¹ ɕuŋ⁴⁴ ɕa⁴⁴ ʔɔ⁵⁵ . ku³⁵ mua⁵² ŋu⁵⁵ŋɦuŋ³¹ li⁴⁴ pe⁵⁵ ɕuŋ³³ ,
我　生　年　七　二　我　有　年龄　　像　三　年
1S　born　year　seven　two　1S　have　age　　be.like　three　year

我生于1972年。我三岁时，

I was born in 1972. When I was three years old,

71 ɕuŋ⁴⁴ ɕa⁴⁴ tʂi⁵⁵ tɕɔ³⁵ tɕɦɔ³¹ lɔ⁵² xen³⁵ . thau²¹ lu⁵⁵ ʂi⁵²xaɯ²¹
年　七　五　些　士兵　大　很　　时候　个　时候
year　seven　five　CL.PL　soldier　big　very　time　CL　time

1975年战争很激烈。当

the war in 1975 was very fierce. When

72 ku³⁵ mua⁵² i⁵⁵ ɕuŋ³³ , ku³⁵ nia²¹ tau⁴⁴ ta³³ ʂi²¹ nen⁵² , tɕai³³ tʂua³³ mua⁵²
我　有　一　年　　我　母亲　得　完　世　　生活　就　只　有
1S　have　one　year　1S　mother　get　finish　lifetime　life　DM　only　have

我一岁的时候，我母亲去世了，就只剩下

I was one year old, my mother passed away, leaving

73 ku³⁵ , ku³⁵ tsi³⁵ , ku³⁵ pɦɔ³¹ , ku³⁵ ʐɦaɯ³¹ sɯ⁵⁵ . pe⁵⁵ tʂe³⁵ nɦen³¹ mua⁵²
我　　我　父亲　我　奶奶　　我　爷　　仅仅　我们　家　人　有
1S　1S　father　1S　grandma　1S　grandpa　only　1PL　family　human　have

我、我爸爸、我奶奶、我爷爷。我们家有

me, my father, my grandma and grandpa. We have

74 plau⁵⁵ len⁵² . lu⁵⁵ ʂi⁵²xaɯ²¹ thau²¹ ɕa⁴⁴ tɕau²¹ tʂi⁵⁵ ntaɯ²¹ , lu⁵⁵ tʂi⁵⁵ li⁴⁴ᐟ³³ ,
四　位　　个　时候　　时候　七　十　五　那　　个　五　月
four　CL　CL　time　time　seven　ten　five　that　CL　five　month

四口人。在1975年5月，

four family members. In May 1975,

75 tɕɔ³⁵ tɕɦɔ³¹ ntaɯ²¹ ʔa³³ma³³li³³ka³³ thia⁵⁵ mplɦɔ³¹ tau⁴⁴ ʂi⁵⁵ntau³³ʂi⁵⁵tua⁴⁴
些　士兵　那　美国　　　　和　老挝　得　(相互缀)打 (相互缀)打
CL.PL　soldier　that　America　and　Laos　get　RECP　fight　RECP　fight

美国和老挝打得很惨烈，

the war between America and Laos was very fierce;

(10) ken⁵⁵kɯ²¹ 经历　　　　　　　　　　　　　　157

76　ŋ̊a³⁵　　xen³⁵．ʔa³³ma³³li³³ka³³　pia²¹　laɯ²¹，tɕai³³　ʔa³³ma³³li³³ka³³　ʐua³⁵tau⁴⁴　thi²¹　　taɯ²¹
　　重　　　很　　美国　　　　　　败　　了　　那么　　美国　　　　　　要得　　　　退　　　出
　　heavy　very　America　　　　lose　PRF　then　America　　　　should　　retreat　out
美国败了，美国得撤出去。
America lost the war so they took their army out.

77　mu³³．lu⁵⁵　ʂi⁵²xaɯ²¹　ntaɯ²¹，tɕɔ³⁵　ʔua³³　ŋɔ⁵⁵　　ntɬɦɔ³¹　tau⁴⁴
　　去　　个　　时候　　　那　　些　　（定标）在　　　　和　　　给
　　go　　CL　time　　　　that　CL.PL　REL　be.located　and　　P

ʔɖaɯ³³phaɯ³³va⁵²pɔ³⁵
　　　　王宝
　　　　Wang Bao

那个时候，王宝的军队
At that time, Wang Bao's military

78　thia⁵²　li⁴⁴　ʐua³⁵tau⁴⁴　taɯ²¹　ntaɯ²¹　lu⁵⁵　te⁵⁵tɕhaɯ³³　lɔ³³tʂua³³　tua⁵²
　　才　　　才　　要得　　　　出　　　那　　　个　　地方　　　　老挝　　　　来
　　just　just　should　　　out　　that　　CL　　place　　　　Laos　　　　come
才必须从老挝
had to pass by Laos

79　mu³³　ʂa⁵⁵　thai⁵⁵　te⁵⁵．pe⁵⁵　tɕɔ³⁵　m̥uŋ⁵⁵　ʔua³³　ŋɔ⁵⁵　tau⁴⁴　ʂa⁵⁵　mplɦɔ³¹
　　去　　边　　泰国　　地　　我们　些　　　苗族　　（定标）在　　　给　　边　　老挝
　　go　　side　Thailand　land　1PL　CL.PL　Hmong　REL　be.located　P　　side　Laos

te⁵⁵
地
land

去泰国。我们那些从老挝
to go to Thailand. Some of us Hmong people

80　ʔua³³　　nɯ³³　taɯ²¹　tua⁵²　tau⁴⁴　ʂa⁵⁵　thai⁵⁵　te⁵⁵，tɕɔ³⁵　ŋɔ⁵⁵　xau³⁵　qaɯ²¹te⁵⁵
　　（定标）他　　出　　　来　　　给　　边　　泰国　　地　　些　　在　　　里　　背　地
　　REL　　3S　　out　　come　　P　　side　Thailand　land　CL.PL　be.located　inside　back　land
来到泰国的苗族，有些原来是住在老挝北部
who came to Thailand from Laos originally lived in

81 sɯ³³li⁴⁴ we⁵⁵sa³³ , tɕai³³ nɯ³³ khia³⁵ taɯ²¹ tua⁵² tau⁴⁴ ʂa⁵⁵
    像   威桑   这样 他 跑 出 来 给 边
    be.like Ngwesaung this way 3S run out come P side

威桑，就跑来泰国欧巴丘孔。
Ngwesaung of Northern Laos; later they moved to Obaqiukong.

82 ʔaɯ³³paɯ³³tɕhaɯ³³khu²¹ thai⁵⁵ te⁵⁵ . tɕai³³ xɔ⁴⁴ ŋɔ⁵⁵ tau⁴⁴ ʂa⁵⁵
    欧巴丘孔   泰国 地 那么 又 在 给 边
    Obaqiukong   Thailand land then again be.located P side

有些原来住在
Some Hmong people who had once lived in

83 saɯ³³na⁵²pu³³we³³, tɕai³³ taɯ²¹ tua⁵² mu³³ tau⁴⁴ ʂa⁵⁵ na⁵² . tɕɔ³⁵ ʔua³³
    沙耶武里   这样 出 来 去 给 边 难 些 (定标)
    Xayaburi   this way out come go P side Nan CL.PL REL

老挝沙耶武里的苗族人，就跑到了泰国的难府。有些
Xayaburi of Laos moved to Nan Province of Thailand. Some

84 ŋɔ⁵⁵ tau⁴⁴ ʂa⁵⁵ lau⁴⁴phua⁵⁵pa³³ , saɯ³³qhua³³ , sen³⁵ xua²¹pha³³ ,
    在 给 边 朗勃拉邦   川圹   省 华潘
    be.located P side Luang Prabang Xiangkhoang province Houaphan

原来住在琅勃拉邦省、川圹省、华潘省的苗族人，
Hmong people who once lived in Luang Prabang, Xiengkhoang and Houaphan Province

85 mu³³ tau⁴⁴ ʂa⁵⁵ ven³³tɕen²¹ ʂa⁵⁵ qa⁵⁵te⁵⁵ , tɕai³³ khia³⁵ taɯ²¹ tua⁵² mu³³
    去 给 边 万象 边 后面地 这样 跑 出 来 去
    go P side Vientiane side lately this way run out come go

就跑到南边的万象，有的接着从万象跑到
moved to Vientiane in South; then some of them came to

86 tau⁴⁴ ʂa⁵⁵ nuŋ²¹qhai²¹ , lɔ³³ zɦɔ³¹ le²¹ . lu⁵⁵ ʂi⁵²xau²¹ ntaɯ²¹ , pe⁵⁵
    给 边 廊开   或 是 黎 个 时候 那 我们
    P side Nong Khai or COP Loei CL time that 1PL

廊开，有的跑到了泰国的黎府。那个时候，我们
Nongkhai, some came to Loei Province of Thailand. At that time, we

(10) ken⁵⁵kɯ²¹ 经历

87 zɦɔ³¹ tɕɔ³⁵ taɯ²¹ tua⁵² mu³³ ŋ⁵⁵ ze⁴⁴ ʈau⁴⁴ saɯ³³na⁵²pu³³we³³
   是   些   出   来   去   在   近   给   沙耶武里
   COP CL.PL out come go be.located close P Xayaburi

跑出去住在靠近沙耶武里的
ran away to live in

88 ntaɯ²¹ lu⁵⁵ me⁵²tɕaɯ³³we³³ ntaɯ²¹ thai⁵⁵ te⁵⁵.
   那   个   湄乍林   那   泰国   地
   that CL Mae Sariang that Thailand land

泰国的湄乍林。
Mae Sariang of Thailand that is near Xayaburi.

89 pe⁵⁵ pfɔ³¹ pe⁵⁵ zɦaɯ³¹ thia⁵⁵ pe⁵⁵ nia²¹ pe⁵⁵
   我们 奶奶 我们 爷 和 我们 母亲 我们
   1PL grandma 1PL grandpa and 1PL mother 1PL

我们的爷爷奶奶和我们的父母
Our grandpa, grandma and parents

90 tsi³⁵ thia⁵²li⁴⁴ tɕɔ⁵² pe⁵⁵ la⁴⁴ lu⁵⁵ ʈuŋ⁵⁵ ntaɯ²¹ tua⁵² mu³³ tau⁴⁴
   父亲 才 才 带 我们 跨 个 山 那 来 去 给
   father just just be.located 1PL cross CL moutain that come go P

才带我们翻过那座山来到
led us over the mountain to reach

91 lu⁵⁵ me⁵²tɕaɯ³³we³³, laɯ³⁵ xu⁴⁴ ʔua⁴⁴ suŋ²¹saɯ³³tua²¹.
   个 湄乍林 他们 叫 做 □ 梢达
   CL Mae Sariang 3PL call make Shaoda

泰国的湄乍林，他们把湄乍林叫作"梢达"。
Mae Sariang of Thailand, which was called "Shaoda"

92 pe⁵⁵ lɔ³³ ŋɔ⁵⁵ ʈau⁴⁴ lu⁵⁵ suŋ²¹saɯ³³tua²¹ ntaɯ²¹ tau⁴⁴ ɕa⁴⁴ ɕuŋ⁴⁴,
   我们 来 在 给 个 梢达 那 得 七 年
   1PL come be.located P CL Shaoda that get seven year

我们在梢达住了七年，
We lived in Shaoda for seven years

93 tsi⁵² thaɯ²¹ ɕuŋ⁴⁴ 1975 tsfɔ³¹ ʈau⁴⁴ ɕuŋ⁴⁴ 1982 . thau²¹ ɕuŋ⁴⁴ 1982
   自   时候   年   1975 到   给   年   1982   时候   年   1982
   since time year 1975 arrive P   year 1982   time   year 1982

从 1975 年到 1982 年。1982 年
from 1975 to 1982. In October 1982,

94 ntaɯ²¹ lu⁵⁵ 10 li⁴⁴ , laɯ³⁵ mua⁵⁵ pe⁵⁵ tshe²¹ taɯ²¹ lu⁵⁵ suŋ²¹saɯ³³tua²¹ ,
   那   个 10 月   他们 拿   我们 撤   出   个   梢达
   that CL ten month 3PL take 1PL withdraw out CL   Shaoda

10 月，他们把我们从梢达撤出来，
they took us out of Shaoda

95 lɔ³³ mu³³ ŋɔ⁵⁵ nʈfɔ³¹ ʈau⁴⁴ tɕɔ³⁵ ŋɔ⁵⁵ tɔ²¹ lu⁵⁵ suŋ²¹ʔdɔ⁵⁵zɔ³³ .
   来 去   在   和   给   些   在   那   个   朵垭
   come go be.located and P   CL.PL be.located that CL Duoya

让我们住在朵垭。
and let us live in Duoya.

96 thau²¹ lu⁵⁵ ɕi⁵²xaɯ²¹ ntaɯ²¹ , tɕɔ³⁵ ʔua³³ tau⁴⁴ ʈaɯ³³ tfɔ³¹ mu³³ ŋɔ⁵⁵
   时候   个   时候   那   些   (定标) 得   跟   兵   去   在
   time   CL time   that   CL.PL REL   get follow soldier go be.located

那个时候，那些跟随部队去
At that time, those Hmong people who followed the military

97 ʈau⁴⁴ thai⁵⁵ te⁵⁵ , nɯ³³ mua⁵² ntaɯ⁴⁴ lu⁵⁵ zaɯ⁵²thɔ⁵²na²¹ ,
   给   泰国   地   它   有   多   个   营 逃 难
   P   Thailand land 3S have many CL camp escape calamity

住在泰国的苗族人，他们住在多个难民营里，
to Thailand lived in several refugee camps,

98 sɯ³³li⁴⁴ lu⁵⁵ zɔ³³ mpa⁵²tɔ³³ ,
   像   个   村子   邦达
   be.like CL village Bangda

比如邦达村，
such as Bangda village,

99 lɔ³³ zfio³¹ lu⁵⁵ ʂɯŋ²¹mpa⁵²tɔ³³, ŋɔ⁵⁵ tau⁴⁴ ʂa⁵⁵ ntaɯ²¹ pha⁵²zau³³ .
    来   是   个   邦达   在   给   边   那   帕尧
    come COP CL Bangda   be.located P side that Phayao
也叫邦达难民营，靠近帕尧府。
which was also called Bangba refugee camp and was close to Phayao Province.

100 lu⁵⁵ ʂi⁵² xaɯ²¹ ntaɯ²¹ pe⁵⁵ zfio³¹ tɕɔ³⁵ ŋɔ⁵⁵ tau⁴⁴ lu⁵⁵ ʂɯŋ²¹saɯ³³tua²¹ .
    个 时候   那   我们   是   些   在   给   个   □   梢达
    CL time   that   1PL COP CL.PL be.located P CL Shaoda
那个时候我们住在梢达。
At that time we lived in Shaoda.

101 tɕɔ³⁵ ŋɔ⁵⁵ tau⁴⁴ ʂa⁵⁵ tɕa³³va²¹len³³ lɔ³³ zfio³¹ ʔdau²¹khai³³ ntaɯ²¹ ,
    些   在   给   边   江万轮   来   是   朵凯   那
    CL.PL be.located P side Jiangwanlun come COP Duokai that
那些住在江万轮或者是朵凯的人，
People who lived in Jiangwanlun or Duokai;

102 ʔi⁵⁵ tɕɔ³⁵ lɔ³³ mu³³ tau⁴⁴ lu⁵⁵ ʂɯŋ²¹fɔ⁵²tha⁵² , ʔi⁵⁵ tɕɔ³⁵ lɔ³³ mu³³
    一   些   来   去   给   个   珐潭   一   些   来   去
    one CL.PL come go   P   CL Pha Tong   one CL.PL come go
一部分迁来珐潭，一部分跑来
some of them moved to Pha Tong, some of them moved

103 tau⁴⁴ lu⁵⁵ ʂɯŋ²¹vi⁵⁵nai³³ . thau²¹ ʂaɯ³⁵ʔdaɯ³³ lɔ³³ tɕuŋ⁵⁵ ʐu⁵²ʐu³³ ,
    给   个   威乃   时候   大家   来   多   (渐多状)
    P   CL Weinai   time   people   come many increasingly
住在威乃。当跑来的人渐渐多起来的时候，
to Weinai. When there were more and more people coming here,

104 laɯ³⁵ ʐua³⁵tau⁴⁴ mua⁵⁵ ʔi⁵⁵ tɕɔ³⁵ kaɯ⁴⁴ tɕia⁴⁴ , lɔ³³ zfio³¹ ʐua³⁵ mua⁵⁵
    他们   要得   拿   一   些   关   保存   或   是   要   拿
    3PL should   take one CL.PL close preserve or COP will take
他们要把一些难民营关闭，或是把
they would shut down some of the refugee camps, or

105 luɨ⁵⁵ suŋ²¹ ntaɨ²¹ kaɨ⁴⁴ tɕia⁴⁴ . luɨ⁵⁵ suŋ²¹ ntaɨ²¹ ʑɦɔ³¹ luɨ⁵⁵
   个   那   关   保存   个   那   是   个
   CL   that close preserve   CL   that COP CL

那个地方关闭。那个难民营是
shut the place down. That was

106 ʑaɨ⁵²tʰɔ⁵² na²¹ na⁵² . mua⁵⁵ luɨ⁵⁵ ʑaɨ⁵²tʰɔ⁵²na²¹ ntaɨ²¹ nɨ³³ tɕɔ⁵² lɔ³³
   营 逃 难   难府   拿   个   营 逃 难   那   它   带   来
   camp escape calamity Nan   take CL   camp escape calamity that 3S   bring come

难府的难民营。把难府的难民营
the refugee camp of Nan Province. Shutting the refugee camp in Nan Province

107 kaɨ⁴⁴, tɕɔ⁵²   mu³³ ntsi³⁵ ʈau⁴⁴ luɨ⁵⁵ tɔ²¹ ʔua⁴⁴ i⁵⁵ luɨ⁵⁵ sɨ⁵⁵ , kɔ²¹
    关   带   去   补   给   个   那   做   一   个   仅仅   让
    close take.along go   supply P   CL   that make one CL   only   let

关闭，把难府难民营和其他的难民营合并为一个，使
down and merging it with other refugee camps as one, making

108 tʂɦaɨ³¹   tʂɦaɨ³¹ , ŋɔ⁵⁵   ʈau⁴⁴ xau³⁵ tɕa⁵²me²¹kau²¹ xai³³ lɔ³³ ʑɦɔ³¹
    少   少   在   给   里   联合国   说   来   是
    RDUP~less   be.located P   inside UN   say   come COP

难民营变少，让联合国或者
refugee camps fewer, so that it would be easy for the United Nations or

109 laɨ³⁵ ʔua⁴⁴ ʑɨ³³ʔen³³ , laɨ³⁵ tʰia⁵² li⁴⁴ ʑua³⁵ ɕai⁵⁵ ɕua³³ ʑuŋ⁵² ʑi²¹ .
    他们   做   U N   他们   才   才   要   看   看   容易
    3PL   make UN   3PL   just   just want   guard guard easy

他们叫做 UN 的，容易管理。
the ones they called "UN" to manage.

110 pe⁵⁵ tɕɔ³⁵ ʔua³³ ŋɔ⁵⁵   ʈau⁴⁴ xau³⁵ luɨ⁵⁵ tɕai⁵² tʰɔ⁵² na²¹   ,
    我们 些   (定标) 在   给   里   个   时间   逃   难
    1PL CL.PL REL   be.located P   inside CL   time   escape calamity

逃难期间的我们，
When we were refugees,

(10) ken⁵⁵kɯ²¹ 经历

111 laɯ³⁵ mua⁵⁵ kaɯ⁴⁴ lu⁵⁵ zaɯ⁵²tho⁵²na²¹ saɯ³³tua²¹, laɯ³⁵ mua⁵⁵ pe⁵⁵ tsa³⁵
他们 拿 关 个 营 逃 难 梢达 他们 拿 我们 移动
3PL take close CL camp escape calamity Shaoda 3PL take 1PL move
他们把我们关在梢达难民营，然后他们把我们转移到
they shut us in the refugee camp of Shaoda; then they transferred us to

112 lɔ³³ mu³³ ŋɔ⁵⁵ ʈau⁴⁴ xau³⁵ lu⁵⁵ zaɯ⁵²thɔ⁵²na²¹ xu⁴⁴ ʔua⁴⁴ nam⁵⁵zɔ³³.
来 去 在 给 里 个 营 逃 难 叫 做 南尧
come go be.located P inside CL camp escape calamity call make Nanyao
一个叫做南尧的难民营。
a refugee camp called Nanyao.

113 ɕuŋ⁴⁴ 1982, pe⁵⁵ thia⁵²li⁴⁴ tau⁴⁴ tau²¹ lɔ³³ mu³³ ŋɔ⁵⁵ ʈau⁴⁴ xau³⁵
年 1982 我们 才 才 得 出 来 去 在 给 里
year 1982 1PL just just get out come go be.located P inside
1982 年，我们才跑出来住在
In 1982, we finally came out and lived in

114 lu⁵⁵ zaɯ⁵²thɔ⁵²na²¹ na⁵⁵mɔ³³. pe⁵⁵ lɔ³³ ŋɔ⁵⁵ xau³⁵ ʔi⁵⁵ ɕuŋ³³ tsɦɔ³¹
个 营 逃 难 南麻 我们 来 在 里 一 年 到
CL camp escape calamity Nanma 1PL come be.located inside one year arrive
一个叫南麻的难民营。我们在南麻难民营住了一年。
a refugee camp called Nanma. We lived in Nanma refugee camp for one year.

115 ʈau⁴⁴ ɕuŋ⁴⁴ 1983. thau²¹ ntaɯ²¹ tʂen²¹fu³⁵ zua³⁵tau⁴⁴ mua⁵⁵ tɕɔ³⁵
给 年 1983 时候 那 政府 要得 拿 些
P year 1983 time that government will take CL.PL
到了 1983 年。那时候政府要把那些
In 1983, the government planned to gradually shut those

116 zaɯ⁵²thɔ⁵²na²¹ tɔ²¹ kaɯ⁴⁴ kɔ²¹ tʂhua³⁵ tʂɦaɯ³¹ ʐu⁵²ʐu³³. ʑɦɔ³¹li⁴⁴ntaɯ²¹,
营 逃 难 那 关 让 剩 少 (缓慢状) 是 像那
camp escape calamity that close let remain less slowly COP be.like that
难民营渐渐关闭。因此，
refugee camps down. Therefore,

117 thia⁵²li⁴⁴ mua⁵⁵ lu⁵⁵ ʐaɯ⁵²thɔ⁵² na²¹ nam⁵⁵ʐɔ³³ nɔ⁴⁴ kaɯ⁴⁴ ,
　　才　　才　拿　个　营　逃　难　南尧　　这　关
　　just just take CL camp escape calamity Nanyao this close

才把南尧难民营关闭，
they shut the Nanyao refugee camp down,

118 mua⁵⁵ tɕɔ³⁵ nɦien³¹ xau³⁵ nɔ⁴⁴ tɕɔ⁵² mu³³ ŋɔ⁵⁵ xau³⁵
　　拿　　些　　人　　里　这　带　　去　在　里
　　take CL.PL human inside this take.along go be.located inside

ʐaɯ⁵²thɔ⁵² na²¹
营　　　逃　难
camp escape calamity

把这个难民营的部分人转移到威乃难民营，
and transferred part of refugees to Weinai refugee camp,

119 vi⁵⁵ nai³³ , ŋɔ⁵⁵ ʈau⁴⁴ xau³⁵ lu⁵⁵ sen³⁵ le²¹ . mua⁵⁵ ʔi⁵⁵ tɕɔ³⁵ sa⁴⁴ mu³³
　　威乃　　　在　　给　里　个　省　　黎　　拿　一　些　送　去
　　Weinai be.located P inside CL province Loei take one CL.PL send go

威乃难民营在黎府。另一部分人转移到
which was in Loei Province. Another group of refugees were transferred to

120 ŋɔ⁵⁵ xau³⁵ lu⁵⁵ ʐaɯ⁵²thɔ⁵²na²¹ mpa⁵⁵ki³³ , ŋɔ⁵⁵ ʈau⁴⁴ sen³⁵
　　在　　里　个　营　　逃　难　　　巴格　　在　　给　省
　　be.located inside CL camp escape calamity Bage be.located P province

pho⁴⁴ʐɔ⁴⁴ .
帕尧
Phayao

一个叫巴格的难民营，这个难民营在帕尧府。
a refugee camp named Bage, which was located in Phayao Province.

121 pe⁵⁵ ʐɦɔ³¹ tɕɔ³⁵ ʔua³³ tɕɦau³¹ sa⁴⁴ mu³³ lu⁵⁵ ʐaɯ⁵²thɔ⁵²na²¹ vi⁵⁵nai³³ .
　　我们　是　　些　　(定标)　被　　送　去　个　营　　逃　难　　　威乃
　　1PL COP CL.PL REL PASS send go CL camp escape calamity Weinai

我们是被送去威乃的难民。

(10) ken⁵⁵kɯ²¹ 经历

We were the refugees who were sent to Weinai.

122 pe⁵⁵ mu³³ ʔua⁴⁴nen⁵² ŋɔ⁵⁵ xau³⁵ lu⁵⁵ ʑaɯ⁵²tʰɔ⁵²na²¹ vi⁵⁵nai³³ tau⁴⁴ 9
　　我们 去 生活 在 里 个 营逃难 威乃 得 9
　　1PL go life be.located inside CL camp escape calamity Weinai get nine
我们在威乃难民营生活了9年，
We lived in Weinai refugee camp for 9 years,

123 lu⁵⁵ ɕuŋ⁴⁴ , ŋɔ⁵⁵ tau⁴⁴ tsɔ²¹ ɲi²¹ kɦaɯ³¹ŋkau³³ . ŋɔ⁵⁵ li⁴⁴ tʰau²¹
　　个 年 在 得 造孽 （极度状） 在 像 时候
　　CL year be.located get poor extremely be.located be.like time
过得非常可怜。
living an extremely hard life.

124 ku³⁵ me⁴⁴ me⁴⁴ tʂi³³ tau⁴⁴ pau⁵⁵ ʔɖa⁵⁵tɕi⁴⁴ , tsɦɔ³¹
　　我 小 小 不 得 知道 什么 到
　　1S RDUP~little NEG get know what arrive
从我很小什么都不知道，到
From knowing nothing to learning to walk,

125 tsaɯ⁵² mu³³ ke³⁵ , ma²¹ ma²¹ lɔ⁵² ʐu⁵²ʐu³³ tua⁵² , ŋɔ⁵⁵ tau⁴⁴ ɕuŋ⁴⁴
　　会 去 路 慢 慢 大 （缓慢状） 来 在 给 年
　　can go road RDUP~slow big slowly come be.located P year
会走路，慢慢长大，到1978、
I gradually grew up; until 1978,

126 1978 , 1979 ntaɯ²¹ , ku³⁵ mua⁵² kɯ³⁵zen³³ li⁴⁴ tau⁴⁴ ɕa⁴⁴ ɕuŋ⁴⁴ ntaɯ²¹ ,
　　1978 1979 那 我 有 估计 像 六 七 年 那
　　1978 1979 that 1S have estimate be.like six seven year that
1979年，我大约有六七岁，
1979, when I was about six or seven years old,

127 ku³⁵ ma²¹li⁴⁴ pi⁵⁵ mu³³ kaɯ²¹ ntaɯ³⁵ . lu⁵⁵ ɕi⁵²xau²¹ ntaɯ²¹ tʂi³³
　　我 才 开始 去 读 书 个 时候 那 不
　　1S just start go read book CL time that NEG
我才开始去读书。那个时候不
I started to go to school. At that time,

128 pau⁵⁵ zua³⁵ zɦu³¹ thau²¹ tɕɯ³¹ , zɦu³¹ ŋu⁵⁵ tɕɯ³¹ , ɕuŋ⁴⁴ tɕɯ³¹ ,
　　知道　要　出生　时候　哪　　出生　天　哪　　年　哪
　　know will born time which born day which year which
知道自己是什么时候、哪天、哪年出生的,
I didn't know when I was born;

129 tɕɔ³⁵ lau³³ tʂi³³ pau⁵⁵ . tɕɔ³⁵ lau³³ tʂua³³ zɦɔ³¹ tia³³ : "zɦu³¹ thau²¹
　　些　　老　　不　　知道　些　　老　　仅仅　是　　道　　出生　时候
　　CL.PL older NEG know CL.PL old only COP QUOT born time
老人不知道。老人只是说:"出生在
the elders didn't know. They just said: "You were born at the time

130 ʔua³³ lu⁵⁵ tɕai⁵² tɕɔ³⁵ mple⁵² tshaɯ³⁵　　tshaɯ³⁵ " . ŋɔ⁵⁵　　tau⁴⁴ ʔɖai²¹ te⁵⁵
　　(定标) 个　时间　些　谷子　抽穗　　　　抽穗　　　在　　　给　　块　地
　　REL CL time CL.PL grain RDUP~heading　　　　 be.located P CL land

nɔ⁴⁴ ,
这
this
稻谷正抽穗的时候。"在这个地方,
of rice heading." At this place,

131 tʂi³³ pau⁵⁵ tia³³ zɦɔ³¹ thau²¹ tɕɯ³¹ . lu⁵⁵ tɕai⁵² ntaɯ²¹ pe⁵⁵ kaɯ²¹
　　不　　知道　道　　是　　时候　哪　　个　　时间　那　　我们　读
　　NEG know COMP COP time when CL time that 1PL read
不知道是什么年代。那个时候我们读书,
I didn't know when I was born. When we would go to school,

132 ntaɯ³⁵ , laɯ³⁵ kua²¹ pe⁵⁵ mu³³ tua³⁵ pɔ⁵⁵ ntʂɦie³¹ , zɦɔ³¹ kɔ⁵² tɕe³⁵ te³³
　　书　　　他们　让　　我们　去　　抓　　根部　耳朵　　是　　你　伸　　手
　　book 3PL let 1PL go catch root ear COP 2S stretch hand
他们叫我们去抓耳根,要是你伸手
we were asked to touch the bottom of our ears; if you can

133 mu³³ tua³⁵ tau⁴⁴ pɔ⁵⁵ ntʂɦie³¹ , tshai³³ tau⁴⁴ tia³³ zu³³ tau⁴⁴ kaɯ²¹
　　去　　抓　　得　　根部　耳朵　　解释　得　道　　自己　得　　读
　　go catch get root ear explain can COMP oneself can read

(10) ken⁵⁵kɯ²¹经历

抓得到自己的耳根，就说明自己可以去读书了。
touch the bottom of your own ear, it means you can go to school.

134 ntaɯ³⁵ . tʰaɯ²¹ lu⁵⁵ ʂi⁵²xaɯ²¹ pe⁵⁵ kʰia³⁵ lɔ³³ mu³³ ŋɔ⁵⁵ ʈau⁴⁴ lu⁵⁵
    书   时候   个   时候   我们 跑   来   去   在   给   个
    book   time   CL time   1PL run come go   be.located P   CL
当我们跑到
When we escaped to

135 zen⁵²tʰɔ⁵²   na²¹   vi⁵⁵nai³³ , ma²¹li⁴⁴ tau⁴⁴ lɔ³³ mu³³ kaɯ²¹ ntaɯ³⁵
    营逃   难   威乃   才   得   来   去   读   书
    camp escape calamity Weinai   just   get   come go   read   book
威乃难民营的时候，才真正能够读书。
Weinai, I could actually go to school.

136 tɕʰia³¹   tɕʰia³¹ . lɔ³³ mu³³ ŋɔ⁵⁵   ʈau⁴⁴ xau³⁵ xau⁵⁵ i⁵⁵ mu³³ tsfiɔ³¹ ʈau⁴⁴
    真   真   来   去   在   给   里   年级   一   去   到   给
    RDUP~real   come go   be.located P   inside grade   one   go   arrive   P
从一年级到
From grade one to

137 xau⁵⁵ ʈau⁴⁴ , lu⁵⁵ ʂi⁵²xaɯ²¹ ntaɯ²¹ pe⁵⁵ kaɯ²¹ ntaɯ³⁵ , ʔi⁵⁵ ȵu⁵⁵ pe⁵⁵
    年级   六   个   时候   那   我们 读   书   一   天   我们
    grade six   CL   time   that   1PL read   book   one   day   1PL
六年级，那时候我们读书，
grade six, we only spent half a day

138 kaɯ²¹ li⁴⁴ ʔi⁵⁵ ta³⁵su⁴⁴ sɯ⁵⁵ . ta⁵⁵ ʂi³³ nɯ⁴⁴ zfio³¹ ʔi⁵⁵ qhɔ⁴⁴ tɕi⁵⁵fe²¹
    读   像   一   中午   仅仅   但是 它   是   一   处   机会
    read be.like one noon   only   but   3S   COP   one   place chance
每天只读半天书。但是它是苗族人
at school. However, it was a good chance for Hmong people

139 zuŋ⁴⁴ ʔua³³ pe⁵⁵ mu³³ ŋɔ⁵⁵ ʔua⁴⁴ke⁴⁴ . mua⁵²zaɯ⁴⁴ʔen³³ , lɔ³³ zfio³¹
    好   (定标) 我们 去   在   一起   有 UN   或   是
    good REL   1PL go   be.located together   have UN   or   COP
在一起的一个好机会。有 UN，或叫

to stay together. We have the UN, the so-called

140 tɕai⁵²me²¹kau²¹xai⁴⁴, lauɯ³⁵ tua⁵² ʂai⁵⁵ ɕua³³. pe⁵⁵ zɦɔ³¹ ʔi⁵⁵ tɕɔ³⁵ nɦien³¹
　　联合国　　　　　他们　来　看　看　我们　是　一些　　人
　　the United Nations　3PL　come　guard　guard　1PL　COP　one　CL.PL　human
联合国，他们来管理。我们是
United Nations to govern us. We were

141 tauɯ³³ tɦɔ³¹ ʔua³³ lɦua³¹ tʂi³³ mua⁵⁵ tsɔ⁵² ke³⁵ tɕi⁵⁵phen⁵² tau⁴⁴ pe⁵⁵.
　　跟　兵　(定标)　人家　不　拿　条　路　自由　　　给　我们
　　follow soldier REL　other　NEG　take　CL　road　freedom　give　1PL
跟着军队来到泰国的难民，人家不给我们自由。
refugees who came to Thailand with the army; we weren't given the right of freedom,

142 pe⁵⁵ zua³⁵ tauɯ²¹ mu³³ qhɔ³⁵ tɦɯ³¹ lɔ³³ tʂi³³ tau⁴⁴, pe⁵⁵ zua³⁵ mu³³
　　我们　要　出　去　处　哪　也　不　得　我们　要　去
　　1PL　want　out　go　place　where　CONJ　NEG　can　1PL　want　go
我们哪里也不能去，我们要去
we could go nowhere; we also couldn't

143 ʔua⁴⁴ ʔi⁵⁵ za²¹ ʔda⁵⁵tʂi⁴⁴ kua²¹ tauɯ³³ li⁴⁴ pe⁵⁵ lu⁵⁵ ɕia⁵⁵ lɔ³³ tʂi³³ tau⁴⁴.
　　做　一样　什么　让　跟　像　我们　个　心　也　不　得
　　do　one style　what　let　follow　be.like　1PL　CL　heart　CONJ　NEG　can
做自己想做的事也不行。
do the things we wanted to.

144 lauɯ³⁵ tua⁵² ʂai⁵⁵ ɕua³³ pe⁵⁵, lauɯ³⁵ tua⁵² pa⁵⁵ tʂhua⁵² len⁵² tɦɯ³¹
　　他们　来　看　看　我们　他们　来　帮忙　检查　位　哪
　　3PL　come　guard　guard　1PL　3PL　come　help　check　CL　who
他们来看管我们，他们来检查看谁
They came to govern us and checked if there's someone

145 mua⁵² mɔ⁵⁵, lauɯ³⁵ pa⁵⁵ tʂhua⁵² tau⁴⁴, tua⁵² pa⁵⁵ thi⁴⁴ken³³ kauɯ²¹
　　有　病　他们　帮忙　药　给　来　帮忙　困难　读
　　have　illness　3pl　help　medicine　give　come　help　hardship　read
生病，他们给药，来帮助读不起书的人。
being ill; they gave us medicine and helped those who couldn't afford to go to school.

(10) ken⁵⁵kɯ²¹ 经历

146 ntaɯ³⁵ ʈau⁴⁴ . len⁵² tɕʰɯ³¹ sa³⁵ mu³³ kaɯ²¹ saɯ³³ khau⁵⁵tɕaɯ³³ , mu³³
　　 书　　 给　　 位　 哪　　想　 去　　 读　　 缝　衣服　　　 去
　　 book　 P　　CL　 who　think　go　 read　sew　cloth　　　 go
谁想去学缝纫，
People who wanted to learn sewing

147 kaɯ²¹ saɯ³³ khau⁵⁵tɕaɯ³³ tau⁴⁴ .len⁵² tɕʰɯ³¹ sa³⁵ mu³³ kaɯ²¹ qhia⁴⁴
　　 读　　 缝　 衣服　　　　 得　 位　 哪　　 想　 去　　读　 告诉
　　 read　sew　cloth　　　　get　 CL　which　think　go　 read　tell
就可以去学缝纫。谁想去学教书
could learn it. People who want to teach

148 ntaɯ³⁵ lɔ³³ mu³³ kaɯ²¹ qhia⁴⁴ ntaɯ³⁵ tau⁴⁴ . lu⁵⁵ ʂi⁵² xaɯ²¹ ntaɯ²¹
　　 书　　 也　去　 读　　告诉　 书　　 得　 个　 时候　 那
　　 book　CONJ　go　read　tell　book　can　CL　time　　that
就去学教书。那个时候
could go to teach. At that time,

149 mua⁵² tɕai⁵² ʈau⁴⁴ pe⁵⁵ kaɯ²¹ ntau⁴⁴ za²¹ . tɕɔ³⁵ mua⁵² tɕai⁵² mu³³
　　 有　　时间　 给　 我们　读　　 多　　样　 些　 有　 时间　 去
　　 have　time　P　　1PL　read　many　style　CL.PL　have　time　go
我们有机会学很多课程。那些有机会去
we had chances to learn many courses. People who had the chance to

150 kaɯ²¹ ntaɯ³⁵ʂua³⁵ , ku⁵² pau⁵⁵ lu³³ ʂua³⁵ pau⁵⁵ ntaɯ³⁵ʂua³⁵ . tɕɔ³⁵ mu³³
　　 读　　 书　汉族　 就　 知道　话　 汉族　知道　书　 汉族　 些　 去
　　 read　book　Han　DM　know　words　Han　know　book　Han　CL.PL　go
学汉语的，就懂汉语汉字。那些
learn Chinese could understand Chinese characters. People

151 kaɯ²¹ ntaɯ³⁵tɕai⁵⁵phen⁵² , laɯ³⁵ ku⁵² pau⁵⁵ ntaɯ³⁵tɕai⁵⁵phen⁵² .
　　 读　　 书　 日本　　　 他们　就　 知道　 书　 日本
　　 read　book　Japan　　　3PL　DM　know　book　Japan
去学日语的，他们就懂日文。
who learned Japanese could understand Japanese writing.

152 tɕɔ³⁵　　mu³³　kaɯ²¹　ntaɯ³⁵ʔen⁵⁵kaɯ⁵²li⁵²ɕi²¹ ,　ku⁵²　pau⁵⁵
　　　些　　　去　　读　　书　　英语　　　　　　　就　　知道
　　　CL.PL　go　　read　book　English　　　　　 DM　know

那些去学英语的，就懂

People who learned English could understand

153 ntaɯ³⁵ʔen⁵⁵kaɯ⁵²li⁵²ɕi²¹ . tɕɔ³⁵　　mu³³　kaɯ²¹　ntaɯ³⁵thai⁵⁵　,　lɔ³³　laɯ³⁵　ku⁵²　pau⁵⁵
　　书　英语　　　　　　　些　　去　　读　　书　　泰国　　　也　　他们　就　　知道
　　book English　　　　　CL.PL go　　read　book Thailand　CONJ 3PL　DM　know

英文。那些去学泰语的，他们也就懂

English. People who had the chance to learn Thai language could understand

154 ntaɯ³⁵thai⁵⁵　. ta⁵⁵ɕi³³ , lu⁵⁵　ɕi⁵²xaɯ²¹　ntaɯ²¹ ,　laɯ³⁵　zua³⁵　mua⁵⁵　ntaɯ³⁵
　　书　泰国　　　但是　　个　　时候　　那　　　他们　要　　　拿　　书
　　book Thailand　but　　CL　time　　that　　3PL　want　take　book

泰文。但是，那个时候，他们教

Thai script. At that time, they taught

155 mplfiɔ³¹　lɔ³³　zfiɔ³¹　ntaɯ³⁵　lɔ³³tʂua³³　qhia⁴⁴　tau⁴⁴　pe⁵⁵　ntau⁴⁴　ʔdua⁴⁴ ,
　　老挝　　或　　是　　书　　老挝　　教　　给　　我们　多　　过
　　Laos　　or　COP　book　Laos　　teach　P　　1PL　much　than

我们老挝语比其他课程更多，

us Lao language much more than other courses;

156 zfiɔ³¹　li⁴⁴ntaɯ²¹ , pe⁵⁵　thia⁵²　tau⁴⁴　kaɯ²¹　ntaɯ³⁵　mplfiɔ³¹ ,　kaɯ²¹　ntaɯ³⁵
　　是　　像那　　我们　才　　得　　读　　书　　老挝　　　读　　书
　　COP　be.like that　1PL　just　can　read　book　Laos　　read　book

因此，我们才得学老挝语，学

therefore, we could learn Lao,

157 thai⁵⁵ ,　kaɯ²¹　ntaɯ³⁵　me³³ka³³ ,　kaɯ²¹　ntaɯ³⁵　ʂua³⁵ ,　pe⁵⁵　tau⁴⁴　kaɯ²¹
　　泰国　　读　　书　　美国　　读　　书　　汉族　我们　得　　读
　　Thailand read　book　America　read　book　Han　1PL　can　read

泰语、学英语、学汉语，我们得学

Thai, English and Chinese; we had to learn

(10) ken⁵⁵kɯ²¹ 经历

158 ntau⁴⁴ za²¹ ntau³⁵ . lu⁵⁵ ʂi⁵²xaɯ²¹ thau²¹ pe⁵⁵ ŋɔ⁵⁵ ʈau⁴⁴ xau³⁵
　　多　 种　 书　　个　 时候　 时候 我们　 在　　给　 里
　　much kind book CL time   time 1PL be.located P inside
多种课程。
many kinds of courses.

159 zaɯ⁵²thɔ⁵²na²¹　　ntau²¹, pe⁵⁵ mua⁵² tɕai⁵² lɔ³³ mu³³ kaɯ²¹ tɕɔ³⁵ ntau³⁵
　　营　逃　难　　　　那　 我们　有　　时间　来　去　读　些　书
　　camp escape calamity that 1PL have time come go read CL.PL book
当我们在难民营的时候，我们有机会去学这些课程，
When we lived in refugee camp, we had the chance to learn these courses,

160 nɔ⁴⁴, pe⁵⁵ xɔ⁴⁴ mu³³ ɕau²¹ ʔua⁵⁴ xau⁵²lɯ²¹ thia⁵⁵ . pe⁵⁵ mua⁵² ʂi⁵²xaɯ²¹ mu³³
　　这　 我们　又　 去　 学　 做　　事情　　也　 我们　有　　时候　　去
　　this 1PL again go learn do matter too 1PL have time go
我们还去学如何做事。
and how to deal with matters.

161 ɕau²¹ ntau³³ pɔ⁵⁵ ŋtɕaɯ³³ pɔ⁵⁵ , ɕau²¹ ntau⁴⁴　　ntau⁴⁴ za²¹ , thia⁵² li⁴⁴ ʔua⁴⁴
　　学　 打　　球　 踢　　　 球　 学　 多　　　　　多　 样　　才　才　 做
　　learn play ball kick ball learn RDUP~many style just just do
有机会去学打球踢球，学很多种，
We had chances to learn basketball, football and many other kinds of sports

162 ʈau⁴⁴ pe⁵⁵ tɕɔ³⁵ ʔua³³ mu³³ ŋɔ⁵⁵ ʈau⁴⁴ xau³⁵ zaɯ⁵²thɔ⁵²na²¹ ntau²¹
　　给　 我们　些　 (定标)　去　 在　　给　 里　 营　逃　难　　　 那
　　P 1PL CL.PL REL go be.located P inside camp escape calamity that

pe⁵⁵
我们
1PL

才使得我们这些难民营中的人，
we who were living in refugee camp

163 tsaɯ⁵² ntau⁴⁴　　ntau⁴⁴ za²¹ . thau²¹ ɕuŋ⁴⁴ 1992 , zɦɔ³¹ lu⁵⁵ ʂi⁵²xaɯ²¹
　　会　　多　　　　多　　样　　时候　 年　1992　是　个　时候
　　can RDUP~many style time year 1992 COP CL time

会很多东西。1992年，
learned to do many things. In 1992,

164 ʔua³³　zua³⁵tau⁴⁴　muɑ⁵⁵　tsɔ³⁵　　zaɯ⁵²thɔ⁵²na²¹　　ntaɯ²¹　kaɯ⁴⁴　kua²¹　ta³³　．
　　　定标　要得　　拿　　些　　　营逃难　　　　那　　关　　让　　完
　　　REL　will　　take　CL.PL　camp escape calamity　that　close　let　finish
所有的难民营都要关闭。
all the refugee camps were going to be shut down.

165 ŋɔ⁵⁵　　　tau⁴⁴　xau³⁵　zaɯ³³ʔen³³　laɯ³⁵　mua⁵⁵　ʔɔ⁵⁵　tsɔ⁵²　xau⁴⁴ke³⁵　tau⁴⁴　pe⁵⁵，
　　　在　　　　给　　里　　　U N　　　他们　　拿　　二　　条　　头路　　给　　我们
　　　be.located　P　inside　UN　　　3PL　take　two　CL　head road　give　1PL
联合国给我们两条出路，
The UN provided us two ways out;

166 tsɔ⁵²　ʔi⁵⁵，mu³³　me³³ka³³，tsɔ⁵²　ʔɔ⁵⁵，tɔ³⁵qa⁵⁵　mu³³　ŋɔ⁵⁵　　　lɔ³³tʂua³³．
　　　条　　一　　去　　美国　　　条　　二　　　回　　去　　在　　　老挝
　　　CL　one　go　America　CL　two　back　go　be.located　Laos
第一条，去美国；第二条，回老挝。
The first one was to go to America; the second one was to go back to Laos.

167 ʂai⁵⁵　pe⁵⁵　zua³⁵　sai³⁵　tsɔ⁵²　tɕhɯ³¹．zu³³　　mu³³　te⁵⁵
　　　看　　我们　　要　　挑　　条　　哪　　　　自己　　去　　回答
　　　look　1PL　want　pick　CL　which　oneself　go　answer
看我们选择哪条。
The choice was ours.

168 tau⁴⁴　laɯ³⁵　xai³³　tia³³　"zu³³　　mu³³　me³³ka³³"，tɕai³³　laɯ³⁵　tɕia⁴⁴li⁴⁴　tɕɔ⁵²
　　　给　　他们　　说　　道　　自己　　去　　美国　　　那么　　他们　　就　　　带
　　　P　3PL　say　QUOT　oneself　go　America　then　3PL　DM　take.along
自己说"自己想去美国"，那么他们就
If you said: "I want to go to America", then they would

169 zu³³　　mu³³　me³³ka³³．zɦɔ³¹　zu³³　　tɯ⁵⁵　xai³³　tia³³　"zu³³　　tɔ³⁵qa⁵⁵　mu³³
　　　自己　　去　　美国　　　是　　自己　　都　　说　　道　　自己　　回　　　去
　　　oneself　go　America　COP　oneself　all　say　QUOT　oneself　back　go
带你去美国。要是自己说"自己想回
take you to America. If you said: "I want to go back to

170 ŋɔ⁵⁵ te⁵⁵tɕhaɯ³³ lɔ³³tʂua³³ ", tɕai³³ laɯ³⁵ tɕia⁴⁴li⁴⁴ sa⁴⁴ zu³³ tɔ³⁵qa⁵⁵
　　在　　　地方　　　老挝　　　这样　　他们　　就　　　送　自己　回
　　be.located place　　Laos　　this way　3PL　DM　send oneself back

老挝",那么他们就送你
Laos", then they would send you

171 mu³³ ŋɔ⁵⁵ te⁵⁵tɕhaɯ³³ lɔ³³tʂua³³ sɯ⁵⁵ . ta⁵⁵ʂi³³ pe⁵⁵ nia²¹ pe⁵⁵ tsi³⁵ pe⁵⁵
　　去　　在　　地方　　　老挝　　仅仅　　但是　我们 母亲 我们 父亲 我们
　　go be.located place　　Laos　　only　　but　1PL mother 1PL father 1PL

回老挝。但是我们的父母我的
back to Laos. However, our parents and

172 pfio³¹ pe⁵⁵ zɦaɯ³¹, laɯ³⁵ tʂi³³ sai³⁵ ʔɔ⁵⁵ tsɔ⁵² ke³⁵ nɔ⁴⁴ , laɯ³⁵ sai³⁵
　　奶奶　我们　爷爷　他们　不　挑选　二　条　路　这　他们　挑
　　grandma 1PL grandpa 3PL NEG pick two CL road this 3PL pick

爷爷奶奶,他们不选这两条路,
grandparents didn't want to choose either.

173 tsɔ⁵² ke³⁵ thi⁵⁵ pe⁵⁵ . laɯ³⁵ tʂi³³ ka²¹ mu³³ me³³ka³³ , thia⁵⁵ laɯ³⁵
　　条　路　第　三　他们　不　愿意　去　美国　　和　他们
　　CL road number three 3PL NEG willing go America and 3PL

他们选第三条路。他们不愿意去美国,他们
They chose the third way. They were not willing to go to America, they

174 tʂi³³ ka²¹ tɔ³⁵qa⁵⁵ mu³³ lɔ³³tʂua³³ , laɯ³⁵ thia⁵²li⁴⁴ tɕɔ⁵² pe⁵⁵
　　不　愿意　回　去　老挝　他们　才　才　带　我们
　　NEG willing back go Laos 3PL just just take.along 1PL

也不愿意回老挝,他们才带我们
were not willing to go back to Laos either; so they took us

175 khia³⁵ tua⁵² mu³³ ŋɔ⁵⁵ tau⁴⁴ tɕhen⁴⁴lai⁴⁴ . pe⁵⁵ tʂi³³ tau⁴⁴ pau⁵⁵ xai³³
　　跑　来　去　住　给　清莱　我们　不　得　知道　说
　　run come go live P Chiang Rai 1PL NEG get know say

跑去清莱住。我们不知道
to Chiang Rai. We didn't know

176 tia³³   mu³³ tɕhen⁴⁴lai⁴⁴ ʐua³⁵ mu³³ ŋɔ⁵⁵ qhɔ³⁵ tɬhɯ³¹ , tʂi³³ pau⁵⁵
     道   去   清莱   要   去   住   处   哪   不   知道
     COMP   go   Chiang Rai   should go   live   place where   NEG   know

去清莱要住在哪里，没有
where to live in Chiang Rai; we didn't have

177 kɯ³⁵ti⁵² , tʂi³³   pau⁵⁵   nen⁵²tʂa⁴⁴ , tʂi³³ pau⁵⁵ ʔi⁵⁵ tu³³ m̥uŋ⁵⁵ ,
     弟兄   不   知道   亲戚   不   知道   一   个   苗族
     brother   NEG   know   relative   NEG   know   one   CL   Hmong

兄弟，没有亲戚，没有一个认识的苗族人，
brothers and relatives; we didn't know any Hmong people

178 tʂi³³   pau⁵⁵   len⁵² tɬhɯ³¹ li⁴⁴ . qhɔ³⁵ ʔua³³ pe⁵⁵ khia³⁵ tua⁵² mu³³ nɔ⁴⁴ ,
     不   知道   位   哪   的   处   (定标) 我们   跑   来   去   这
     NEG   know   CL   where   PRT   place REL   1PL   run   come   go   this

没有一个认识的人。我们跑来清莱，
or anyone. We moved to Chiang Rai

179 vi²¹   ʐfiɔ³¹   mua⁵² i⁵⁵   tɛɔ³⁵   sau⁵⁵ ,   lɔ³³   ʐfiɔ³¹   laɯ³⁵   xu⁴⁴   ʔua⁴⁴
     因为   是   有   一   些   菩萨   或   是   他们   叫   做
     because COP   have   one CL.PL   Bodhisattva   or   COP   3PL   call   make

sau⁵⁵ŋtʂua⁵⁵sɯ²¹ .
菩萨 爪叟
Bodhisattva Zhuasou

是因为有一个菩萨，人们叫作"爪叟"的菩萨。
because there's a Bodhisattva called "Zhuasou".

180 thau²¹ ʔu⁵⁵   ŋɔ⁵⁵   tau⁴⁴   te⁵⁵tɕhaɯ³³   lɔ³³tʂua³³ , sau⁵⁵ŋtʂua⁵⁵sɯ²¹
     时候   以前   在   给   地方   老挝   菩萨 爪叟
     time   before be.located P   land   Laos   Bodhisattva Zhuasou

以前在老挝的时候，爪叟菩萨
In old time in Laos, Bodhisattva Zhuasou

181 tau⁴⁴ xai³³ ʔi⁵⁵   tɛɔ³⁵   lu³³   tʂfie³¹ , xai³³ tia³³ len⁵² tɬhɯ³¹ sa³⁵ kɔ²¹ m̥uŋ⁵⁵
     得   说   一   些   话   保留   说   道   位   哪   想   让   苗族
     get   say   one   CL.PL   words   preserve   say   QUOT   CL   who   want let   Hmong

说过一些话，说的是"谁想让苗族
once said: "Those who want Hmong people

182 lu⁵⁵ nen⁵² ʐuŋ⁴⁴, zua³⁵tsu²¹ khia³⁵ tua⁵² mu³³ ŋɔ⁵⁵ tau⁴⁴ ʔa³⁵ʂa⁵⁵sen⁵⁵kau²¹,
　　 个　 生活　好　　要得　　 跑　　来　 去　 在　　给　 安杉圣皋
　　 CL　 life　good　should　 run　come　go　be.located　P　Anshanshenggao
生活好，就要跑来安杉圣皋住，
to live a better life should live in Anshanshenggao

183 ma³³ thia⁵²li⁴⁴ zua³⁵ pɔ²¹ m̥uŋ⁵⁵ lu⁵⁵ nen⁵², m̥uŋ⁵⁵ lu⁵⁵ nen⁵² thia⁵²li⁴⁴
　　(顺承连词)　才　才　要　见　苗族　个　生活　　苗族　个　生活　才　才
　　 CONJ　　just just　want　see　Hmong　CL　life　　Hmong　CL　life　just just
苗族的生活才有希望，苗族的生活才
So that Hmong people's life can be hopeful and be

184 zua³⁵ ʐuŋ⁴⁴." zɦo³¹ li⁴⁴ntaɯ²¹, pe⁵⁵ tɕɔ³⁵ lau³³ lau³⁵ ɳtʂɦen³¹ ʔi⁵⁵
　　 要　 好　　是　 像那　　我们　些　 老　他们　相信　　一
　　 want good　COP　be.like that　1PL　CL.PL old　3PL　believe　 one
会好"。因此，我们的老人他们相信
better". Therefore, our elders also believed

185 tɕɔ³⁵ lu³³ sau⁵⁵ li⁴⁴nɔ⁴⁴, pe⁵⁵ tɕɔ³⁵ lau³³ thia⁵²li⁴⁴ tɕɔ⁵² pe⁵⁵
　　 些　 话　菩萨　　像这　　我们　些　 老　　才才　　带　　我们
　　 CL.PL words Bodhisattwa be.like this　1PL　CL.PL old　just just　take.along　1PL
khia³⁵
跑
run
菩萨说的这些话，我们的老人才带我们跑
these words that Boghisattwa said; so they took us

186 tua⁵² mu³³ ŋɔ⁵⁵ ʔa³⁵ʂa⁵⁵sen⁵⁵kau²¹. ʔa³⁵ʂa⁵⁵sen⁵⁵kau²¹ ntaɯ²¹
　　 来　去　在　　安杉圣皋　　　　 安杉圣皋　　　　那
　　 come go be.located Anshanshenggao　Anshanshenggao that
来安杉圣皋。安杉圣皋
to Anshanshenggao. Anshanshenggao

187 nɯ³³　zɦɔ³¹　ŋɔ⁵⁵　　ʈau⁴⁴　ntaɯ²¹　tɕhen⁴⁴lai⁴⁴　lu⁵⁵　ɳʈɦuŋ³¹　tɕen²¹sai³³　,
　　　它　　是　　在　　　给　　那　　　清莱　　　个　　城市　　　清盛
　　　3S　　COP　be.located　P　　that　　Chiang Rai　CL　city　　Chiang San

位于清莱的清盛城,
is located in the Chiang San city of Chiang Rai;

188 ʂa⁵⁵　ti²¹　nɔ⁴⁴　zɦɔ³¹　thai⁵⁵ ,　ʂa⁵⁵　ti²¹　zɦɔ³¹　mplɦɔ³¹ ,　ʂa⁵⁵　pe²¹　zɦɔ³¹
　　　边　　那　　这　　是　　泰国　　　边　　那　　是　　老挝　　　边　　上面　　是
　　　side　that　this　COP　Thai　　side　that　COP　Laos　　　side　above　COP

安杉圣皋的这边是泰国, 对面是老挝, 上面是
Anshanshenggao has Thailand on this side, Laos on the other side, and Myanmar

189 pha⁵⁵ma⁵² . tɕɔ³⁵　lu³³　　sau⁵⁵　　　nɔ⁴⁴　nɯ³³　xai³³　tia³³　"kɔ⁵²　mu³³　ŋɔ⁵⁵
　　　缅甸　　　　些　　话　　菩萨　　　　这　　它　　说　　道　　　你　　去　　在
　　　Myanmar　　CL.PL　words　Bodhisattwa　this　3S　say　QUOT　2S　go　be.located

缅甸。菩萨这些话说"你去住在
to the North. Bodhisattwa said: "If you

190 ʈau⁴⁴　ʔa³⁵ʂa⁵⁵sen⁵⁵kau²¹ ,　tɕai³³　　　m̥uŋ⁵⁵　lu⁵⁵　nen⁵²　zua³⁵　zuŋ⁴⁴ ." qhɔ³⁵
　　　给　　安杉圣皋　　　　　(顺承连词)　　苗族　　个　　生活　　要　　好　　　处
　　　P　　Anshanshenggao　　CONJ　　　　Hmong　CL　life　　will　good　place

安杉圣皋的话, 你的生活会变好。"
live in Anshanshenggao, your life will be better."

191 zɦɔ³¹　ʔi⁵⁵　qhɔ³⁵　ke³⁵ɳtʂɦen³¹　ntaɯ²¹　tɕɔ³⁵　lau³³ ,　thia⁵²li⁴⁴　tɕɔ⁵²　　　pe⁵⁵
　　　是　　一　　处　　　路相信　　　　那　　　些　　老　　　　才　　才　　带　　　我们
　　　COP　one　place　road believe　that　　CL.PL　old　　just　just　take.along　1PL

这是老人的信仰, 才带我们
This was elders' belief so they took us

192 khia³⁵　tua⁵²　ŋɔ⁵⁵　ʈau⁴⁴　tɕhen⁴⁴lai⁴⁴ .　ta⁵⁵ʂi³³　tua⁵²　ŋɔ⁵⁵　tɕhen⁴⁴lai⁴⁴
　　　跑　　　来　　住　　给　　清莱　　　　但是　　来　　　住　　清莱
　　　run　　come　live　P　　Chiang Rai　but　　come　live　Chiang Rai

跑来清莱住。但是来清莱
here to live in Chiang Rai. But after coming to Chiang Rai

(10) ken⁵⁵kɯ²¹ 经历

193 tau⁴⁴ nen³³ ŋkau²¹ ʈau⁴⁴ ɕuŋ⁴⁴ ʈau⁴⁴ ta²¹ʂi²¹nɔ⁴⁴ , pe⁵⁵ tua⁵² thau²¹ ɕuŋ⁴⁴ 1992 ,
　　　得　　二　　十　　六　　年　　给　　现在　　　　　我们　来　　时候　年　1992
　　　get　two　ten　six　year　P　　now　　　　　1PL　come　time　year　1992
生活了 26 年直到现在。我们 1992 年到这里，
we have lived here for 26 years till now. We arrived here in 1992;

194 lɔ³³ tsɦɔ³¹ ʈau⁴⁴ ta²¹ʂi²¹nɔ⁴⁴ . zɦɔ³¹ 2018 .
　　　来　　到　　给　　现在　　　　　是　　2018
　　　come arrive P　　now　　　　　COP　2018
现在是 2018 年。
now it's 2018.

195 qhɔ³⁵ nɔ⁴⁴ zɦɔ³¹ qhɔ³⁵ pe⁵⁵ ʔua⁴⁴ nen⁵² ʂai⁵⁵ tʂi³³
　　　处　　这　　是　　处　　我们　做　　生活　看　　不
　　　place this COP place 1PL make life look NEG
这是我们不知道
We don't know

196 pɔ²¹ tɔ²¹ xau³⁵ nte⁵² , pe⁵⁵ tɕia⁴⁴li⁴⁴ sa³⁵ xai³³ tia³³ pe²¹ ʐuŋ⁴⁴ , pe⁵⁵
　　　见　　那　　里　　前面　　我们　就　　　　想　　说　　道　　上面　好　　我们
　　　look that inside front 1PL DM　　want say COMP above good 1PL
以后的生活会怎样，我们只是单纯地认为上面好，我们
what our life will be in the future; we simply thought it's good for us to stay here,

197 tɕia⁴⁴li⁴⁴ khia⁴⁴ mu³³ laɯ²¹ sɯ⁵⁵ . qhɔ³⁵ nɔ⁴⁴ zɦɔ³¹ ʔi⁵⁵ qhɔ³⁵ ʔua³³ pe⁵⁵
　　　就　　跑　　去　　了　　仅仅　处　　这　　是　　一　　处　　(定标) 我们
　　　DM run go PRF only place this COP one place REL 1PL
就跑去了。这是因为
so we came here. It is because

198 tɕɔ³⁵ lau³³ tʂi³³ mua⁵² tsɔ⁵² ke³⁵kau²¹ , tʂi³³ pɔ²¹ lu⁵⁵ nen⁵² tɔ²¹ nte⁵²
　　　些　　老　　不　　有　　条　　路　　读　　不　　见　　个　　生活　那　　前面
　　　CL.PL old NEG have CL road read NEG see CL life that front
我们老一辈没有读书，看不见未来
our old generaton had never received education and couldn't foresee the future,

177

199 tɕai³³ la²¹ tau⁴⁴ la²¹ khia³⁵ , ŋɔ³⁵ lɦua³¹ xai³³ sɯ⁵⁵ tai³³ la²¹ mu³³
　　就　　胡乱　　得　　胡乱　　跑　　　听见　人家　说　　仅仅　就　随便　　去
　　DM　recklessly　get　recklessly　run　　hear　others　say　only　DM　informal　go

la²¹
胡乱
recklessly

就胡乱地跑，只是听别人的话就随便做决定。
they just went to anywhere recklessly and made decision only by others' words.

200 ʔua⁴⁴ . ta⁵⁵ ʂi³³ ku⁵² zuŋ⁴⁴ʂia⁵⁵ . zuŋ⁴⁴ʂia⁵⁵ ʔua³³ pe⁵⁵ tau⁴⁴ ŋɔ⁵⁵ ʔi⁵⁵ lu⁵⁵
　　做　　　但是　可　好　心　　　好　心　　(定标)　我们　得　在　　　一　个
　　make　but　can　good　heart　good　heart　REL　1PL　get　be.located　one　CL

但是很高兴。高兴的是我们住在
However, we are pleased. We are happy that we live in

201 te⁵⁵tɕhaɯ³³ ʔua³³ nɯ³³ zen⁵² mua⁵² tsɔ⁵² ke³⁵ zaɯ⁵²phen⁵² ,
　　地方　　　　(定标)　它　　确实　有　　条　　路　　自由
　　place　　　REL　　　3S　　indeed　have　CL　road　freedom

zaɯ⁵²ʂia⁵⁵zaɯ⁵²ɳtaɯ³³ .
由　心　由　肺
from heart from lung

一个自由的国家，我们自由自在。
a free country. We are free.

202 tau⁴⁴ tsai³³ tsɔ⁵² ke³⁵ pa⁵⁵ lɔ³³ ntaɯ²¹ tʂen²¹fɯ³⁵ . tʂen²¹fɯ³⁵ laɯ³⁵ pa⁵⁵
　　得　　接　　条　　路　帮忙　来　　那　　政府　　　　　政府　　　　他们　帮忙
　　get　receive　CL　road　help　come　that　government　government　3PL　help

能够得到政府的帮助。
We can get assistance from the government.

203 tau⁴⁴ pe⁵⁵ nia³² ɳu⁵⁵ nɔ⁴⁴ ta²¹ʂi²¹nɔ⁵⁴ nɯ³³ zuŋ⁴⁴ ntaɯ⁴⁴ za²¹ . sɯ³³li⁴⁴
　　给　　我们　年　　天　　这　　现在　　　　它　　好　　多　　样　　　像
　　give　1PL　year　day　this　now　　　　　3S　good　many　style　be.like

政府帮助我们，现在给了我们很多种好政策。
The government offers help to us with many beneficial policies.

(10) ken⁵⁵kɯ²¹ 经历

179

204 ʑfiɔ³¹ ke³⁵khɔ⁴⁴mɔ⁵⁵, ʑfiɔ³¹ len⁵² tɕfiɯ³¹ mua⁵² mɔ⁵⁵, zen⁵² tʂi³³ puŋ⁵⁵
  是 路医病 是 位 哪 有 病 确实 不 丢
  COP road doctor ill COP CL who have ill indeed NEG lose
比如医疗，要是谁生病了，不用花钱，
Take medical treatments as an example, people who get ill don't have to pay on their own

205 ȵia⁵², khɔ⁴⁴ mɔ⁵⁵ ʔdaɯ⁵⁵. pe⁵⁵ tɕɔ³⁵ mi⁴⁴ ŋua²¹ tshua⁴⁴ tshua⁴⁴ len⁵² tɯ⁵⁵
  钱 医 病 白白 我们 些 小 孩子 全   全 位 都
  money doctor ill vain 1PL CL.PL little kid RDUP~all CL all
免费治病。我们的每一个孩子都
and can enjoy free medical treatment. Every child of ours can all

206 zua³⁵tau⁴⁴ kaɯ²¹ ntaɯ³⁵, kaɯ²¹ ntaɯ³⁵ ʔdaɯ⁵⁵, tsfiɔ³¹ thau²¹ ʔua³³ nɯ³³ kaɯ²¹
  要得 读 书 读 书 免费 到 时候 (定标) 他 读
  can read book read book free arrive time REL 3S read
要能够读书，读书免费，直到他读
receive education freely until they go to

207 mu³³ ʈau⁴⁴ qe⁵⁵ʂia⁵⁵, ma²¹ li⁴⁴ the²¹ ȵia⁵². qhɔ³⁵ nɔ⁴⁴ ʑfiɔ³¹ ʔi⁵⁵ qhɔ³⁵
  去 给 大学 慢 才 支付 钱 处 这 是 一 处
  go P college slow just pay money place this COP one place
大学时，才交学费。这是一个
college. This is a

208 ʐuŋ⁴⁴ ʈau⁴⁴ pe⁵⁵ tɕɔ³⁵ mi⁴⁴ ŋua²¹ ʔua³³ tau⁴⁴ tsau⁵²ntau⁵⁵tsaɯ⁵²ntaɯ³⁵. ʔua³³
  好 给 我们 些 小 孩子 (定标) 得 会 布 会 书 一
  good P 1PL CL.PL little kid REL get can fabric can book one
让我们孩子能上学的好政策。
good policy for our children to receive education.

209 qhɔ³⁵ ntsi³⁵, ʑfiɔ³¹ ɴqe⁴⁴ ʔde⁵² , ɴqe⁴⁴ ḻua³⁵tau³³sɔ⁵⁵ lɔ³³ pe⁵⁵ tʂi³³ tau⁴⁴
  处 接 是 费用 水 费用 火   雷 也 我们 不 得
  place connect COP fee water fee fire thunder CONJ 1PL NEG get
下一个政策，水费、电费我们也不用
Next policy is that we don't have to pay for the water and electricity.

210 the²¹ . qhɔ³⁵ nɔ⁴⁴ zɦɔ³¹ ʔi⁵⁵ qhɔ³⁵ ʔua³³ zuŋ⁴⁴ tau⁴⁴ pe⁵⁵ tɕɔ³⁵ m̥uŋ⁵⁵ ŋɔ⁵⁵
支付 处 这 是 一 处 (定标) 好 给 我们 些 苗族 在
pay place this COP one place REL good P 1PL CL.PL Hmong be.located

交。这是一个对我们这里的苗族有好处的政策。
This is a policy which is beneficial to us Hmong people here.

211 ntaɯ²¹ nɔ⁴⁴ . nɯ³³ mua⁵² ntau⁴⁴ za²¹ zuŋ⁴⁴ thia⁵⁵ . xai³³ tsɦɔ³¹ lu⁵⁵ nen⁵²
那 这 它 有 多 样 好 也 说 到 个 生活
that this 3S have many style many too say about CL life

这样的政策还有很多。说起
There are still so many policies like these. When we talk about

212 pɦua³¹ thau²¹ me⁴⁴ me⁴⁴, pe⁵⁵ ʂaɯ³⁵ʔdaɯ³³ zen⁵² tsɔ²¹ɲi²¹ xen³⁵. ve²¹ zɦɔ³¹
(远指) 时候 小 小 我们 大家 确实 造孽 很 因为 是
DIST time RDUP~little 1PL people indeed poor very because COP

小时候的生活，我们大家真的很可怜。因为
our life as a child, we were really pathetic. Because

213 pe⁵⁵ pɦɔ³¹ pe⁵⁵ zɦaɯ³¹ laɯ³⁵ tʂi³³ tsaɯ⁵²ntaɯ⁵⁵tsaɯ⁵²ntaɯ³⁵ , ku³⁵
我们 奶奶 我们 爷 他们 不 会 布 会 书 我
1PL grandma 1PL grandpa 3PL NEG can fabric can book 1S

我们的爷爷奶奶没有读过书，我
our grandparents had never received education, my

214 zɦaɯ³¹ lɔ³³ tʂen²¹ xau³³ zen⁵⁵ , ku³⁵ tsi³⁵ lɔ³³ xau³³ zen⁵⁵ thia⁵⁵, tɕai³³
爷 也 还 喝 烟 我 父亲 也 喝 烟 也 (顺承连词)
grandpa CONJ still drink smoke 1PL father CONJ drink smoke too CONJ

爷爷还吸罂粟，我爸爸也吸罂粟，他们
grandpa took opium and my father also took opium; they

215 tʂi³³ tsaɯ⁵² ntaɯ⁵⁵ tʂi³³ tsaɯ⁵² ntaɯ³⁵ , zɦɔ³¹li⁴⁴ntaɯ²¹ pe⁵⁵ ʔua³³ ʔi⁵⁵ lu⁵⁵
不 会 布 不 会 书 是 像那 我们 做 一 个
NEG can fabric NEG can book COP be.like that 1PL make one CL

没有读过书，因此，我们的生活
never went to school; therefore, our life

（10） ken⁵⁵kɯ²¹ 经历

216 nen⁵² tsɔ²¹ŋe²¹ xen³⁵ , ʔua³³ tʂi³³ mua⁵² ȵia⁵² ʂi³⁵ . tsi⁵² li⁴⁴ thau²¹ zu³³
　　生活　造孽　　很　　（定标）　不　有　　钱　　用　　自从　像　　时候　自己
　　life　poor　very　REL　NEG have money use　since be.like time oneself

很可怜，没有钱用。从自己长大
was pathetic and poor. Since I became

217 lɔ⁵⁵ tsia³⁵ tsi³⁵ lɔ³³ mu³³ , zu³³ ma²¹ li⁴⁴ mu³³ khɯ³⁵ , ma²¹ li⁴⁴ zua³⁵
　　大　　成　　父亲　来　去　　自己　慢　　才　去　　劳苦　　慢　才　　要
　　big become father come go oneself slow just go　toil　　slow just want

成人起，自己就去劳苦，去娶
an adult, I started to work hard, to get

218 pɔ⁵²ȵia²¹ . ʔi⁵⁵ lu⁵⁵ tai³³ lɔ³³ zu³³ zua³⁵ tʂi²¹ , ʔi⁵⁵ tʂa⁵⁵ ʔdia³⁵ lɔ³³ zu³³
　　老婆　　　一　　个　　碗　　也　　自己　要　　置办　　一　　把　　勺　　也　自己
　　wife　　one CL bowl CONJ oneself want buy　　one CL spoon CONJ oneself

老婆。一个碗得自己买，一把勺子也得自己
married. I have to buy a bowl on my own, and also a spoon

219 ma²¹ tʂi²¹ , ʔi⁵⁵ lu⁵⁵ tɦɔ³¹ lɔ³³ zu³³ ma²¹ tʂi²¹ , tshua⁴⁴za²¹ tshua⁴⁴tʂa³⁵
　　慢　　置办　　一　个　　凳子　也　　自己　慢　　置办　　全　　样　　全　　种
　　slow buy　　one CL chair CONJ oneself slow buy　　all　　style all　kind

买，一个凳子也得自己想办法，每一样东西
and a chair; I had to buy every single thing

220 tɯ⁵⁵ ma²¹ tʂi²¹ . qhɔ³⁵ nɔ⁴⁴ zɦɔ³¹ ʔi⁵⁵ qhɔ³⁵ tia³³ ku³⁵ thia⁵²li⁴⁴ pɔ²¹ zu³³
　　都　慢　置办　　　处　　这　是　　一　　处　　道　我　　才　　才　见　自己
　　all slow buy　　place this COP one place way 1PL just just see oneself

都得自己置办。这样的生活我自己才
on my own. Only I know

221 tsɔ⁵² ke³⁵ tsɔ²¹ŋe²¹ zuŋ⁴⁴ li⁴⁴tɕa³³ . thau²¹ zu³³ mu³³ pɔ²¹ ʔi⁵⁵ tu³³ ti⁵⁵nɦen³¹
　　条　　路　造孽　　　好　　怎样　　　时候　自己　去　见　一　个　人
　　CL road poor　　good how　　time oneself go see one CL human

知道有多可怜。当我自己看见别人
how pathetic my life was. When I see other poor

222 nɯ³³ tsɔ²¹ŋe²¹, zu³³ thia⁵² pau⁵⁵ xai³³ tia³³ tsɔ⁵² ke³⁵ tsɔ²¹ŋe²¹
　　　他　　造孽　　自己　才　知道　说　道　条　路　造孽
　　　3S　　poor　　oneself juts know say　COMP CL road poor

很可怜时，自己才能体会可怜的生活
people, I can understand what a pathetic life

223 zuŋ⁴⁴ li⁴⁴tɕa³³ . zɦɔ³¹li⁴⁴ntaɯ²¹ , nia⁵² ŋu⁵⁵ nɔ⁴⁴ zu³³ thia⁵² zua³⁵
　　　好　怎样　　是　像那　　　年　天　这　自己　才　要
　　　good how　　COP be.like that year day this oneself just want

是怎样的。因此，今天自己才要
looks like. Therefore, today I want to

224 tau⁴⁴ thia³⁵ ʔi⁵⁵ tsɔ⁵² xau⁴⁴ke³⁵ mu³³ pa⁵⁵ tɕɔ³⁵ ti⁵⁵nɦien³¹ tsɔ²¹ŋe²¹ ,
　　　得　　找　　一　条　头　路　去　帮忙　些　人　　造孽
　　　can find one CL head road go help CL.PL human poor

想办法去帮助那些贫困的人，
find ways to help those poor people,

225 ve²¹ zɦɔ³¹ zu³³ tɯ⁵⁵ tau⁴⁴ tsɔ²¹ŋe²¹ ʔdua⁴⁴ lɔ³³ laɯ²¹ . ku³⁵ lu⁵⁵
　　　为　是　自己　都　得　造孽　过　来　了　我　个
　　　for COP oneself all get poor spend come PRF 1S CL

因为自己曾经贫困过。
because I was poor once.

226 nen⁵² pɦua³¹ thau²¹ me⁴⁴ me⁴⁴ lɔ³³ tsɦɔ³¹ nia⁵² ŋu⁵⁵ nɔ⁴⁴ ,
　　　生活 (远指) 时候　小　　小　来　到　年　天　这
　　　life DIST time RDUP~little come arrive year day this

我的生活从小时候到现在，
My life since I was a child to now;

227 thau²¹ ŋɔ⁵⁵ tau⁴⁴ te⁵⁵tɕhaɯ³³ lɔ³³tʂua³³ zɦu³¹ ku³⁵ ,
　　　时候　在　给　地方　　老挝　　生　我
　　　time be.located P place Laos born 1S

在老挝出生，我
I was born in Laos;

(10) ken⁵⁵kɯ²¹ 经历

228 ku³⁵ mua⁵² pe⁵⁵ ɕuŋ³³, khia³⁵ lɔ³³ mu³³ ŋɔ⁵⁵ tau⁴⁴ ʂa⁵⁵ thai⁵⁵ te⁵⁵,
　　我　　有　　三　　年　　跑　来　去　在　　给　边　泰国　地
　　1S　have　three　year　run　come　go　be.located　P　side　Thailand　land

三岁时，跑来住在泰国，在
When I was three years old, I moved to Thailand and lived in

229 ŋɔ⁵⁵ tau⁴⁴ lu⁵⁵ zen⁵²thɔ⁵² na²¹ sauɯ³³tua²¹ ɕa⁴⁴ ɕuŋ⁴⁴. n̪u⁵⁵ŋɦuŋ³¹
　　在　　给　个　营　逃　难　梢达　　七　年　年龄
　　be.located　P　CL　camp　escape　calamity　Shaoda　seven　year　age

梢达难民营住了七年。我
Shaoda refugee camp for seven years.

230 ku³⁵ mua⁵² li⁴⁴ kau²¹ ɕuŋ⁴⁴, xɔ⁴⁴ khia³⁵ mu³³ lu⁵⁵ zen⁵²thɔ⁵²na²¹
　　我　　有　像　　十　年　　又　跑　去　个　营　逃　难
　　1S　have　be.like　ten　year　again　run　go　CL　camp　escape　calamity

nam⁵⁵ mu³³
难　　去
calamity　go

十岁的时候，又跑去难府难民营
When I was ten years old, I moved to refugee camp of Nan Province and lived for

231 ʔi⁵⁵ ɕuŋ³³, ku³⁵ mua⁵² n̪u⁵⁵ŋɦuŋ³¹ kau²¹ ʔi⁵⁵ ɕuŋ³³. ʔthau⁴⁴ ntaɯ²¹ xɔ⁴⁴
　　一　年　　我　有　年龄　　十　一　年　　过　那　又
　　one　year　1S　have　age　ten　one　year　spend　that　again

一年，我有十一岁。之后又
one year till I was eleven. Later

232 khia³⁵ mu³³ lu⁵⁵ zen⁵²thɔ⁵²na²¹ tau³³ tɕɦo³¹ ve⁵⁵nai³³ tau⁴⁴ tɕua⁵²
　　跑　　去　个　营　逃　难　　　跟　　士兵　　威乃　　得　九
　　run　go　CL　camp　escape　calamity　follow　soldier　Weinai　get　nine

跟随军队跑到威乃难民营住了九年，
I went to Weinai refugee camp and lived for nine years

233 ɕuŋ³³, ku³⁵ mua⁵² n̪u⁵⁵ŋɦuŋ³¹ li⁴⁴ 20 ɕuŋ⁴⁴. thau²¹ ɕuŋ⁴⁴ 1992 ntaɯ²¹,
　　年　　我　　有　年龄　像　20　年　　时候　年　1992　那
　　year　1S　have　age　be.like　20　year　life　year　1992　that

我有二十岁。1992 年,
till I was twenty. It was in 1992

234 thia⁵² li⁴⁴ tau⁴⁴ tauɯ²¹ tua⁵² mu³³ ŋɔ⁵⁵　　tau⁴⁴ ʂa⁵⁵ tɕhen⁴⁴lai⁴⁴ , ŋɔ⁵⁵
　　 才　才　得　出　来　去　在　　　 给　边　清莱　　　 在
　　 just just get out come go be.located P　side Chiang Rai　be.located

才跑到清莱府去住,
that I finally move to Chiang Rai Province and

235 tau⁴⁴ nen³³ ŋkau²¹ tau⁴⁴ ɕuŋ³³ , tɔ²¹ʂi³³nɔ⁴⁴ ku³⁵ mua⁵² ɳu⁵⁵ɳɦuŋ³¹ zɦɔ³¹
　　 得　二　十　六　年　　现在　　我　有　年龄　是
　　 get two ten six year now 1S have age COP

住了 26 年,我现在有
have lived here for 26 years; I am

236 plau⁵⁵ tɕhau³¹ tʂi⁵⁵ ɕuŋ³³ .
　　 四　十　五　年
　　 four ten five year

45 岁。
45 years old now.

经历

　　大家好，我是嘎英才融，我姓王。我住在泰国，在清莱府。现在我四十五岁，我在政府里工作。在村里的工作是管治村庄。我要讲一些我的经历，说我从哪里来，我的父母叫什么，大家看看我的生活怎么样。

　　我是一个苗族孩子，我出生在老挝那边，我生于1972年。当我三岁的时候，老挝在打战，有美国人、法国人，他们来老挝打仗。

　　我刚出生的那个时候，我们苗族分为两帮。我们有一些苗族加入老挝王国军队，老挝王国军队的领袖是王宝，老挝王国军队受美国政府领导。老挝苗族有一部分加入共产党，也就是跟随共产党，例如菲黄罗陪幺、杨陶朵等多位苗族人。那个时候，老挝共产党和老挝王国军队打仗，老挝王国军队输给了老挝共产党军队。因此，美国军队只得撤回自己的国家，法国军队也只得撤回自己的国家。那个时候，美国从老挝撤军回国。在两军打仗的时候，我们的父母们，他们只得从战争国逃往泰国，才带着我们这些小孩来泰国。

　　我们的父母在来老挝沙耶武里省之前，我的父母生在老挝乌多姆赛省的一座山上，这座山他们叫作普陀山。他俩在那里长大在那里结婚，他俩在乌多姆赛省结婚。后来由于逃避战争才来到老挝博胶省会晒市，又跑到琅勃拉邦山，住在黑山。从黑山跑到沙耶武里省，住在沙耶武里省的一个边境村，这个村子叫岩爱村。我爷爷奶奶他们来乌多姆赛省之前，我的父母快要出生了。我爷爷叫绍楞，我爷爷奶奶他们从丰沙里省跑来，跑到乌多姆赛省，才生下我父亲。

　　我们的曾祖父叫岩绍，我们的高祖父叫棕邹。但是我不知道从高祖父棕邹到曾祖父岩绍这两代人，他们从哪里来。在他们跑来丰沙里省之前，我相信高祖棕邹和曾祖岩绍住在越南那边，后来他们才跑到丰沙里省。他们跑到丰沙里省的时候，才生下我爷爷绍楞。丰沙里那边有战事，我们的爷爷绍楞才跑来乌多姆赛省，生下了我爸爸。我爸爸叫泰。生我父亲的那个时候，战事频繁，他们才跑到会晒。从会晒跑来琅勃拉邦山，从琅勃拉邦山跑到沙耶武里省。那个时候我不知道他们在一个地方住了多久才跑到另一个地方，或者说在一个地方住多久。因为在那之前还没有生我。但是，根据我的绍楞奶奶给我讲的家史，根据她所讲的事情和她带我去看过的以前他们住过的老地方，我相信高祖棕邹和曾祖岩绍他们以前住在越南。

　　我出生在沙耶武里省芒平县奈娘村。我生于1972年。我三岁时1975年战争很激烈。当我一岁的时候，我母亲去世了，就只剩下我、我爸爸、我奶奶、我爷爷。我们家有四口人。

　　1975年5月，美国和老挝打得很惨烈，美国败了，美国得撤出去。那个时候，王宝的军队必须从老挝去泰国。我们那些从老挝来到泰国的苗族，有些原来是住在老挝北部威桑，就跑来泰国欧巴丘孔。有些原来住在老挝沙耶武里的苗族人，就跑到了泰国的难府。有些原来住在琅勃拉邦省、川圹省、华潘省的苗族人，就跑到南边的万象，有的接着从万象跑到廊开，有的跑到了泰国的黎府。那个时候，我们跑出去住在靠近沙耶武里的泰国的湄乍林。我们的爷爷奶奶和我们的父母才带我们翻过那座山来到泰国的湄乍林，他们把湄乍林叫作"梢达"。我们在梢达住了七年,从 1975 年到 1982 年。

1982 年 10 月,他们把我们从梢达撤出来,让我们住在朵垭。那个时候,那些跟随部队去住在泰国的苗族人,他们住在多个难民营里,比如邦达村,也叫邦达难民营,靠近帕尧府。那个时候我们住在梢达。那些住在江万轮或者是朵凯的人,一部分迁来珐潭,一部分跑来住在威乃。当跑来的人渐渐多起来的时候,他们要把一些难民营关闭,或是把那个地方关闭。那个难民营是难府的难民营。把难府的难民营关闭,把难府难民营和其他的难民营合并为一个,使难民营变少,使联合国(苗族人把联合国叫做 UN)容易管理。

逃难期间,他们把我们关在梢达难民营,然后他们把我们转移到一个叫作南尧的难民营。1982 年,我们跑出来住在一个叫南麻的难民营。我们在南麻难民营住了一年,住到 1983 年。那时候政府要把那些难民营渐渐关闭。因此,要把南尧难民营关闭,把这个难民营的部分人转移到威乃难民营。威乃难民营在黎府。另一部分人转移到一个叫巴格的难民营,这个难民营在帕尧府。我们是被送去威乃的难民。我们在威乃难民营生活了 9 年,过得非常可怜。

从我很小的时候,到会走路,慢慢长大。到 1978、1979 年,我大约有六七岁的时候,我才开始去读书。那个时候不知道自己是什么时候、哪天、哪年出生的,老人也不知道。老人只是说:"出生在稻谷正抽穗的时候。"在这个地方,不知道是什么年代。那个时候他们叫我们抓耳根,要是你伸手抓得到自己的耳根,就说明自己可以去读书了。当我们跑到威乃难民营的时候,才真正能够读书。从一年级到六年级,我们每天只读半天书。但是,这是苗族人在一起的一个好机会。

UN,或叫联合国,他们来管理我们。我们是跟着军队来到泰国的难民,人家不给我们自由。我们哪里也不能去,我们要去做自己想做的事也不行。他们来看管我们,他们来检查看谁生病,他们给药,他们来帮助读不起书的人。谁想去学缝纫,就可以去学缝纫。谁想去学教书就去学教书。那个时候我们有机会学很多课程。那些有机会去学汉语的,就懂汉语汉字。那些去学日语的,他们就懂日文。那些去学英语的,就懂英文。那些去学泰语的,他们就懂泰文。但是,那个时候,他们教我们老挝语比其他课程要多,因此,我们才得学老挝语,也学泰语、学英语、学汉语,我们学了多种课程。当我们在难民营的时候,我们有机会去学这些课程,我们还去学如何做事。有机会去学打球踢球,学很多种,才使得我们这些难民营中的人,会很多东西。

1992 年,所有的难民营都要关闭。联合国给我们两条出路,第一条,去美国;第二条,回老挝。看我们选择哪条。自己说"自己想去美国",那么他们就带你去美国。要是自己说"自己想回老挝",那么他们就送你回老挝。但是我们的父母我们的爷爷奶奶,他们不选这两条路,他们选第三条路。他们不愿意去美国,他们也不愿意回老挝,他们才带我们跑去清莱住。我们不知道去清莱要住在哪里,没有兄弟,没有亲戚,没有一个认识的苗族人,没有一个认识的人。

我们跑来清莱,是因为有一个菩萨,人们叫作"爪叟"的菩萨。以前在老挝的时候,爪叟菩萨说过一些话,说的是"谁想让苗族生活好,就要跑来安杉圣皋住,苗族的生活才有希望,苗族的生活才会好"。因此,我们的老人他们相信菩萨说的这些话,我们的老人才带我们跑来安杉圣皋。安杉圣皋位于清莱的清盛城，安杉圣皋的这边是泰国，对面是老挝，上面是缅甸。菩萨这些话说"你去住在安杉圣皋的话，你的生活会变好。"这是老人的信仰。所以，老人才带我们跑来清莱住。

　　来清莱生活了 26 年直到现在。我们 1992 年到这里，现在是 2018 年。当时我们不知道以后的生活会怎样，我们只是单纯地认为上面好，我们就跑去了。这是因为我们的老一辈没有读书，看不见未来就胡乱地跑，只是听别人的话就随便做决定。

　　但是很高兴。高兴的是我们住在一个自由的国家，我们自由自在。能够得到政府的帮助。政府帮助我们，现在给了我们很多种好政策。比如医疗，要是谁生病了，不用花钱，免费治病。我们的每一个孩子都能够读书，读书免费，直到他读大学时，才交学费。这是一个让我们孩子能上学的好政策。下一个政策，水费、电费我们也不用交。这是一个对我们这里的苗族有好处的政策。这样的政策还有很多。

　　说起小时候的生活，我们大家真的很可怜。因为我们的爷爷奶奶没有读过书，我爷爷还吸罂粟，我爸爸也吸罂粟，他们没有读过书，因此，我们的生活很可怜，没有钱用。从自己长大成人起，自己就去劳苦，去娶老婆。一个碗得自己买，一把勺子也得自己买，一个凳子也得自己想办法，每一样东西都得自己置办。这样的生活我自己才知道有多可怜。当我自己看见别人很可怜时，自己才能体会可怜的生活是怎样的。因此，今天自己才要想办法去帮助那些贫困的人，因为自己曾经贫困过。

　　我的生活从小时候到现在，在老挝出生，我三岁时，跑来住在泰国，在梢达难民营住了七年。我十岁的时候，又跑去难府难民营一年，直到我十一岁。之后又跟随军队跑到威乃难民营住了九年，直到我二十岁。1992 年，才跑到清莱府去住，住了 26 年，我现在有 45 岁。

Personal Experience

Hello everyone, my name is Gayingcairong, and my last or family name is Wang. I live in Chiang Rai Province of Thailand. Now I'm 45 years old and I'm working in the government. I'm responsible for the management and government of the village. I'm going to talk about my experience, about where I come from, what my parents' names are. So you can see how my life is going on.

I am a Hmong child, who was born in Laos in 1972. When I was three years old, Laos was at war; Americans and French also came here to fight.

When I was just born, we Hmong people were divided into two groups. Some of us joined the Lao Royal Army, of which the leader was Wang Bao. The troop was led by the U.S. government. Some of the Hmong people in Laos joined the Communist Party, namely they followed the Communist Party, such as Feihuangluopeiyao, Yang Taoduo and other Hmong people. At that time, Lao Communist party was at war with the Lao Royal Army, and the Royal Army lost the war to the troops of the Communist Party of Laos. Therefore, the U.S. military and French military had to retreat back to their country. At that time, the American troops retreated from Laos back to America. When the two sides were fighting, our parents had to run away to Thailand. So they took us little kids to Thailand.

Before my parents came to Xayaburi Province of Laos, they were born in a mountain in Oudomxay Province of Laos, which was called "the Putuo Mountain". They grew up and get married there in Oudomxay. Later in order to escape from the war, they moved to Houayxay, Bokeo Province of Laos, and then came to Luang Prabang Mountain and lived in the Black Mountain. Then they moved from the Black Mountain to Xayaburi Province and lived in a border village which was called Ngai'ai village. Before my grandparents came to Oudomxay Province, my parents were almost about to be born. My grandpa's name is Shaoleng; my grandparents ran away from Phongsaly Province to Oudomxay Province, and then gave birth to my father.

Our great-grandfather was called Yanshao and great-great-grandfather was called Zongzou. But I don't know where the two generations of my great-grandfather and great-great grandfather came from. Before they came to Phongsaly, I believe that my great-great-grandfather Zongzou and great-grand father Yanshao lived in Vietnam and moved to Phongsaly Province later. When they came to Phongsaly, my grandfather Shaoleng was born. Because the war in Phongsaly, my grandfather escaped to Oudomxay Province, only then could they give birth to my father, whose name is Tai. It was always war when my father was born, so they moved to Houayxay. Then they escaped to Luang Prabang Mountain and then came to Xayaburi Province. I don't know how long they lived in one place before they moved to another place at that time; in other words, I don't know how long they lived in one place. It is because I wasn't born yet at that time. However, according to the family history and the stories my grandmother Shaoleng told me, and the old places where they once lived, which she showed me, I believe that my great-great-grandfather Zongzou and great-grandfather Yanshao lived in Vietnam before.

I was born in Nainiang village of Mangping County, Xayaburi Province in 1972. The war in 1975 was extremely fierce when I was three. My mother passed away when I was one year old, leaving me, my father, my grandmother and my grandfather. So we have four family members.

In May 1975, the war between America and Laos was very fierce. America lost the war, so they had to take their army out of Laos. At that time, Wang Bao's army had to pass by Laos to go to Thailand. Some of us Hmong people who came to Thailand originally lived in Ngwesaung of Northern Laos, later they moved to Oubaqiukong of Thailand. Some Hmong people who lived in Xayaburi of Laos moved to Nan Province of Thailand. Those who originally lived in Luang Prabang Province, Xiengkhoang Province and Houaphan Province moved to Vientiane in the south, and some of them immediately moved to Nong Khai, and some came to Loei Province of Thailand. At that time, we run away to live in Mae Sariang of Thailand that is nearing Xayaburi. Our grandpa, grandma and parents led us over the mountain to reach Mae Sariang of Thailand, which was called "Shaoda". We lived in Shaoda for seven years from 1975 to 1982.

In October 1982, they took us out of Shaoda and let us live in Duoya. At that time, those Hmong people who followed the military to Thailand lived in several refugee camps, such as Bangda village, which was also called Bangba refugee camp. It was close to Phayao Province. At that time we lived in Shaoda. Some of the people who lived in Jiangwanlun or Duokai moved to Pha Tong, and some came to Weinai. When there were more and more people coming here, they would shut down some of the refugee camps, or shut the place down. That was refugee camp of Nan Province. Shutting the refugee camp in Nan Province down and merging it with other refugee camps as one, making refugee camps fewer, so that it would be easy for the United Nations (Hmong people call it "UN") to manage.

When we were refugees, they shut us in the refugee camp of Shaoda; then they transferred us to a refugee camp called "Nanyao". In 1982, we finally came out and lived in a refugee camp called "Nanma". We lived in Nanma refugee camp for one year. In 1983, the government planned to gradually shut those refugee camps down. Therefore, they shut the Nanyao refugee camp down, and transferred part of refugees to Weinai refugee camp, which was in Loei Province. Another group of refugees were transferred to a refugee camp named "Bage", which was located in Phayao Province. We were the refugees who were sent to Weinai. We lived in Weinai refugee camp for 9 years, living an extremely hard life.

From when I was very little to being able to walk, I gradually grew up. Until 1978 or 1979, I was about six or seven years old, I started to go to school. At that time, I didn't know when I was born, the elders also didn't know. They just said: "You were born at the time of rice heading." At this place, I don't know when I was born. When we would go to school, we were asked to touch the bottom of our ears; if you can touch the bottom of your ears, it means you can go to school. After we escaped to Weinai refugee camp, I could actually go to school. From grade one to grade six, we only spend half a day at school every day. However it was a good chance for Hmong people to stay together.

We had the UN, the so-called United Nations to govern us. Because we were refugees who came to Thailand with the army, we weren't given the right of freedom. We could go nowhere and we also couldn't do things we wanted to. They came to govern us and check if there's someone being ill; they gave us medicine and helped those who couldn't afford to go to school. People who wanted to learn sewing could learn it. People who want to teach could go to teach. At that time, we had chances to learn many courses. People who had the chance to learn Chinese could understand Chinese characters. People who learned Japanese could understand Japanese writing. People who learned English could understand English. People who had the chance to learn Thai language could understand the Thai script. However at that time, they taught us the Lao language much more than other courses; therefore, we could learn Lao, Thai, English and Chinese; we had to learned many kinds of courses. When we lived in refugee camp, we had the chance to learn these courses, and learn about how to deal with matters. We had chances to learn basketball, football and many other kinds of sports so that we who were living in refugee camp could learn to do many things.

In 1992, all the refugee camps were going to be shut down. The UN provided us two ways out. The first one was to go to America; the second one was to go back to Laos. The choice was ours. If you said: "I want to go to America", then they would take you to America. If you said: "I want to go back to Laos", then they would send you back to Laos. However our parents and grandparents didn't want to choose either. They chose the third way. They were not willing to go to America or go back to Laos; so, they took us to Chiang Rai. We didn't know where to live in Chiang Rai; we didn't have brothers and relatives; we didn't know any Hmong people or anyone.

We moved to Chiang Rai because there's a Bodhisattva called "Zhuasou". In old time in Laos, Bodhisattva Zhuasou once said: "Those who want Hmong people to live a better life should live in Anshanshenggao, so that the Hmong people's life can be hopeful and be better". Therefore, our elders also believed these words that Bodhisattva said; so they took us to Anshanshenggao, which is located in the Chiang San city of Chiang Rai and has Thailand on this side, Laos on the other side, and Myanmar to the North. Bodhisattva said: "If you live in Anshanshenggao, your life will be better." This was elders' belief, so they took us here to live in Chiang Rai.

We have lived in Chiang Rai for 26 years till now. We arrived here in 1992; now it's 2018. We didn't know what our life would be in the future at that time; we simply thought it would be good for us to stay here, so here we came. It is because our old generations had never received education and couldn't foresee the future; they just went to anywhere recklessly and made their decision only by others' words.

However, we are pleased. We are happy to live in a free country. We are free. We can get assistance from government. The government offers help to us with many beneficial policies. Take medical treatments as an example, people who get ill don't have to pay on their own; they can enjoy free medical treatments. Every child of ours can all receive education freely until they go to college. This is a good policy for our children to receive education. Next policy is that we don't have to pay for the water and electricity. This is a policy which is beneficial to us Hmong people here. There are still so many policies like these.

When we talk about our life as a child, we were really pathetic. Because our grandparents had never received education, my grandpa took opium and my father also took opium; they never went to school; therefore, our lives were pathetic and poor. Since I became an adult, I started to work hard, to get married. I had to buy a bowl on my own, and also a spoon and a chair; I had to buy every single thing on my own. Only I know how pathetic this kind of life was. When I see other poor people, I can understand what a pathetic life looks like. Therefore, today I want to find ways to help those poor people, because I was poor once.

This is my life since I was a child to now. I was born in Laos; when I was three years old, I moved to Thailand and lived in Shaoda refugee camp for seven years. When I was ten years old, I moved to refugee camp of Nan Province and lived for one year till I was eleven. Later I went to Weinai refugee camp and lived there for nine years till I was twenty. It was in 1992 that I moved to Chiang Rai Province and have lived here for 26 years. I am 45 years old now.

(11) ke⁴⁴ ʔua⁴⁴nen⁵² 生活之道

路　　生活
road　life

1 ʐua³⁵ ʔua⁴⁴ li⁴⁴ tɕa³³ tʰia⁵² li⁴⁴ mua⁵² nɔ⁵² mua⁵² xau³³ ?
　要　怎么办　　才　　有　吃　有　喝
　should how to do　just　have eat have drink

要怎么办才能有吃有喝？

How can one live the good life?

2 ʐɦɔ³¹ len⁵² tɕʰɯ³¹ sa³⁵ kua²¹ lu⁵⁵ nen⁵² mua⁵² nɔ⁵²
　是　位　谁　想　让　个　生活　有　吃
　COP CL who want let CL life have eat

谁想要有吃有喝，

People who want to live the good life

3 mua⁵² xau³³, ʐua³⁵tau⁴⁴ ʔua⁴⁴ tau³³ ni⁴⁴ ntau²¹ nɔ⁴⁴.
　有　喝　　要得　　做　跟　这　那　这
　have drink should　do follow this that this

就得这样做。

should do as follows.

4 ɴqe⁴⁴ ʔi⁵⁵, ʐua³⁵tʂu²¹ ɴqɦua³¹, tʂi³³ tsʰɔ⁵⁵ ŋken³³.
　条　一　要得　　勤奋　　不　别　懒惰
　CL one should　diligent NEG IRR.NEG lazy

第一，要勤奋，别懒惰。

Firstly, be diligent and stop being lazy.

5 ʂaɯ³⁵ ntsɔ³⁵ me⁴⁴ ɳtʂi³³, ɴqɦua³¹, lau³⁵　ʔua⁴⁴
　起　早　小　些　　勤奋　别人　　做
　get up early little CL.PL diligence other people do

(11) ke⁴⁴ ʔua⁴⁴nen⁵² 生活之道

起早些，勤奋，
Get up early to be a diligent person;

6 ʔḍa⁵⁵ tʂi⁴⁴ lɔ³³ ɀua³⁵tau⁴⁴ mu³³ pa⁵⁵ ʔua⁴⁴ ,
  什么   也   要得   去   帮 做
  what   CONJ should   go help do

别人做什么都要得去帮，
learn to offer help no matter what other people do,

7 ɀua³⁵tʂu²¹ tau⁴⁴ mu³³ ɕau²¹ ʔua⁴⁴ , tʂi³³ tshɔ⁵⁵ xai³³ tia³³ :
  要得   得   去   学   做   不   别   说   道
  should   should go learn do   NEG IRR.NEG say QUOT

要得去学做，
you should learn to help others,

8 "ʔu³⁵ ku³⁵ ŋken³³ ŋken³³ ni⁴⁴, tʂi³³ sa³⁵ ʔua⁴⁴ ."
  哦   我   虚弱   虚弱   呢   不   想   做
  INT   1S RDUP~weak   IP   NEG think do

别说"哦，我好累啊，不想做。"
instead of saying "Oh, I'm so tired and I don't want to do that."

9 ɀua³⁵tʂu²¹ ɴqɦua³¹ pɫɦia³¹ , tʂi³³ xai³³ xau⁵² lɯ²¹ ʂi⁵⁵ xau⁵² lɯ²¹
  要得   勤快   迅捷状   不   说   活儿   轻   活儿
  should   diligent quickly NEG say   works   slight works

要勤快，不计较活儿轻重，
You should be diligent and don't care whether the work is light or heavy,

10 ŋa³⁵ , lɔ³³ kɔ⁵² tʂi³³ tshɔ⁵⁵ sai³⁵ , ʔua⁴⁴ tɦa³¹ ntɦɔ⁴⁴ ,
   重   也   你   不   别   挑   做   完   完结状
   heavy CONJ 2S NEG IRR.NEG pick   do   finish completely

你都别挑，全都要做完，
don't be picky and finish all the work.

11 tʂua³⁵ ʐɦɔ³¹ ʔua⁴⁴ tau⁴⁴ tɕɔ⁵² lɔ³³ tau⁴⁴ ɀu³³ nɔ⁵² ,
   只   是   做   得   领   来   给   自己   吃
   only COP   do   get   lead come give oneself eat

只要能够挣钱吃饭，赶紧做。
Do it quickly so you will be paid to live a good life;

12 ka³⁵ tɕi³⁵ ʔua⁴⁴ . ɴqe⁴⁴ ʔɔ⁵⁵ , ʐua³⁵tʂu²¹ ntsaɯ²¹ ,
    赶紧   做   第二   要得   麻利
    quickly do secondly should efficient

第二，要麻利。
Secondly, be efficient.

13 lu⁵⁵ ʂi⁵² xaɯ²¹ kɔ⁵² mu³³ ʔua⁴⁴ xau⁵² lɯ²¹ ntaɯ²¹ ,
    个 时候 你 去 做 活儿 那
    CL time 2S go do works that

当你做事的时候，
When you're working,

14 tʂi³³ tshɔ⁵⁵ ŋken³³ ŋken³³ thia⁵⁵ ʔua⁴⁴ ʂɔ⁴⁴ tɯ⁵⁵ zu²¹ ,
    不 别 懒 懒 和 做 歇息 悄悄状
    NEG IRR.NEG RDUP~lazy and do rest silently

不要偷懒，做做歇歇，
don't be lazy and take rests frequently,

15 ke⁴⁴ ʔua⁴⁴ ke⁴⁴ ʂɔ⁴⁴ , ʐua³⁵tʂu²¹ ʔua⁴⁴ kua²¹ ntsaɯ²¹ ntsuŋ³³ ,
    路 做 路 歇息 要得 做 让 麻利
    road do road rest should do let efficient

边做边歇，要做得麻利，
work a little, rest a little; You have to be highly efficient,

16 kɔ⁵² tɕɔ³⁵ xau⁵² lɯ²¹ ntaɯ²¹ thia⁵² li⁵¹ tia³⁵ ʂai⁴⁴ ,
    你 些 活儿 那 才 完成 快
    2S CL.PL works that just complete quick

你的活儿才能完成得快，
so that can you complete your works quickly;

17 thia⁵² li⁵¹ ta³³ ʂai⁴⁴ , nɯ³³ thia⁵² tau⁴⁴ taɯ²¹ lɔ³³ mu³³ ʂai⁴⁴ ,
    才 完 快 它 才 得 出 来 去 快
    just finish quick 3S just can out come go quick

才能完成得快，事情才能很快地做完，
so that can you complete your works quickly; things can be done quickly;

18 kɔ⁵² zi²¹ ʔua⁴⁴ ntsaɯ²¹ zi²¹ tau⁴⁴ ntau⁴⁴ ,
　　你　越　做　麻利　越　得　多
　　2S　more　do　efficient　more　get　much

你做得越快得到的就越多，
the quicker you work, the more you will get;

19 tʂi³³ tshɔ⁵⁵ ʔua⁴⁴ ɴqen⁵⁵ ɴqen⁵⁵ , kɔ⁵² ʔua⁴⁴ ntsaɯ²¹ , kɔ⁵² ʔua⁴⁴ ʂai⁴⁴ .
　　不　别　做　慢　慢　你　做　麻利　你　做　快
　　NEG　IRR.NEG　do　RDUP~slow　2S　do　efficient　2S　do　quick

别慢吞吞地做，你做得麻利，你做得快，
Don't be slow; if you do things efficiently and quickly,

20 tɕai³³ ʔi⁵⁵ n̥u⁵⁵ nɔ⁴⁴ pe⁵⁵ mua⁵² ʂi⁵² xaɯ²¹
　　那么　一　天　这　我们　有　时候
　　then　one　day　this　1PL　have　time

我们每个人每天都一样的有
each of us have the same

21 nen³³ ŋkau²¹ plau⁵⁵ su⁵⁵ muŋ⁴⁴ ʔi⁵⁵ za²¹ , kɔ⁵² zi²¹ ʔua⁴⁴
　　二　十　四　小时　一　样　你　越　做
　　two　ten　four　hour　one　same　2S　more　do

二十四个小时，
24 hours a day.

22 ʂai⁴⁴ mpau²¹ tɕa³³ , nɯ³³ zi²¹ tau⁴⁴ ntau⁴⁴ mpau²¹ li⁴⁴
　　快　多　怎么　它　越　得　多　多　像
　　quick　much　how　3S　more　get　much　much　be.like

你做得越快，事情就完成得越多，
The quicker you work, the more work can be done;

23 ntau²¹ , qhɔ³⁵ nɔ⁴⁴ zɦɔ³¹ ʔua⁴⁴ kua²¹ ntsaɯ²¹ . qhɔ³⁵ pe⁵⁵ ,
　　那　处　这　是　做　让　麻利　处　三
　　that　place　this　COP　do　let　efficient　place　three

这就是做得麻利。第三,
that's efficiency. Thirdly,

24 kɔ⁵² zua³⁵tʂu²¹ the³⁵ , lɔ³³ zɦɔ³¹ kɔ⁵² zua³⁵tʂu²¹ ɲia⁵² ntsen²¹ ,
   你   要得   刻苦   也   是   你   要得   坚韧
   2S should hardworking CONJ COP 2S should tenacity
你要刻苦,你还要坚韧。
be hardworking and tenacious.

25 tʂi³³ xai³³ tʂha³⁵ ku⁵⁵ lɔ³³ nɦa³¹ ,
   不   说   阳光   烫   来   雨
   NEG say   sunlight hot come rain
不管天晴下雨,
Whether it's sunny or rainy,

26 kɔ⁵² zua³⁵tʂu²¹ the³⁵ kua²¹   tau⁴⁴ , lɔ³³ zɦɔ³¹ kɔ⁵² zua³⁵tʂu²¹
   你   要得   耐   尽可能   得   也   是   你   要得
   2S should endure as far as possible can CONJ COP 2S should
你都要坚持住,
you must endure;

27 mua⁵² tsɔ⁵² ke³⁵ ɲia⁵² ntsen²¹ , kɔ⁵² sa³⁵ ʔua⁴⁴ qhɔ³⁵ ʂi⁵⁵
   有   条   路   坚韧   你   想   做   处   轻
   have CL   road tenacity   2S   want do   part   light
你要有坚韧的品质,你只想做轻活,
you should be tenacious; if you only want to do light work,

28 ʂi⁵⁵ suɯ⁵⁵ , qhɔ³⁵ ŋa³⁵ , kɔ⁵² tʂi³³ sa³⁵ ʔua⁴⁴ lau²¹ ,
   轻   仅仅   处   重   你   不   想   做   了
   light only   part heavy 2S   NEG want do   PRF
你不想干重活了,
you don't want to do heavy work,

29 lɔ³³ zɦɔ³¹ kɔ⁵² sa³⁵ ʔua⁴⁴ qhɔ³⁵ ʔua³³ ntsuŋ³⁵ ntsuŋ⁴⁴ suɯ⁵⁵ ,
   也   是   你   想   做   处   (定标) 阴凉   仅仅
   CONJ COP 2S want do   place REL   shade   only

或者你只想待在阴凉的地方，
or you just want to stay in the shade,

30 ŋɔ⁵⁵ ʈau⁴⁴ xau³⁵ tɕhaɯ⁴⁴ tʂe³⁵ vɔ³⁵ tsia³³ tsia³³ sɯ⁵⁵ ,
   在   给   里   处   家   盖   凉   凉   仅仅
   be.located give inside place home cover RDUP~cool only

只想待在凉爽的家里。
or only stay in your cool house.

31 mu³³ ʈau⁴⁴ xau³⁵ tʂha³⁵ ku⁵⁵ lɔ³³ tʂha³⁵ ti³⁵ nɦa³¹ ,
   去   给   里   阳光   烫   也   场地   抵   雨
   go give inside sunlight hot CONJ place resist rain

不去日晒或者淋雨的地方，
Going where the sun burns and the rain comes

32 tɕhaɯ⁴⁴ ʑia⁵⁵ ʑia⁵⁵ tʂha³⁵ , lɔ³³ zɦɔ³¹ mu³³ ti³⁵ tʂha³⁵ ti³⁵ nɦa³¹ ,
   地方   晒   晒   阳光   也   是   去   抵   阳光   抵   雨
   place RDUP~bask sunlight CONJ COP go resist sunlight resist rain

去日晒淋雨，
to suffer from sunburn and rain,

33 kɔ⁵² tʂi³³ sa³⁵ ʔua⁴⁴ laɯ²¹ . qhɔ³⁵ ntaɯ²¹ zɦɔ³¹ ,
   你   不   想   做   了   处   那   是
   2S NEG want do PRF place that COP

你不想干了。
you don't want to do that.

34 qhɔ³⁵ kɔ⁵² tʂi³³ mua⁵² ke³⁵ ȵia⁵² ntsen²¹ . kɔ⁵² tʂi³³ the³⁵ ,
   处   你   不   有   路   坚韧   你   不   耐
   place 2S NEG have road tenacity 2S NEG endure

那就是你没有坚韧的品质。
Then you have no tenacity.

35 kɔ⁵² zua³⁵ tʂi³³ mua⁵² nɔ⁵² mua⁵² xau³³ . qhɔ³⁵ plau⁵⁵ ,
   你   要   不   有   吃   有   喝   处   四
   2S want NEG have eat have drink place four

你不能吃苦，你将没有吃的喝的。第四，
If you cannot bear hardship, you won't be able to live a good life.

36 kɔ⁵² ʐua³⁵tʂu²¹ tsɦua³¹ ntshi³³ . kɔ⁵² khɯ³⁵ tau⁴⁴ mpau²¹ li⁴⁴tɕa³³ ,
　　你　　要得　　　节约　　点　　 你　　苦　　 得　 多　　　怎么
　　2S　should　　thrift　bit　　2S　bitter　get　much　how
你要得节约点。你挣得再多，
Fourthly, be a thrifty person. No matter how much you get paid,

37 ʐɦɔ³¹ kɔ⁵² tʂi³³ tsɦua³¹ , kɔ⁵² mua⁵⁵ ɕi³⁵ ta³³
　　是　　 你　 不　 节约　　 你　 把　 用　 完
　　COP　2S　NEG　thrift　　2S　PT　use　finish
如果你不节约，你把它用完花完，
if you're not thrifty, you immediately spend it all;

38 ʐa⁵² ta³³ ʐɦɔ³¹ , n̥u⁵⁵ nɔ⁴⁴ kɔ⁵² khɯ³⁵ tau⁴⁴ lɔ³³ pe⁵⁵ pua³³ ,
　　完状　　完　　 完状　　　天　 这　 你　　苦　　得　 来　 三　 百
　completely finish completely day this 2S bitter get come three hundred
今天你挣了三百，
For instance, you earn three hundred yuan today

39 kɔ⁵² tɯ⁵⁵ ɕi³⁵ mu³³ pe⁵⁵ pua³³ lauu²¹ thia⁵⁵ ,
　　你　　都　　用　　去　　三　　百　　了　　也
　　2S　all　use　go　three hundred　PRF　too
你也用了三百，
and also spend all of the three hundred;

40 tɕai³³ ta³³ lauu²¹ . qhɔ³⁵ nɔ⁴⁴ ʐɦɔ³¹ qhɔ³⁵ kɔ⁵²
　　那么　　完　 了　　 处　　 这　　是　　 处　　你
　　so　finish PRF　place this COP place 2S
那么就花完了。
then your money is used up.

41 ʐua³⁵tʂu²¹ tau⁴⁴ tsɦua³¹ ntshi³³ . khɯ³⁵ tau⁴⁴ lɔ³³ ʔi⁵⁵ pua³³ ,
　　要得　　　　 得　　 节约　　 点　　　苦　　 得　 来　 一　 百
　　should　　should thrift　point　bitter get come one hundred

（11）ke⁴⁴ ʔua⁴⁴nen⁵² 生活之道

这就需要你节约了。
You should be thrifty.

42 kɔ⁵² ʐua³⁵tʂu²¹ ɕi³⁵ li⁴⁴ tʂi⁵⁵ tɕɦau³¹ suɯ⁵⁵ ,
   你 要得   用   像   五   十   仅仅
   2S should   use be.like five ten   only

挣来一百，你只花五十，
When you earn one hundred, you only spend fifty;

43 qhɔ³⁵ nɔ⁴⁴ zɦɔ³¹ qhɔ³⁵ tsɦua³¹ ntshi³³ . qhɔ³⁵ tsua³³ ntsi³⁵ ,
   处   这   是   处   节约   点   处   接   补
   place this COP place thrift   bit   place next supply

这就是节约。下一条是，
this is thrift. Next,

44 kɔ⁵² ʐua³⁵tʂu²¹ pau⁵⁵ zɦuŋ³¹ lɦua³¹ luɯ²¹ tu³³ ,
   你 要得   知道 学习   人家   另外 个
   2S should   know study other person other CL

你得知道向别人学习。
you should know to learn from others.

45 ta²¹ ɕi³³ nɔ⁴⁴ lɦua³¹ nʈhia³⁵ nɔ⁵² nʈhia³⁵ xau³³ li⁴⁴tɕa³³ ,
   现在   人家   找   吃   找   喝   怎么
   now   other person find eat   find   drink how

现在人家怎么去挣钱，
How people earn money now,

46 kɔ⁵² ʐua³⁵tʂu²¹ tau⁴⁴ mu³³ zɦuŋ³¹ ʈaɯ³³ lɦua³¹ ,
   你 要得   得   去   学习   跟   人家
   2S should   should go   learn follow others

你要跟人家去学，
you should learn from others;

47 lɦua³¹ mu³³ ʔua⁴⁴ ɖe⁵² ʔua⁴⁴ nu²¹ li⁴⁴tɕa³³ thia⁵² li⁴⁴ tau⁴⁴ ɲia⁵² ,
   人家 去   做   活   做   活   怎么   才   得   钱
   others go   do   work do   work how   just   get   money

别人怎样干活才能挣到钱，
What people do to earn money,

48 kɔ⁵² ʐua³⁵ tau⁴⁴ ʐɦiuŋ³¹ ʈaɯ³³ lɦua³¹ . lɦua³¹ tɯ⁵⁵ mu³³
　　你　　要得　　　学习　　跟　　人家　　人家　都　去
　　2S　should　　learn　follow　others　others　all　go

你要得跟人家学着做。
you should learn from others.

49 ʈau⁴⁴ tsɔ⁵² ke³⁵ va²¹ men⁵² , lɦua³¹ mu³³ nʈhia³⁵ nɔ⁵²
　　给　条　路　发达　　　人家　去　找　吃
　　give　CL　road　prosperous　others　go　find　eat

人家都去走发达的路，
People have already gone on the way to prosperity,

50 nʈhia³⁵ xau³³ ŋɔ⁵⁵　　ʈau⁴⁴ xau³⁵ nʈua⁵⁵ nʈɦiuŋ³¹ ,
　　找　　喝　　在　　　　给　　里　　中　　城市
　　find　drink　be.located　give　inside　middle　city

人家去大城市里求生存，
and gone to the city to strive;

51 mu³³ ʔua⁴⁴ ʔɖe⁵² ʔua⁴⁴ nu²¹ ʈau³³ te⁵² thai⁵⁵ ʔɖaɯ³³ zi⁵² ,
　　去　做　活　做　活　跟　些　泰族人
　　go　do　work　do　work　follow　CL.PL　Tai　people

去为泰族人干活挣钱，
they work for the Thai people,

52 lɔ³³ ʐɦɔ³¹ te⁵² za²¹ ʔua³³ nɯ³³ va²¹ men⁵² .
　　也　　是　　些　　样　（定标）　它　　繁荣
　　CONJ　COP　CL.PL　look　REL　3S　prosperity

或者是走发达的路。
or work on the way to prosperity.

53 ta⁵⁵ ʂi³³ zu³³ tʂen²¹ nia⁵² ŋu⁵⁵ mu³³ nʈhia³⁵ tɔ²¹ xa³⁵ ʐuŋ³⁵ ,
　　但是　　自己　正　　年　　天　去　找　那　谷　森林
　　but　oneself　right　year　day　go　find　that　valley　forest

但是自己还天天去森林里打猎，

But you're still hunting in the forest every day,

54 ʐu³³ tʂi³³ pau⁵⁵ ʑɦuŋ³¹ lɯ²¹ tu³³ , qhɔ³⁵ ntaɯ²¹ ʑɦɔ³¹ qhɔ³⁵ ʔua³³
　 自己　不　知道　学习　另外　个　　处　那　是　处　(定标)
　 oneself NEG know learn other CL place that COP place REL

自己不知道向别人学习，

not knowing to learn from other people;

55 ʐu³³ mu³³ ɳʈuŋ⁴⁴ tʂi³³ tau⁴⁴ lu⁵⁵ xu⁵⁵ ȵia⁵² ,
　 自己　去　找　不　得　个　缸　钱
　 oneself go find no get CL jar money

这就是你没有找到钱缸，

you didn't find a money jar,

56 lɔ³³ ʑɦɔ³¹ ʐu³³ mu³³ tʂi³³ tɬɦau³¹ tsɔ⁵² ka⁵⁵ ʔua³³ mua⁵² ȵia⁵² ,
　 或　是　自己　去　不　中　条　路　(定标) 有　钱
　 or COP onself go no middle CL road REL have money

或者说自己没有走上发财之路，

or you didn't go on the path to fortune;

57 qhɔ³⁵ ntaɯ²¹ ʑɦɔ³¹ qhɔ³⁵ ʔua³³ ʔua⁴⁴ tau⁴⁴ ʐu³³ tʂi³³ mua⁵²
　 处　那　是　处　(定标) 做　给　自己　不　有
　 place that COP place REL do give oneself NEG have

那就是你让自己没吃没喝。

Then it is your own fault that you have nothing to eat or drink.

58 nɔ⁵² tʂi³³ mua⁵² xau³³ . ʑɦɔ³¹ li⁴⁴ntaɯ²¹ ʐu³³ ʐua³⁵tʂu²¹
　 吃　不　有　喝　　是　那样　自己　要得
　 eat NEG have drink COP that way oneself should

这样，你自己得知道向别人学习。

Therefore, you should know to learn from others.

59 tau⁴⁴ pau⁵⁵ ʑɦuŋ³¹ lɦua³¹ lɯ²¹ tu³³ . te⁵² lau³³ lɦua³¹ xai³³
　 得　知道　学习　人家　另外　个　些　老　人家　说
　 should know learn others other CL CL.PL old others say

老人有一句话说：
The old folks say:

60 ʔi⁵⁵ lɔ⁴⁴ lu³³ xai³³ tia³³ ：kɔ⁵² sa³⁵ ntʂe⁴⁴，kɔ⁵² ʐua³⁵tʂu²¹
　　一　句　话　说　道　　你　想　聪明　　你　要得
　　one CL words say COMP 2S want clever 2S should

你想变聪明，
If you want to be smart,

61 mu³³ ɳtɕʰiɔ³¹ tɕɔ³⁵ nɦien³¹ ntʂe⁴⁴，kɔ⁵² sa³⁵ mua⁵² ɲia⁵²
　　去　和　些　人　聪明　你　想　有　钱
　　go and CL.PL human clever 2S want have money

你就得跟着聪明人，你想要有钱，
you must follow the smart ones; if you want to be rich,

62 kɔ⁵² ʐua³⁵tʂu²¹ tau⁴⁴ mu³³ tɕau²¹ tɕɔ³⁵ nɦien³¹ mua⁵² ɲia⁵²，
　　你　要得　　得　去　跟随　些　人　有　钱
　　2S should should go follow CL.PL human have money

你得跟着有钱人，
you should follow those who are wealthy

63 mu³³ ɳtɕʰiɔ³¹ lauɯ³⁵ tha²¹ xai³³ tia³³ lauɯ³⁵ ʔua⁴⁴ ʔda⁵⁵ tʂi⁴⁴，
　　去　和　他们　讲　说　道　他们　做　什么
　　go and 3PL speak say COMP 3PL do what

去和他们交谈看看他们做什么，
and talk with them to find out what they do

64 thia⁵² li⁴⁴ mua⁵² nɔ⁵² mua⁵² xau³³．
　　才　　　有　吃　有　喝
　　just have eat have drink

才有吃有喝。
to live the good life.

生活之道

要怎么办才能有吃有喝？谁想要有吃有喝，就得这样做。

第一，要勤奋，别懒惰。起早些，勤奋，别人做什么都要得去帮，要得去学做，别说："哦，我好累啊，不想做。"要勤快，不计较活儿轻重，你都别挑，全都要做完，只要能够挣钱吃饭，赶紧做。

第二，要麻利。当你做事的时候，不要偷懒，做做歇歇，边做边歇，要做得麻利，你的活儿才能完成得快，你做得越快得到的就越多，别慢吞吞地做，你做得快。我们每个人每天都一样的有二十四个小时，你做得越快，事情就完成得越多，这就是做事麻利。

第三，你要刻苦，你还要坚韧。不管天晴下雨，你都要坚持住，你要有坚韧的品质。你只想做轻活，你不想干重活，或者你只想待在阴凉的地方，只想待在凉爽的家里，不去日晒或者淋雨的地方，你不想干了。那就是你没有坚韧的品质。你不能吃苦，你将没有吃的喝的。

第四，你要得节约。你挣得再多，如果你不节约，你把它用完花完。今天你挣了三百，你也用了三百，那么就花完了。这就需要你节约了。挣来一百，你只花五十，这就是节约。

下一条是，你得知道向别人学习。现在人家怎么去挣钱，你要跟人家去学。别人怎样干活才能挣到钱，你要得跟人家学着做。人家都去走发达的路，人家去大城市里求生存，去为泰族人干活挣钱，或者是走发达的路。但是自己还天天去森林里打猎，自己不知道向别人学习，这就是你没有找到"聚宝盆"，或者说自己没有走上发财之路，那就是你自己让自己没吃没喝。这样，你自己得知道向别人学习。老人有一句话说：你想变聪明，你就得跟着聪明人，你想要有钱，你得跟着有钱人，去和他们交谈，看看他们做什么，才有吃有喝。

How to Live a Good Life

How can one live a good life? People who want to live a good life should do as follows.

Firstly, be diligent and stop being lazy. You should get up early and be diligent; learn to offer help no matter what other people do, instead of saying "Oh, I'm so tired that I don't want to do that." You should be diligent and don't care whether the work is light or heavy. Don't be picky and finish all the work. Do it quickly so you will get paid to live a good life.

Secondly, be efficient. You can't be lazy and rest frequently while working. You can't work a little and rest a little. You have to be highly efficient so that can you complete all your work quickly. The quicker you complete the more you will get, so don't be sloppy. Each of us has the same 24 hours a day. The quicker you work, the more work can be done. That's efficiency.

Thirdly, be hardworking and tenacious. Whether it's sunny or rainy, you must endure. You should be tenacious. If you only want to do light work rather than heavy work, or you just stay in the shade or in your cool house; if you don't want to go where the sun burns and the rain comes to suffer from sunburn and rain, then you have no tenacity. If you cannot bear hardships, you won't be able to live a good life.

Fourthly, be a thrifty person. No matter how much you get paid, if you're not thrifty, you will immediately spend it all. For instance, you earn three hundred today and you also spent all of three hundred, then your money is used up. Thus, you should be thrifty. Thrift means that you only spend fifty when you earn one hundred. This is thrift.

Next, you should learn from others. You should learn from others about how to earn money and how to work. People have already gone on the way to prosperity, and gone to the city to strive; they work for the Thai people. However you're still hunting in the forest every day, not knowing to learn from other people. This is because you haven't found the money jar, or in other words, you've not gone on the path to fortune. Then it's your own fault that you have nothing to eat or drink. Therefore, you should learn from other people. The old folks say: If you want to be smart, you must follow the smart ones; if you want to be rich, you must follow those who are wealthy. You should talk with them to find out what they do to live a good life.

（12）ka⁵⁵ ke³⁵ ʔua⁴⁴ nɔ²¹ 为官之道

道路　　　做　　官
road　　　be　　an official

1 len⁵² tɕʰɯ³¹ ʑua³⁵ sa³⁵ ʔua⁴⁴ nɔ²¹ , ʑua³⁵tʂu²¹ mua⁵² ʈau⁴⁴ ʑa²¹
位　哪　要　想　做　官　要得　有　六　样
CL　who　want　want do　official　should　have　six　kind

谁想要做官，就得具备这六个条件。
People who want to be an official should fulfill six conditions.

2 su³³ li⁴⁴ ntau²¹nɔ³⁵/⁴⁴ . ʑa²¹ ʔi⁵⁵ , ʑua³⁵tʂu²¹ pau⁵⁵ . pau⁵⁵ ʑɦɔ³¹
像　像　这里　样　一　要得　懂　懂　是
be.like be.like here　kind one should understand understand be

第一，要博学。
Firstly, be erudite.

3 lau³⁵ tʰa²¹ tsʰɔ³¹ ʔda⁵⁵tʂi⁴⁴ , kɔ⁵² ʑua³⁵tʂu²¹ pau⁵⁵ tsʰua⁴⁴ ʑa²¹ ,
他们 讲 到 什么 你 要得 懂 全部 种类
3PL speak about whatever 2S should understand all kind

"博学"就是别人说什么，你都懂，
"Erudite" means you understand whatever other people say;

4 tsau²¹ pau⁵⁵ tʂi³³ ta³³ tsʰua⁴⁴ ʑa²¹ , lɔ³³ kɔ⁵² ʑua³⁵ pau⁵⁵
就 懂 不 完 全部 种类 也 你 要 懂
although understand no completely all kind CONJ 2S should understand

就算不是全都懂，但也要尽可能多懂。
know as much as you can even if you can't understand all.

5 kua²¹ ntau⁴⁴ ntau⁴⁴ . lau³⁵ tʰa²¹ tsʰɔ³¹ ʔda⁵⁵tʂi⁴⁴ lɔ³³ kɔ⁵² pau⁵⁵ ,
使 多 多 他们 讲 到 什么 也 你 懂
make RDUP~many 3PL speak about whatever CONJ 2S understand

别人谈到什么你都懂,
You know everything people talk about,

6 tha²¹ tsfiɔ³¹ za²¹ pe²¹ lɔ³³ kɔ⁵² pau⁵⁵ , tha²¹ tsfiɔ³¹
  讲   到   种类 上面 也 你 懂   讲   到
  speak about kind above CONJ 2S understand speak about
说到上面的你懂,
including things above

7 za²¹ ɲta²¹ lɔ³³ kɔ⁵² pau⁵⁵ , tha²¹ tsfiɔ³¹ ke³⁵ plau⁵⁵ntfiu³¹
  样   下面 也   你   懂   讲   到   路   事情
  kind below CONJ 2S understand speak about road matter
谈到下面的你也懂,谈到世间伦理你也懂,
and things below; you know how the world works

8 lɔ³³ kɔ⁵² pau⁵⁵ , tha²¹ tsfiɔ³¹ ke³⁵ kaɯ²¹ntau⁵⁵kaɯ²¹ntaɯ³⁵
  也   你   懂   讲   到   路   读   布   读   书
  CONJ 2S understand speak about road read fabric read book
谈到诗书礼仪你也懂,
and you're rich in poetry and etiquette;

9 lɔ³³ kɔ⁵² pau⁵⁵ , tha²¹ tsfiɔ³¹ ke³⁵ va²¹men⁵² lɔ³³ kɔ⁵² pau⁵⁵ ,
  也   你   懂   讲   到   路   兴盛   也   你   懂
  CONJ 2S understand speak about road prosperity CONJ 2S understand
谈到兴盛之路你懂,
You also know the way to prosperity,

10 tha²¹ tsfiɔ³¹ m̥uŋ⁵⁵ ka⁵⁵li³³ke³⁵tɕai⁴⁴ lɔ³³ kɔ⁵² pau⁵⁵ .
   讲   到   苗族   传统文化   也   你   懂
   speak about Hmong traditional culture CONJ 2S understand
谈到苗族传统文化你也懂。
as well the traditional Hmong culture.

11 qhɔ³⁵nɔ⁴⁴ zfiɔ³¹ pau⁵⁵ . ɴqe⁴⁴ ʔɔ⁵⁵ , tsaɯ⁵² . kɔ⁵² zua³⁵ ʔua⁴⁴
   这里   是   懂   条   二   会   你   要   做
   here   be understand CL two   can   2S should do

(12) ka⁵⁵ ke³⁵ ʔua⁴⁴ nɔ²¹ 为官之道   207

这就是博学。第二，是能干。
This is what we call erudition. Secondly, be competent.

12 nɔ²¹   kɔ⁵²   zua³⁵tʂu²¹   tsaɯ⁵² . laɯ³⁵ xai³³ tia³³: "kɔ⁵² ʔua⁴⁴
    官   你   要得   会   他们   说   道   你   做
    official 2S   should   can   3PL   say   QUOT   2S   be

你想要当官你就得能干。
You have to be competent if you want to be an official.

13 ʔi⁵⁵ tʂa⁵⁵ ntaɯ³⁵ ʈau⁴⁴ pe⁵⁵ sa⁴⁴ mu³³ tho³⁵ ȵia⁵² lɔ³³
    一   封   书   给   我们   送   去   讨   钱   来
    one   CL   book   give   1PL   send   go   ask for money come

他们说："你写一封信去讨钱来帮助百姓。"
If they say: "You should write a letter to ask for money to help the people."

14 pa⁵⁵   pe⁵²sen²¹ ." kɔ⁵²   zua³⁵tʂu²¹   tsaɯ⁵² lɔ³³   mu³³   ʔua⁴⁴
    帮忙   百姓   你   要得   会   来   去   做
    help   people   2S   should   can   come   go   be

你就得会写这封信。
You have to be able to write the letter.

15 tʂa⁵⁵ ntaɯ³⁵ . ʔi⁵⁵ za²¹ li⁴⁴ , laɯ³⁵ xai³³ tia³³ :
    封   信   一   样   的   他们   说   道
    CL   letter   one   style PRT   3PL   say   QUOT

同样的，他们说：
Likewise, when they say:

16 "kɔ⁵² tʂa³⁵ tʂhe⁵⁵ pe⁵⁵ mu³³ pe²¹ ʈuŋ⁵⁵   pe²¹ ."
    你   开   车   我们   去   上面   山   上面
    2S   drive car   1PL   go   up   mountain up

"你开车，我们去山上面去。"
"You should drive us up to the mountain."

17 kɔ⁵² zua³⁵tʂu²¹ tsaɯ⁵² tʂa³⁵ tʂhe⁵⁵ , zɦo³¹ kɔ⁵² tʂi³³ tsaɯ⁵²,
    你   要得   会   开   车   是   你   不   会
    2S   should   can   drive car   be   2S   NEG   can

你得会开车，要是你不会，
You have to be able to drive, otherwise,

18　kɔ⁵² tʂa³⁵ tʂi³³ tau⁴⁴ lu⁵⁵ tʂhe⁵⁵ mu³³ pe²¹ ʈuŋ⁵⁵ .
　　你　 开　 不　 得　 个　 车　 去　 上面　山
　　2S drive no can CL car go up mountain

你开不了车去山上。
You can't drive them up to the mountain.

19　lauɯ³⁵ xai³³ tia³³ kua²¹ kɔ⁵² ʔua⁴⁴ za²¹ tɔ²¹ , kɔ⁵² zua³⁵tʂu²¹ tsauɯ⁵² ʔua⁴⁴ .
　　他们　 说　 道　 让　 你　 做　 样　 那　 你　 要得　 会　 做
　　3PL say QUOT let 2S be kind that 2s should can be

他们叫你办那件事情，你得会做。
You should do what they want you to do.

20　"kɔ⁵² ʂi²¹ qhia⁴⁴ pe⁵⁵ ʂai⁵⁵ , zua³⁵ ʔua⁴⁴li⁴⁴tɕa³³ ,
　　 你　 试　 教　 我们　看　 要　 怎么办
　　 2S try teach 1PL look should what to do

"你试着教我们看看，要怎么做,
"Please try to teach us how to do,

21　zua³⁵ pi⁵⁵ li⁴⁴tɕa³³ , zua³⁵ mu³³ sau³³ li⁴⁴tɕa³³ ."
　　要　 开始　 怎么　 要　 去　 结束　怎么
　　should begin how should go end how

要怎么开始，怎么结束。"
how to start and how to end."

22　kɔ⁵² zua³⁵tʂu²¹ tsauɯ⁵² lɔ³³ qhia⁴⁴ tau⁴⁴ kɔ⁵² tɕɔ³⁵ ti⁵⁵nɦen³¹
　　你　 要得　 会　 来　 教　 给　 你　 些　 人
　　2S should can come teach P 2S CL.PL people

你得会教你所管的那些人，
You have to teach those who are under you,

23　ntauɯ²¹ xai³³ tia³³ : "kɔ⁵² pi⁵⁵ kɔ⁵² zua³⁵ ʔua⁴⁴ li⁴⁴ nɔ⁴⁴ ,
　　那　 说　 道　 你　 开始　 你　 要　 做　 像　 这
　　that say QUOT 2S begin 2S should be be.like this

(12) ka⁵⁵ ke³⁵ ʔua⁴⁴ nɔ²¹ 为官之道

对他们说:"开始你要这样做,
and say to them: "At beginning you should do like this;

24 thau²¹   sau³³   kɔ⁵²   ʐua³⁵   ʔua⁴⁴   li⁴⁴   nɔ⁴⁴."   qhɔ³⁵nɔ⁴⁴   ʑɦɔ³¹   tsaɯ⁵² .
   时候   结束   你   要   做   像   这   这里   是   会
   time   end   2S   should   do   be.like   this   here   be   can

结束的时候你要这样做。"这就是"能干"。
and do it this way when it ends." That's competence.

25 pau⁵⁵   thia⁵⁵   tsaɯ⁵²   nɯ³³   tʂi³³   ʐuŋ⁴⁴   ʔi⁵⁵   ʐa²¹ .
   懂   和   会   它   不   好   一   样
   understand   and   can   3S   NEG   good   one   kind

"博学"和"能干"不相同。
Erudition and competence are not the same.

26 tu³³   ti⁵⁵nɦien³¹   pau⁵⁵   ta⁵⁵ʂi³³   nɯ³³   tʂi³³   tsaɯ⁵² ,
   个   人   懂   但是   他   不   会
   CL   human   understand   but   3S   NEG   can

博学的人但他不能干,
If one is erudite but not competent,

27 tu³³   nɔ⁴⁴   ʔua⁴⁴   tʂi³³   tau⁴⁴   nɔ²¹ ,   vi²¹   ʑɦɔ³¹   nɯ³³   pau⁵⁵   sɯ⁵⁵ .
   个   这   做   不   得   官   因为   是   他   懂   仅仅
   CL   this   do   NEG   can   official because   be   3S   understand   only

这个人就当不了官,因为他仅仅博学而已。
he can't be qualified to be an official because he is only erudite.

28 thau²¹   laɯ³⁵   kua²¹   nɯ³³   ɴqe³³   te³³   ʔua⁴⁴ ,   nɯ³³   ʔua⁴⁴   tʂi³³   tau⁴⁴ .
   时候   他们   让   他   下   手   做   他   做   不   得
   time   3PL   let   3S   down   hand   do   3S   do   no   can

当别人叫他动手做的时候,他做不了。
So he is not able to do work practically when people demand.

29 ɴqe⁴⁴   pe⁵⁵ ,   ȵtɕa⁵²ȵtɕen³³ .   kɔ⁵²   ʐua³⁵   ʔua⁴⁴   ʔi⁵⁵   tu³³   nɔ²¹ ,
   条   三   公正   你   要   做   一   个   官
   CL   three   justice   2S   should   do   one   CL   official

第三，公正。你想当官，
Thirdly, be a just man. If you want to be an official,

30 kɔ⁵² zua³⁵tʂu²¹ mua⁵² tsɔ⁵² ke³⁵ ȵtɕa⁵²ȵtɕen³³ .
　　你　　要得　　　有　　条　　路　　公正
　　2S　 should　　have　CL　road　justice

你得公正。
you should persist in justice.

31 lauɯ³⁵ mua⁵⁵ ʔi⁵⁵ pɔ⁵⁵ ȵia⁵² tau⁴⁴ kɔ⁵² tɕɔ⁵² lɔ³³ mu³³ pa⁵⁵ pe⁵²sen²¹ ,
　　他们　　拿　　一　　包　　钱　　给　 你　 带　 来　 去　 帮忙　百姓
　　3PL　 take　 one　pack　money give　2S　bring come go　help　people

他们拿一包钱给你，让你去帮助百姓，
They give you a pack of money to help the people,

32 kɔ⁵² zua³⁵tʂu²¹ tɕɔ⁵² lɔ³³ mu³³ pa⁵⁵ pe⁵²sen²¹ tɦia³¹ tɦia³¹ ,
　　你　　要得　　　带　　来　去　 帮忙　百姓　 真　　　真
　　2S　 should　 bring come go　help　people　RDUP~really

你就真的要拿去帮助百姓，
you should actually take it to help the people.

33 kɔ⁵² tʂi³³ tshɔ⁵⁵ mua⁵⁵ ʔi⁵⁵ qhɔ⁴⁴ tɕɔ⁵²
　　你　 不　　别　　　拿　　一　　处　　带
　　2S　NEG IRR.NEG take　one　part　bring

你不要拿一些装在自己的腰包里，
Don't pocket some of the money,

34 lɔ³³ ȵtʂɯ³³ tau⁴⁴ xau³⁵ ȵa⁵⁵ tʂhɔ³³ ,
　　来　　塞　　　给　　里　　袋　　衣服
　　come stuff　P　inside pack cloth

拿一些去帮助百姓，
then use the rest of the money to help the people;

35 ʔe³³ mua⁵⁵ ʔi⁵⁵ qhɔ⁴⁴ mu³³ pa⁵⁵ pe⁵²sen²¹ , kɔ⁵² zua³⁵tʂu²¹ mua⁵² tsɔ⁵²
　　(顺承连词) 拿　 一　 处　 去　 帮忙　百姓　　你　要得　　　有　 条
　　CONJ　 take　one　part　go　help　people　2S　should　have　CL

(12) ka⁵⁵ ke³⁵ ʔua⁴⁴ nɔ²¹ 为官之道   211

你得走廉洁公正的道路。
you should keep clean-fingered and just.

36 ke³⁵ ʔdɯ⁵⁵ xu³⁵ ɲtɕa⁵²ɲtɕen³³ . thau²¹ lu⁵⁵ ʂi⁵²xaɯ²¹
   路   白   干净 公正   时候 个 时候
   road white clean justice   time CL time

有时候，有一些百姓，
Sometimes, when some people

37 mua⁵² ʔi⁵⁵ tɕɔ³⁵ pe⁵²sen²¹ , laɯ³⁵ tua⁵² ʔua⁴⁴ plau⁵⁵ , kɔ⁵²
   有   一   些   百姓   他们 来   做   事   你
   have one CL.PL people   3PL come do   thing   2S

他们来办事，
come to ask for something,

38 tʂi³³ tshɔ⁵⁵ mu³³ ɲtɬɦo³¹ ʔi⁵⁵ tu³³ tɔ²¹ , lɔ³³ zɦo³¹ mu³³ ɲtɬɦo³¹ tu³³ tɔ²¹ ,
   不   别   去   和   一   个   那   或   是   去   和   个   那
   NEG IRR.NEG go and   one CL that or   be   go   and   CL   that

你不要偏袒这一个，也不要偏袒那一个，
you shouldn't be biased towards this one or that one,

39 mu³³ pa⁵⁵ tu³³ tɔ²¹ nɔ⁴⁴ lɔ³³ zɦo³¹ mu³³ pa⁵⁵ tu³³ tɔ²¹ .
   去   帮忙 个   那   这   或者 是   去   帮忙 个   那
   go   help CL that this or   be   go   help CL that

去帮这个或者是去帮那个。
Or only help this one or that one.

40 kɔ⁵² zua³⁵tʂu²¹ mua⁵² tsɔ⁵² ke³⁵ ɲtɕa⁵²ɲtɕen³³ tau⁴⁴ ʔɔ⁵⁵ tu³³ pe⁵²sen²¹ ntaɯ²¹ .
   你   要得   有   条   路   公正   给   两   个   百姓   那
   2S   should   have CL   road justice   P   two CL   people   that

你要坚持公平，平等对待双方。
You should insist on impartial treatment towards both sides.

41 tsia³⁵ plau⁵⁵ ʈau⁴⁴ laɯ³⁵ kua²¹ ɲtɕa⁵²ɲtɕen³³ ,
   砍   事   给   他们   使得   公正
   chop matter give 3PL   make justice

公正地给他们断案，
Justly issue verdicts for them,

42 kɔ⁵² zua³⁵ tʂi³³ tua⁵² len⁵² tɕʰɯ³¹ tɕʰɔ³¹ . tʰau²¹ lu⁵⁵ ʂi⁵²xau²¹ kɔ⁵²
　　你　　要　　不　　来　位　　哪　　头　　　时候　个　时候　　你
　　2S　should　NEG　come　CL　who　head　　time　CL　time　　2S

你要不偏袒任何一方。当你有一些物资的时候，
and don't take sides. If you have some supplies,

43 mua⁵² ʔi⁵⁵ qhɔ⁴⁴ khɯŋ²¹ , kɔ⁵² zua³⁵ mua⁵⁵ tɛɔ⁵² 　 mu³³ pa⁵⁵ ṭau⁴⁴ lau³⁵ ,
　　有　　一　　处　　东西　　你　　要　　拿　　带　　　去　帮忙　给　他们
　 have　one　thing　thing　2S　should　take　take.along　go　help　P　3PL

你要拿去资助他们，
you should use it to help them;

44 kɔ⁵² zua³⁵tʂu²¹ tʂi³³ tsʰɔ⁵⁵ 　 mu³³ tɛai³³ xai³³ tia³³ : "tɛɔ³⁵ nɔ⁴⁴
　　你　　要得　　不　　别　　　去　　隔开　说　　道　　　些　　这
　　2S　　should　NEG　IRR.NEG　go　divide　say　QUOT　CL.PL　this

你要不分亲疏远近，不要说："这些是我的兄弟，
don't show favoritism according to relationships and say: "These are my brothers

45 ʐɔ³¹ ku³⁵ tɛɔ³⁵ kɯ³⁵ti⁵² , tɛɔ³⁵ nɔ⁴⁴ tʂi³³ ʐɔ³¹ ku³⁵ tɛɔ³⁵ kɯ³⁵ti⁵² ."
　　是　我　些　　兄弟　　　些　　这　不　是　我　些　　兄弟
　　be　1S　CL.PL　brother　CL.PL　this　NEG　be　1S　CL.PL　brother

这些不是我的兄弟。"
and those are not,"

46 ʔe³³ 　 kɔ⁵² zua³⁵ mu³³ mua⁵⁵ ṭau⁴⁴ zu³³ tɛɔ³⁵ kɯ³⁵ti⁵² sɯ⁵⁵ ,
　(语助)　你　　要　　去　　拿　　给　自己　些　兄弟　仅仅
　　IP　　2S　should　go　take　give　oneself　CL.PL　brother　only

而你只把东西分给了自己的兄弟，
only distributing supplies to your own brothers,

47 tʂi³³ mua⁵⁵ ṭau⁴⁴ tɛɔ³⁵ qhua⁴⁴ . qhɔ³⁵nɔ⁴⁴ ʐɔ³¹ tsɔ⁵² ke⁴⁴ ŋtɛa⁵²ntɛen³³
　　不　拿　　给　　些　　客人　　这里　　　是　条　　路　　公正
　　no　take　give　CL.PL　guest　　here　　be　CL　road　justice

(12) ka⁵⁵ ke³⁵ ʔua⁴⁴ nɔ²¹ 为官之道　　　　213

不分给关系远的人。
but not to those who are outsiders.

48　ʔua³³　　kɔ⁵²　ʐua³⁵tʂu²¹　tau⁴⁴　mu³³　pa⁵⁵　ţau⁴⁴　tshua⁴⁴　tshua⁴⁴　len⁵² .
　　(定标)　你　　要得　　　得　　去　　帮忙　给　全　　　全　　　位
　　REL　　2S　　should　　should　go　help　P　　RDUP~all　　　CL
这就是公正，它要求你公平地帮助每个人。
This is justice, which requires you to impartially help everyone.

49　ɴqe⁴⁴　plau⁵⁵，mua⁵²　pen³⁵ʂi²¹ . kɔ⁵²　ʐua³⁵　ʔua⁴⁴　ʔi⁵⁵　tu³³　nɔ²¹　　，
　　条　　四　　　有　　本事　　　你　　要　　做　　一　　个　　官
　　CL　four　　have　capability　2S　should do　one CL　official
第四，有本事。你要当官，
Fourthly, be capable. If you want to be an official,

50　kɔ⁵²　ʐua³⁵tʂu²¹　ʐɦo³¹　ʔi⁵⁵　tu³³　nɦien³¹　mua⁵²　pen³⁵ʂi²¹　，
　　你　　要得　　　　是　　一　　个　　人　　　　有　　　本事
　　2S　should　　　be　one　CL　human　have　capability
你得是个有本事的人。
you should be a capable person.

51　ka³⁵　xai³³，ka³⁵　ʔua⁴⁴，xai³³　lauɯ²¹　ma³³　ʔua⁴⁴，ʔua⁴⁴　li⁴⁴　qho³⁵　ʐu³³　xai³³ .
　　敢说　　敢做　　　说了　　　　就　做　　　做　　像　　处　自己　说
　　dare say　dare do　say　PRF　DM　do　　do　be.like　place　oneself　say
敢说，敢做，说了就要做，怎么说就要怎么做。
Dare to speak and act, and perform what you said.

52　lauɯ³⁵　xai³³　tia³³　：''ʔu⁵⁵，tɕua⁴⁴　tʂhua⁵⁵　pe⁵⁵　tɕɔ³⁵　va⁵²　tʂe³⁵
　　他们　　说　　道　　　哦　　　风　　　　吹　　　我们　些　　围栏　家
　　3PL　say　QUOT　　INT　wind　　blow　　1PL　CL.PL fence home
他们说："哦，风把我们的家吹毁了，
They say: "oh, the wind blew our house to pieces;

53　pua³³　ta³³　lauɯ²¹，kɔ⁵²　mu³³　pa⁵⁵　xai³³　nɔ²¹　　，
　　损坏　　完　了　　　　你　　去　　帮忙　说　　官
　　destroy　finish　PRF　2S　go　help　say　official

你帮忙去向政府汇报，

you should help to report to the government,

54　lɔ³³　　mu³³　pa⁵⁵　thɔ³⁵　ʔi⁵⁵　tɕɔ³⁵　vua³³　tua⁵²　tau⁴⁴　pe⁵⁵　vɔ³⁵　tʂe³⁵　."

　　或者　　去　　帮忙　讨　　一　　些　　瓦　　来　　给　　我们　盖　　家

　　or　　　go　　help　ask　one　CL.PL　tile　come　give　1PL　build　home

或者帮忙讨一些瓦来给我们盖房子。"

or ask for some tiles for us to rebuild our house."

55　kɔ⁵²　ʐua³⁵tʂu²¹　mua⁵²　pen³⁵ʂi²¹　mu³³　xai³³　,

　　你　　要得　　　　有　　　本事　　　去　　说

　　2S　　should　　　have　capability　go　　speak

你得有本事去说，

You should be capable of giving a full account,

56　lɔ³³　ʐɦɔ³¹　mu³³　qhia⁴⁴　qhɔ³⁵　ten⁵⁵men²¹　nɔ⁴⁴　tau⁴⁴　lauɯ³⁵　,

　　或　　是　　去　　教　　　处　　事情　　　　这　　给　　他们

　　or　　be　　go　　teach　　place　matter　　this　　P　　3PL

或者是把这件事向政府汇报，

or representing this situation to the government,

57　kua²¹　nɔ²¹tsɯ³⁵　lauɯ³⁵　mua⁵⁵　ɲia⁵²　mu³³　pa⁵⁵　ʐua³⁵　vua³³　,

　　让　　官府　　　　他们　　拿　　钱　　去　　帮忙　要　　瓦

　　let　government　　3PL　　take　money　go　　help　ask　tile

让官府拿钱去帮忙买瓦，

to ask the government to provide the money to buy tile,

58　tɕɔ⁵²　lɔ³³　vɔ³⁵　tʂe³⁵　tau⁴⁴　tɕɔ³⁵　nɦien³¹　tɕɦau³¹　ke³⁵　tsɔ²¹ɲi²¹　ntauɯ²¹ .

　　带　　来　　盖　　家　　给　　些　　人　　　着　　　路　　困难　　　那

　　bring　come　build　home　give　CL.PL　human　hit.the.mark　road　hard　that

带来盖房子给那些受灾的人。

and build houses for those who are suffering from the disaster.

59　lɔ³³　ʐɦɔ³¹　xai³³　tia³³　: "ʔau⁵²　, mua⁵²　ʔi⁵⁵　tu³³　nɔ²¹　tua⁵²　pe²¹　lu⁵²　,

　　或　　是　　说　　道　　　噢　　　有　　一　　个　　官　　来　　上面　啦

　　or　　be　　say　　QUOT　INT　　have　one　CL　official　come　above　IP

(12) ka⁵⁵ ke³⁵ ʔua⁴⁴ nɔ²¹ 为官之道

或者说："噢，有个领导来到上面这里啦，
or they say: "Ah, a higher official happens to come here,

60 kɔ⁵² mu³³ pa⁵⁵ xai³³ ʈau⁴⁴ tu³³ nɔ²¹ pe²¹ ,
　　你　 去　 帮忙　说　 给　 个　 官　 上面
　　2S　 go　 help　say　 P　 CL　official above

你帮忙去找上面那个领导，
you should help by going to talk to the higher official;

61 pe⁵⁵ tɕɔ³⁵ pe⁵²sen²¹ tsɔ²¹ɲi²¹ xen³⁵ , kua²¹ nɯ³³ ɳʈhia³⁵ ke³⁵ tua⁵²
　　我们　 些　　 百姓　　 困难　 很　　让　他　 找　　路　 来
　　1PL　CL.PL　people　 hard　very　let　3S　find　road come

我们老百姓很困难，让他想办法来帮助我们，
we live a hard life so please ask him to find way to help us;

62 pa⁵⁵ pe⁵⁵ , kua²¹ nɯ³³ tua⁵² ʔua⁴⁴ ke³⁵ tʂhe⁵⁵ ʈau⁴⁴ pe⁵⁵ .
　　帮忙　我们　 让　 他　 来　 做　 路　 车　 给　 我们
　　help　1PL　let　 3S　come make road car　 P　 1PL

让他来给我们修路。
ask him to make a road for us."

63 lɔ³³ zɦɔ³¹ tia³³: "pe⁵⁵ tʂi³³ mua⁵² ʔde⁵² xau³³ , tua⁵² ʔua⁴⁴ ʔde⁵² ʈau⁴⁴
　　或　 是　 道　 我们　 不　 有　 水　 喝　　 来　 做　 水　 给
　　or　 be　QUOT 1PL　NEG have water drink　come make water P

或者说："我们没有水喝，让他来通水。"
or they say: "We don't have water to drink, please ask him to provide water."

64 pe⁵⁵ xau³³ ." kɔ⁵² zua³⁵tʂu²¹ mua⁵² pen³⁵ɕi²¹ mu³³ xai³³ qhɔ³⁵
　　我们　喝　　 你　 要得　　 有　 本事　　 去　 说　 处
　　1PL drink　2S　should　 have capability go　say　place

你得有本事去把事情告诉上面那个领导。
You should have the capability to represent this situation to the higher official.

65 ten⁵⁵men²¹ nɔ⁴⁴ ʈau⁴⁴ tu³³ nɔ²¹ pe²¹ . qhɔ³⁵nɔ⁴⁴ zɦɔ³¹ pen³⁵ɕi²¹ .
　　事情　　　 这　 给　 个　 官　 上面　　这个　　 是　 本事
　　matter　　this　P　 CL official above　this　　 be　capability

这就是本事。
This is capability.

66 ŋqe⁴⁴ tʂi⁵⁵ , kɔ⁵² ʑua³⁵tʂu²¹ mua⁵² ɲia⁵² . kɔ⁵² ʑua³⁵ ʔua⁴⁴ ʔi⁵⁵ tu³³ nɔ²¹ ,
   条   五   你 要得   有   钱   你   要   做   一 个 官
   CL   five 2S should   have money 2S want do one CL official

第五，你得有钱。你想要当官，
Fifthly, you have to be rich. If you want to be an official,

67 kɔ⁵² ʑua³⁵tʂu²¹ mua⁵² ɲia⁵² . thau²¹ lu⁵⁵ ʂi⁵²xaɯ²¹
   你   要得   有   钱   时候   个   时候
   2S should   have money time   CL   time

你就得有钱。当百姓有困难的时候，
you have to be rich. When the people are in trouble,

68 pe⁵²sen²¹ tsɔ²¹ɲi²¹ , ʑu³³ mu³³ thɔ³⁵ tʂi³³ tau⁴⁴ ʔi⁵⁵ qhɔ³⁵ ɲia⁵²
    百姓   困难   自己   去   讨   不   得   一   处   钱
   people difficulty oneself go ask   NEG   get one part money

自己去哪里都讨不到钱来帮助他们，
and you can't ask for money from anywhere to help them;

69 qhɔ³⁵ tɬɯ³¹ lɔ³³ pa⁵⁵ pe⁵²sen²¹ laɯ²¹ , ʑu³³ ʑua³⁵tau⁴⁴ ntɦɔ⁴⁴
   处   哪   来   帮忙 百姓   了   自己   要得   插
   place where come help people PRF   oneself should   stick

自己就得先掏腰包来帮助他们。
you have to pay out of your pocket to help them.

70 xau³⁵ ʑu³³ ŋa⁵⁵ tʂhɔ⁴⁴ mu³³ pa⁵⁵ ʔua⁴⁴ nte⁵² . ʑau²¹ nɔ⁴⁴ ,
    里   自己   袋   衣服   去   帮忙 做   前面   次   这
   inside oneself bag cloth go   help do   front   time this

这次，
This time,

71 ʑua³⁵ mu³³ khia³⁵ ʔi⁵⁵ tʂa⁵⁵ ʔɖe⁵²nu²¹ lɔ³³ mu³³ pa⁵⁵ ʑu³³
    要   去   跑   一   样   事情   来   去   帮忙 自己
   should go run   one kind matter   come go   help oneself

(12) ka⁵⁵ kɛ³⁵ ʔua⁴⁴ nɔ²¹ 为官之道

自己要想办法帮老百姓解决问题。
you should figure out ideas on your own to help solve problems for the people.

72 tɕɔ³⁵ ti⁵⁵nɦien³¹ , pa⁵⁵ tɕɔ³⁵ kɯ³⁵ti⁵² nen⁵²tʂa⁴⁴ ,
 些　　人　　　　帮忙 些　兄弟　　亲戚
 CL.PL human　　help CL.PL brother　relatives

帮助亲朋好友，帮助自己的老百姓，
Help your relatives, friends, and your people;

73 pa⁵⁵ zu³³ tɕɔ³⁵ pe⁵²sen²¹ , tʂi³³ mua⁵² ȵia⁵² , kɔ⁵² zua³⁵tau⁴⁴ mua⁵⁵
 帮忙 自己 些　 百姓　　　 不　 有　 钱　　 你　 要得　　　 拿
 help oneself CL.PL people　NEG have money 2S should take

没有钱，你得拿自己的钱来出车费、
If they don't have money, you have to pay for the car fare,

74 kɔ⁵² tɕɔ³⁵ ȵia⁵² lɔ³³ ʔua⁴⁴ ɴqe⁴⁴ tʂhe⁵⁵ , ɴqe⁴⁴ nɔ⁵² ɴqe⁴⁴ xau³³ ,
 你　 些　　 钱　 来　 做　 费用　 车　　 费用 吃　 费用 喝
 2S CL.PL money come do fare car fare eat fare drink

伙食费、
room and board expenses,

75 ɴqe⁴⁴ the²¹ tɕhaɯ⁴⁴ pɯ⁴⁴ , mu³³ khia³⁵ kua²¹ tau⁴⁴
 费用 支付 处　　 睡　　 去　　 跑　 让　 得
 fare pay place sleep go run let get

住宿费，
hotel expenses;

76 qhɔ³⁵ xau⁵²lɯ²¹ nɔ⁴⁴ tɕɔ⁵² lɔ³³ mu³³ pa⁵⁵ kɔ⁵² tɕɔ³⁵ pe⁵²sen²¹ .
 处　 事情　　　 这　 带　 来　 去　 帮　 你　 些　 百姓
 place thing this bring come go help 2S CL.PL people

想办法让事情办成，来帮助你的百姓。
if you want the things to be done to help your people,

77 qhɔ³⁵nɔ⁴⁴ zɦɔ³¹ ʔi⁵⁵ qhɔ³⁵ ʔua³³ kɔ⁵² zua³⁵tʂu²¹
 这个　　　 是　　 一　 处　　 (定标) 你　 要得
 this　　　 be　　 one place REL 2S should

这就是你得是一个有钱人。
you have to be a rich man.

78 zfiɔ³¹ ʔi⁵⁵ tu³³ nɦen³¹ mua⁵² ɲia⁵² . ɴqe⁴⁴ tau⁴⁴ ,
   是   一   个   人   有   钱   条   六
   be one CL people have money CL six

第六,
Sixthly,

79 lɔ³³ zfiɔ³¹ ɴqe⁴⁴ kɦauɯ³¹ , kɔ⁵² zua³⁵ ʔua⁴⁴ ʔi⁵⁵ tu³³ nɔ²¹ ,
   也   是   条   最后   你   要   做   一   个   官
  CONJ be   CL   last   2S want do one CL official

也是最后一条,你要做官,
also the last one, if you want to be an official,

80 kɔ⁵² zua³⁵tʂu²¹ ɕia⁵⁵ lɔ⁵² ɕia⁵⁵ ʔda³⁵ .
   你   要得   心   大   心   宽
   2S   should   heart big heart wide

你得心胸宽广。
you should be generous.

81 ɕia⁵⁵ lɔ⁵² ɕia⁵⁵ ʔda³⁵ zfiɔ³¹ thau²¹ kɔ⁵² mua⁵² ʔi⁵⁵ tʂa³⁵ pe⁵² sen²¹ ,
   心   大   心   宽   是   时候   你   有   一   种   百   姓
  heart big heart wide   is   time   2S have one CL people

心胸宽广是指当你有一些老百姓,
Being generous means when

82 lauɯ³⁵ tua⁵² xai³³ tia³³ : "ʔau⁵⁵ zfiauɯ³¹ lɔ⁵⁵ , ku³⁵ tʂi³³ mua⁵² ɲia⁵² lauɯ²¹ ,
   他们   来   说   道   哦   爷   大   我   不   有   钱   了
   3PL come say QUOT   INT   lord   big   1S   NEG   have money   PRF

他们来对你说:"哦,领导,我没有钱了,
some people say "Oh, Official, I have no money,

83 lai³⁵ , ɕai⁵⁵ kɔ⁵² pua³³ pa⁵⁵ tau⁴⁴ mi⁴⁴ ntʂi³³ ɲia⁵²
   嘞   看   你   是否   帮   得   小   些   钱
   IP   see   2S   Q   help can small CL.PL money

(12) ka⁵⁵ ke³⁵ ʔua⁴⁴ nɔ²¹ 为官之道

看你可否给些钱
could you please give me some?

84 ʈau⁴⁴ ku³⁵ tɕɔ⁵² mu³³ ʐua³⁵ ʔɔ⁵⁵ tʂa⁵⁵ tia²¹ tɔ²¹ ,
　　给　　我　　带　　　　去　　要　　两　　把　　刀　　那
　　give　1S　take.along　go　want　two　CL　knife　that
给我去买那两把刀，
I want to buy a few knife,

85 lɔ³³ ʐɦo³¹ ʐua³⁵ ʔi⁵⁵ tɕɔ³⁵ tʂhua⁵² tɕɔ⁵² mu³³ pa⁵⁵ ku³⁵ pɔ⁵²nia²¹ ,
　　或　　是　　要　　一　　些　　药　　　带　　　　去　　帮忙　我　　妻子
　　or　　be　want　one　CL.PL　medicine　take.along　go　help　1S　wife
或是买一些药带回去给我妻子治病，
or bring some medicine back to help my wife;

86 tɔ²¹ʂi²¹nɔ⁴⁴ ku³⁵ pɔ⁵²nia²¹ mɔ⁵⁵ ŋa³⁵ xen³⁵ ."
　　现在　　　　　我　　妻子　　　　痛　　重　　很
　　now　　　　　1S　wife　　　hurt　heavy　very
现在我妻子病得很重。"
now my wife is seriously ill."

87 zu³³ ʐua³⁵tau⁴⁴ ɳʈhɔ⁴⁴ lɔ⁴⁴ mua⁵⁵ ʈau⁴⁴ nɯ³³ ,
　　自己　　要得　　　插　　　快速　拿　　给　　他
　　oneself　should　stick　rapidly　take　give　3S
自己得赶快从口袋里拿钱给他，
You should immediately get your money out of pocket for him;

88 zu³³ tsaɯ²¹ pu⁵⁵ tʂi³³ tau⁴⁴ ʈau⁴⁴ nɯ³³ ,
　　自己　就　　　赠　　不　　得　　给　　他
　　oneself　although　give　NEG　can　give　3S
就算自己不能送给他钱，
even if you can't give him your money,

89 lɔ³³ zu³³ ʐua³⁵tau⁴⁴ tsai⁴⁴ pu⁵⁵ ʈau⁴⁴ nɯ³³ . ʐau²¹ nɔ⁴⁴ ,
　　也　　自己　　要得　　　借　　赠　　给　　他　　次　　这
　　CONJ　oneself　should　lend　give　give　3S　time　this

自己也得借给他。这次,
you should lend to him. This time,

90 tɕua⁴⁴ tʂhua⁵⁵ lɔ³³ zɦɔ³¹ tʂe³⁵ ku⁵⁵ȵia⁵⁵, lu⁵⁵ tʂe³⁵ tɔ²¹ ku⁵⁵ȵia⁵⁵ lauɯ²¹,
  风   吹   或   是   家   烧焦 , 个   家   那   烧焦   了
  wind   blow   or   be   home   burn   CL   home   that   burn   PRF

是风灾或是火灾,那个房子烧毁了,
whether be it wind disaster or fire disaster, the house gets burned down,

91 zu³³ zua³⁵tau⁴⁴ ntʂhia³⁵ tsɔ⁵² xau⁴⁴ ke³⁵ lɔ³³ zɦɔ³¹ zu³³
  自己   要得   找   条   头   路   或   是   自己
  oneself   should   find   CL   head   road   or   be   oneself

自己得寻求外援,或者是自己
you have to seek assistance, or

92 zua³⁵tau⁴⁴ mua⁵⁵ te⁵² lau⁵²kau⁵⁵ tai³³ ʔdia³⁵ tɕe³⁵ pua³⁵
  要得   拿   些   锅   碗   勺   身   把
  should   take   CL.PL   pot   bowl   spoon   CL   PT

得拿些锅、碗、勺、
offer some pots, bowels, spoons and clothes

93 ti³³ tʂhɔ⁴⁴ tɕɔ⁵² mu³³ pa⁵⁵ tau⁴⁴ zi²¹ ntauɯ²¹.
  裤子   衣服   带   去   帮   给   家   那
  pants   cloth   take.along   go   help   P   home   that

衣服去帮助受灾的那家人。
to help the family who are suffering.

94 qhɔ³⁵nɔ³⁵/⁴⁴ zɦɔ³¹ ʔi⁵⁵ qhɔ³⁵ ke³⁵ zu³³ ɕia⁵⁵ lɔ⁵² ɕia⁵⁵ ʔda³⁵,
  这里   是   一   处   路   自己   心   大   心   宽
  here   be   one   place   road   oneself   heart   big   heart   wide

这是自己要心胸宽广的地方,
This is the reason why you should be generous;

95 zu³³ zua³⁵tau⁴⁴ mu³³ pa⁵⁵ kɯ³⁵ti⁵² nen⁵²tʂa⁴⁴.
  自己   要得   去   帮忙   兄弟   亲戚
  oneself   should   go   help   brother   relatives

(12) ka⁵⁵ ke³⁵ ʔua⁴⁴ nɔ²¹ 为官之道 221

自己得去帮助亲朋好友。
you should help your friends and relatives.

96 tʂi³³ xai³³ tu³³ qhua⁴⁴, lɔ³³ʂi³³ kɯ³⁵ti⁵², laɯ³⁵ tua⁵² tsi⁵⁵ tsɦɔ³¹
　　不　　说　　个　客人　　　或者　　兄弟　　　他们　来　叫　到
　　NEG say CL guest　　　or　　 brother　3PL come call about

不管是外人，还是亲人，
Whether they are outsiders or relatives,

97 zu³³ thau²¹ tɕɦɯ³¹ laɯ²¹, zu³³ zua³⁵tʂu²¹ tau⁴⁴ ʔua⁴⁴
　　自己　时候　　哪　　了　　自己　　要得　　　得　　做
　　oneself time　when PRF oneself should　should do

他们来叫自己的时候，自己得把心肠放软，
when they ask you for help, you should be softhearted

98 lu⁵⁵ zɦɔ³¹ mɦua³¹, zua³⁵tau⁴⁴ mu³³ pa⁵⁵ lɦua³¹,
　　个　　力量　　软　　　要得　　　去　　帮　　人家
　　CL power soft　　 should　　 go　 help other people

要得去帮助人家，
and offer them help

99 kua²¹ tau⁴⁴ qhɔ³⁵ xau⁵²lɯ²¹ ntaɯ²¹ tau⁴⁴ lɦua³¹ .
　　使得　　处　　事情　　那　　　给　　人家
　　make can place thing that give other people

让别人的困难得到解决。
to solve their difficulties.

100 qhɔ³⁵nɔ⁴⁴ zɦɔ³¹ qhɔ³⁵ ʔua³³ zu³³ zua³⁵tau⁴⁴ ʔua⁴⁴ ʔi⁵⁵ tu³³ nɦien³¹
　　这里　　　是　　　处　（定标）自己　　要得　　　做　一　个　人
　　here　　 be　place REL oneself should　　 do　one CL human

这是心胸宽广的人要做到的。
This is what a generous person should do.

101 ɕia⁵⁵ lɔ⁵² ɕia⁵⁵ ʔda³⁵ . tʂi³³ tʂhɔ⁵⁵ xai³³ tia³³ : "ʔɔ⁵⁵, tɕia⁴⁴ ku³⁵ sa³⁵ tʂɔ⁴⁴,
　　心　大　心　宽　　　不　别　　说　道　　　啊　　让　我　想　让
　　heart big heart wide NEG IRR.NEG say QUOT INT let 1S think let

不要说：“啊，先让我想想，
Don't say: "Ah, let me see first;

102 ʔɔ⁵⁵ , ne⁵² mu³³ ʔua⁴⁴nte⁵² , ku³⁵ ma²¹ tua⁵² ."
　　 啊　　你们　去　　先　　　　我　　慢　　来
　　 INT　 2PL　 go　 first　　　 1S　 slow　come

啊，你们先去，我稍后来。"
ah, you go first and I'll follow later on."

103 zu³³ 　ʑua³⁵tau⁴⁴ 　mu³³ 　ta²¹ɕi²¹ntɯ²¹/³⁵ .
　　 自己　 要得　　　　 去　　 当时
　　 oneself should　　　go　　 at that moment

自己得马上去。
You should go right away.

104 zɦo³¹ xai³³ tia³³ 　qhɔ³⁵ xau⁵²lɯ²¹ ntaɯ²¹ nɯ³³ tɕen³⁵ 　　 tɕen³⁵ ,
　　 是　　 说　　道　　 处　　事情　　　 那　　　它　　 紧　　　　 紧
　　 be　　 say　COMP place matter　　　 that　 3S　 RDUP~tight

要是说那件事情很紧急，
If it is an emergency,

105 kɔ⁵² ʑua³⁵tau⁴⁴ ʔua⁴⁴ lu⁵⁵ ɕia⁵⁵ lɔ⁵² ɕia⁵⁵ ʔda³⁵ .
　　 你　　要得　　　 做　　个　　心　　大　　心　　宽
　　 2S　 should　　 do　　CL　 heart big　 heart wide

你得沉着。
You must stay calm.

106 ta³³ 　ŋtɕhɔ⁴⁴　 tɕɔ³⁵ 　nɔ⁴⁴ 　zɦo³¹ tau⁴⁴ za²¹ ke³⁵ ʔua³³ kɔ⁵²
　　 完　　完状　　　 些　　　这　　 是　　 六　　样　 路　（定标）你
　　 finish completely CL.PL this　 be　 six　 kind road REL　 2S

以上这些就是当官的六个要求，
These above are the six requirements to be an official.

107 ʑua³⁵ ʔua⁴⁴ ʔi⁵⁵ tu³³ nɔ²¹ , lɔ³³ ʑua³⁵ ʔua⁴⁴ ʔi⁵⁵ tu³³
　　 要　　做　　一　　个　　官　　 或　要　　做　　一　　个
　　 need　do　 one　 CL　 official　or　 want　do　 one　 CL

（12）ka⁵⁵ ke³⁵ ʔua⁴⁴ nɔ²¹ 为官之道

你要当官、当一个好领导，

If you want to be a good official,

108 thaɯ⁵² tɕɔ⁵² ʐuŋ⁴⁴ , kɔ⁵² ʐua³⁵tʂu²¹ ʔua⁴⁴ tau⁴⁴ ʑa²¹ nɔ⁴⁴ .
　　头　　带　　好　　你　要得　做　　六　样　　这
　　head　lead　good　2S　should　do　six　kind　this

你得做到这六条。

you must live up to the six conditions.

为官之道

  谁想要做官,就得具备这六个条件。
  第一条,要博学。"博学"就是别人说什么,你都懂,就算不是全都懂,但也要尽可能多懂。别人谈到什么你都懂,说到上面的你懂,谈到下面的你也懂,谈到世间伦理你懂,谈到诗书礼仪你也懂,谈到兴盛之路你懂,谈到苗族传统文化你也懂。这就是博学。
  第二条,是能干。你想要当官你就得能干。他们说:"你写一封信去讨钱来帮助百姓。"你就得会写这封信。同样的,他们说:"你开车,我们去山上面去。"你得会开车,要是你不会,你就开不了车去山上。他们叫你办那件事情,你得会办。比如老百姓对你说:"你试着教我们看看,要怎么做,要怎么开始,怎么结束。"你得会教他们。对他们说:"开始的时候你要这样做,结束的时候你要这样做。"这就是"能干"。"博学"和"能干"不一样。博学的人但他不能干,这个人就当不了官,因为他仅仅博学而已。当别人叫他动手做的时候,他做不了。
  第三条,公正。你想当官,你得公平公正。他们拿一包钱给你,让你去帮助百姓,你就真的要拿去帮助百姓,你不要拿一些装在自己的腰包里,只拿一些去帮助百姓,你得走廉洁公正的道路。有时候,有一些百姓来办事,你不要偏袒这一个,也不要偏袒那一个,去帮这个或者是去帮那个。你要坚持公平,平等对待双方。公正地给他们断案,你要不偏袒任何一方。当你有一些物资的时候,你要拿去资助他们,你要不分亲疏远近。不要说:"这些是我的兄弟,这些不是我的兄弟。"而你只把东西分给了自己的兄弟,不分给关系远的人。这就是公正,它要求你公平地帮助每个人。
  第四条,有本事。你要当官,你得是个有本事的人。敢说,敢做,说了就要做,怎么说就要怎么做。他们说:"哦,风把我们的家吹毁了,你帮忙去向政府汇报,或者帮忙讨一些瓦来给我们盖房子。"你得有本事去说,或者是把这件事向政府汇报,让官府拿钱去帮忙买瓦,来盖房子给那些受灾的人。或者说:"噢,有个领导来到上面这里啦,你帮忙去找上面那个领导,我们老百姓很困难,让他想办法来帮助我们,让他来给我们修路。或者说:"我们没有水喝,让他来通水。"你得有本事去说服上面那个领导。这就是本事。
  第五条,你得有钱。你想要当官,你就得有钱。当百姓有困难,而自己去哪里都讨不到钱来帮助他们的时候,自己就得先掏腰包来帮助他们。这次,自己要想办法帮老百姓解决问题。帮助亲朋好友,帮助自己的老百姓。没有钱,你得拿自己的钱来出车费、伙食费、住宿费,想办法让事情办成,来帮助你的老百姓。这需要你是一个有钱人。
  第六条,也是最后一条。你要做官,你得心胸宽广。心胸宽广是指当有一些老百姓来对你说:"哦,领导,我没有钱了,你可否给我一些钱,让我去买两把刀,或是买一些药带回去给我妻子治病,现在我妻子病得很重。"自己得赶快从口袋里拿钱给他,就算自己不能送他钱,也得借给他。若是风灾或火灾,那个房子烧毁了,自己得寻求外援,或者是自己

（12）ka⁵⁵ ke³⁵ ʔua⁴⁴ nɔ²¹ 为官之道

得拿些锅、碗、勺、衣服去帮助受灾的那家人。这是自己要心胸宽广的地方，自己得去帮助亲朋好友。不管是外人，还是亲人，他们来求自己的时候，自己得把心肠放软，要得去帮助人家，让别人的困难得到解决。这是心胸宽广的人要做到的。不要说："啊，先让我想想，啊，你们先回去，我稍后来。"自己得马上去。要是说那件事情很紧急，你得沉着应对。以上这些就是当官的六个条件。你要当官、当一个好官，你得做到这六条。

How to be an Official

People who want to be an official should fulfill six conditions.

Firstly, be erudite. "Erudite" means you know whatever other people say. You know as much as you can even if you can't understand all. You know everything people talk about, including things above and things below; you know how the world works and you're rich in poetry and etiquette. Meanwhile, you also know the way to prosperity as well the traditional Hmong culture. That's what we call erudition.

Secondly, be competent. You have to be competent if you want to be an official. When people say: "You should write a letter to ask for money to help the people", you should be able to do it. Likewise, when people say: "You should drive us up to the mountain", you should be able to drive. Otherwise, you can't drive them up to the mountain. You should have the competence to do what people want you to do. For instance, when people say that "Please try to teach us how to do, how to start and how to end", you should help them understand and tell them "you should do it like this at the beginning and do it like that when it ends". That's competence. Erudition and competence are not the same. If one is erudite but not competent, he can't be an official because he is only erudite. He is not able to do work practically when people demand.

Thirdly, be a just man. You should persist in justice if you want to be an official. You should actually help when they give you a pack of money and ask you to help the people. Don't pocket some of the money and only use the rest of the money to help them. You should keep clean-fingered and just. Sometimes, when some people come to ask for something, you shouldn't be biased towards this one or that one. Justly issue verdicts for them and don't take sides. If you have some supplies, you should use it to help them; don't show favoritism according to relationships and say: "These are my brothers and those are not", only distributing supplies to your own brothers but not to those who are outsiders. This is justice, which requires you to impartially help everyone.

Fourthly, be capable. You should be a capable person who dares to speak and act, and actually perform what you said, if you want to be an official. When people say that "Oh, the wind blew our house into pieces, you should help us report to the government, or ask for some tiles for us to rebuild our house", you should be capable of giving a full account or representing this situation to the government to ask the government to provide money to buy tiles and build houses for those who are suffering from the disaster. Or they say: "Oh, a higher official happens to come here, you should help by going to talk to him, because we live a hard life so please ask him to find way to help us; ask him to make a road for us." Or they say: "We don't have water to drink, please ask him to provide water." You should have the capability to represent this situation to higher official. This is capability.

Fifthly, you have to be rich. You have to be a rich man if you want to be an official. When the people are in trouble, and you can't ask for money from anywhere to help them; you have to pay out of your own pocket to help them. This time, you should figure out ideas on your own to solve their problems. Help your relatives, friends, and your people. If they don't have money, you should pay for the car fare, room and board expenses. If you want things to be done to help your people, you have to be a rich man.

Sixthly, also the last one, if you want to be an official, you should be generous, which means that when people say to you "Oh, official, I have no money so could you please give me some to buy a few knifes or bring some medicine back to help my wife who is seriously ill", you should immediately get your money out of pocket for him; even if you can't give the money to him freely, you should lend to him. Whether by wind disaster or fire disaster, if the house got burnt down, you have to seek for assistance, or offer some pots, bowels, spoons and clothes to help the family who are suffering. This is the reason why you should be generous. You should help your relatives and friends. Whether they are outsiders or your relatives, you should be softhearted and offer help to solve their difficulties when they ask you for help. This is what a generous person should do. Don't say: "Let me see first; you go first and I'll follow later on". You should do it right away. If it's emergency, you must stay calm.

These above are the six requirements to be an official. If you want to be a good official, you must live up to the six conditions.

（13）lu⁵⁵nen⁵²lia²¹ 糟糕的生活

个　生活　烂
A　Life　Terrible

1 zɦɔ³¹　len⁵²　tɦɯ³¹　ʔua⁴⁴　tɑɯ³³　li⁴⁴　　　ntɯ²¹　nɔ⁴⁴，lu⁵⁵　nen⁵²　zua³⁵　lia²¹．
　是　　位　　哪　　做　　跟　　像　　　那　　这　　个　　生活　要　　烂
　COP　CL　who　do　follow　be.like　that　this　CL　life　will　rot
要是谁照这样做，生活要毁掉。
People who do as follows will ruin their own life.

2 ŋqe⁴⁴　ʔi⁵⁵，ʔdʑia³¹　nɔ⁵²　ʔdʑia³¹　xau³³．zɦɔ³¹　xai³³　tia³³　　kɔ⁵²　zɦɔ³¹　ʔi⁵⁵
　条　　一　　骗　　　吃　　骗　　　喝　　是　　说　　道　　你　　是　　一
　CL　one　decieve　eat　decieve　drink　COP　say　COMP　2S　COP　one
第一条，骗吃骗喝。
Firstly, lying and cheating for food and drink.

3 tu³³　ti⁵⁵　nɦien³¹　ʔdʑia³¹　nɔ⁵²　ʔdʑia³¹　xau³³，ʔdʑia³¹　ʔi⁵⁵　ŋu⁵⁵　ʔtʰau⁴⁴　ʔi⁵⁵
　个　　人　　　　　骗　　　吃　　骗　　　喝　　骗　　　一　　天　　过　　　一
　CL　human　　　decieve　eat　decieve　drink　decieve　one　day　pass　one
如果说你是一个骗吃骗喝的人，骗一天过一天，
If you're a person who lies and cheats for food and drink,

4 ŋu⁵⁵，ʔdʑia³¹　ʔi⁵⁵　m̥ɔ³³　ʔtʰau⁴⁴　ʔi⁵⁵　m̥ɔ³³．kɔ⁵²　tsi³³　　mua⁵²　ȵia⁵²，
　天　　骗　　　一　　晚　　过　　　一　　晚　　你　　不　　有　　钱
　day　decieve　one　night　pass　one　night　2S　NEG　have　money
骗一晚过一晚。你没有钱，
deception is the only way you can count on to live. You have no money,

5 kɔ⁵²　mu³³　ŋqe³⁵　lɦua³¹　le⁴⁴　ȵia⁵²，kɔ⁵²　ʔdʑia³¹　xai³³　tia³³　：
　你　　去　　借　　人家　　的　　钱　　你　　骗　　　说　　道
　2S　go　borrow　others　PRT　money　2S　decieve　say　QUOT

（13）lu⁵⁵nen⁵²lia²¹ 糟糕的生活

你去跟人家借钱，你骗人家说：
so you go to borrow from others and lie to them:

6 "tsai³³ kɔ⁵² ʔi⁵⁵ qhɔ³⁵ ȵia⁵² ʈau⁴⁴ ku³⁵ , ʔɔ⁵⁵ pe⁵⁵ ṉu⁵⁵ ma²¹ the²¹ kɔ⁵² ."
　　借　　你　一　点　钱　　给　我　，两　三　天　慢　还　你
　　borrow 2S one point money give 1S two three day slow repay 2S

"你借给我一点钱，过两三天还你。"
"Please lend me some money and I will repay you in two or three days."

7 ʔthau⁴⁴ lɔ³³ lau²¹ kau²¹ tau²¹ ṉu⁵⁵, kɔ⁵² ʐua³⁵ tsi³³ mu³³ the²¹ .
　　过　来　了　十　出　天　你　　要　　不　去　还
　　pass come PRF ten out day 2S need NEG go repay

过了十多天，你没有去还。
However over ten days pass, you still didn't return the money.

8 kɔ⁵² mu³³ ʔdɦa³¹ tu³³ tɔ²¹ : "tsai³³ kɔ⁵² ʔɔ⁵⁵ sen³⁵ mple⁵² ʈau⁴⁴
　　你　去　骗　个　那　　借　　你　两　袋　谷子　给
　　2S go decieve CL that borrow 2S two bag rice give

你去骗另外一个："你借两袋米给我吃，
Then you lie to another one, saying "please lend a few bags of rice,

9 ku³⁵ nɔ⁵² , ʔɔ⁵⁵ pe⁵⁵ ṉu⁵⁵ ma²¹ the²¹ ȵia⁵² ʈau⁴⁴ kɔ⁵² , lɔ³³
　　我　吃　两　三　天　慢　还　钱　　给　你　　也
　　1S eat two three day slow return money give 2S CONJ

过几天再还你米钱，
I will return to you the money

10 zɦɔ³¹ ku³⁵ ma²¹ the²¹ ʔɔ⁵⁵ pe⁵⁵ sen³⁵ ʈau⁴⁴ kɔ⁵² ."
　　是　我　慢　还　两　三　袋　给　你
　　COP 1S slow return two three bag give 2S

或者我再还你几袋米。"
or some bags of rice in a few days."

11 ʔthau⁴⁴ lau²¹ tʂhen⁵² ɕuŋ⁴⁴, kɔ⁵² tsi³³ the²¹ ʈau⁴⁴ lau³⁵ .
　　过　了　成　年　你　不　还　给　人家
　　pass PRF become year 2S NEG return give others

过了一年，你还不还给人家。
A year passed and you still didn't repay them.

12 qhɔ³⁵ nɔ⁴⁴ ʐɦɔ³¹ ʔi⁵⁵ qhɔ³⁵ ke³⁵ ˀɖɦa³¹ nɔ⁵² ˀɖɦa³¹ xau³³ .
　　处　 这　 是　 一　 处　 路　 骗　　 吃　 骗　　 喝
　　place this　COP　one place road decieve eat decieve drink

这就是骗吃骗喝。
This is lying and cheating for food and drink,

13 nɯ³³ ʐua³⁵ tsia³⁵ kɔ⁵² tsɔ⁵² xau⁴⁴ ke³⁵ , kɔ⁵² ʐua³⁵ tʂi³³ mua⁵² nɔ⁵² mua⁵² xau³³ .
　　它　 要　 砍　 你　 条　 头　 路　　 你　 要　 不　 有　 吃　 有　 喝
　　3S　need chop　2S　CL　head road　　2S　need NEG have eat have drink

它会阻断你的路，你将没有吃的喝的。
which will hinder your way to prosperity and lead to a bad life.

14 ŋqe⁴⁴ ʔɔ⁵⁵ , tɯ³⁵ tsia⁵² ʐua²¹ pɔ³⁵ . kɔ⁵² ʐɦɔ³¹ ʔi⁵⁵ tu³³ nɦen³¹
　　条　 二　　 赌　 钱　 押　 宝　　 你　 是　 一　 个　 人
　　CL　two　 gamble money pledge treasure　2S　COP one CL human

第二条，赌钱押宝。
Secondly, gamble and pawn.

15 ɲia²¹ tɯ³⁵ tsia⁵² . thau²¹ kɔ⁵² mu³³ tɯ³⁵ tsia⁵² ,
　　喜欢 赌　 钱　　 时候 你　 去　 赌　 钱
　　like gamble money time　2S　go　gamble money

你是一个好赌的人。当你去赌钱的时候，
You're a gambler. When you go to gamble,

16 kɔ⁵² tau⁴⁴ tai³³ ʐuŋ⁴⁴ lu³³ . ta⁵⁵ ʂi⁵⁵ thau²¹ kɔ⁵² puŋ⁵⁵ tɦa³¹ ,
　　你　 得　 的话 好　 咯　　 但是　 时候 你　 丢　 完
　　2S　get　if　 good IP　 but　 time　2S　lost finish

你赢的话就好咯。但是当你输完的时候，
it's good to win, but when you lose all your money,

17 kɔ⁵² ʐua³⁵ mua⁵⁵ kɔ⁵² te⁵² pɔ³⁵ xau²¹ tɔ²¹ tʂe³⁵ tɕɔ⁵² mu³³ ʐua²¹ .
　　你　 要　 拿　 你　 些　 宝物　 那　 家　 带　　 去　 押
　　2S　need take　2S　CL.PL treasure that home take.along go pledge

(13) lu⁵⁵nen⁵²lia²¹ 糟糕的生活　　231

你把你家里的宝物拿去押。
you have to pledge your valuables.

18 kɔ⁵² mu³³ ʐua²¹, ʐua²¹ ʔi⁵⁵ ʑa²¹, ʐua²¹ ʔɔ⁵⁵ ʑa²¹, ʐua²¹ pe⁵⁵ ʑa²¹.
　　你　去　押　　押　一　样　　押　两　样　　押　三　样
　　2S　go　pledge　pledge one kind　pledge two kind　pledge three kind
你去押，押一样，押两样，押三样。
You have to pledge one, two or three valuable things,

19 mua⁵² te⁵² ʑa²¹ ʐuŋ⁴⁴ ʐuŋ⁴⁴ ŋɔ⁵⁵ tɔ²¹ tʂe³⁵ kɔ⁵² tɛɔ⁵² mu³³ ʐua²¹,
　　有　　些　样　好　　好　　在　那　家　你　带　去　押
　　have　CL.PL kind RDUP~good　be.located that home 2S take.along go pledge
家里有什么好的你都拿去押，
you pledge whatever's the most valuable in your home

20 tɛɔ⁵² mu³³ tɯ³⁵ tsia⁵². thau²¹ kɔ⁵² tɛɔ⁵² mu³³ tɯ³⁵ tsia⁵² ta³³,
　　带　　去　赌　钱　　时候　你　带　　去　赌　钱　完
　　take.along go gamble money time 2S take.along go gamble money finish
拿去赌。当它们被你赌完的时候，
to do gambling. When you gamble them all away,

21 kɔ⁵² lu⁵⁵ nen⁵² kɔ⁵² te⁵² ɲia⁵² tsɦia³¹ kua³³ kɔ⁵² khɯ³⁵ tau⁴⁴ ntaɯ²¹,
　　你　个　生活　你　些　钱　钱　(定标) 你　苦　得　那
　　2S CL life 2S CL.PL money money REL 2S bitter get that
你辛苦挣来的钱和家产，
the money and estate you have earned with great effort

22 nɯ³³ ʐua³⁵ ta³³ ʐu⁵² ʐu³³. thau²¹ kɔ⁵² tɛɔ³⁵ ɲia⁵² ta³³ ʐu⁵² ʐu³³,
　　它　要　完　渐渐　　时候　你　些　钱　完　渐渐
　　3S need finish gradually time 2S CL.PL money finish gradually
它会慢慢败完。
will be gradually squandered.

23 kɔ⁵² mua⁵² pe³³ tʂɦaɯ³¹ ʑa²¹ khuŋ²¹ tɕen²¹ tɕen⁵⁵,
　　你　有　多少　　样　东西　正经
　　2S have how much kind thing decent

当你的钱渐渐花完的时候，你有多少样拿得出手的东西，
After all of your money runs out, whatever good things you have

24 pe³³ tʂɦaɯ³¹ za²¹ khuŋ²¹ zuŋ⁴⁴, kɔ⁵² zua³⁵ mua⁵⁵
　　多少　　　样　东西　好　　你　要　拿
　　how much　style　thing　good　2S　should　take

你有多少样好东西，
however many, good things you have

25 tɕɔ⁵²　　mu³³ zua²¹, tɕɔ⁵² lɔ³³ tɯ³⁵ tsia⁵², ʔua⁴⁴ kua²¹　　ta³³ .
　　带　　　去　押　带　　来　赌　钱　　做　尽可能　　　完
　　take.along　go　pledge　take.along　come　gamble　money　do　as far as possible　finish

你要拿去押，拿去赌钱，赌到精光。
you have to pledge them, take them for gambling until nothing is left.

26 thau²¹ ta³³　laɯ²¹, kɔ⁵² zua³⁵ mua⁵⁵ pɔ⁵²nia²¹ mi⁴⁴ ŋua²¹
　　时候　完　了　　你　要　拿　妻子　　小　孩子
　　time　finish　PRF　2S　should　take　wife　　little　kid

当赌到精光的时候，你把妻儿拿去做抵押，
Then in the end, you have to pledge your wife and kids

27 tɕɔ⁵²　　mu³³ zua²¹, kɔ⁵² mua⁵² tu⁵⁵ mua⁵² ntshai³³ ,
　　带　　　去　押　你　有　儿子　有　女儿
　　take.along　go　pledge　2S　have　son　have　daughter

你有儿有女的话，你会拿去抵押。
if you have sons or daughters, you'll use them for a pledge.

28 kɔ⁵² zua³⁵ tɕɔ⁵²　　mu³³ zua²¹ . qho³⁵ nɔ⁴⁴ zɦɔ³¹ kɔ⁵² tʂi³³ tʂɔ⁴⁴ tʂɦe³¹ ,
　　你　要　带　　　去　押　处　这　是　你　不　放弃
　　2S　need　take.along　go　pledge　place　this　COP　2S　NEG　give up

赌博这事要是你还不放弃，
In this case, you're still not willing to give up gambling,

29 kɔ⁵² lu⁵⁵ nen⁵² zua³⁵ lia²¹ . ŋqe⁴⁴ pe⁵⁵ , qua³⁵ zen⁵² qua³⁵ tʂhua⁵² .
　　你　个　生活　要　烂　条　三　　毒品
　　2S　CL　life　going to　rot　CL　three　drugs

（13）lu⁵⁵nen⁵²lia²¹ 糟糕的生活　　　233

你的生活将会毁掉。第三条，毒品。
your life will be ruined. Thirdly, take drugs.

30　zɦɔ³¹　xai³³　tia³³　kɔ⁵²　tʂi³³　tʂo⁴⁴　tʂfie³¹　tsɔ⁵²　ke³⁵
　　是　　说　　道　　你　　不　　放　　弃　　条　　路
　　COP　say　COMP　2S　NEG　give　up　　CL　road

如果说你不戒掉毒瘾，
If you don't get out of the drug addiction,

31　qua³⁵　ʑen⁵⁵　qua³⁵　tʂhua⁵²　mua⁵²　ʑen³³　, kɔ⁵²　lu⁵⁵　nen⁵²　ʑua³⁵　lia²¹ .
　　屎　　烟　　屎　　毒　　　　有　　瘾　　　你　个　生活　　要　烂
　　shit　smoke shit　drugs　　　have addiction 2S CL life　going to rot

你的生活会毁掉。
your life will be ruined.

32　kɔ⁵²　qua³⁵　ʑen⁵⁵　nɯ³³　tʂua³³　mua⁵²　ta³³　ʑu⁵²　ʑu³³　sɯ⁵⁵ ,
　　你　　毒品　　　　它　　只　　有　　完　　渐渐　　　只
　　2S　drugs　　　　3S　only　have finish gradually only

你的毒品只会慢慢用完，
Your drugs will be gradually used up;

33　kɔ⁵²　xau³³　tɕɔ³⁵　tʂhua⁵²　mua⁵²　ʑen³³　ntau²¹　ntau⁴⁴　ntau⁴⁴ ,
　　你　喝　　些　　毒品　　　　　那　　多　　　多
　　2S drink CL.PL drugs　　　　　that RDUP~much

你吸很多毒品，
the large quantities of drugs you've taken,

34　ʔi⁵⁵　ɳtʂi³³　nɯ³³　ʔua⁴⁴　ṭau⁴⁴　kɔ⁵²　lu⁵⁵　l̥ɯ⁵⁵　ʑua³⁵　pua²¹ .
　　一　　些　　它　　做　　给　　你　个　脑子　要　　坏
　　one CL.PL 3S　do　give　2S　CL brain going to bad

过一会儿，它会损害你的大脑。
after a while, will do harm to your brain.

35　kɔ⁵²　mua⁵²　pe³³　tʂɦau³¹　ʑa²¹　kɔ⁵²　ʑua³⁵　tɕɔ⁵²　mu³³　mfiua³¹ ,
　　你　　有　　多少　　　样　　你　要　　领　　去　　卖
　　2S have how much look 2S should lead go sell

你有多少家产你都拿去卖,
You have to sell all your estate

36 tɕɔ⁵² lɔ³³ zua³⁵ za²¹ tʂhua⁵² mua⁵² zen³³ ntaɯ²¹ . kɔ⁵² tʂi³³
   带   来   要   样   毒品   那   你   不
   bring come should kind drugs   that   2S   NEG

用来买那些毒品。
to buy drugs.

37 tʂɦie³¹ tsɔ⁵² ke³⁵ qua³⁵ zen⁵⁵ qua³⁵ tʂhua⁵² nɔ⁴⁴ , kɔ⁵² lu⁵⁵ nen⁵² zua³⁵ lia²¹ .
   放弃   条   路   毒品   这   你   个   生活   要   烂
   give up CL   road drugs   this 2S   CL life going to rot

你不戒掉毒品,你的生活要毁掉。
If you don't end drug addiction, your life will be ruined.

38 ɴqe⁴⁴ tsua³³ ntsi³⁵ mu³³ , qua³⁵ tɕaɯ³⁵ .
   条   接   补   去   酒瘾
   CL   next supplement go   alcoholism

下面一条,酒瘾。
Next is alcoholism.

39 zɦɔ³¹ kɔ⁵² tʂi³³ tʂɦie³¹ tsɔ⁵² ke³⁵ qua³⁵ tɕaɯ³⁵ , kɔ⁵² nia⁵² ɲu⁵⁵ xau³³ tɕaɯ³⁵ ,
   是   你   不   放弃   条   路   酒瘾   你   年   天   喝   酒
   COP 2S   NEG give up CL   road alcoholism   2S   year day   drink wine

如果你戒不掉酒瘾,你天天喝酒,
If you don't quit drinking, drinking every day,

40 tau⁴⁴ ʔi⁵⁵ qhɔ³⁵ ɲia⁵² kɔ⁵² mu³³ zua³⁵ tɕaɯ³⁵ lɔ³³ xau³³ ,
   得   一   点   钱   你   去   要   酒   来   喝
   get   one point money 2S   go want wine   come drink

得一点钱你拿去买酒喝,
every penny that you earn you use on drinking alcohol;

41 mua⁵² tʂhuŋ⁵⁵ mua⁵² kɔ³³ kɔ⁵² mu³³ xau³³ , kɔ⁵² tʂi³³ zɦɔ³¹ xau³³ ʈaɯ³³ tshen⁵² tshen²¹
   有   婚宴   你   去   喝   你   不   是   喝   跟   尺寸
   have wedding party   2S   go drink   2S NEG COP drink follow size

(13) lu⁵⁵nen⁵²lia²¹ 糟糕的生活　　235

有婚宴你就去喝，你喝酒没有分寸，
you drink at every wedding party and have no limits;

42 kɔ⁵² zɯ⁵²　　mu³³ xau³³　luɯ⁵² xau³³ lia²¹ ,
　 你　放任　　去　　喝　　烂　　喝　　烂
　 2S　indulge　go　drink　rot　drink　rot

你放任自己无节制地喝，
You binge on drinking indulgently,

43 xau³³ ntau⁴⁴ tʂha⁵² le⁴⁴ lauɯ³⁵ te⁵²　tshen⁵² tshen²¹ .
　 喝　　多　　过　　的　人家　些　　尺寸
　 drink　much　pass　PRT　others　CL.PL　size

喝过了人家的尺度。
crossing the line of others'.

44 thau²¹ tʂi³³　mua⁵² tʂhuŋ⁵⁵ mua⁵² kɔ³³ , tʂi³³　mua⁵² ʈuŋ⁵² ɴqai⁵² ʈuŋ⁵² n̥ɔ⁴⁴ .
　 时候　不　　有婚宴　　　　　　　　不　　有　　酒肉饭菜
　 time　NEG　have wedding party　　NEG　have　food and wine

当没有婚宴的时候，没有酒肉。
When there's no wedding party and no food and wine,

45 lɔ³³　　kɔ⁵² mu³³ zua³⁵ lɔ³³　ʈau⁴⁴ kɔ⁵² xau³³ , xau³³ ta³³ ŋu⁵⁵ ta³³ m̥ɔ⁴⁴ .
　 也　　你　去　　买　　来　　给　你　喝　喝　没日没夜
　 CONJ　2S　go　buy　come　give　2S　drink　drink　day and night

你也去买给自己喝，没日没夜地喝。
you also buy wine for yourself to drink day and night.

46 qhɔ³⁵ ntauɯ²¹ ʑɦɔ³¹ kɔ⁵² tʂi³³ tʂɔ⁴⁴ tʂɦie³¹ , kɔ⁵² lu⁵⁵ nen⁵² zua³⁵　lia²¹ .
　 处　　那　　是　　你　　不　　放弃　　你　个　生活　要　　烂
　 place　that　COP　2S　NEG　give up　2S　CL　life　going to rot

嗜酒这事你不放弃的话，你的生活一样要毁掉。
If you don't quit drinking, your life will also be ruined.

47 ʔi⁵⁵ za²¹ ŋkau³³ . ɴqe⁴⁴ tsua³³ ntsi³⁵　　mu³³ , ʑɦɔ³¹ tha²¹ ɭua³³ ŋkau⁵² .
　 一样　　正好　条　接　　补　　　去　　是　谈　　姑娘
　 one kind　perfectly　CL　next　supplement　go　COP　talk　girl

下一条，婚外情。
The next one is extramarital affairs.

48 ʔi⁵⁵ tu³³ tsi³⁵ nen⁵² ʔua³³ kɔ⁵² tɯ⁵⁵ mua⁵² tɕua⁵⁵ mua⁵² ʑɦi³¹ lau̯²¹ ,
　一　个　男人　　(定标)　你　都　有　　家　　有　　户　　了
　one　CL　man　　REL　　2S　all　have　home　have　house　PRF

一个已有家室的男人，
If you are a married man,

49 lɔ³³ ʑɦɔ³¹ kɔ⁵² tɯ⁵⁵ mua⁵² pɔ⁵² nia²¹ mi⁴⁴ ŋua²¹ lau̯²¹ ,
　或　是　你　都　有　　妻子　　小　孩子　了
　or　COP　2S　all　have　wife　　little　kid　PRF

或者你已经有妻儿了，
who has a family with a wife and children,

50 kɔ⁵² tʂi³³ tʂɦie³¹ tsɔ⁵² ke³⁵ tʰa²¹ l̪ua³³ ŋkau⁵² ,
　你　不　　放弃　　条　路　谈　姑娘
　2S　NEG　give up　CL　road　talk　girl

你还不放弃婚外情，
you are still not willing to give up your extramarital love,

51 kɔ⁵² nia⁵² ŋu⁵⁵ mu³³ tʰa²¹ l̪ua³³ ŋkau⁵² ɴtɕe⁴⁴ tɔ⁵² ɴqe³³ tɦau³¹ .
　你　年　天　去　谈　姑娘　　　上上下下
　2S　year　day　go　talk　girl　　up and down

你天天到处去找情人。
and spend all everyday with your lovers.

52 kɔ⁵² mua⁵² ɲia⁵² ntau⁴⁴ mpau²¹ le⁴⁴ tɕa³³ , kɔ⁵² zua³⁵ mua⁵⁵ tɕɔ⁵² mu³³ tau⁴⁴
　你　有　钱　多　多　　　怎么　　你　要　拿　　带　　去　给
　2S　have　money　much　much　how　　2S　want　take　take.along　go　give

你有再多的钱，你都拿去给你那边的那个情人，
You give all the money you have to the lover of yours over there,

53 kɔ⁵² tu³³ l̪ua³³ ŋkau⁵² tɔ²¹ , tau⁴⁴ tu³³ pe²¹ , tau⁴⁴ tu³³ nta²¹ .
　你　个　姑娘　　那　给　个　上面　给　个　下面
　2S　CL　girl　　that　give　CL　above　give　CL　below

(13) lu⁵⁵nen⁵²lia²¹ 糟糕的生活　　237

给上面的那个情人，给下面的那个情人。
the lover up above and the one down below,

54　pɔ⁵² nia²¹　mi⁴⁴ ȵua²¹　ʐuŋ⁴⁴ tʂhai⁵⁵ ʐuŋ⁴⁴ ɴqhe³³　．
　　妻子　　小　孩子　　忍饥受渴
　　wife　　little kid　　suffering from hunger and thirst

妻儿忍饥受渴。
leaving your wife and children to suffer from hunger and thirst.

55　qhɔ³⁵ nɔ⁴⁴ zɦɔ³¹ kɔ⁵² tʂi³³　tʂɔ⁴⁴ tʂɦie³¹ , kɔ⁵² lu⁵⁵ nen⁵² ʐua³⁵　lia²¹ .
　　处　这　是　你　不　　放弃　　　你　个　生活　要　烂
　　place this COP 2S NEG give up　2S CL life going to rot

婚外情这事儿要是你不放弃，你的生活要毁掉。
Your life will be ruined if you don't end your extramarital affairs.

56　ɴqe⁴⁴ tsua³³ ntsi³⁵　tɔ²¹ qa⁵⁵ nɔ⁴⁴ , tu⁵⁵ ŋken³³ tu⁵⁵ ŋkɦi³¹ .
　　条　接　补　　　那　后面 这　　懒惰
　　CL next supplement that later this　laziness

最后一条，懒惰。
The last one is laziness.

57　kɔ⁵² tsau²¹ ʐua³⁵ mua⁵² ȵia⁵² ntau⁴⁴ mpau²¹ le⁴⁴ tɕa³³ , lɔ³³ zɦɔ³¹ kɔ⁵² lu⁵⁵ nen⁵²
　　你　　就　　要　　有　　钱　　多　　多　　怎么　　或　是　你　个　生活
　　2S DM need have money much much how　or COP 2S CL life

即使你有再多的钱，或者你的生活有多好，
No matter how much money you have or how good your life is,

58　ʐuŋ⁴⁴ mpau²¹ le⁴⁴ tɕa³³ , zɦɔ³¹ xai³³ tia³³　kɔ⁵² tʂi³³ ɴqɦua³¹ ,
　　好　　多　　怎么　　是　说　道　你　不　勤劳
　　good much how　COP say COMP 2S NEG diligence

如果说你不勤劳，
if you're not diligent,

59　kɔ⁵² tu⁵⁵ ŋkɦien³¹ tu⁵⁵ ŋkɦi³¹ , tʂi³³ ʔua⁴⁴ nɔ⁵² tʂi³³ ʔua⁴⁴ xau³³ , kɔ⁵² lɔ³³ ŋɔ⁵⁵　nɔ⁵²
　　你　懒惰　　　　　　　　　不　做　吃　不　做　喝　你　来　在　　吃
　　2S laziness　　　　　　　NEG do eat NEG do drink 2S come be.located eat

你懒惰，不劳动，你只在家里吃吃喝喝，
but lazy, and don't do work, only staying at home drinking and eating,

60 ŋɔ⁵⁵　　　xau³³　, tʂi³³　nte³⁵　, kɔ⁵² tɕɔ³⁵　ɲia⁵²　ntaɯ²¹　nɯ³³　ʐua³⁵　tsaɯ⁵² ta³³　.
　　在　　　喝　　不　长　　你　些　　钱　　那　　它　　要　　会　完
　　be.located　drink　NEG　grow　2S　CL.PL　money　that　3S　going to　can　finish

不久，你的那些钱要被用光。
sooner or later, your money will run out.

61 thau²¹ nɯ³³ ta³³　laɯ²¹, kɔ⁵² lu⁵⁵ nen⁵² ʐua³⁵　tʂi³³　mua⁵² nɔ⁵²
　　时候　它　　完　　了　　你　个　生活　要　　　不　　有　　吃
　　time　3S　finish PRF　2S　CL　life　going to　NEG　have　eat

当钱花光的时候，
When the money runs out,

62 tʂi³³　mua⁵² xau³³　ʔi⁵⁵ ʑa²¹　ŋkau³³　.
　　不　　有　　喝　　一　样　　正好
　　NEG　have　drink　one style　perfectly

你会没有吃的喝的。
you will have a bad life with nothing to eat or drink.

糟糕的生活

要是谁照下面这样做，生活一定会毁掉。

第一条，骗吃骗喝。如果说你是一个骗吃骗喝的人，骗一天过一天，骗一晚过一晚。你没有钱，你去跟人家借钱。你骗人家说："你借给我一点钱，过两三天还你。"过了十多天，你没有去还。你去骗另外一个人："你借两袋米给我吃，过几天再还你米钱，或者我再还你几袋米。"过了一年，你还不还给人家。这就是骗吃骗喝。它会阻断你的路，你将没有吃的喝的。

第二条，赌钱押宝。你是一个好赌的人。当你去赌钱的时候，你赢的话就好咯。但是当你输完的时候，你把你家里的宝物拿去押。你去押，押一样，押两样，押三样。家里有什么好的你都拿去押，拿去赌。当它们被你赌完的时候，你辛苦挣来的钱和家产，会慢慢败完。当你的钱渐渐花完的时候，你有多少样拿得出手的东西，你有多少样好东西，你都要拿去押，拿去赌钱，赌到精光。当赌到精光的时候，你把妻儿拿去做抵押。赌博这事要是你还不放弃，你的生活将会毁掉。

第三条，毒品。如果说你不戒掉毒瘾，你的生活会毁掉。你的毒品只会慢慢用完，你吸很多毒品，过一段时间，它会损害你的大脑。你有多少家产都拿去卖，用来买那些毒品。你不戒掉毒品，你的生活要毁掉。

第四条，酒瘾。如果你戒不掉酒瘾，你天天喝酒，得一点钱你拿去买酒喝，有婚宴你就去喝。你喝酒没有分寸，你放任自己无节制地喝，喝过了人家的尺度。当没有婚宴的时候，没有酒肉，你就去买给自己喝，没日没夜地喝。嗜酒这事你不放弃的话，你的生活一样要毁掉。

第五条，婚外情。一个已有家室的男人，或者你已经有妻儿了，你还不放弃婚外情，你天天到处去找情人。你有再多的钱，你都拿去给你那边的那个情人，给上面的那个情人，给下面的那个情人。妻儿忍饥挨饿。婚外情这事儿要是你不放弃，你的生活要毁掉。

第六条，懒惰。即使你有再多的钱，或者你的生活有多好，如果说你不勤劳，你懒惰，不劳动，你只在家里花天酒地，不久，你的那些钱要被用光。当钱花光的时候，你会没有吃的喝的。

A Warning Against Ruining Your Life

People who do as follows will certainly ruin their own life.

Firstly, lying and cheating for food and drink. If you're a person who lies and cheats for food and drink, deception is the only way that you can count on to live. You have no money so you have to borrow from others and lie to them: "Please lend me some money and I will repay you in two or three days." However over ten days passed, you still didn't return the money. Then, you lie to another one that "Please lend me a few bags of rice and I promise I will return the money or some bags of rice in a few days." But a year passed and you still didn't repay the money or rice. This is cheating for food and drink, which will hinder your way to prosperity and lead you into a bad life.

Secondly, gamble and pawn. If you're a gambler, it's lucky of you to win when you go to gamble, but when you lose all your money, you have to pledge your valuables. You have to pledge one, two or three valuable things; you pledge whatever's the most valuable in your home to gamble. When you gamble all of them away, all the fortune and estate that you earned with great effort will be gradually squandered. After all your money runs out, no matter how many good things you have, you have to pledge them and take them for gambling, until nothing is left. Then in the end, you have to pledge your wife and kids. In this case, if you still not willing to give up gambling, your life will be ruined.

Thirdly, take drugs. If you don't get out of the drug addiction, your life will be ruined. Your drugs will be gradually used up. The large quantities of drugs you've taken will do harm to your brain after a while. You have to sell all your estate to buy drugs. Thus, if you don't end drug addiction, your life will be destroyed.

Fourthly, alcoholism. If you don't quit drinking, drinking every day, and every penny that you earn will be used on drinking alcohol. You drink at every wedding party and have no limits. You always binge on drinking indulgently until you cross the line of other's. You will also buy yourself wine to drink day and night when there's no wedding party. Your life will be ruined if you don't quit drinking.

Fifthly, extramarital affairs. If you're a married man who has a family with wife and kids, you still not willing to give up your extramarital love and spend all the time with your lovers. Besides, you give all your money you have to the lovers of yours over there, the lover up above and the lover down below, however leaving your wife and kids suffer from hunger and thirst. Your life will be ruined if you don't end your extramarital affairs.

Sixthly, laziness. No matter how much money you have or how good your life is, if you're not diligent but lazy, and don't do work, only staying at home eating and drinking, sooner or later, your money will run out. When all your money runs out, you will live a bad life with nothing to eat or drink.

附录　清莱白苗话语音系统

该语法标注的调查点是泰国清莱府通县搭普岛镇拉克撒村（英文地址：Banratraksa，Tabtao，Thoeng，Chiang Rai）。该村有85户，560人，全部是白苗。有杨、王、马、陶、黄、侯六姓。村民种植水稻、苞谷、芒果、姜、卷心菜等，养猪、牛、鸡、狗。年轻人大多去县里、府、曼谷以及韩国、澳大利亚打工。

该村保留苗族传统习俗。丧俗吹芦笙打鼓，习惯于族内婚。婚恋自由，若男女双方中意，男方把女方带回家，男方家用一只鸡进行宗教迎接仪式，三天之后告知女方父母即可。传统宗教盛行，跳神仪式就有6种（nen^{55}ʂi^{35}zi̩^{31}、nen^{55}kaɯ^{21}、nen^{55}ʂau^{55}、nen^{55}sua^{44}mple^{21}、nen^{55}ʔdia^{44}、nen^{55}khau^{55}taɯ^{55}）。

本音系发音人叫嘎英才融（苗语音译），姓王。1972年生于老挝沙耶武里（Xaignabouli，Laos），1975年来到泰国。父母都是白苗。母亲姓王，父亲姓杨。嘎英才融的母亲生于老挝乌多姆赛省，后从乌多姆赛省迁至博胶省的会晒（Ban Houayxay），从会晒迁往琅勃拉邦（Luangphrabang），从琅勃拉邦迁到老挝和泰国交界的老挝沙耶武里省（Xaignabouli）南波村（Namphouy），此时是1972年，生下了发音合作人。在南波村，发音人的母亲去世了。在这个村住了3年，到1975年，发音人从老挝沙耶武里省南波村迁到了泰国难府（Nan）的湄乍林（Mae Charim）。在湄乍林的难民营（Soptouang Refuge，Mae Charim）住了7年。然后来到了难府波县（Pua）的难民营（Ban Nam yao Refuge，Pua），在这里住了1年。再从难府波县的难民营迁徙到黎府巴宗难民营（Ban Vinai Refuge，Pak Chom，Loei），在这里住了9年，此时发音人已有20岁了。1992年，发音人嘎英才融从黎府巴宗难民营迁到清莱府通县搭普岛镇拉克撒村，也就是现居地。在这个村子已经生活了25年。嘎英才融说：老挝的很多人跟他们家走一样的迁徙路线。老挝的苗族有部分是从中国来到老挝的凤沙里（Pgongsaly）和琅南塔（Luangnamtha），有部分来到了老挝华潘、会晒、琅勃拉邦、川圹；老挝的苗族又从老挝琅南塔省迁到泰国清莱府，从老挝沙耶武里省迁到泰国难府。"

该村约有20%的人掌握老挝苗文。五六年前，村里有苗语广播，下午5点播放新闻或歌曲，电视普及之后，广播被替代了。

发音人在镇政府工作，负责管理村寨。他热爱苗族文化，参与苗族电影电视的拍摄和表演，懂苗语、泰语和英语三种语言。他会五种苗文，第一种是拉丁苗文，也就是老挝苗文；第二种是庞豪苗文（Pa Hawh），第三种是把刀苗文（Paj Ntaub），第四种是波自苗文（Puaj Txwm），第五种老凤苗文（Lauj Foom）。

（一）声母

该点白苗话有56个声母。其声母系统的特点是：（1）舌尖后有塞音、塞擦音、擦音三套，为出现合并；（2）鼻音声母有清化和非清化的对立；（3）绿苗的声母 tl̥ 变异为伴随前喉塞的ʔd，绿苗的声母 tl̥h 和 ntl̥h 变异为伴随前喉塞的ʔth，绿苗的声母 ntl̥ 变异为 nt。

1. 声母表

p	ph	mp	mph	m	m̥	f	v
pl	phl	mpl	mphl	ml	m̥l		
ts	tsh	nts	ntsh			s	
t	th	nt	nth	n	n̥	l	l̥
ʔd	ʔth						
ʈ	ʈh	ɳʈ	ɳʈh				
tʂ	tʂh	ntʂ	ntʂh			ʂ	ʐ
tɕ	tɕh	ɲtɕ	ɲtɕh	ɲ	ɲ̥	ɕ	ʑ
k	kh	ŋk	ŋkh			x	
q	qh	ɴq	ɴqh				

2. 声母例词

p	pa⁵⁵	帮助	pɔ⁵⁵	包
ph	pha⁵⁵	旁边	phua²¹	帕子
mp	mpa⁵⁵	手臂	mpɔ⁵²	（一）群
mph	mpha³⁵	碰	mphuŋ⁴⁴	撒（药粉）
m	ma⁵²	麻（名词）	mɔ⁵⁵	疼
m̥	m̥a⁵⁵	藤蔓	m̥ɔ⁵⁵	腻虫
f	fa⁵⁵	荒	fai⁵⁵	分开
v	va⁵⁵	簸箕	vɔ³⁵	盖
pl	plau⁵⁵	毛	plɔ⁵²	消失
phl	phlau⁵⁵	壳	phlu⁴⁴	脸
mpl	mplai³³	（一）瓣	mplau²¹	糯
mphl	mphlai⁵⁵	戒指	mphlɔ³³	捆
ml	mlua³⁵	扁	mlfiuŋ³¹	听
m̥l	m̥lɔ³³	凹		
ts	tsa⁵²	床	tsɔ⁵⁵	辣椒
tsh	tsha⁵⁵	伤口	tshɔ⁵⁵	别
nts	ntsai³³	吸	ntsa⁴⁴	坟
ntsh	ntshai³³	女孩	ntsha⁵⁵	陡峭
s	sai³³	掐	sɔ³⁵	线
t	tu⁵⁵	儿子	tɔ⁵⁵	深
th	thu³⁵	松树	thɔ⁵⁵	掏（粪）
nt	ntua³⁵	吐	ntɔ³⁵	倒（水）
nth	nthua³⁵	打开	ntha⁵⁵	楼层
n	nuŋ⁵⁵	种子	nen³³	马
n̥	n̥u⁵⁵	太阳	n̥ɔ³⁵	听到
l	lu⁵⁵	个	len³³	认领

l̥	l̥ɔ⁵⁵	长（大）	l̥ai³³	割（肉）
ʔd	ʔdua³⁵	腰	ʔdia³⁵	勺子
ʔtʰ	ʔtʰua³⁵	腻	ʔtʰia⁴⁴	跳
t	tau⁴⁴	六	tuŋ⁵²	门
tʰ	tʰai³³	插	tʰɔ⁴⁴	拔
nt	ntau⁴⁴	（牛）打架	ntɔ⁴⁴	（水）浑
ntʰ	ntʰia³⁵	找	ntʰuŋ⁵⁵	绑腿
tʂ	tʂe³⁵	房子	tʂɔ⁴⁴	放（水）
tʂʰ	tʂʰau⁴⁴	筛（米）	tʂʰɔ⁵⁵	瓢
ntʂ	ntʂe³³	鱼	ntʂai³³	眨（眼）
ntʂʰ	ntʂʰaɯ⁴⁴	想要	ntʂʰa³⁵	血
ʂ	ʂa⁵⁵	（一）边	ʂɔ³⁵	热
ʐ	ʐai³³	藏（东西）	ʐɔ³⁵	守
tɕ	tɕaɯ³³	皱	tɕu⁵⁵	蒸
tɕʰ	tɕʰaɯ³³	穿行	tɕʰɔ⁵⁵	穿（针）
ntɕ	ntɕua³⁵	粑粑	ntɕɔ⁴⁴	思念
ntɕʰ	ntɕʰua³⁵	倒（水）	ntɕʰɔ⁴⁴	冒（烟）
ɲ̥	ɲ̥a⁵⁵	媳妇	ɲ̥u⁵²	牛
ɲ	ɲa³⁵	重	ɲu³⁵	肠子
ç	çuŋ⁴⁴	年	ça⁴⁴	七
ʑ	ʑuŋ⁴⁴	挨饿	ʑa⁴⁴	飞
k	ku⁵⁵	（牛）角	kau²¹	十
kʰ	kʰu⁵⁵	脏	kʰau⁴⁴	鞋子
ŋk	ŋkau⁵²	歌	ŋkau⁵⁵	蛋黄
ŋkʰ	ŋkʰi⁵⁵	树桠	ŋkʰaɯ⁵⁵	烟尘
x	xau³³	喝	xau⁴⁴	盖子
q	qai⁵⁵	鸡	qu⁵⁵	旧
qʰ	qʰia³⁵	姜	qʰua⁴⁴	客人
ɴq	ɴqai⁵²	肉	ɴqa⁴⁴	提
ɴqʰ	ɴqʰi³³	渴		

3. 声母说明

（1）v 的实际读音是 pv，双唇先接触后发 v。例如 va⁵⁵"簸箕"的实际读音是 pva⁵⁵。

（2）l̥ 前带有擦音 h，其实际读音是 hl̥。如：hl̥ɔ⁵⁵"长大"、hl̥ai³³"割"等。

（3）清化音 m̥、n̥、l̥、ŋ̊ 伴随强送气。

（4）ʔd 和 ʔtʰ 伴随前喉塞，是复杂的单辅音声母。

（二）韵母及例词

该点白苗话有 13 个韵母，其中单韵母 6 个（i、e、a、ɔ、u、ɯ）、复合元音韵母 5 个（ai、ia、ua、au、aɯ）、鼻韵母 2 个（en、uŋ）。

i	ti⁴⁴	靠近	ti⁵²	哥哥
e	te³³	手	te⁵²	（那）些
a	nta⁴⁴	（一）半	nta⁵²	刀
ɔ	tɔ⁴⁴	通（洞）	tɔ⁵²	山坡
u	tu⁴⁴	断	ntu⁵²	天
ɯ	tɯ⁴⁴	尾巴	tɯ³³	削
ai	ʔɖai⁴⁴	吊	tai⁵²	祈求
au	tau⁴⁴	得	xau⁴⁴	锅盖
ia	tia⁵⁵	裙子	tia⁵²	平
aɯ	taɯ⁴⁴	指（动词）	taɯ³⁵	皮
ua	tua⁴⁴	杀	tua⁵²	来
en	ten⁵⁵	摆放	ten³⁵	积（水）
uŋ	thuŋ⁵⁵	桶	thuŋ⁵²	坨

（1）单韵母 i 能够与所有声母相拼。如：tsi³⁵nen⁵⁵ "巫师"、si⁵⁵fɯ⁵⁵ "拳师"、ɴqhi³³ "渴" 等。

（2）该点单韵母 u 有 u 和 o 两个变体。与舌面、舌根、小舌声母相拼时读 u。如：ŋu⁵² "牛"、tɕu⁵⁵ "蒸"、khu⁵⁵ "脏"、qu⁵⁵ "旧" 等，与舌尖中音相拼时读 o，如：to⁴⁴ "断"。

（三）声调

古苗语的 8 个调类在该点白苗话对应 7 个调值，第 4 调气嗓音消失，与第 7 调合并，读为 33 调值。第 6 调保留气嗓音（用 ɦ 表示），该点气嗓音的特点是强送气。

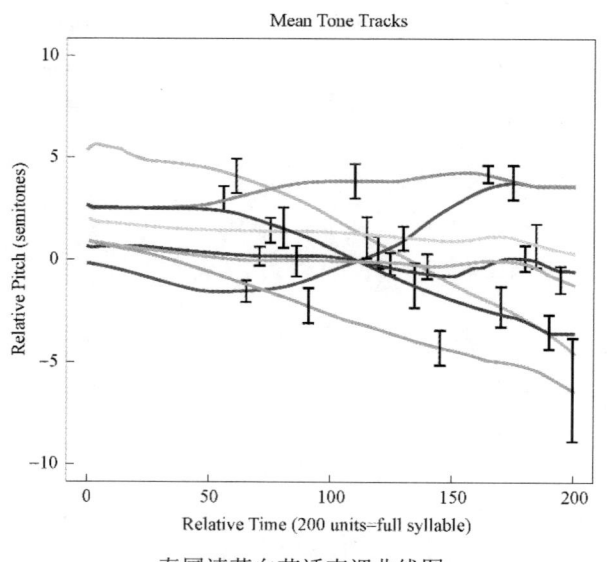

泰国清莱白苗话声调曲线图

声调曲线图的实验调值大致与听感调值相同，差别只有：（1）第 6 调实验调值是 42，听感调值是 31。听感调值低于实验调值是由于第 6 调伴有明显的气嗓音，气嗓音最突出的特点是送气和使听感调值降低一度，故本文将第 6 调记为 31。（2）第 8 调的实验调值是 31，听感调值是 21，读音短促，且其来源是阳入调，故而记为 21。

古苗语调类在泰国清莱白苗话中的实验调值与听感调值

调序	1 橙色	2 粉色	3 蓝色	4 红色	7 灰色	5 黄色	6 紫色	8 绿色
实验调值	55	52	35	33	33	44	42	31
听感调值	55	52	35	33	33	44	31	21
中国苗文标记	b	x	d	l	k	t	s	f
泰国白苗苗文标记	b	j	v	s	无标记	g	m	

1. 声调例词

调类	调值	例词 1		例词 2	
第一调	55	pɔ⁵⁵	包	tau⁵⁵	瓜
第二调	52	pɔ⁵²	雌性	tau⁵²	芭茅草
第三调	35	pɔ³⁵	丢	tau³⁵	朵（量词）
第四调	33	pɔ³³	刺	tau³³	能够
第五调	44	sɔ⁴⁴	咬	tau⁴⁴	得到
第六调	31	pɦɔ³¹	奶奶	tɦau³¹	沿着
第七调	33	pɔ³³	蒙	tau³³	斧头
第八调	21	pɔ²¹	看见	tau²¹	豆

调类	调值	例词 3		例词 4	
第一调	55	tʂɔ⁵⁵	棵（量词）	te⁵⁵	回答
第二调	52	tɔ⁵²	油	te⁵²	些
第三调	35	tʂɔ³⁵	老虎	te³⁵	剥开
第四调	33	tɯ³³	柴	te³³	手
第五调	44	tʂɔ⁴⁴	放（水）	te⁴⁴	霜
第六调	31	tɦɔ³¹	肥	tɦɔ³¹	沉
第七调	33	kau³³	伞	tau³³	点（灯）
第八调	21	tʂɔ²¹	镜子	tɕau²¹	追

调类	调值	例词 5	
第一调	55	pe⁵⁵	我们
第二调	52	pa⁵²	花
第三调	35	nte³⁵	长

第四调	33	na³³	老鼠
第五调	44	nte⁴⁴	烤（火）
第六调	31	ʑɦua³¹	梳子
第七调	33	ʐai³³	藏
第八调	21	ʑi²¹	八